The Yorkshire Law Society
1786 – 2015

A Personal Tribute

TONY LAWTON

TO THE

PRESIDENT AND MEMBERS

OF THE

YORKSHIRE LAW SOCIETY,

THIS TREATISE

IS

WITH GREAT DEFERENCE

INSCRIBED,

BY

THEIR MOST OBEDIENT

HUMBLE SERVANT,

THE

PUBLISHER.

Shortly will be publiſhed
And may be had of Mr. Teſſyman and Mr. Frobiſher,
Bookſellers in YORK,

A SHORT TREATISE on the LAW, relative to ARBITRATION

Containing adjudged CASES on that uſeful Subject to the preſent Time, digeſted and arranged under the familiar Heads.
With an APPENDIX of uſeful Precedents.

By JOHN WILSON

MEMBER of the YORKSHIRE LAW SOCIETY

To the PUBLIC.

A Ready Reference to the Deciſions of the Superior Courts on the Subject of theſe Sheets is the publiſher's principal Aim, and if, in the ſtolen Hours from the executive Branch of a laborious Profeſſion, he ſhould in ſome Degree have accompliſhed that End, or that by the Attempt the Labours of others may be facilitated, he will conſider himſelf amply rewarded

HULL, Aug. 6, 1791.

Dedication to the President and members of the Yorkshire Law Society from A Short Treatise on the Law relative to Arbitrations by John Wilson (Hull 1972) together with advertisement from the York Courant.

To my grandchildren
That they may know a little more
about what happened before they were born

The Yorkshire Law Society 1786 – 2015

A Personal Tribute

*I hold every man a debtor
to his profession*

Francis Bacon – *The Elements of the Common Law*

Tony Lawton

Skelton York 2016

© Tony Lawton, 2016

Published by Tony Lawton

All rights reserved. No part of this book may be reproduced, adapted, stored in a retrieval system or transmitted by any means, electronic, mechanical, photocopying, or otherwise without the prior written permission of the author.

The rights of Tony Lawton to be identified as the author of this work have been asserted in accordance with the Copyright, Designs and Patents Act 1988.

A CIP catalogue record for this book is available from the British Library.

ISBN 978-0-9955603-0-7

Book layout and jacket design by Clare Brayshaw

Prepared by:

York Publishing Services Ltd
64 Hallfield Road
Layerthorpe
York YO31 7ZQ

Tel: 01904 431213

Website: www.yps-publishing.co.uk

CONTENTS

List of Illustrations	ix
Preface and Acknowledgements	xi
Prologue	1
Chapter One – The Legal and Social Background	15
Chapter Two – Gentlemen of the Law	37
Chapter Three – Costs, Conveyancers & Low Practitioners	51
Chapter Four – Communications	63
Chapter Five – The Doldrums 1815-1849	81
Chapter Six – The Last Days of the Ancien Régime 1850 – 1886	101
Chapter Seven – A Centenary Interlude 1886	123
Chapter Eight – The Dawn of the Modern Age 1886 – 1814	137
Chapter Nine – Armageddon – The Great War 1914 – 1918	163
Chapter Ten – Between the Wars 1919 – 1939	183
Chapter Eleven – The Second World War 1939 – 1945	209
Chapter Twelve – The Post War Years 1945 – 1960	231
Chapter Thirteen – Modern Times – The First Stirings 1960 – 1986	251
Chapter Fourteen – The Bicentenary and Beyond	279
Epilogue	305
Appendix A – English Law and the English Legal Profession	325
Appendix B – Some Former Members	357
Appendix C – The Society's Library	393

Appendix D – Land Registration	419
Sources & Select Bibliography	429
Table of Statutes	433
Table of Cases	443
Index	445

LIST OF ILLUSTRATIONS

1. Dedication to the President and Members of the Yorkshire Law Society from *A Short Treatise on the Law relative to Arbitrations* by John Wilson (Hull 1792) together with advertisement from the *York Courant* — Frontispiece
2. Title page of Burke's *Reflections on the Revolution in France* — 4
3. *Slavers throwing overboard the Dead and Dying* by JMW Turner, Museum of Fine Arts, Boston — 19
4. Reverend Robert Gilbert — 29
5. The Handbill convening the Society's first meeting 20 March 1786 — 38
6. Lord Macclesfield, the provincial attorney from Derbyshire who became Lord Chancellor, but ended in disgrace © National Portrait Gallery — 44
7. Improved Travel Facilities in the 18th century — 64
8. *Tolls to be Lett* – Notice of Meeting from the *Leeds Intelligencer* 1798 — 67
9. *Dover Harbour* in the late 18th or early 19th century – artist unknown. Image courtesy of the Dover Museum and Bronze Age Boat Trust — 71
10. York Law Library – Proprietary Member's certificate, 21 January 1828 — 86
11. First page of Indenture dated 20 August 1885 transferring the contents of York Law Library to the Yorkshire Law Society — 87
12. *Doctors Commons, Knightrider Street, London* – Ackermann Print 1808 — 107

13.	An Excusion to Whitby 1886 – Programme Introduction	128
14.	Centenary Celebrations 1886 – Mrs Walker 'At Home' as President's wife and Lady Mayoress	130-131
15.	*Captain Boycott* – Spy Cartoon, January 1881	141
16.	*Thiepval Memorial and Harveng Churchyard* – © Commonwealth War Graves Commission	175
17.	*Curious! I seem to hear a child weeping!* – Cartoon by Will Dyson 1919	184
18.	An extract from page 181 of the Lincoln's Inn Call Register	204
19.	*Blake Street York* ankle-deep in glass and rubble 29 April 1942 Photo ©York Press	211
20.	*Braunschweig-Querum Law Society* – Oflag79, Lower Saxony Photo courtesy of Peter Knowles	215
21.	*Temporary Rules 1940* – Richmond Golf Club	217
22.	*Fiat iustitia, ruat caelum* – A procession into a fire-blackened and roofless York Guildhall for the reading of the Assize Commission, 1942. Photo courtesy of David Wilson	218
23.	Legal Aid *in forma pauperis* from The Attorney's Compleat Pocket Book 1743	238
24.	*Poor Man's Lawyer Service* – Letter (redacted) 1952	243
25.	*Assembly Rooms, Blake Street, York* – Photo courtesy York Conservation Trust	279
26.	A print of James Scarlett, 1st Baron Abinger ©National Portrait Gallery	284
27.	*Hoisting of American Colors over Louisiana* – Thure de Thulstrup, Cabildo Museum, New Orleans	327
28.	Presentation of silver vinaigrette to Presiding Judge at York's Mansion House February 1968. © York Press	335
29.	York's Bloody Assize	338

PREFACE AND ACKNOWLEDGMENTS

This book owes its origin to a chance conversation with a former President of the Society, Raymond Burn, on the pavement outside his office at 11 Lendal York, next door to the former Judges' Lodgings in the days of the assizes – now a hotel of that name. Until 1970 this was where my own office had been located when I first arrived in York in 1966 and had long been the site of various solicitors' practices ever since George Hicks Seymour (1793-1872) had set up in practice there as Seymour & Blyth. It was Raymond who had suggested that I write a history of the Society. The idea slowly grew on me but was a long time in gestation. I was still very much in practice at the time and the pressures of 'busyness' on solicitors seemed to be ever increasing (and have increased much further since!). But when I finally retired in 2008 being in practice ceased to be available as an excuse.

My first step was to retrieve (with the Society's permission) the archive material which had been deposited with the County Archivist at Northallerton some years previously. Two things fairly soon became apparent. Firstly, that I was in no way qualified to approach the task on a formal academic basis for which I had neither temperament nor training: merely being 'interested in history' is no more a sufficient preparation for writing it than 'being interested in food' is a preparation for being a professional chef. Secondly, I would have to give some thought to the broader social and historical context in which solicitors conduct the affairs of their clients. I could see that this inevitably involved selection. Professional historians may not approve of either the topics which I have selected or my treatment of them, but so be it. Those I have sought to incorporate include the very notion of what constitutes a profession, its social make up, the development of communications, reform of civil and criminal law and practice in the 19th and 20th centuries and the background to the abolition of capital punishment, the legal, political and constitutional impact of Ireland and Irish affairs, colonial expansion, the impact of two world wars and the dire consequences of the fulminating anti-semitism of the 20th century, of which not-so-faint echos are with us still, and finally the effect of the shortcomings in our political culture of recent years. Clearly, over time, individual members of the Society may not have been directly involved in any of these matters but they will certainly have been affected by them as they will have formed the background to their professional work. For this social and historical perspective I have essentially depended on my own somewhat haphazard reading, so any faults of commission or omission have been mine.

Thirdly I would like to thank both present and past solicitor colleagues and staff at Grays for their friendly guidance and support which they have generously bestowed on me in all sorts of direct and indirect ways since my retirement in 2008, in particular by providing me with my own office space, my own pc and general back office support which has greatly assisted my task. In this connection I would like to express my particular thanks to Brian Mitchell. In addition to the onerous role of being Grays' managing partner, with all that entails, Brian also doubles as an in-house IT manager of whose exceptional expertise in that cabalistic art all at Grays are in awe. As a particular beneficiary myself in that respect, I ruefully call to mind the young subaltern on whose confidential report his superior had noted "This officer never makes the same mistake twice but seems to have made most of them once." Where my own IT mistakes are concerned, no counsel, however dedicated, could make even that ambivalent plea in mitigation on my behalf.

I would also like to thank the following for their guidance and help: successive Presidents, Secretaries and Council Members of the Yorkshire Law Society for encouragement and support over a long period and in particular for entrusting me with custody of the Society's extensive archive material without which my task would not have been possible; likewise various members of the Society for the supply of valuable information about former members; the staff of the Law Society's library in Chancery Lane, the Reference Department of York City Library and the Leeds Law Society for general help and guidance; the Secretary and members of the Norfolk and Norwich Law Society for information about the Norwich Guildhall Court of Record; and finally Duncan Beal, Director and

Clare Brayshaw, Design Manager, at York Publishing Services Ltd. for their friendly and tolerant support of my shortcomings.

I gratefully acknowledge the permission given by the following for the use of their copyright or other material:

The present partners at Grays for various information and material contained in *A History of Grays of York 1695-1988* by WHC Cobb, especially relating to the Assizes at York on pp. 336 to 337.

Peter Knowles for the group portrait of members of the Braunschwig-Querum Law Society on p. 215.

LexisNexis for the use I have made of "The Languid Leader and the Ducal Action" from *Forensic Fables* by 'O' republished by Butterworths 1961 on p. 256 and *History of a Publishing House* by H Kay and W Gordon 2nd ed. Butterworths 1997 on pp. 307-308.

David Manthey for the use of his Wyld font at various locations.

Dover Museum and Bronze Age Boat Trust for the image of Dover Harbour on p. 71.

York Conservation Trust for the photograph of the Assembly Rooms in Blake Street on p. 279.

The National Portrait Gallery for the print of Lord Macclesfield on p. xxx and of James Scarlett, 1st Baron Abinger on p. 284.

Sir Tatton Sykes Bt for permission to photograph and use the portrait of the Reverend Robert Gilbert at Sledmere shown on p. 29.

Thomson Reuters for the long title of the Continuance of Acts etc Act 1749 on p. 439 and other material on p. 96.

The Treasurer and Benchers of Lincoln's Inn for permission to use the extract from their Call Register in respect of Dr Heinrich Lietzmann on p. 204.

David Wilson for the photograph of the Opening of the Assize 1942 in a roofless Guildhall on p. 218.

Wikimedia Commons: for The Slave Ship by JMW Turner's p. 19, Peace and Future Cannon Fodder by Will Dyson's on p. 184 and Hoisting of the American Colors over Louisiana by Thure de Thulstrup's on p. 327.

York Museums Trust for the portrait of John Brook on p. 356.

York Press for the photograph on p. 335 of the Lady Mayoress at the Mansion House presenting a silver vinaigrette to Lawton J to mark the holding of the assizes, February 1968; also, the photograph on p. 211 of Blake Street following the air-raid of 22/23 April 1942.

York Race Committee for the use of material in their museum on the Knavesmire and Yorkshire Post Newspapers for re-working an article of mine which originally appeared in the *Yorkshire Post* on 17 May 2000, both relating to the case of *Burdon v Rhodes* in Chapter 1.

Finally, on the home front I must express my deep gratitude to my wife Catherine for her patience and fortitude in coping with my excessively proprietary attitude to our study at home, not least on account of my insistence on using every available horizontal surface for lodging the Society's extensive archive. Some of these items, it must be said, did match two at least if not all three of the qualities attributed by Lord Westbury to the title deeds of his day, *viz* "difficult to read, disgusting to touch and impossible to understand".

Tony Lawton
September 2016

PROLOGUE

To anyone other than its members any account of the history of a local law society might seem a matter of domestic or parochial concern. Even where the society in question shares its title with the greatest county of England – greatest at least in the eyes of those privileged to reside in it – the general reader must justifiably wonder whether it is going to be of sufficient interest to merit his attention. Besides, to those unfamiliar with the origins of this very special *appellation*, the title of "The Yorkshire Law Society" is misleading.[1] In 1786, the year of its establishment, the City of York was still, officially at least, the second city of England after London and the only assize town of the entire county. Inevitably, therefore, it was the focus of attention for Yorkshire lawyers and it was perfectly natural that those lawyers should have adopted the county name. The industrial revolution which was to transform parts of Yorkshire, particularly the West Riding,[2] had already started to stir in the last two decades of the 18th century. Few could have predicted the course it was to take but new ideas and new attitudes were beginning to take root; and new men too had appeared who were no longer content with the old ways. For the time being, however, the new men had perforce to accept the old structures and for lawyers the structure in 1786 was "Yorkshire". That explains why at the Society's first meeting members of the profession came from all parts of the county; from Bradford, Dewsbury, Doncaster, Easingwold, Halifax, Kippax, Knaresborough, Leeds, Malton, Northallerton, Pocklington, Richmond, Ripon, Rotherham, Scarborough, Sheffield, Thorne and Wakefield as well as from York itself and a few from places beyond the county boundary such as Clitheroe and Durham, together with two representatives from London.

The Society's Yorkshire monopoly was to last less than twenty years. In January 1805 the Leeds Law Society was formed – marking the beginning of a shift in population and economic clout which was to make that city in our own day one of the pre-eminent legal centres outside London. But in 1786 that was still very much in the future. Even in 1831 the members of the Leeds Society numbered no more than 21 and only 39 by 1870, the year of its incorporation. This slowness of local development on the part of Leeds would seem to be confirmed by the fact that only three of is practitioners are recorded as attending the National Conference in York in 1886 when there were five from Bristol, 16 from Liverpool and 10 from Newcastle, all further afield. There were only 129 by the end of the century and 250 by 1970. Today its membership stands at over 1,300 among an estimated total of 2,500 solicitors who practise there. Other local law societies in various parts of Yorkshire followed and there are now a dozen or so altogether, although some were to be established much later. Sheffield & District Law Society, for example, did not appear until 1875. But despite this multiplication the original 'Yorkshire' society never saw any good reason to change its name. Perhaps such a trade mark was just too valuable to lose! But it is interesting to note that one of the founder members of the Leeds Law Society and its first President, Mr Lucas Nicholson, was equally a founder member of the Yorkshire Law Society, having been present at its inaugural meeting at the house of Mr Ringrose in York on 21 March 1786, before even the first rules were adopted. But despite his involvement in the founding of not one but *two* local law societies, there was something of a shadow over Mr Nicholson's subsequent career. Having served as town clerk of Leeds, President of the Yorkshire Law Society in 1795, first President of the Leeds Law Society in 1805, he unfortunately become bankrupt in 1812 albeit as a result of his involvement as a partner in a banking company. This inevitably meant his having to give up the town clerkship and presumably also his legal practice. He does not seem to have suffered excessively thereby. He was succeeded by his son James as Town Clerk and continued to share with him his Royal Exchange insurance agency.

    Yorkshire was not the first of the provincial law societies. That privilege falls to Bristol which was founded in 1770 but Bristol has no surviving minutes before 1774 and none likewise for the whole of the critical period between 1780 and 1819. When embarking on the task of writing about the Yorkshire Law Society I did start with one great advantage. The Society's records, of which details can be found in the bibliography, are largely complete. However, its antiquity and the comprehensiveness of its records are not sufficient in themselves to confer on its affairs a more general interest. For this we must look to the light it sheds on the very idea of a profession as it developed in this country from the late 18th century onwards. But before doing so we need to consider for a moment the nature of associations of any kind in England.

In 1781 Edmund Burke, himself son of a Dublin attorney, became MP for Malton, a seat he was to retain until 1794. For the previous six years he had represented Bristol in parliament but the Bristolians had taken against him for his championship of causes which were displeasing to them, in particular the freeing of Irish trade[3] and Catholic emancipation. We think of him today as one of the founding fathers of political conservatism, the progenitor of classic Tory principles. In his own day, however, he was very much a Whig although he was eventually to fall out with them in 1791, not sharing in any way their sympathetic view of the French Revolution – a sympathy shared at that time it must be said by Prime Minister William Pitt. The two had clashed on 9 February the previous year in a Commons debate on the army estimates. Burke was one of the few to have judged the situation in France correctly from the outset. Pitt, who generally had a shrewd grasp of foreign affairs, had initially failed to appreciate the significance of what was happening across the channel. "The present convulsions in France" he had cheerfully observed in the course of the debate, "must, sooner or later, terminate in general harmony".

For Burke the Revolution was a disaster. The French he claimed "had shewn themselves the ablest architects of ruin that had hitherto existed in the world. In that very short space of time they had completely pulled down to the ground; their monarchy; their church; their nobility; their law; their revenue; their army; their navy; their commerce; their arts; and their manufactures." He went on to refer to "the excesses of an irrational unprincipled, proscribing, confiscating, plundering, ferocious, bloody and tyrannical democracy". As to religion, Burke foresaw the danger of the French example as being "no longer from intolerance, but from Atheism; a foul, unnatural vice, foe to all the dignity and consolation of mankind; which seems in France, for a long time, to have been embodied into a faction, accredited and almost avowed." He equally deprecated the French tendency to grandiloquent declarations of general principle, such as "the Rights of Man",[4] and their attempts to construct a system of government which would accommodate those rights. The year 1790 had also seen the

> REFLECTIONS
>
> ON THE
>
> REVOLUTION IN FRANCE,
>
> AND ON THE
>
> PROCEEDINGS IN CERTAIN SOCIETIES
> IN LONDON
>
> RELATIVE TO THAT EVENT.
>
> IN A
>
> LETTER
>
> INTENDED TO HAVE BEEN SENT TO A GENTLEMAN
> IN PARIS.
>
> BY THE RIGHT HONOURABLE
>
> EDMUND BURKE.
>
> ———
>
> THE SIXTH EDITION.
>
> ———
>
> LONDON:
> PRINTED FOR J. DODSLEY, IN PALL-MALL.
> M.DCC.XC.

Title page of Burke's Reflections.

The book was an instant success. First published in November 1790, eight thousand copies were sold within five weeks and by September 1791 it had gone through eleven editions. Napoleon had a copy which he took with him into exile on St Helena following his final defeat.

publication of his *Reflections on the Revolution in France*. It was widely read and much criticised at the time. It was only the shock of the execution of Louis XVI and Marie Antoinette and the Terror in 1793 which brought home to Burke's politically correct English contemporaries that perhaps this maverick Irishman was right about events in France after all. The book is still in print.

This misreading of France and the French by the English governing classes is surprising in some ways but of course we know "what happened next". Burke was indeed one of the few to have judged the situation in France correctly from the outset. Even the British Ambassador in Paris, the Duke of Dorset, was convinced in the summer of 1789 that the Revolution was "actually concluded" – so much so that he arranged with his cricketing friend, Lord Tankerville, to get a team together to go over to France to teach the natives the principles of the game and *le fair-play*. The English tourists, largely made up of members of Chertsey CC, included, as well as Lord Tankerville himself, his butler, William Bedster and his gardener, the demon bowler Edward "Lumpy" Stevens, to whom, incidentally, the game owes the introduction of the third stump.[5] Apart from Dorset, who was supposed to be in Paris, they all duly assembled at Dover on 10 August 1789 but before they could embark they were dismayed to meet HM Ambassador himself hurriedly coming the other way – never to return. The cricketing duke (who, according to scurrilous and improbable gossip, was supposed to have had an affair with Marie Antoinette and given her a cricket bat as a souvenir – an amatory gesture of which only an Englishman would have been capable) had discovered that far from the revolution being "actually concluded", the fall of the Bastille on 14 July was merely the beginning. Accordingly, the French were left to get on with cutting off the heads of their noble lords, and the English to playing cricket with theirs. As Churchill was later to remind the House of Commons in 1942 "The Almighty, in His infinite wisdom, did not see fit to create Frenchmen in the image of Englishmen". Indeed not.

All this, however, was in the future when the founding fathers of the Yorkshire Law Society first met on the evening of Tuesday 21 March 1786. They would not have known of the passing reference of the Malton MP in his *Reflections* to "the little platoon" – a phrase which has since passed into our political language.[6] They would not have realised that what they were setting up was just such a "little platoon" as the author had in mind when he wrote "To be attached to the subdivision, to love the little platoon we belong to in society, is the first principle (the germ as it were) of public affections. It is the first link in the series by which we proceed towards a love to our country and to mankind. The interests of that portion of social arrangement is a trust in the hands of all those who compose it … ". The political insight which it was Burke's genius to grasp was that a healthy society was built from the bottom up, not from the top down and that the "little platoons" of people, freely associating together for this purpose or that, was the best guarantee of stable and beneficent government and a guarantee against the tyranny of "the state". Such associations were not of course established with these self-conscious political motives in mind – they just happened and by and large the British state let them happen. There were exceptions. The French Revolution itself and political unrest in Ireland were to make governments here nervous of anything which smacked of sedition or "Jacobinism" and at a later time there was an equal distrust of trade unionism or "combinations". But they were indeed exceptions.

The French state by contrast has never shaken off the inheritance of 1789. Even today a village sports club, local history group or similar "association", never mind a professional body, still has to have its constitution approved by the local Prefect, before it can be recognised for any purpose whatsoever, even opening a bank account and, of course, because the concept of a trust as we understand it is wholly absent from French law, "non-recognition" is conclusive. The Prefect is the representative of central government and without government "recognition" nothing can "exist" and therefore the state ultimately, and not always benevolently, controls what any association can or cannot do. It was entirely within this tradition that religious orders became unlawful and were effectively expelled from France following the Law of 9 December 1905 concerning the Separation of Church and State.

It was this freedom of association and freedom from state interference which the English enjoyed which was to influence the particular way in which the very concept of a profession was to develop in this country. This would not have been obvious in 1786 but it was to become obvious to later generations. How did it all start? Until about thirty years ago I had never given any thought as to whether the essential nature of a profession in England – any profession, not just my own – differed from that to be found in any other country. It was an article in *The Times* by Professor Dahrendorf (1929-2009) which first alerted me to its rather special character.

Dahrendorf had arrived in England from his native Germany as a young and impressionable postgraduate student in 1952. Thirty-one years later on 31 October 1983, as Ralf Dahrendorf, KBE, FBA, he was to deliver the Jephcott Lecture to the Royal Society of Medicine. Its title was *In Defence of the English Professions*. The article in *The Times* which had first attracted my attention was merely a summary. At the time of his lecture Dahrendorf was a distinguished academic and director of the London School of Economics but had not yet taken out UK citizenship. He was clearly intrigued by the particular features which distinguished the professions in England from those on the continent of Europe. He recognised the defining characteristics of a profession, as the practising of a body of knowledge or art, a concern with an educational process and the upholding of a standard of professional qualifications as well as a standard of conduct. These were all matters which were traditionally taken for granted in this country, but which were by no means universal. The crucial point was that all this was done by the profession itself without extraneous, ie state, intervention.

Dahrendorf did not claim to be the first to focus on these aspects. He freely acknowledged his debt to an American, WE Wickenden (1882-1947), a former President of the American Institute of Electrical Engineers, quoting in particular his conclusion: "Professional status is therefore an implied contract to serve society over and beyond all specific duty to client and employer in consideration of the privileges and protection society extends to the profession." Dahrendorf continued:

> Perhaps one has to be a continental to see anything special in this statement; I am a continental, and therefore I do. What is special is the notion of an "implied contract" between society and the professions which has no intermediary, no outside guarantor, and which nevertheless works ... Professions are private bodies with public functions; at least this is true for the English professions. They serve needs which extend far beyond the immediate relationship between the professional person and his or her client; but they serve them by rules and standards which are defined and upheld by the professions themselves. At the same time their protection and privileges are provided if not as a matter of course then through voluntary agreement.

The defining characteristic as Dahrendorf saw it was that the professions in England "are part of a society which does not require the state to govern all its affairs but which recognizes the independence of those who provide a public service. In this sense their story is, by the same token, that of freedom in Britain." This may sound somewhat high-flown to the English ear but not only was Dahrendorf a respected academic with a very wide-ranging career – at various times a German academic, member of the German federal parliament, English academic, European Commissioner, and member of the House of Lords, but as he himself put it, he was a *continental* and therefore an outsider looking in. Outsiders often see things which we don't. He, however, was in no doubt: " . . it is my contention that the condition of the British professions is an index of the state of liberty in this country, and that what they do, and what happens to them, has a great deal to do with whether Britain remains a model of a free society for the rest."

These words were spoken over thirty years ago. It would be interesting to know how Dahrendorf would have viewed the present state of the professions, particularly the medical profession (which he was addressing in his lecture) and our own legal profession. In recent years governments have shown an increasing tendency to meddle in a way which would have astonished our forebears in 1786 and even the generation immediately preceding our own. One wonders too what our predecessors would have made of solicitors being encouraged by our own professional body to refer no longer to our clients but to our "customers". As one colleague put it to me "We are supposed to be on the same side as our clients. Are we on the side of our *customers* in the same way?" By way of contrast we now have government websites in which social work is described as a "profession" and social workers themselves who invariably refer to their "clients". This is no reflection on social work or social workers, merely a comment on what seems to indicate some confusion of language and possibly of thought likewise.

The Society's President for 2008-2009, Peter Hannam, made a similar point from a slightly different perspective. Referring to the efforts of the national Law Society in Chancery Lane in the current climate he observed:

They work on a much altered playing-field on which there are many who would prefer to regard lawyers simply as business people attempting to make as much money as they can at the expense of the consumer. Any idea that respect for lawyers and the legal system is a necessary part of the civilised society and essential for the protection of the constitutional and private rights of every citizen seems long forgotten.[7]

But in 1786 all that was very much in the future.

How to tell the story of the Yorkshire Law Society and bind all these threads together? My first thought was that solicitors are so intimately involved with the affairs of their clients, with the whole of society in effect, that their activities can only be understood in the context of that society. It was this notion of context which prompted me to begin with an account of four cases of the period, three civil and one criminal. None of them can exactly be described as typical and of the four, only two *Burdon v Rhodes* and *Gilbert v Sykes* were Yorkshire cases. However, in their different ways, each provides a clue as to how some aspects at least of late 18th century legal life are so utterly remote from the world with which we are familiar as to be almost unrecognisable. Yet human nature does not change and there are still many aspects of late 18th and early 19th century society with which we are all too familiar today.

In 1795, for example, Patrick Colquhoun, accounted England's first stipendiary magistrate, was claiming that crime rates were rising because "the morals and habits of the lower ranks in society are growing progressively worse" and blaming it on the decline of religion and the influence of pubs and the popular music of his day.[8] And thirty years later, commenting on the banking and financial crisis of 1825, a York paper was to write:

> ... that man must have strong nerves who can look, without emotions of deep sympathy and regret for the unfortunate sufferers, on the dreadful effects produced [by the crisis] ... Many instances of private wretchedness which it has occasioned, have been brought to our knowledge; but of the general mass of misery, the interruption to trade, and the aggregate loss which must be incurred, no estimate can be formed .... farmers without the means of paying their rent, the shopkeepers without customers, every class of workmen without employment ... Neither experience nor theory, however, lead us to expect any beneficial result from a crisis which is

to begin in insolvency, to proceed in starvation and riots, and to end probably in the co-operation of all who have any thing to lose, to repress by any expedients the excesses which would arise out of these calamities.[9]

In the words attributed to Mark Twain, history does not repeat itself but it rhymes.

I cannot claim, of course, to have written a social history; such a task would be wholly outside my capabilities and the intended scope of this book. Nevertheless, I have tried to give an account of the Society against the background of what was happening in the wider world, being mindful of Hugh Trevor-Roper's very necessary warning: " ... every age has its own social context, its own intellectual climate, and takes it for granted ... It also deserves respect ... ".[10] Any attempt to include such "social context" must of necessity be on a very selective basis and I can only hope that it will go some way to assist in understanding and provide some appeal to the general reader who is not necessarily a solicitor nor with any particular connection to Yorkshire. This was an aim unlikely to be achieved by a bare chronological account of "what happened next". The Jesuit historian, Fr Philip Caraman,[11] must have faced a similar task. In the introduction his *University of the Nations* (the history of another rather specialised institution, the Gregorian University in Rome originally established by St Ignatius in 1551), he commented:

> It was my good fortune many years ago to belong to a small group of students who met every week in the rooms of Sir Maurice Powicke, the Regius Professor of History at Oxford, who would talk about long-forgotten bishops, kings and statesmen as though he had just come from entertaining them in the hall of his college. All that I learned then about the thirteenth century I have now forgotten, but one lesson I took away with me, namely, that there need never be an excuse for making history dull.

I have done my best to bear Sir Maurice Powicke's example in mind but I am deeply conscious that Philip Caraman was not only a distinguished historian but a close friend of the likes of Evelyn Waugh, Graham Greene and Muriel Spark. I, for my part, am a retired solicitor and my only qualification for writing this account is to have been a member of the Yorkshire Law Society for nearly fifty years. For this reason too, I am hesitant to describe it as a *history* of the Society and happier describing it as a tribute, accepting as I do Bacon's dictum that every man is a debtor to his profession. But insofar as my tribute is a history of sorts, it is for my readers to judge whether or not I have managed to avoid making it dull. I have done what I could and can only echo the words which appear on the title page of Richard Tottell's 1565 edition of *Fitzherbert's Abridgement*[12] of which the Society once had a copy in its library "Ne moy reprous sauns cause car mon entent est de bon amour" which may be loosely translated "Don't chide me unfairly because what I do, I do for love".

NOTES

1. Such misnomers may perhaps be forgiven. That most eminent historian of the law, FW Maitland, once observed somewhat tartly "In England it is not to be expected that the territorial arrangement that serves for any one purpose, will serve for any other … " *Justice and Police* (1885).

2. Sheffield had an older industrial tradition. Its cutlery was renowned even in Chaucer's day. Describing the roguish miller of Trumpington, the Reeve recounts "Ther was no man for peril dorste him touche – A Sheffield thwitel [large knife] baar he in his hose" – from *The Canterbury Tales*. There was seemingly less legislative concern over "knife crime" in the 14th century.

3. Ever since Tudor times England had sought to restrict Irish trade in support of its own commercial interests. Scotland had enjoyed free trade with England and its "Dominions and Plantations" since the Union with Scotland Act 1706 which came into force on 1 May 1707. Ireland, however, was not so lucky and for the whole of the 18th century Irish commercial interests were subordinated to those of Great Britain (ie England and Scotland). The effects of this commercial discrimination can be seen to this day. It was responsible for the development of the Ulster linen industry (prompted by the prohibition on the export of Irish wool by the Westminster parliament). It equally had the unintended effect of encouraging Irish involvement in wine and spirit production in the Bordeaux region of France – hence the world famous Hennessy cognac and the celebrated "Irish" Châteaux of Lynch-Bages, Palmer, Clarke, Kirwan etc. Maurice Healey (1887-1943) a well-known Irish member of the Bar, raconteur and wit of his generation, even went so far as to suggest that the first growth Médoc "Haut-Brion" was simply a Gallic corruption of "O'Brien", but then he never was one to let the facts get in the way of a

good story. Free trade between Great Britain and Ireland was not to be finally achieved until the Act of Union (Ireland) 1800 which came into force on 1 January 1801.

4. The debate on aspects of this fundamental difference of approach is still on-going. Lord Hoffman, in a lecture to the Judicial Studies Board at the Inner Temple on 9 March 2009, offered a detailed critique of the approach adopted by the Strasbourg-based European Court of Human Rights. The nub of his argument is that the ECHR moves from general principles to the actual *application* of those principles in circumstances where they do not and cannot have the necessary background knowledge.

5. For readers who adopt the Wisden approach to such matters, the full team was to consist of Yalden (Captain) Attfield, Edmeads, Tankerville (Earl), Wood, Bedster, Stevens, Fry, Etheridge, Harding and Dorset (Duke).

6. Burke's "little platoons" was one of David Cameron's favorite historical allusions in the run-up to the 2010 election.

7. *President's Column* Yorkshire Law Society – Report of the Council for 2008-2009. Solicitors are well-used to requests to act as counter-signatories on passport applications. If they find such a task irksome, they may find it pays to make a close study of the detailed requirements on the government's website: www.ips.gov.uk with a view to spreading the burden. The list which they provide, includes "a bank/building society official", and a "trade union officer" which members of the Society will no doubt find reassuring.

8. Patrick Colquhoun *A Treatise on the Police of the Metropolis* (1795). Colquhoun (1745-1820) was a prominent Scottish merchant and statistician who founded the Glasgow Chamber of Commerce and served as Lord Provost of Glasgow before moving to London in 1785. There he founded the Thames River Police and was appointed as a stipendiary magistrate in the East End. Drunkenness of course was endemic in Georgian and early Victorian England. A London newspaper the *Public Advertiser* for 23 August 1787 reported that "The gin shops about St Paul's have greatly added to the nightly riots and disturbances of neighbourhood. When abandoned women have drunk themselves to intoxication, they lie before the doors and the watchmen, constables etc. are the bait of their profligate abuse …". Plus ça change …

9. *Yorkshire Gazette* 24 December 1825. The next ten years were to see the beginnings of a fundamental change in the ways in which banking was conducted in Britain. In 1826, the year after the crisis, all 554 of our banks

were private, with not a single joint-stock bank among them. By 1836 the number of private banks had reduced to 407 but there were in addition 100 joint-stock banks. The rapid expansion of railways was to give added impetus to this change.

10. Hugh Trevor-Roper (1914-2003) *The Past and the Present – History and Sociology* (London 1969).

11. Philip Caraman SJ (1911-1998) He is probably best known for *John Gerard – The Autobiography of an Elizabethan* translated from the Latin and published in 1951 with an introduction by Graham Greene and *The Lost Paradise – An Account of the Jesuits in Paraguay 1607-1768* published in 1975. The story of the latter might have been familiar only to Latin American specialists and those interested in Jesuit history had not Hollywood and the award-winning script writer Robert Bolt combined to make a film *The Mission* starring Robert de Niro, Jeremy Irons and Liam Neeson among others, which won the top prize at Cannes in 1986, thus bringing it to a much wider audience than would necessarily have interested itself in 18th century Jesuit missionary activity in Paraguay. A similar fate is unlikely to overtake the present work.

12. *La Grande Abridgement* – a work first published in 1514 – see Appendix C p. 398. It was written in Norman French and the work of Sir Anthony Fitzherbert (1470-1538) a member of Gray's Inn and a Justice of the Common Pleas.

Chapter One

THE LEGAL AND SOCIAL BACKGROUND

"The past is a foreign country: they do things differently there"

LP Hartley *The Go-Between*

Foreign countries can be difficult for us to understand and, in the case of the one we know as the past, our true understanding is not always helped by knowing what happened next. We have the benefit of hindsight without the responsibility for the exercise of any foresight and are tempted in consequence to be overly critical of what we see as the shortcomings of our predecessors. They for their part do not have any opportunity to be critical, overly or otherwise, of our shortcomings. Any history of a local law society which reaches back into the past for over two hundred years cannot be considered in isolation from the legal and social world which gave it birth. It was this thought, coupled with Cicero's dictum that "not to know what happened before you were born is to be a child for ever" which prompted me to begin this account with four cases which may help to convey some flavour of those early years following that meeting on 21 March 1786 when the founding members first resolved "at Mr Ringrose's House in York"[1] to set about the establishment of the Society which we know today. Those signatures recorded in the Society's first minute book bear names which seem so familiar. One of them, William Gray, was a partner of the firm which still bears his name today and of which I myself was a partner for nearly forty years. Not only that but I have been a member of the Society for just over one fifth of its entire history, so in a manner of speaking the 230 or so years which separate us from those founding members represent a mere five or six successive professional generations. When we reflect on that our origins somehow do not seem quite that remote.

In 1786 George III had been on the throne for more than quarter of a century. Twenty years had passed since the young Austrian virtuoso, Wolfgang Amadeus Mozart, had been performing on a visit to London in the decidedly down-market pub, the *Swan and Hoop* in Cornhill. Only three years had passed since the Treaty of Versailles in 1783 had finally ended the war of American independence although its outcome had hardly been in doubt since the surrender at Yorktown in 1781. Louis XVI was still King of France (a title incidentally still claimed at that time by our very own George III)[2] and within living memory British cabinet meetings had to be conducted in French, at least when George I insisted on attending, as he didn't speak English, or at least not well enough for that purpose. And the French Revolution had not yet happened. Old men at the time could doubtless recall the Jacobite rebellion of 1745 and the Battle of Culloden, the last land battle to be fought on British soil. Indeed, one of the High Sheriff's trumpeters in William Gray's time when he was under sheriff was Harry Rowe who had served in that capacity for 45 consecutive years. He certainly would have remembered the battle as he had actually fought in it. Bonnie Prince Charlie and Flora Macdonald were both still alive, the latter living quietly at Kingsburgh on the Isle of Skye where she had been visited just thirteen years earlier by Dr Johnson and James Boswell in the course of their celebrated Hebridean tour.[3] As we shall see, the Atlantic slave trade was still operating as it always had and until 1790 there were still offences for which women could be, and were, sentenced to be burnt at the stake.

The Yorkshire Law Society was established as the result of the meeting on 21 March 1786 although its formal constitution was not adopted until 1 August of that year. Five years earlier, on 6 September 1781, the slave ship *Zong*, originally a Dutch vessel which had been captured as a British prize, left its last port of call, Sao Tomé off the coast of West Africa bound for Jamaica. It was the start of the notorious "middle passage" of the slave trade. She had taken 442 African slaves on board and was owned by a consortium of Liverpool merchants, John, William and James Gregson, Edward Wilson and James Aspinall. Her master, Luke Collingwood (a former slaving ship's surgeon) was assisted by his second captain Edward

Howard and a crew of twenty. The voyage should have lasted six to nine weeks but it was on 28 December, well over three months later, that the *Zong* finally arrived at the port of Black River on the south coast of Jamaica.

The exceptional length of the passage was occasioned by a navigational error. The *Zong* had arrived at the island of Hispaniola (now shared between Haiti and the Dominican Republic) which the captain had mistaken for Jamaica. One hopes but rather doubts that Collingwood's surgical expertise was greater than his skill in navigation. That unfortunately was not the only mishap of the voyage. At 110 tons, a relatively small ship for a slaver, she had taken on board far more African slaves than the number for which she was "designed", even by the notorious standards of the slavers of the day. This doubtless was to contribute to the exceptional rate of sickness and mortality on board. By the first landfall at Hispaniola at the end of November this had already claimed the lives of seven crew and sixty slaves and many of the remaining slaves were seriously ill. Collingwood was a worried man. He was well aware that his employers' profits were at risk. He was also aware of the terms of their policy of marine insurance: if the slaves perished from "natural causes", in other words death from sickness, the underwriters were not liable. However, if the "cargo" was jettisoned for the protection of the ship then they were liable – to the extent of £30 per head. His chosen solution had the virtue of simplicity if nothing else: jettison the cargo and claim that it was for the safety of the ship. Over the next three days a total of 133 slaves thought least likely to survive were thrown overboard, chained ankle by ankle. Collingwood had sought to justify his actions by alleging that they were necessary due to a shortage of water. He was clearly being "economical with the truth" but unlike Sir Robert Armstrong of Spycatcher fame, Collingwood was careful to die before he could be cross-examined in court. In fact, when the *Zong* eventually arrived at Black River on 28 December it had over 400 gallons of fresh water on board. The matter was not to rest there.

Gregson v Gilbert (1783)

On 6 March 1783, less than two years after that fateful departure from Africa, the case of *Gregson v Gilbert* came on for trial in the Court of King's Bench where the *Zong's* owners were initially successful in their claim against the underwriters in the trial at the Guildhall before Mansfield CJ and a jury. The factual basis of the original trial, however, was somewhat uncertain. Captain Collingwood having prudently chosen to die shortly after the arrival of the *Zong* at Black River and the ship's log having mysteriously disappeared, not only the moral but the legal basis of the original verdict was clearly open to doubt. Furthermore new evidence had subsequently emerged that the last group of slaves had been thrown overboard the day after a heavy fall of rain had enabled the ship's water supply to be replenished. On this basis the defendants were able to seek an order for a new trial. This application was heard on 22 May before three judges (Mansfield CJ, Willes and Buller JJ) and was successful; it is duly to be found in the law reports (1783) 3 Dougl 233; (1783) 99 ER 629. The second trial never took place, the plaintiffs having prudently decided to withdraw their claim, no doubt sensing that public (and legal) opinion was beginning to change. The facts of the case were extraordinary enough but even more extraordinary to the modern mind was the argument put forward by the plaintiffs' counsel, Yorkshire-born Solicitor-General and former Recorder of Doncaster, John Lee:

> What is this claim that human people have been thrown overboard? This is a case of chattels or goods. Blacks are goods and property; it is madness to accuse these well serving and honourable men of murder. They acted out of necessity and in the most appropriate manner for the cause. The late Captain Collingwood acted in the interests of his ship to protect the safety of his crew. To question the judgment of an experienced, well-travelled captain held in the highest regard is one of folly, especially when talking of slaves. The case is the same as if horses had been thrown overboard.

Mansfield of course had been the judge in the earlier well-known case of *Somerset v Stewart*.[4] James Somerset was a black slave whose master had brought him to England from Virginia and sought to return him there forcibly. The issue as to whether he was entitled to do this came before the court on a writ of *Habeas Corpus*. Mansfield upheld Somerset's claim to liberty on the basis that slavery was a concept unknown to the common law although the words at the end of the case often attributed to him "Let the black go free" may have been uttered by counsel.

Slavers throwing overboard the Dead and Dying – Typhon coming on ("The Slave Ship) 1840 by JMW Turner, Museum of Fine Arts, Boston.

Mansfield was a humane and enlightened man by the standards of the age. My own particular interest in his career is prompted in part by the fact that when he was at the Bar my father occupied the very same chambers at 5, King's Bench Walk in the Temple. On a holiday visit in August 2002 to the Mansfield family home at Scone Palace in Perthshire, no doubt like many before and since, I was very struck by a charming picture once attributed to Zoffany of Lady Elizabeth Murray, Mansfield's great-niece, and a black woman, Dido Elizabeth Belle, who was her cousin.[5] Dido was the illegitimate daughter of Mansfield's nephew, Sir John Lindsay, a captain in the Royal Navy. Her mother had been a black slave whom her father had encountered on a Spanish vessel in the West Indies and brought to England where Dido was born. Possibly unaware of Dido's paternity at the time, Mansfield was quite happy to accept her into his London household. Indeed, he eventually became very fond of her in an avuncular way, providing for her education and remembering her in his will. At the family's London home in Bloomsbury Square and subsequently at Kenwood House, she seems to have been on friendly and familiar terms with her cousin Elizabeth and to have occupied a quasi *au pair* status unknown in 18th century England. This seems to have unsettled one contemporary, Thomas Hutchinson, former Governor-General and Chief Justice of Massachusetts – and doubtless others. Recalling a family dinner party at the Mansfields in 1779 Hutchinson observed "A Black came in after dinner and sat with the ladies and after coffee, walked with the company in the gardens, one of the young ladies having her arm within the other." He also described her rather sniffily as "pert".

Twenty-four years after the *Zong* case, in 1807, William Wilberforce, then MP for Hull, and friend of William Gray, finally managed to achieve his life's ambition of securing the abolition of the slave trade by the enactment of the Slave Trade Act 1807 – 47 Geo.3 c.36. Many great fortunes had been raised on the foundations of this abominable traffic, particularly in the ports of Bristol and Liverpool, and those who benefited from it were extremely vociferous and influential. Due to the enormous vested mercantile interests involved,[6] abolition proved to be a much more difficult exercise in legal reform than the abolition of burning at the stake for women which is the subject of the next case *R v Murphy* which follows. But public opinion on this and other matters was slowly turning.

R v Murphy (1789)

Until it was abolished by the Treason Act 1790 (itself not actually repealed until the Crime and Disorder Act 1998) – women could still be sentenced to be burnt at the stake in public for High or Petty Treason – the former including coining offences and the latter including the murder of a husband, employer or other "superior". The last person to be executed at York in this way was Elizabeth Bordingham on 30 March 1776 – for doing away with her husband.

The reason why women were treated differently from men in this respect was that the penalty for treason in the case of men was hanging, drawing (ie disembowelling) and quartering but this was thought to be too indelicate a public spectacle in the case of women. But 18th century crowds were not that squeamish – it is said that the execution by burning of Elizabeth Herring for Petty Treason at Tyburn in 1773 attracted an estimated crowd of 20,000 – huge by 18th century standards. But even that was modest compared with the number attracted to the execution at Newgate in 1807 of three murderers, including a woman, Elizabeth Godfrey (albeit not by burning) which attracted an estimated crowd of 40,000 and provoked a stampede which led to the deaths of about a hundred spectators. (By way of comparison, the population of York in 1801 was only 16,846 and that of Leeds 30,669 according to the census of that year).

Since the beginning of the century executioners dealing with women sentenced to be burnt at the stake had adopted the practice of strangling them first, although their efforts to temper the rigour of the law with some semblance of humanity were not always attended with success. But on 18 March 1789 there took place the last judicial burning of a woman in England, Catherine Murphy, a Newgate prisoner condemned for a coining offence. The Sheriff of London at the time, who was responsible for the supervision of this gruesome procedure, was Sir Benjamin Hammett. He also happened to be a prominent city alderman, a partner in the banking firm of Esdaile, Hammett and Esdaile – and an MP. The experience had affected him deeply and in May of the following year he introduced a bill for the abolition of this appalling penalty. It passed with little debate or controversy although a bill introduced by William Wilberforce just four years earlier had passed through the Commons equally without controversy but had been thrown out by the Lords.[7]

Burdon v Rhodes (1791)

Unlike *Gregson v Gilbert and R v Murphy*, this and the next case were very much Yorkshire ones. The plaintiff, Thomas Burdon, owned a horse, *Centaur*, which had won a race at the May meeting on the Knavesmire earlier that year, with seventy year old "Kitty" Rowntree on board. The defendant, Robert Rhodes, the clerk of the course who held the stake monies, was being sued for debt. At the instigation of the unsuccessful owners he had refused to hand over the sum of £123 to the winner. The others claimed that it was a condition of the race that horses were only to be ridden by *gentlemen* and Rowntree they said was no gentleman. The race was a sweepstake, each subscriber to deposit ten guineas, and the horses all to be hunters and their *bona fide* property. Owners were not obliged to ride their horses themselves: the restriction to *gentlemen* riders was evidently intended to exclude "professional" riders – jockeys, grooms and the like. They, by definition, were not gentlemen. The question before the court, therefore, was very simple: what were the essential qualifications of a "gentleman" and did the unfortunate Rowntree possess those qualifications?

A popular hanging could hardly have provided better free entertainment to the ordinary citizens of York than a vulgar public spat between members of the gentry about who was entitled to call himself a gentleman and thus be entitled to the winnings of a sweepstake. The lawyer of today would have found some aspects of the proceedings curious, quite apart from the subject matter of the case itself. For one thing, it was listed for hearing at 7 pm; even then it did not begin on time, the judge apparently being so incensed at the tumult in the streets surrounding York's Guildhall that he chose to appear an hour late.[8] That was only the beginning. An anonymous pamphlet,[9] the author of which chose to describe himself simply as "A Bystander", produced shortly after the hearing, makes it quite apparent that the tumult was by no means confined to the streets:

> Before eight the judge arrived, evident symptoms of discontent at the unseasonable croud, and apparent occasions of tumult, were manifest in his countenance. The box was ordered to be cleared for the special jury,[10] which after much difficulty, and amidst great confusion, was at last effected. The judge's officer then made the usual proclamation for silence; it seemed however to have little effect, the tumult rather increased than diminished. The officer then gave notice that if there was any more disturbance, or if any person was guilty of making a noise, so as to interrupt the proceedings of the court, he would bring them into court,[11] and the judge would commit them. The effect of this second notice was not visible, except in the increasing tumult of the witnesses pressing to get into the box set apart for them, and in a temper of mind not much fitted to bear resistance. The judge then rose in no little displeasure, and addressing himself to the surrounding auditors, "If there is any more interruption or noise, I shall certainly take especial notice of those concerned in it." A voice immediately replied "I hope I shall be the first object of your lordship's notice." In consideration of the situation of the gentleman concerned, I shall forbear to mention his name. It was uttered in the vexation of the moment, in the inconsiderateness of youthful ardor. Much do I fear it did not escape the ear of the bench; to the good sense and moderation of the judge, it owed its escape from public notice; the

impression it made on him was visible, (in the opinion of the writer of this) he sunk instantly on the bench; grief, indignation and surprise sat strongly pourtrayed on his countenance. A partial silence however ensued this (I had almost said insult) and Mr Law, as senior counsel for the plaintiff, was suffered to open his case.

Various representatives of the local landowning gentry were called to say what they understood by the term "gentleman" and whether Kitty Rowntree could properly be described as such. It was clear from the evidence, particularly of a respected sporting baronet, Sir William Foulis, that Rowntree was an honourable character but was that enough?

Sir William Foulis Bart

Q   Do you know anything of his general character?
A   I know nothing against him; but on the contrary have a good opinion of him, and think myself obliged to him for assisting me in preserving game on my estate.
Q   Did you ever know him do a dirty action?
A   I never did.

The witnesses called on behalf of the defendant were less accommodating to Rowntree:

Christopher Wilson Esq (one of the subscribers)

Q   You must of course see Rowntree. Is he such a man as you would conceive to come within the meaning of the term Gentleman, as intended by you when you subscribed to the sweepstakes?
A   I saw Rowntree on the race-ground; he is certainly not such a man as we intended should ride; he would be objected to on any race-ground in England. I have rode in similar sweepstakes for several, for the Prince of Wales, and I am certain if Rowntree had attempted to ride on such occasions, he would have been kicked off the course.

Other witnesses, whilst generally acknowledging that he was an *honourable* man, objected to his appearance and dress: "an old gentleman [sic!] with one eye, dirty leather breeches, and an old wig not worth eightpence" as one described him. Another cause of disqualification it seemed was that he dined with farmers on market days "at an ordinary, where the expenses seldom exceed one shilling per head". The term "ordinary" referred to "an ordinary eating-house" roughly equivalent to the present day pub – clearly not the kind of establishment frequented by "gentlemen". The court heard evidence about Rowntree keeping hounds and holding a licence to kill game, of his having ridden in a race at "Red-Carr for a saddle" and the value of his property – one "estate" estimated to be worth £120 and another "little estate which may be worth £40 per annum". One witness, asked whether he considered "Rowntree to keep hounds" replied "No more than I do a pack of Archdeacons". Another, asked whether he regarded him as a gentleman, answered "No more than I regard myself to be a rhinoceros". It was all good knockabout stuff and clearly occasioned much mirth to the public in a packed Guildhall and much irritation to the judge: "Gentlemen of the jury ... If I had not been already convinced of the necessity of courts of law to set their faces against actions of this nature , I think the tumult and indecency I have been a witness to ... would be sufficient, in my mind, to point out the necessity of refusing them admittance here. As the law however, now stands, they are recognised ..." He clearly thought that unseemly rows about entitlement to sweepstake winnings should not be aired in public – and certainly not to the botheration of His Majesty's judges.[12]

The other subscribers' real objection to Rowntree was that he was not "one of them" but a social inferior. Even a Yorkshire special jury were not impressed and the plaintiff duly had his verdict later that night. The plaintiff's leader, Mr Edward Law,[13] had left the jury in little doubt as to his own views:

> Gentlemen of the jury, I have now sat almost three hours to hear a man, confessedly allowed by all parties to be a man of probity and worth, degraded and vilified as the outcast of mankind, as the refuse and scum of the earth. One witness has told us that if he had dared to lay claim to the rank of gentleman on any race-ground in England, he would infallibly have been kicked off the course. Gentlemen, amidst all this obloquy, all this wanton and ungenerous abuse of a respectable character, amidst all this arrogance and pride, too often the appendages of high rank or fortune, and which have been most lavishly displayed this night, amidst all this opposition to the pretensions of Mr Rowntree to the appellation

of gentleman, no one has favoured us with a definition of that term. Since therefore my learned friends have not indulged us with their definition of the word, it may not be perhaps amiss, if I take the liberty of offering mine.

This learned counsel then proceeded to do, in eloquent and sympathetic terms towards the unfortunate Mr Rowntree. After pointing out that he was undoubtedly in possession of an hereditary estate of £160 per annum,

> … descended to him from his father, (and let me say, with this clear income, his situation may be more independent than that of many gentlemen whose rent-rolls are infinitely larger). Not that I think this enjoyment of an hereditary estate adds any merit to his character, regarding as I do the fortune acquired by industry as the most honourable one.

Counsel's closing words were very much in the spirit of the age: after referring in terms to "the Rights of Man"[14] he continued, referring to himself and the other members of the Bar, "There are perhaps those who may deny to us, exercising here an honourable profession, the claims to that distinction." Counsel himself would of course have been very much a aware that he was not a "mere" solicitor or attorney but he was certainly conscious that in the eyes of some he himself was not *quite* a gentleman. After the close of speeches the judge retired to his lodgings,[15] (it must by that time have been very late) and it was arranged that the jury would attend there as soon as they had reached their verdict. It was but a short walk from the Guildhall, down Coney Street. Apparently, however, the tumult which had occurred before and during the sitting of the court did not abate after the retirement of the judge. Shortly afterwards the jury followed him back to the lodgings with their verdict, "amidst a great number of people, who, on hearing that it was found for the plaintiff, were very liberal of their acclamation …" Notwithstanding, therefore, the "tumult and indecency" associated with the proceedings, the unfortunate Rowntree (who of course was not a party to the action) was adjudged to be a "gentleman". But as the "bystander" author of the account of the trial noted at the time, it was "a vague and indefinite term… The servant when referring to his co-equal by the term *gentleman* …the man of rank and independence to those who he regards as on a par with himself, will demand each of them a different construction."

Nevertheless, the city's weekly newspaper, *The York Courant*, for 16 August 1791, after providing a detailed account of *Burdon v Rhodes* added the following laconic postscript: "The same day at the Guildhall, Abraham Robertshaw, convicted of Forgery, received sentence of death." Clearly who was or was not entitled to be classed as a gentleman was considered at the time to be much more newsworthy than the life or death of a convicted felon.

Gilbert v Sykes

York seemed to attract wagering cases at his period. Two decades later its citizens were similarly entertained by the case of *Gilbert v Sykes*. It came on for hearing at the Spring Assizes in 1812 before Thompson B[16] and yet another special jury. However, the events giving rise to the case had occurred some years previously in 1802. The defendant, Sir Mark Masterman Sykes Bt of Sledmere had given a dinner party. The plaintiff, the Reverend Robert Gilbert, then Vicar of Settrington, was one of the guests. After the table had been cleared and the ladies had retired, the conversation turned to politics. The great subject of dinner party conversation at the time was a certain Napoleon Bonaparte. The United Kingdom and France were then at peace following the Treaty of Amiens in March 1802 but there seemed to be a general opinion that he was at great risk from assassination. Certainly Sir Mark was of this opinion; so much so indeed that he incautiously suggested that he would "venture to receive one hundred guineas to pay a guinea a day during the life of Bonaparte". "Will you Sir Mark – Done!" immediately interjected the Reverend Gilbert. According to the detailed account in the *Sporting Magazine* Sir Mark appeared surprised and rather displeased that his offer should have been so hastily accepted and there was a general cry from the other guests of "No bet!" The Vicar of Settrington seemed to be somewhat abashed at their reaction and said to his host "If you will submit, Sir Mark, to ask it as a favour, you may be off" but Sir Mark was not prepared to settle on those terms. His reply made it clear that he would not ask any favour or make any concession at his own table or in his own house.

Later attempts were made by Sir Mark through an intermediary to settle the matter by payment of £500 but they came to nought. Sir Mark duly paid up for a while until the "guinea a day" had reached the appreciable sum of £970 but then stopped, no doubt thinking that honour had been satisfied. For some years nothing happened and then, in January 1812 the Reverend Gilbert commenced proceedings, claiming a total of £2,296.7s 0d from Sir Mark, being the accrued amount said to be due under the "contract". A number of witnesses were called. One of them, another clergyman, conceded under cross-examination, that "those present did not drink water to their dinner" and was unable to say that Sir Mark "was remarkable for his abstemiousness", adding "the glass was circulated very freely" although another guest, John Robert Foulis,[17] conceded that he "did not mean to represent the company as being drunk."

Given the absence of any admission on the part of the defendant and the strict rules against hearsay, the Reverend Gilbert clearly had a problem: strict proof would be required that Napoleon was still alive at the commencement of proceedings in January 1812. This posed certain evidential difficulties for his advisers. It is now known of course that Napoleon was very much alive, but how was this to be proved to the satisfaction of a judge and jury sitting in York in the course of a major European war under the conditions prevailing in the early 19th century? The solution was to call a Mr Anderson, a messenger employed at the US consulate in London. He gave evidence to the effect that in the course of his visits to Paris he had seen Napoleon "repeatedly". More specifically, that he had left Paris on 30 January with dispatches for the American *Chargé d'Affaires* in London; that he had seen the Emperor reviewing his troops at the Tuilleries in "January or December"; and that he was mounted on "a white charger".[18] However, he admitted under cross-examination that the Emperor (if indeed it were he) was too far away for him to have recognised his features. Rather defensively, he admitted that it was not very easy to get close to the Emperor when he was engaged in reviewing 30,000 troops! Asked about Napoleon's apparent health, the witness attempted to get his own back on counsel and regain lost ground: "I am very sorry to inform you that he will probably live thirty or forty years longer; when I saw him near five years since he had an oval Italian face but is now grown fat, and as good-looking and quite as embonpoint as yourself! I repeatedly saw him and his lady in a barge at Amsterdam and subsequent to his grand military entrée into that city."

The plaintiff was lucky to have been able to get any evidence at all from American consular staff in March 1812. Less than three months after the hearing any special relationship with the United States had gotten a little less special as by then the Americans had declared war on Britain. By August of that year British forces had captured Detroit and two years later had occupied Washington and burned the White House to the ground. But it did him no good. In his closing speech to the jury Mr Topping, counsel for Sir Mark, can have left them in little doubt as to his own views on the plaintiff's conduct; having been paid £970 by his client "in consequence of an unguarded expression used in a moment of jollity at his own table, amongst those whom he imagined his friends; and in addition to this, the plaintiff seeks to recover by your verdict £2,296.7s.0d. This is what this worthy clergyman, this ornament of the established church, now seeks through your means to obtain from the defendant." He went on to quote Lord Ellenborough[19] "that it would be well for some persons, before they came into court, to inquire if there is not something more valuable than money; but there are persons who have so little value and feeling for character, that if you were to put 5/- in one scale and character in the other, they would run away with the money and leave character to kick the beam." The jury found for Sir Mark.

As luck would have it, Lord Ellenborough, having been quoted by counsel for Sir Mark, then found himself hearing an application by counsel for Mr Gilbert for a rule to show cause why the jury's verdict for the defendant should not be set aside and a new trial ordered on the grounds that it was against all the evidence. Counsel's argument was that the trial judge, Thompson B, in his charge to the jury, had treated the contract as an annuity rather than a wager. Lord Ellenborough, although he clearly regarded the proceedings with some distaste, decided that unless there was some element of immorality or that was contrary to public policy in the agreement it could and should be enforced as any other legal contract, the existence of which seemed to have been established by the fact that the defendant had gone on paying for three years. That being so, he considered that the jury had gone beyond their remit in finding for the defendant.

On Friday 12 June the matter came before the judges of the King's Bench (Lord Ellenborough CJ, Bayley, Le Blanc and Grose JJ), and the matter was fully argued by counsel for both parties. It is clear from the report[20] that the four judges were not entirely *ad idem* as to the precise reason for refusing to order a new trial but they were all agreed that it should be refused. On the one hand a wager on the life of Napoleon gave the plaintiff an interest in keeping Napoleon (an enemy of the king) alive; on the other, it gave the defendant an interest in encompassing his death by means other than lawful warfare. Either way, it was contrary to public policy and they were not having it. The decision was to be later criticised as being of "doubtful authority"[21] but has nevertheless been cited and found its way into legal textbooks across the English-speaking common law world – the lawyer's version perhaps of the chaos theory where a host's chance remark at a dinner party in rural East Yorkshire in 1802 can lead to a reference in an Australian law report over two hundred years later.[22]

The level of legal representation on both sides in this case was equally remarkable. Of four counsel appearing on behalf of the Reverend Robert Gilbert, William Garrow (1760-1840) was to become Solicitor-General that same year and Attorney-General the following year before being elevated to the Bench in the Court of Exchequer and (in 2009) becoming the subject of a BBC television programme *Garrow's Law*. James Alan Park (1762-1858) became a judge in the Court of Common Pleas and Joseph Littledale (1761-1842) a judge of the Court of King's Bench. As for the youngest member of the team, Henry Brougham MP (1778-1868), he went on to be leading counsel for Queen Caroline at her trial in 1820 and later still to become Lord Chancellor and a leading law reformer of the age. On Sir Mark's side, James Scarlett (later Lord Abinger) was advising the Society in 1815 in an effort to secure a more equitable basis of taxation of costs in the common law courts – see Chapter 3 note 5 – and went on to become Attorney-General under both Canning and Wellington's administrations before briefly becoming MP for Malton and later Chief Baron of the Court of Exchequer, of which John Hullock

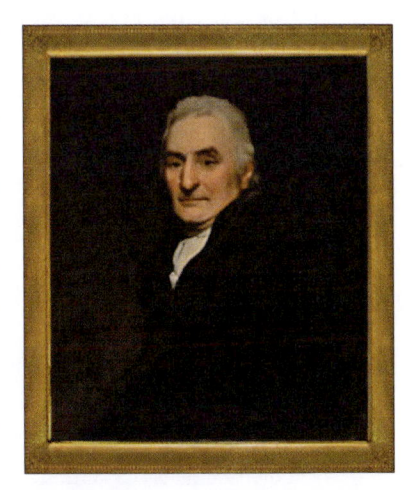

The portrait, believed to be of the Reverend Robert Gilbert, now on display at Sledmere.

Photo John Knowles

was equally to become a judge. Indeed, of the seven counsel engaged, only one, the Yorkshireman, Mr Topping eventually failed to make it to the Bench. Although described about this time by an anonymous author[23] as the "senior practising counsel in the Court of King's Bench" he seems to have been somewhat aggressive in court even by the standards of a rough age. The same observer commented " … there is no counsel who has been so frequently interrupted by the Bench with a sort of gentle hint that more restraint would be becoming … he has sometimes appeared as it were overwhelmed in the foam of his own wrath …" Remarking also on Topping's pronounced Yorkshire accent, which apparently he made a somewhat unsuccessful effort to disguise, he adds "In the North I have heard his Yorkshire brogue (if it may be so called) is of considerable use to him; but it is much to be regretted that he could never leave much of it behind him." Seemingly all this was less acceptable to the establishment when it came to judicial appointments than the acknowledged urbanity of James Scarlett. But at least peace has now been established between the Sykes family and their former vicar: a portrait believed to be of the Reverend Robert Gilbert is now to be seen on display at Sledmere.

NOTES

1. "Mr Ringrose's house", also known as Bluitt's Inn, was a fashionable York hostelry of the day situated in what was then Little Blake Street or Lop Lane. In 1784 in the pre-election meeting prior to the adoption of William Wilberforce as a parliamentary candidate for Yorkshire in the election of that year it is known that Wilberforce himself and other supporters of Pitt dined at the York Tavern whilst the Foxites dined at Bluitt's – See *The Life of William Wilberforce* by his sons Robert Isaac and Samuel Wilberforce. Lop Lane disappeared from the streetscape of York in the 1860s. In 1859 York Corporation was planning a new approach road to Lendal Bridge and, by arrangement with Dean Duncombe, this was extended towards the Minster. The widened thoroughfare became known as Duncombe Place. Bluitt's Inn was located roughly where Thomas's now is in Museum Street, just around the corner from the Assembly Rooms.

2. Formal legal documents in the 18th century invariably referred to the sovereign as being " … of Great Britain France and Ireland King Defender of the Faith etc". Although the Treaty of Amiens in March 1802 did not specifically deal with the issue, renunciation of the claim by British

sovereigns to be "King of France" had been one of the demands of the Directory in the abortive peace negotiations at Lille in 1797, along with the return to France of the Channel Islands and much else besides. However, the 1802 treaty did refer to the contracting party of the other part as being "His Majesty the King of the United Kingdom of Great Britain and Ireland". Following the execution of Louis XVI in 1793 George III's claim to the French throne had become even more academic than it had been previously. Moreover, a much more credible pretender was the Comte de Provence (the future Louis XVIII) who was living in London at the time.

3. *The Journal of a Tour to the Hebrides with Samuel Johnson* by James Boswell (1740-1795) had only just been published (1785) although the journey itself had been accomplished in the summer of 1773. The book was an instant success. The following year (1786) Boswell was admitted to the English Bar, having previously been called as an advocate in Scotland. He hardly practised in England although he did sit as recorder of Carlisle from 1788 to 1790. At the time of their journey Scotland was still subject to the Disarming of the Highlands etc Act 1745 which proscribed the wearing of highland attire (kilt, tartan etc) following the Jacobite uprising of 1745. However, by the time Boswell's account came to be published parliament had already repealed these provisions by the Use of Highland Dress Act 1782. This was to have the slightly quixotic effect of enabling later generations of Scots to adopt as an iconic symbol of their national identity a form of dress formerly confined to the remoter parts of their country and closely associated with an essentially alien cultural, religious and rebellious political faction.

4. Loft 1 *sub nom Sommersett's Case*; 20 State Trials 1; (1772) 98 ER 499.

5. The story of James Somerset has long been familiar to lawyers and those interested in the history of slavery and the slave trade but that of Dido much less so. This has been rectified by the release in June 2014 of the film *Belle* directed by Amma Asante with Gugu Mbatha-Raw in the title role and Leeds born Tom Wilkinson as Mansfield. The film also coincided with the commissioned publication of *Belle:The True Story of Dido Belle* by Paula Byrne – Harper Collins 2014.

6. The English at this period had acquired a taste for sugar which is still with us. Many a family fortune was based on sugar and one benefit that is also still with us is the "Tate" Gallery and "Tate" Britain (as in "Tate & Lyle"). Indeed, it was the demand for sugar that largely drove the Carribean slave trade. It was only when the growing and processing of beet

was developed, prompted by the Napoleonic wars which had disrupted the export of cane sugar to Europe, that our economic dependence on the West Indies began to decline. Nevertheless, statutory abolition of the slave trade notwithstanding, our indirect commercial involvement in slavery lingered on for some years. In *Santos v Illidge* (1860) CB (NS) 861 the court had to consider the case of a claim by a Brazilian plaintiff against an English company trading in Brazil for non-delivery of slaves which the defendants had contracted to deliver. *Quaere* whether the contract was illegal under the statutes against slave trading. Apparently not according to a majority in the Court of Exchequer Chamber (an appellate court dealing with appeals from the courts of King's Bench, Exchequer and Common Pleas and made up of judges from the two courts not involved at first instance). Slavery was not abolished in Brazil until 1888.

7. The bill was "For regulating the Disposal after Execution of the Bodies of Criminals and for Changing the Sentence pronounced upon Female Convicts in certain cases of High and Petty Treason". The proposals were described by Lord Loughborough, the leading Whig lawyer, as "raw, jejune, ill-advised and impracticable". He further argued that the incorporation of burning into a death sentence made it more severe "than mere hanging" – quoted by William Hague *William Wilberforce* Harper Press 2007 p.99.

8. There was much less uniformity about court hours in the 18th and early 19th centuries and they were very much up to individual judges. The great William Blackstone himself at Bristol Assizes once tried to insist on proceedings starting at 7am but was confronted with a barristerial mutiny. By way of contrast, in the 1960s a judicial attempt at Oxford Assizes to dispose of a case by sitting on a Saturday met with the ready concurrence of counsel and solicitors but was defeated by the jury. Oxford City had an important home match on the day in question and it became abundantly clear that the court could do what it liked but an Oxford jury had its own priorities. However, provided the lawyers and the jury were prepared to co-operate, the discretion of judges as to court hours could be astonishing to the modern mind. All night sittings were not unknown. In February 1781 Lord George Gordon, the leader of the Protestant Association, was being tried for treason on the basis of his alleged conduct provoking the "Gordon Riots" the previous year. The case of was presided over by Lord Mansfield, who had not thought it necessary to recuse himself despite the fact that his own house in Bloomsbury Square had been burnt to the ground by the rioters and his other residence, Kenwood House on Hampstead Heath, had very nearly suffered the same fate. The proceedings began at

8am on a Monday morning, continued throughout that day and were not concluded until 5.15am the following morning. Not altogether surprisingly Mansfield's summing up to the jury in the early hours of Tuesday morning seemed to lack his customary succinctness and clarity. On several occasions Gordon's counsel, Thomas Erskine, the future Lord Chancellor, and indeed Gordon himself, had to interrupt him to point out that he had misstated or omitted material facts. Perhaps the jury merely wished to get to bed after this marathon session; after they had retired for only half-an-hour Gordon was acquitted.

9. Its full title was "The Famous Turf Cause of Burdon against Rhodes, Tried at the Guildhall, York before Mr Baron Thomson and a Special Jury, on Wednesday the 10th day of August, 1791, to which are added, Some Observations on the Merits of the Case, as well as on the Singular Circumstances attending the trial". I am indebted to the York Race Committee for kindly allowing me to make use of the copy in the Racecourse Library. This account is also based, with their permission, on an article which I wrote for the *Yorkshire Post* © which appeared on 17 May 2000.

10. Either party could apply for a "special jury" drawn from the special jury list maintained by the sheriff of persons of the degree of esquire or similar, merchants, bankers etc. Special juries were finally abolished by the Labour government after the war except for commercial cases tried in London – see S.27(1) Juries Act 1949. The last recorded instance of the use of a City of London special jury was in 1950 and special juries were abolished for all purposes by S.35(7) of the Courts Act 1971.

11. "Bring them into court" – ie within the "Bar" of the courtroom. Junior counsel are "bar-risters" because they have been called *to* the Bar and are thus entitled to appear *at* the Bar. If, and when they are appointed "Queen's Counsel" they become members of the court and are thus entitled to appear "within the Bar". This is why junior counsel were sometimes referred to as "utter (or outer) barristers".

12. Ever since the Gaming Act 1710 parliament had interested itself in correcting *abuses* in gaming and wagering. However, it was not until the Gaming Act 1845 that wagers as such became unenforceable by action – a position reversed only recently by S 335(1) of the Gambling Act 2005 which came into force on 1 September 2007. Scots law has always taken a more Presbyterian view of such matters and refused to enforce contracts relating to wagers on the grounds that they were *sponsiones ludicrae* and thus beneath the dignity of their courts.

13. Edward Law (1750-1818) was a noted Northern Circuiteer who went on to become Attorney-General in 1801 and Chief Justice of the King's Bench. He was leading counsel for Warren Hastings on his impeachment.

14. Part 1 of the work of this title by Thomas Paine had been published in London in February 1791 price 3/-, and was the subject of great interest and controversy. The concept embodied by the phrase had appeared a few years before in the American Declaration of Independence on 4 July 1776. Thirteen years later at the beginning of the French Revolution on 26 August 1789 the phrase (in French) had appeared as "La déclaration des droits de l'homme et du citoyen". Paine's pamphlet had appeared in answer to Burke's *Reflections on the Revolution in France* first published on 1 November 1790, see Prologue p. 5. It is safe to assume that counsel would have been fully familiar with these contemporary issues as they were the political correctness of the age. Linguistic usage, of course, changes with the years and it is no longer considered seemly to talk about "the Rights of *Man*". Were he alive today, Mr Law would no doubt have been a member of Matrix Chambers and practised in the field of *Human* Rights.

15. The York lodgings at this date (1791) were still in Judges Court off Coney Street, subsequently the offices of Messrs Sykes, Lee & Brydson, solicitors now incorporated in Ware & Kay LLP. The subsequent "Judges Lodgings" in Lendal (now a hotel of that name) did not come into use as such until 1806. They became a hotel in 1979 following the abolition of the assize system under the Beeching reforms when York ceased to be a first tier trial centre.

16. By a strange coincidence these two remarkable sporting cases, *Burdon v Rhodes* and *Gilbert v Sykes*, were both tried in York by the same judge. Thompson's judicial reputation was high. He was described by the eminent law reformer, Sir Samuel Romilly, in a debate in the House of Commons on 17 February 1813 as being "as conscientious and as intelligent a judge as ever sat on the bench" – Hansard HC Debates Vol 24 Col 570. Park J in *Shackell v Rosier* (1836) 2 Bing NC 634 described him as "one of the most eminent judges of his time". See also York's Bloody Assize – Appendix A p. 338.

17. Robert Foulis was Sir Mark's brother-in-law and son of Sir William Foulis who had given evidence as to how he had "a good opinion" of jockey Kitty Rowntree and felt obliged to him "for assisting me in preserving game on my estate" in the case of *Burdon v Rhodes* – a family as well as a judicial link between the two cases.

18. The story of Napoleon's famous white charger *Marengo*, said to have been acquired in 1799 in the course of his Egyptian campaign and ridden in all his major campaigns thereafter up to and including Waterloo, is doubtful. A white horse supposedly belonging to the Emperor was certainly captured by British forces following the battle and brought back to England where it died in 1831, its skeleton now being preserved in the National Army Museum. However, Napoleon is known to have had several horses killed under him in the course of his campaigns; he is also known to have had a preference for white or grey horses.

19. Edward Law first Baron Ellenborough. See Note 13 above.

20. (1812) 16 East. 150; 104 ER 1045

21. By Parke B in *Egerton v Earl Brownlow* (1853) 4 HLC 124

22. *Cattanach v Melchior* [2003] HCA 38; 215 CLR 1

23. *Criticisms on the Bar including Strictures on the Principal Counsel Practising in the Courts of King's Bench, Common Pleas, Chancery and Exchequer* by "Amicus Curiæ" – London 1819. This irreverent and subjective precursor of *Chambers* or *The Legal 500* is a surprisingly lively read. Despite the author's attempt to preserve anonymity, it quickly became known that he was John Payne Collier (1789-1883) a journalist and critic on the *Morning Chronicle*. He had entered the Middle Temple but was not called until 1829, partly due to his indiscretion in publishing his *Criticisms on the Bar*.

Chapter Two

GENTLEMEN OF THE LAW

"He is not a gentleman, he works"

William Cavendish (Fifth Duke of Devonshire) on his
distinguished scientist cousin Henry Cavendish

The numerous lawyers attending the Assizes for the County and City of York which began on the 11 March 1786 may have been intrigued to receive a copy of a handbill which was being distributed that week in all the places where they were accustomed to congregate on such occasions. York being the only assize centre of the largest county in England, many of them will have come some distance and would doubtless have been staying in town for the whole period of the assizes or at least until their business was done. A copy of that handbill has survived and we know from where the "many gentlemen" came[1] who attended that meeting on Tuesday 21 March 1786 because their names are in the carefully handwritten minute book before me as I write – duly signed by the Town Clerk of York, George Townend, the Society's first President.

For the most part nowadays the term "gentlemen" is merely descriptive of gender, although the more politically correct local authorities and universities insist on marking the doors of their conveniences "Men" and "Women" or "Male" and "Female". Otherwise it is used simply to denote a man who can be relied upon to behave with a reasonable degree of propriety and formality towards others and who, if he sometimes fails to polish his shoes, at least has a pair capable of being polished and is aware that he ought perhaps to do so. It may occasionally be used ironically but it is difficult for the modern mind to grasp the importance which

The Handbill of March 20, 1786

> YORK, March 20, 1786.
>
> # MEETING
>
> OF
>
> ATTORNIES and SOLICITORS.
>
> MANY Gentlemen being of Opinion that General Meetings, to be occasionally held, will be of public Utility and productive of useful Regulations; and as a Bill in Parliament is intended, which may materially affect the Profession, a General Meeting of ATTORNIES and SOLICITORS resident in the County and City of York, and of such others as attend the present Assizes, is requested to be held at the House of Mr. RINGROSE, in YORK, on TUESDAY EVENING next, the 21ft of March instant, precisely at SEVEN o'Clock, to consider of the Heads of the proposed Bill, and fix upon a proper Plan for establishing General Meetings in future.

our forebears attached to the term as indicative of social status. Social *status* mattered in former times, and was one of the considerations which prompted the formation of the Society on that March evening over two hundred years ago so it is worth considering in detail the extent to which it mattered.

Let us suppose for a moment that it was not Kitty Rowntree who had been riding *Centaur* in that controversial race on the Knavesmire in May 1791 but John Foljambe (1741-1792), a founder member of the Society. Would the subscribers to that sweepstake have objected to him too? After all, he may not have been personally possessed of an estate, even a "little" one and may have kept neither a pack of hounds nor even of archdeacons. And we know nothing about his wig, although he did have the advantage that like many good aristocratic names, its pronunciation

"Full-jum" would doubtless have been a trap for the unwary farmer who dined at an ordinary.[2] Unfortunately, however, Foljambe was a leading lawyer in Rotherham in his day. At one stage of his career he was a steward of the manorial courts and legal adviser to Thomas, third Earl of Effingham, although he features in the *Rotherham Directory* for 1784 simply as "Attorney-at-Law". The Foljambes were a very prominent Yorkshire/Derbyshire family who could reliably trace their origins to the mid 13th century. The first Sir Geoffrey Foljambe who died in 1376 (Arms: *Sable, a Bend between Six Escallops Or*; Crest: *A Leg in Armour, Couped at the Thigh, Quarterly Or and Sable*) was a close associate of John of Gaunt. John Foljambe the solicitor or "attorney-at-law" certainly seems to have been connected to the branch of the family based at Aldwarke Hall[3] near Rotherham who claimed, somewhat improbably, descent from Scandinavian royalty of the 10th century. But even as a member of a family claiming royal, albeit Scandinavian, descent, John Foljambe suffered one great handicap in the gentlemen stakes: he was an *Attorney-at-Law*. Would this have disqualified him from riding *Centaur* without objection?

It is not a question to which it is easy to give a clear answer. For nearly the whole of the 18th century social protocol was ostensibly rigid. The fifth Duke of Devonshire was certainly not in any doubt. Forbidding his notoriously unconventional wife Georgiana to visit the laboratory of his own cousin, the distinguished scientist, Henry Cavendish,[4] he observed peremptorily: "He is not a gentleman; he works." But the social effects of the industrial revolution and for that matter the French Revolution were beginning to be felt and by the Regency period at least, if you were smart, witty and knew how to adapt, it was just possible over time to break the rigid 18th century glass ceiling of low birth. After all, that iconic dandy of the period, Beau Brummell (1778–1840) although of prosperous middle class parentage (Eton, Oriel for one year only, and even the 10th Royal Hussars until thy were posted to Manchester and he resigned in disgust) was the grandson of a valet.

However, questions of social status apart, the sad fact is that for far longer than anyone can remember lawyers have had a bad press. It would be tempting to believe that Shakespeare started it all with his famous exchange between Dick and Cade:[5]

Dick   The first thing we do, let's kill all the lawyers.
Cade   Nay, that I mean to do.

But it goes back much further than that. In 15th century Hull the borough court had half-a-dozen attorneys sworn to act for those unable or unwilling to conduct their own cases. From what they were enjoined *not* to do it may be inferred that professional standards were low. "They were not to foment lawsuits, not to trick the court into considering matters not within its jurisdiction, not to take any fee from the party against whom they were acting but to be true to their clients, not to urge any client to take elsewhere a case within the jurisdiction of the court, and not to retain money due to clients for their own profit but to pay it out to them immediately." [6]

Standards in Hull were no different from anywhere else. As one historian put it "Although there were many honest and able attorneys and solicitors, collectively they were a rabble, needing no formal qualifications and subject to no sort of control. The attorney had become the butt of every dramatist and his calling was despised."[7] By the beginning of the 18th century various attempts were made to introduce reforms but it was parliamentary petitions from the West and East Riding justices and the Liberty of St Peter in York which were referred to a committee presided over by Sir William Strickland, MP for Scarborough and a Lord of the Treasury. This eventually prompted the Attorneys and Solicitors Act 1729 which came into force on 1 December 1730. The provisions of the act are well summarised by Robert Robson:[8]

> After that date, no person was to be admitted as an attorney unless he had taken the prescribed oath, and had been duly admitted and enrolled in one of the courts. Before they admitted any clerk, the judges were "to examine and inquire, by such ways and means as they shall think proper, touching his fitness and capacity to act as an attorney". Clerks were to serve an apprenticeship of five years to an attorney "duly sworn and admitted", and no attorney was to have more than two clerks at any one time. Attorneys of one court were permitted to sue out writs in another if they had the permission of an attorney of the court so to do, but those attorneys who allowed persons to practise in their names who had not been admitted were to be debarred from practice, and those suing out the writs fined £50. Sworn attorneys were able to practise as solicitors, without paying

an additional fee. They were obliged to put their names on all writs before delivering them, and were not to begin any action for the recovery of fees until one month after the delivery of their bills.[9] After June 1729, the names of all who were admitted were to be enrolled on lists kept in the respective courts. Nothing in the act was to be held as either requiring or authorising the judges to admit a greater number of attorneys "than by the ancient custom and usage of such court hath heretofore been allowed".

According to James Boswell[10] attitudes to attorneys had not much changed in Dr Johnson's time: "...much enquiry having been made concerning a gentleman, who had quitted a company where Johnson was, and no information being obtained; at last Johnson observed, that 'he did not care to speak ill of any man behind his back, but he believed the gentleman was an *attorney*'". But was Dr Johnson's description of the absent attorney as a *gentleman* intended as irony or an oxymoron? Many solicitors are doubtless familiar with the old saw that they are only gentlemen "by act of parliament". Certainly it seems to have been received as accepted fact throughout the 19th century. The best known source[11] seems to have been Charles Dickens in *The Old Curiosity Shop*:

> "Gentlemen," said Brass, laying his right hand on his waistcoat, and looking towards the father and son with a smooth smile – "Gentlemen, I appeal to you – really, gentlemen – consider, I beg of you. I am of the law. I am styled 'gentleman' by Act of Parliament. I maintain the title by the annual payment of twelve pound sterling for a certificate. I am not one of your players of music, stage actors, writers of books, or painters of pictures, who assume a station that the laws of their country don't recognise. I am none of your strollers or vagabonds. If any man brings his action against me, he must describe me as a gentleman, or his action is null and void. I appeal to you – is this quite respectful? Really, gentlemen …"

However, in *Portrait of a Profession: A history of the Solicitor's Profession 1100 to the present day* the author Harry Kirk,[12] who has clearly gone into the matter in some detail, after referring to the character of Mr Brass in the above extract from *The Old Curiosity Shop*, observed:

> The idea that an attorney was a gentleman by statute was probably of long standing … there is no statute which expressly so provides, but it has been suggested that it is implied in the Attornies and Solicitors Act

1729, which confirmed the status of attorneys and solicitors as officers of the court. As early as 1534 court officers were sometimes given the title of "generoso" and Camden refers to a fifth grade of esquire arising from status as an official and which he traces back to the reign of Richard II. On a similar tack is Coke's statement of the rule at common law that "a man may have an addition of gentleman within this statute [ie 1 Hen. 5 c. 5] if he be a gentleman by office (though he be not by birth).... and clerks, being officers in the King's Court of Record....so long as they continue in their office they ought to be named gentleman as their due addition."

Even at the time of the Society's centenary celebrations in 1886 there were still members of the profession who were clearly preoccupied by questions of social status.[13]

To bring the matter forward, at least to the 20th century, the well-known historian AJP Taylor used the term "other ranks" to describe solicitors in his Leslie Stephen lecture[14] in 1961. Taylor himself started as an articled clerk in his uncle's firm: " ... from the first day I realised I had made a ghastly mistake. The work, such as it was, bored me ... after six months of solitary unhappiness I broke my articles and became a free man".[15] The uncle in question was WH Thompson whose firm, now Thompsons, claims to have "more experience of winning personal injury claims than any other firm" and one of the largest to be licensed as an Alternative Business Structure (ABS). More than fifty years after Taylor's lecture it is difficult to imagine any serious commentator making a similar remark, although in the days of Lloyd George (which was the subject matter of his lecture) and even until the 1960s and beyond, the description may have been partially accurate. The late Sir David Napley,[16] still thought it necessary in his book *Not Without Prejudice* published in 1982 to mention some of the sillier aspects of the Bar's rules regarding their relationship with solicitors. He describes one occasion at St Albans Quarter Sessions in the 1950s where he had instructed a very young junior counsel. At the luncheon adjournment Napley, being unfamiliar with the area, enquired where they could get some lunch. Counsel mentioned a pub which was fairly good so Napley invited him to join him there. Counsel agreed and went off to the robing room. When they met up as arranged the young man, with great embarrassment, had to explain to his intended lunching companion that they would be unable to eat together. He had mentioned their proposed arrangement to a more senior member of the Bar and had been advised that the pub in question was used as the Bar Mess and that he could not have lunch there with a solicitor. Napley, familiar with the Bar rules, assured counsel that he quite understood.[17] Arriving at the pub, he found it fairly crowded. Whilst he was looking around to see where he could safely sit without breaching the Bar's self-imposed apartheid, he was spotted by the senior enforcer who had "warned off" the young barrister from having lunch with him. In a barristerial voice clearly audible throughout the room he intoned "Right, Napley, now you choose where you want to sit, and we will then go and sit somewhere else." "No," replied Napley, "that will not be necessary; I will lunch elsewhere." Picking up his hat and coat he departed. Unable to find anywhere else in St Albans suitable to get something to eat, he spent the next hour wandering around in the cold in considerable exasperation.

In theory the Bar's rules were directed against the practice of "attorney-hugging" as it was known – or in modern parlance "touting'. In practice by the beginning of the second half of the 20th century its practical manifestations had as much to do with lingering notions of snobbery. Certainly there is nothing in my own professional experience remotely comparable to that of Sir David Napley in the 1950s. Attending county courts in South Wales as an articled clerk in the mid-1960s, solicitors and counsel mixed freely at lunchtime – even with the opposition. Later still in the 1990s, when involved in a five day civil case in Newcastle, both I and our leading counsel (from Liverpool) were invited by junior counsel to stay at the Northern Counties Club where he was a member and which was serving at the time as the de facto Bar Mess. Not only was it a sensible arrangement from a purely professional point of view, it enabled us to follow Tranio's injunction in *The Taming of the Shrew* "And do as adversaries do in law – Strive mightily, but eat and drink as friends." To which incidentally, Gremio's response is "O excellent Motion".

One has to remember, of course, that in AJP Taylor and David Napley's time there were far fewer members of the Bar and they were generally more socially and professionally cohesive than solicitors who had tended for most of the previous two hundred years or so to be recruited from a wider social spectrum. But even at the Bar there were doubtless those whom some at least of the founder members of the Society would have regarded as "low practitioners", more particularly perhaps those who practised in the criminal courts. Equally, there was a noticeable tendency throughout the 19th century for even the most patrician families to encourage younger sons to become solicitors: it was, after all helpful to have somebody close at hand who was able to deal with the family estates. Perhaps it was this that encouraged John Foljambe of Rotherham to become an attorney. Indeed, there is some evidence to suggest that even in the 18th century the social distinction between the Bar and "other ranks" was not *quite* so great as some at least of the former might have imagined. Among those who attained high judicial office were several former attorneys or articled clerks or who had at least started their legal life in an attorney's office. They included no less than four future Lord Chancellors although admittedly one of them ended his career in total disgrace and another had the distinction as an undergraduate of being sent down from Cambridge.

Lord Macclesfield, the provincial attorney whose stratospheric albeit picaresque career took him first to the woolsack but ultimately to the Tower of London for equally stratospheric bribery (about £100,000 or £11M in modern money)

© *National Portrait Gallery*

The first of these, Lord Macclesfield (1666-1732), was himself the son of an attorney from Leek in Staffordshire, and actually practised as such in Derby before being called to the Bar in 1691. It is something of a mystery as to how he acquired sufficient education for a career at the Bar. He seems to have been taught to read by his mother and certainly spent two or three years at the local (free) grammar school at Newport (Shropshire) where he picked up a smattering of Greek and Latin but, as Lord Campbell[18] remarked of him "he knew little more than the peasantry among whom he was reared, and never having had any further instruction, he must be considered as in a great measure self-taught." In all events he completed his articles and was duly admitted as an attorney. At first he was somewhat overawed by the barristers on whom he attended but, as Lord Campbell put it, it was not long before "his reverence for these dignitaries gradually dwindled away" and "he began sometimes to think he himself could have examined witnesses quite as well as the barristers employed by him, and even by making a better speech to the jury have won verdicts which they lost", adding "he was likewise hurt by the distance at which he was in public kept by all members of the superior grade of the profession" although conceding that "some of them were intensely civil to him in private": – a problem that David Napley would certainly have recognised. Nevertheless the progress of this provincial self-taught grammar school boy from the provinces was rapid and steady. Having elected to practise on the Midland Circuit, it wasn't long before he became its leader. In due course he became not only Recorder of Derby but its MP, Bencher of the Inner Temple and Chief Justice of the Queen's Bench before finally attaining the Woolsack as Lord Chancellor in 1718.

At an earlier stage in his career he had even achieved the distinction of being appointed a Regent of Great Britain following the death of Queen Anne on 1 August 1714. A temporary regency had been necessary because George I, busy as Elector of Hanover at the time, was not able to reach England and claim his throne until 18 September. Four years later, as Lord Chancellor, Macclesfield even found himself having to read the King's Speech in the House of Lords, the King's English being unequal to the task. Seemingly he got on very well with King George, although having neither German nor French he was obliged to converse with him in his very limited schoolboy Latin. Unfortunately, his lord chancellorship did not last long: in 1725 he was impeached for corruption – he is supposed to have taken more than £100,000 in bribes, about £11M in today's money – subsequently convicted and fined £30,000. Unable to pay the fine as all his property had been confiscated, he was sent to the Tower. Nevertheless, despite his eventual disgrace, he still seems to have been the only one-time attorney ever to have exercised royal power, albeit merely as regent.

Then there was The Lord Thurlow (1731-1806) who was at one time articled to a solicitor, after having been sent down from Caius College Cambridge for misconduct, and before being called to the Bar. Lord Hardwicke (1690-1764) was articled to a Mr Salkeld, attorney at the age of fourteen but quickly showed such promise that after four years his principal arranged for him to join the Middle Temple and he was eventually called to the Bar in 1715. As Lord Chancellor from 1737 to 1756, he was responsible *inter alia* for the trial of the Jacobite leaders after the 1745 rising and the Marriage Act 1753 "An Act for the Better Prevention of Clandestine Marriage", better known as "Lord Hardwicke's Act". Yet another 18th century judge to obtain high office but who started legal life as an attorney or at least as an articled clerk was Lord Kenyon. He was articled to WJ Tompkinson of Nantwich, Cheshire but following completion of his articles, he opted for the Bar where he eventually succeeded Lord Mansfield as Chief Justice. Whilst still at the Bar he was leading counsel for Lord George Gordon (Thomas Erskine with him) on a charge of high treason following the Gordon Riots in 1780. Between them they secured his acquittal. Not the least notable aspect of this acquittal was that Mansfield was the presiding judge, notwithstanding that his own London property in Bloomsbury Square had been burnt to the ground, together with its contents in the course of the riots.[19] A modern judge would doubtless have recused himself but even by 18th century standards Mansfield's decision not to do so was thought to have been somewhat indelicate.

In our own time perhaps the best-known judge to have begun legal life as a solicitor was RE Megarry (1910-2006), eventually to become a much respected judge of the Chancery Division and later still, Vice-Chancellor. More recently, of course, it has become possible for a solicitor to become a High Court judge directly. The first to achieve this distinction in 1993 was Michael Sachs (1932-2003). He was followed by Lawrence Collins, Henry Hodge (1944-2009) and most recently by Henry Hickinbottom. Lawrence Collins was the first solicitor to be appointed to the High Court Bench directly from private practice (where he was a partner in Herbert Smith from 1971 until his appointment to the Bench in 2000) eventually becoming a Lord Justice of Appeal and replacing Lord Hoffman in the House of Lords. As a Lord of Appeal in Ordinary he was one of the first justices of the newly-formed Supreme Court of the United Kingdom on its formation in 2009 where he remained until his retirement in 2011.

The real distinction between "low practitioners" and those who can fairly be described as "professionals" has best been drawn by a distinguished Italian lawyer Piero Calamandrei, less inclined perhaps to share the purely class prejudices of the English: "The difference," he observed "between the true lawyer and those men who consider the law merely a trade is that the latter seek to find ways to permit their clients to violate the moral standards of society without overstepping the letter of the law, while the former look for principles which will persuade their clients to keep within the limits of the spirit of the law in common moral standards.[20] The words were carefully chosen: there was no suggestion that the practice of the law was not "a trade" – at one level it clearly is and has to be – rather he was saying that it was not *merely* a trade because it has a significant moral content and purpose and that any practitioner who fails to understand this cannot claim to be a "true lawyer". From the beginning of its existence the story of the Yorkshire Law Society has been in part at least an attempt to hold that crucial distinction in view.

NOTES

1. See Prologue p. 1

2. 'An ordinary eating house" – see Chapter 1 p. 24

3. A rather splendid early Georgian property judging from an old photograph but demolished in 1898 to make way for Aldwarke steelworks. By that time the whole area had become completely industrialised.

4. Henry Cavendish FRS (1731-1810) was the discoverer of hydrogen – "inflammable air" as he termed it – as well as Ohm's Law and was perhaps the greatest scientist of his age. Unfortunately, he was also so secretive that many of his discoveries were attributed to others. William Cavendish, the seventh duke (1808-1891) had a rather different attitude to work and indeed to science from that of the fifth duke. After becoming second wrangler at Trinity College Cambridge he was a Fellow of the Royal Society at the age of 21 and was later to become Chancellor of the University until his death. He was responsible for the funding the world famous Cavendish Laboratory which bears his name and where Ernest Rutherford first split the atom.

5. Henry VI Part 2 Act IV sc. 2

6. *A History of Hull* Edward Gillett and Kenneth A Macmahon OUP for the University of Hull 1980 citing the Bench Book (Hull City Archives) f55b

7. M Birks *Gentlemen of the Law* Stevens & Sons 1961 quoted by Judy Slynn *A History of Freshfields* Freshfields 1984

8. *The Attorney in Eighteenth Century England* Cambridge University Press 1959. Chapter 4, *The Provincial Law Societies*, devotes several pages to the early activities of the Yorkshire Law Society based on the Society's first *Minute Book* 1786-1839 referred to at the beginning of this chapter and which had been made available to the author by the then Hon. Secretary, John Shannon. Robert Robson (1929-1995) was a Fellow of Trinity College Cambridge. His obituary in *The Independent* (24 January 1995) said of this book that it "can be seen in retrospect to have pioneered the modern study English professionalism and the development of the middle class."

9. A statutory rule incidentally that is still applicable – see S69 Solicitors Act 1974.

10. James Boswell *Life of Johnson* (1791)

11. Dickens generally knew his law. *The Old Curiosity Shop* first appeared in 1840-41 but nevertheless some years later in *Tuton v Sanoner* (1858) 3 H & N 280 it was held that if the grantor of a bill of sale or a witness *was an attorney or an attorney's clerk* the bill was invalidated by describing him in the necessary affidavit of due execution as a "gentleman". Not only would this seem to contradict Mr Brass's claim, it is also a shattering example of the absurd technicalities of the law even in the middle of the 19th century.

12. Oyez 1976. See also an article by Sir Thomas Lund in the *Law Society Gazette* for February 1956 *"Gentleman" by Act of Parliament – A Hoary Problem Solved*.

13. See Chapter 7 p. 125.

14. *Lloyd George: Rise and Fall* – Cambridge University Press (1961).

15. AJP Taylor *A Personal History* – Atheneum (1983)

16. Sir David Napley (1915-1994) was President of the Law Society from 1976 to 1977. Chapter 7 of this book "Legal Politics" provides several similar examples.

17. In Lord Kingsdown's *Recollections of his Life at the Bar and in Parliament* (1868 but recently republished) the author recalls how "at Lancaster Summer Assizes I was present at the usual saturnalia, where, however, there was less fun and more seriousness than I fancy is usual on such occasions. The present Chief Baron Pollock was tried for what was treated as a really grave offence, having dined with an attorney during the circuit."

18. Lord Campbell – *Lives of the Chancellors* London 1845-7. Campbell himself subsequently served as Lord Chancellor from 1859-1861.

19. Lord Mansfield's country property on Hampstead Heath, Kenwood House, very nearly suffered the same fate. Fortunately for the nation and Historic England it escaped as the result of quick thinking by Lord Mansfield's steward who got wind of the rioters' intentions. He nipped down to the local pub, *The Spaniards' Inn* (an Elizabethan hostelry which still exists) and, in cahoots with the landlord who was suitably primed with Mansfield funds, the two of them ensured that when the rioters stopped for some suitable liquid refreshment before proceeding with their incendiary intent, they were not disappointed. They tarried too long and eventually decided to go back to town although their decision was doubtless reinforced by the arrival of a squadron of dragoons.

20. Piero Calamandrei (1889-1956) *L'Elogio dei Giudici* (1935). English translation *Eulogy of Judges* 50th Anniversary edition American Law Institute – American Bar Association 1992.

Chapter Three

COSTS, CONVEYANCERS & LOW PRACTITIONERS

"It cannot be denied ... that the profession is disgraced by some low practitioners whose names are familiar in every cause list"

The Society's memorandum to the Protonotaries of the Court of Common Pleas 10th December 1814

At its second meeting on the evening of 1 August 1786, Mr Townend the Town Clerk of York in the chair, the Society had established its first rules by unanimous resolution. These rules are perhaps worth quoting in full as they give a clear indication of what was in the minds of the Society's founders:

> RESOLVED, that Attornies and Solicitors residing in the County of York, the City of York and the Town of Kingston-upon-Hull, and the County of the said Town, who shall be admitted in pursuance of, and act agreeable to, the adopted Rules, shall form a Society, and shall be called "The Yorkshire Law Society".
>
> The objects of the Society were: The preservation of the privileges of Solicitors, the protection of their interests, the promotion of honourable practice; the repression of malpractice, the settlement of disputed points of practice; the decision of questions of professional usage, or courtesy, the use of hospitality, and the promotion of social intercourse amongst the members of the Society by the continuance of such entertainments as have hitherto been provided for the members of the Society, or for the Committee, or any other means.

The consideration of any proposed alteration of the law affecting solicitors and the promotion and support of, or opposition to, the same, either alone, or in conjunction with, any other person or persons including any Society or Association, either by means of a grant from the funds of the Society, or by such other means as may be deemed expedient.

The settlement of any question affecting the interests of the profession, and for this purpose the initiation and prosecution, or the defence of any legal proceedings, or the stating of a special case, or cases, for the opinion of counsel, or the grant of money from the funds of the Society, for any such purposes.

The acquisition by purchase, lease or otherwise, of lands or buildings in the City of York, and the erection of new, or alteration of existing buildings on any land, which the Society might from time to time think proper to acquire as aforesaid, and the letting, sale, surrender, or disposition of such lands or buildings, or any part thereof, the promotion of the cause of legal Education, either by a grant or grants, or by offering, or other rewards, or by donation, or annual subscription to any Society or person engaged in legal educational work, or by such other means as may be deemed expedient, the relief of necessitous persons, being Solicitors, or their widows or children, by grants from time to time from the funds of the Society.

The officers of the Society to consist of a President, a Vice-President, a Treasurer, and a Secretary. The Committee and officers to be elected annually.

The annual meeting of the Society to be held in York, in the month of January, the day to be fixed by the President, at which meeting the Treasurer shall present his report and balance sheet. Five members personally present shall form a quorum. The members of the Society may, by resolution at any special general meeting, may appoint any person, or persons, (whether Solicitors or not) not exceeding three, in any one year, honorary members of the Society. The property of the Society shall be vested in the Trustees, in pursuance of the provisions of the Trust Deed. The above form the constitution of the Society.

It was agreed that all Members should be elected by ballot; and a code of Rules was adopted.

If the relative importance of the objects of the Society to its members were to be judged by the order in which they appear above, then clearly "the preservation of the privileges of Solicitors" took pride of place. However, it would be a mistake to assume that this was the only or even the main motivation of the Society's founders. With "privileges" went obligations and there was a genuine desire to establish and maintain professional standards of competence and behaviour. Six months after that August meeting, on 13 March 1787, it was unanimously resolved to present a petition to parliament which was signed by a total of 70 attornies and solicitors practising in the City and County of York.

What concerned the Society were the problems associated with unqualified conveyancers. After reciting "That whereas your Petitioners before they can be admitted to practice, in any of his Majesty's Courts of Law or Equity are compelled to serve a regular Clerkship and undergo an Examination touching their capacity and fitness for the conduct of business in those Courts" and reciting the various laws and regulations to which they were subject "which have proved highly beneficial to the Profession at large, and calculated to bind your Petitioners to the due and punctual performance of their duty to their respective clients" the petition continued "That a branch of the Profession of the Law which your Petitioners also carry on jointly with the proper business of an Attorney and Solicitor in the said Courts, and which consists in the preparing and writing deeds, and other solemn contracts for the passing and assuring real and personal estates and rights and interests therein, is wholly excluded from the benefits of the aforesaid regulations and may be carried on and practised by persons of every description without any previous admission or qualification required by Law, which in the apprehension of your Petitioners is attended with inconvenience and prejudice as well to the parties concerned as to the Public in general, inasmuch as persons of mean fortune, character, and education are thereby permitted to intrude themselves into that branch of the Profession."

In modern language what the petitioners were seeking was a level playing-field: they were regulated (and taxed) but those who practised solely as conveyancers were not, "whereby the Fees and Profits of Business to which your Petitioners would be entitled are diminished, whilst others are admitted to participate with them, without incurring the same expense, disabilities or burthens." The petition also suggested an increase in the duty on articles of clerkship. But it was evidently not just the intrusion of "persons of mean fortune, character, and education" into the business of conveyancing which concerned the Society. The Society was also jealous of counsel. At a general meeting on 24 July 1787 it was unanimously resolved "that any Counsel who shall by himself or his Clerk or otherwise, for any fee or Reward to himself or his Clerk, write or engross upon stamped Paper or Parchment any Deed or Instrument (except awards made by such Counsel as Arbitrator) or make out the Abstract of any Title for the Inspection of any other Person or Persons, or do any Act in any Suit, Prosecution or Appeal where no Attorney is imployed (unless it be for Prisoners making out their own Case) will not deserve the countenance or support of this Society." Whoever drafted this resolution clearly did so with care and was anxious to cover all possible eventualities. Members were requested to report to the President the names of any defaulting counsel.

The conveyancing and other issues of concern were not going to go away, the 1787 petition to parliament notwithstanding. They rumbled on for another thirty years. Two documents during this period stand out.[1] The earliest, dated 13 March 1815, is described as the *First Report of the Committee for obtaining an Augmention of the Allowance of Costs de Incremento*. It was concerned with the inadequacy of costs allowed on party and party taxations in the common law courts (the Chancery Court was apparently more generous). There were two grounds of complaint, namely inadequate allowances to witnesses for attending to give evidence and for attorneys for attending trials. In the summer of 1814 a sub-committee had been appointed consisting of Mr Charles Frost, Mr Jonathan Gray and Mr Richard Garland. Their brief was to go to London and present a memorial to the judges of the common law courts on the subject and generally to make representations on behalf of the Society. The prime instigator was Mr Frost. It was he who had written to the President earlier in the year, setting out in detail his complaints about "the inadequate taxation of their costs by the master or prothonotary".[2] The letter ended "to obtain redress from these evils which daily result from the present system, if such it may be called, of taxation, it is only requisite I trust that the matter be brought fairly under discussion and be properly represented to the authorities in whom is reposed the power of the revision and augmentation of costs."

A vain hope as it turned out. A later generation of lawyers with a greater collective experience of dealing with "the authorities" would doubtless have been less sanguine as to the outcome. However, Mr Frost's letter to the President was duly considered and a resolution passed that the costs *de incremento* at present allowed in the several courts of law in *Nisi Prius* causes are inadequate to meet the exigences of the times and the additional burthens recently imposed … That the present system of taxation of costs is greatly defective in the allowance to attorneys for their attendance and expenses on the trial of causes and loss of time whereby the successful party to a suit is subjected to very serious loss, arising from the difference between the sums which he feels himself bound by every equitable principle to pay to his attorney and to the witnesses and the costs allowed by the master or Prothonotary on taxation."

The memorial drafted by the committee was addressed to "the Right Honourable Edward Lord Ellenborough,[3] Lord Chief Justice of His Majesty's Court of King's Bench and the other judges presiding in that honourable court". The draft was submitted to counsel (Mr Parke) who "handsomely declined" the proffered fee of five guineas. Counsel suggested "various alterations" which were adopted. In due course the three members of the sub-committee arrived in London on 14 November 1814, the Hon Treasurer having been instructed "to furnish them with such sums as they might have occasion for".

Lord Ellenborough was out of town. However, the Lord Chief Justice of the Common Pleas promised to consult with the judges of his court and indicated that they would afterwards communicate with the other judges. A similar promise of attention was eventually received from Lord Ellenborough.

A supporting memorandum addressed to the prothonotaries is of particular interest as it sought to establish the principle in 1814 that was eventually applied only in 1986[4] with the abolition of the party and party basis of taxation, "that the successful party to a suit ought to be indemnified against the attendant expenses by the losing party. Practice however is in opposition to this principle … It therefore becomes a question of whether this fact be attributable to the inadequacies of the costs allowed on taxation or to the exorbitancy of the attorney's charges."

A particular source of irritation on taxation was the practice of reducing the allowance to the attorney for attending trial if he had more than one case in the list at the same assize. The prothonotaries also appeared to entertain some doubt as to whether the personal attendance of the attorney (as opposed to an agent) was necessary – "it cannot for a moment be contended" says the memorandum, "that the interests of a suitor ought to be confided to an agent who ... could not possibly, amidst the multiplicity of business which would be thus thrown into his hands at the moment of the assizes, so far make himself master of the case as to be able to give counsel those instructions and generally to take those steps which the various unforseen turns of the case might require". The memorandum ends on a slightly defensive note: "it cannot be denied on the other hand that the profession is disgraced by some low practitioners whose names are familiar in every cause list ... But this evil is not without remedy; as instances must frequently occur in the career of the practice of such person, which would fully justify the judges in making them a summary example to the profession ..."

These representations by the Yorkshire Law Society in November 1814 only met with very limited success. In the following term there was a test case from Yorkshire: "Messieurs Thomas and Charles Frost from Hull had a bill to tax in a cause of some importance, so gave their agents particular instructions to attend the taxation and to obtain all possible information on the subject. The result showed that no alteration whatever had been made in the measure of allowance ... " After giving further details of the taxation, the report continues " ... finding from this taxation, that the prayer of the memorials had not been attended with the success which we expected, we thought it proper to ascertain whether any official answer had been given to the memorials and we had the satisfaction to learn through a channel which we are precluded from naming, that a communication in writing had been made from the judges of the court of the King's Bench to their officers on the subject. We accordingly wrote to Mr Le Blanc to request he would favour us with a copy thereof. In reply to our application, Mr Le Blanc stated that when Lord Ellenborough handed the paper to him, he said "You will give publicity to it among the practitioners in any way you think proper but I desire it may not be put in the newspapers or anything of that sort"'. The instruction (or practice direction as it would now be termed) was not encouraging: " ... upon mature consideration of the subject of the several memorials which have been presented to them, it appears to the judges of this court that the practice which has hitherto prevailed in this particular shall still be observed and that they will not be warranted in departing therefrom". It was signed "Ellenborough, S Le Blanc, J Bayley and H Dampier".

When the Sub-Committee's first report was considered at a meeting at Clark's Hotel in York on 15 March 1815, the Committee was not satisfied and their three representatives were requested to return to London at the beginning of the Trinity term and attend personally to, as well as on the application to the Court of King's Bench for a review. Mr Gray reported that "it was not in his power to attend in London" and Mr Paul was appointed in his place. By this time the members of the Society were once again concerned with the topic which had seized their attention back in 1786/7, namely unqualified conveyancers, so further instructions were given to the London delegation.

As far as costs were concerned, the second visit to London was no more fruitful than the first. The test case for taxation was *Atkinson v Sadler*, a case from Hull which had been set down for trial at the previous Spring Assizes. The bill to be taxed amounted to £380.6.1 "and was prepared expressly with the view of raising the question of objectionable allowances in the several items of loss of time and maintenance of witnesses in different stations of life – attendance of the attorney at the assizes and charges for consultation". The bill was taxed by Master Le Blanc and the sum disallowed amounted to £115.0.4.

The next step was the preparation of an affidavit in support of a motion for a rule to show cause why the master should not be directed to review his taxation. No less than three counsel were briefed, Mr Scarlett, Mr Bullock and Mr James Parke,[5] all Northern Circuiteers,[6] "with such fees as the deputation judged to be proper on the occasion and suitable to the respectability of the Society when the business was brought forward".

The application seems to have been something of a disaster. "On the 10th June last, Mr Scarlett made his motion but the deputation regret to state that notwithstanding the perfect conviction of Mr Scarlett and the other counsel retained that a *Rule Nisi* would at all events be granted such a rule was refused".

One reason for the lack of success was that the whole question of costs was under consideration by the judges at that time in any event. This is clear from an observation of Mr Justice Le Blanc (whose relationship to Master Le Blanc, whose taxation it was sought to review, was not stated).

Also, the judge observed that "it would lead to terrible consequences if witnesses of every description were to be allowed according to the value of their time." However, it was another King's Bench judge who was the subject of specific criticism "for the assertion of Mr Justice Bailey that a labourer out of 5/- a day allowed him for maintenance and loss of time, might take home to his family 2/6 a day and his illiberal remark that 'all attornies are anxious to enter their causes the last', cannot be treated as serious."

Mr Scarlett subsequently returned to the attack on 14 June 1815 (the last day of term), armed with a further affidavit on the specific issue of the 5/- a day allowed to "witnesses of the description of *Labourers*". On this second occasion, the Chief Justice was sitting – he had been absent at the time of the original application – and appears to have been conciliatory, recognising the principle that a successful party ought to be indemnified against all reasonable expenses but observing "that the court could hardly make a general rule for the allowance to witnesses, as living is cheaper and there are a greater number of public houses in some places than others."

The deputation concluded that "the master will in future make a more liberal allowance to witnesses attending the Assizes in the County of York (the peculiar circumstances of which County was recognised by all the Judges) than has hitherto been made." The attempt on the other hand to secure any measure in the allowance to the attorney for attending court had clearly failed. The only bright note was the fact that the "fees which they left with the Briefs for Mr Scarlett, Mr Bullock and Mr James Parke, were returned by those gentlemen in the most handsome manner."

The report concludes with "a remark as to the conduct of the Judges relative to the procedures upon the memorials presented to them on the subject of costs". The deputation clearly felt that they had been encouraged by the judges in their original response to the memorials to take a test case by way of review of taxation, that had then been summarily rejected "with this result, that the court has, by refusing to grant a *Rule Nisi* declared that it will not even hear the arguments which the profession have to offer upon the subject."

The other topic with which the sub-committee was concerned on their second visit to London was unqualified conveyancers. They had brought with them from York a second memorial, this time addressed to "The

Right Honourable Nicholas Vansittart, Chancellor of His Majesty's Exchequer."[7] The memorial recited the history and membership of the Society and drew attention to the fact that attornies and solicitors had to serve five years' articles, pay stamp duties on their articles and on admission amounting to £130. The memorial continued: "That these taxes have been highly beneficial to the public by increasing the respectability of attornies and solicitors and diminishing the evils occasioned by the errors and misconduct of ignorant needy practitioners, that conveyancing has always formed the principal and most lucrative part of the business of an attorney and a solicitor. That it requires more extensive and abstruse learning than any other branch of the law etc, etc." The cause of complaint then appears, namely that "the Stamp Act of 44th year of the King required persons practising conveyancing to be members of an Inn of Court but this provision is quite insufficient because the expenses of obtaining such an admission amount only to twenty-eight pounds or thereabouts and the benchers of an Inn of Court cannot be expected to enquire into the character of all its members. That persons admitted as members of an Inn of Court under the Act enabled them to take out certificates of practise as conveyancers without keeping any number of terms or producing any testimonials of their having any professional education whatever, means ignorant and incompetent persons are enabled to practice as conveyancers to the disgrace of the profession and to the injury of the public."

The Society wanted such conveyancers to have kept twelve terms at an Inn of Court and to pay stamp duty "equal at least to the amount of Stamp Duties paid by an attorney and a solicitor upon his Articles of Clerkship". The memorial was sent to the Chancellor of the Exchequer with a covering letter. The deputation received a reply from the Chancellor the same day, inviting them to contact Mr Neyle, the Chairman of the Board of Stamps and Mr Kaye, the solicitor of the Bank of England. A meeting with Neyle was duly arranged and he admitted that the arguments adduced by the deputation had made a considerable impression on him and he agreed to see the Chancellor again on the subject. There were, however, parliamentary difficulties and problems of introducing measures of control into a money Bill. A further meeting was arranged at Westminster Hall the following day attended by the Attorney-General, the Solicitor-General and other interested parties.

This meeting lasted nearly two hours. In addition to problems of parliamentary procedure, there was a question as to the propriety of imposing "any tax whatsoever upon persons of this description, in as much as such a proceeding would be a direct sanction to their practice – that on the contrary, as the property of individuals might be endangered by want of competent skill in persons professing to act as conveyancers, it became a matter of public importance that the practice of certificated conveyancers should be restricted to such persons as should have received a proper education as conveyancers."

The suggestion was made that such regulation ought to be the subject of a separate act as the proposed increase of duty on articles of clerkship and the increased fee on admissions and attornies' practising certificates would undoubtedly lead to a great increase in the number of certificated conveyancers. This was conceded by both law officers and the Attorney-General agreed that the attention of parliament ought to be called to the point.

Allowances on the taxation of costs and certificated conveyancers, the two subjects that had so exercised the Society in 1814 and 1815 as to prompt two deputations to London, were still unresolved. In July 1815 there was correspondence with Mr Hexney, the Secretary of the London Law Society from which it appears that the latter had arranged a meeting with Mr Justice Dallas and Mr Brian Richards "at Mr Justice Dampier's". They went through the whole of the *Atkinson v Sadler* bill item by item, explaining why the increase had been sought. The judges naturally declined to give any opinion on the specific points but promised that the subject would receive the attentive consideration of all the judges during the long vacation. The discussion apparently occupied "several hours".

Both topics were still under discussion by the Society the following year. A committee minute of 13 March 1816 recorded that "no intention exists in the London Law Society to prosecute any measures for the regulation of Certificated Conveyancers". However, the committee were able to record having received "a pamphlet published officially, whereby the Society will perceive that some increase has been made in the allowance of costs as between party and party".

In March 1817, a Mr James Anderton, solicitor, petitioned the House of Commons complaining of "the interference of unqualified persons in the Practice of conveyancing". By this time the Society appears to have become slightly battle weary: "whilst your committee feel the grievance complained of to be one which calls for redress, they apprehend the single application of Mr Anderton to Parliament is likely to be productive of no advantage and also that any application to the legislature, in order to be effective, must be followed up by carrying a bill through both houses at an enormous expense. It appears therefore to your committee that a representation to the Lord Chancellor and the Judges and also if necessary to the Chancellor would be a more profitable means of obtaining the relief sought by Mr Anderton's petition than any application to Parliament".

The matter was again before the committee in July 1817 when certain amendments were recommended to the Bill then before Parliament, although the committee agreed that "the Bill in its present form is very desirable". A petition to the House of Commons was subsequently drafted and after the usual recitals, continued, "Your Petitioners therefore most humbly pray that the Honourable House will be pleased to take the subject into immediate consideration that an Act may be passed for preventing uneducated and incompetent persons from practising as Conveyancers and for regulating the examination and admission of such persons as may in future be admitted to practice …".

The bill was still before parliament the following year and in March 1818 the committee agreed to contribute £50 to Mr Anderton in support of the measure. The bill appeared eventually to have passed into law, although whether in a form altogether acceptable to the Society is not clear. The practice of conveyancing and the identity and qualifications of those entitled to undertake it is still not entirely resolved even today, two hundred years after that meeting with the law officers in Westminster Hall in the Trinity Term of 1815. As a Mr Leach is reported to have observed on that occasion, "there might be some difficulty in determining precisely what regulations ought to be adopted respecting the education of conveyancers but it was certainly a matter of great public importance and legislative interference would be very properly exercised on the subject". That is surely still the case.

NOTES

1. The remainder of this chapter is largely based on the author's article *Costs and Conveyancers* which appeared in the *Law Society Gazette* on 16 October 1986 Vol 83 No 37 to mark the Yorkshire Law Society's bicentenary.

2. Or "protonotary", a curious Greek/Latin *mélange* (like "television") meaning "chief clerk" – the "h" appeared in mediæval times. The term is still in current use in some American, Canadian and Australian jurisdictions and in the Vatican.

3. See Chapter 1 note 19

4. Since 1986 there has been a major upheaval to the whole basis on which costs are allowed or recovered.

5. James Scarlett (1769-1844) was born in Jamaica where his father owned a sugar plantation on which the family fortunes were based. He took silk in 1816 and for the remainder of his time at the Bar he was one of its leading members and his annual income was reputed to have attained the colossal sum of £18,500. He subsequently became Attorney-General and (in 1830) MP for Malton, and Chief Baron of the Court of Exchequer (1834). Created Baron Abinger in 1835, he was the father of General Sir James Yorke Scarlett who led the charge of the Heavy Brigade at Balaclava in 1854. James Scarlett's other claim to fame concerns an incident at Lancaster Summer Assizes in 1819. Having been obliged by some organisational mishap to hurry into court without his wig and gown, he apologised to the judge and expressed the hope that the time would shortly come when these "mummeries" would be entirely discarded. In accordance with his wish all counsel attending court the following day appeared without the usual barristerial accoutrements. The fashion was not to last and only in our own day under the influence of Lord Phillips and others have some inroads been made in "these mummeries". The Abinger title is still extant.

   James Parke (1782-1868) was also to become a judge of the King's Bench in his later career although he subsequently transferred to the Exchequer. In 1856 he was created Baron, curiously at first as a Life Peer until the Committee of Privileges decided that the Crown had lost the power of creating life peerages through disuse.

6. York was part of the Northern Circuit except for a short period between 1864 and 1876 when an entirely new North-Eastern Circuit was created out of the eastern part of the Northern Circuit and the northern part of the Midland Circuit which then included York and Leeds. Legend has it that a coin was tossed to determine whether the truncated Northern or the new North-Eastern Circuit was to retain the "Northern" name. The North-East lost.

7. Nicholas Vansittart, First Baron Bexley (1766-1851). Before becoming Chancellor (1812-1823) he had been First Secretary to the Treasury under Pitt of whom he was a keen supporter.

Chapter Four

COMMUNICATIONS

"Several waggons were set fast and the coach was in the greatest danger of overturning ... All the outside passengers of weight alighted and had to wade through much mud and dirt to the great discomfort of their persons."

Margaret Gray (daughter of Jonathan Gray) aged 13 describing a family trip from York to Manchester 31 July 1822

The founding of the Society in York in 1786 was not the only event of that year which was to have a significant effect on the life of York and Yorkshire. As far as most York citizens were concerned, they would doubtless have been more immediately aware of the establishment of the *Edinbro' Mail*, a new stage coach service between London and Edinburgh.[1] It was in three sections: London-York, York-Newcastle and Newcastle-Edinburgh, each operated by a different company working in close collaboration with the others. The first leg of the journey north was by way of Ware, Royston, Huntingdon, Stilton, Stamford, Newark, East Retford, Bawtry, Doncaster, Ferrybridge and Tadcaster before arriving at the Black Swan in Coney Street – the site now occupied by British Home Stores – a distance of 197 miles. Its best time was 24 hours 54 minutes, including all stops for changing horses etc, although 36 hours or thereabouts was the norm. By 1796 three coaches a day were running to London, two to Leeds and a Royal Mail coach ran to Liverpool. *The Edinbro' Mail* continued to operate until 1842 by which time it was possible to reach London from York by train. In 1706, eighty years before the inauguration of the Edinbro' Mail the coach journey from London to York had taken four days and even thirty years later, in 1754,

Improved Travel Facilities in the 18th Century

In 1719 at the tender age of thirteen the future Lord Mansfield had been dispatched by his father from the family home at Scone Palace in Perth to London so that he might be enrolled as a scholar at Westminster School. His father had provided him with a pony but he was expected to get himself there unaccompanied. He may have been delayed by the distractions that are apt to beset all unaccompanied teenagers on such a journey but he arrived safely in London after 54 days on the road.

The EDINBURGH STAGE COACH, for the better accommodation of Paſſengers will be alter'd to a new genteel Two end Glaſs Machine hung of Steel Springs, exceedingly light and eaſy, to go in Ten days in ſummer and Twelve in winter.

Perform'd if GOD permits by your dutiful Servant HOSEA EASTGATE

Advertisement for a fortnightly service in 1754 from Dean Street, Soho, to John Somervell's Canongate Edinburgh

---

THE MERCURY COACH
Carrying SIX INSIDE PASSENGERS

With a Guard all the Way from
London to Newcaſtle

Sets out from Mr. Batty's at the Black-Swan, Coney Street York every Morning at Five o'clock to London and arrives at Saracen's Head Snow Hill London the next day about Two o'clock; Sets out from the Black Swan, the George and the York Tavern alternately every Morning at Six o'clock, and arrives at Mr. Turner's the Queen's Head, Newcaſtle, early the ſame Evening.

Fare from York to London	2l. 10s.
Outſide	1l. 5s.
From York to Newcaſtle	1l. 4s.
Outſide	12s.

Short Stages, 3 1/2d. per mile – Outſide, Half-Price

From the York Courant, *Tuesday, 16 August 1791*

a contemporary advertisement tells us that the journey along the whole length of the Great North Road between London and Edinburgh took ten days in summer and twelve in winter.

This improvement in travel between York and London at the end of the 18th century was to have an inevitable effect on the city's future. This would scarcely have been foreseen at that inaugural meeting of the Society "at Mr Ringrose's House" but it meant that London would no longer be below the psychological horizon for the Yorkshire gentry and the attornies and solicitors who were their professional advisers. The infamous highwayman, Dick Turpin, convicted and hanged in York in 1739, is reputed to have ridden his mare Black Bess from London to York in twenty-four hours but this has long been discounted as a myth. Such a feat would have been well-nigh impossible for a single horse as horses do not possess that degree of combined speed and distance stamina. Riding a single horse was one thing; coach traffic on better roads, with efficient provision for changing horses, was another. Following a meeting with Prime Minister William Pitt on Sunday 29 November 1795, William Wilberforce was reckoned at the time to have performed a remarkable feat by getting himself up the Great North Road to York to urge support for the government in time for an important political meeting at the Guildhall on Tuesday 1 December. With the loan of one of Pitt's own carriages and four of his horses he was able to cover the 67 miles to Alconbury by the Sunday night and the further 106 miles to Ferrybridge by Monday night. He arrived in York on the Tuesday just in time for the meeting.[2] It was of course the improved state of the roads which made possible the achievements of the *Edinbro' Mail* and the Prime Minister's supporter. Even so, as is evident from Margaret Gray's account of a coach journey between York and Manchester in 1822, even road travel in summer could be problematic although to be fair their problems had arisen on that occasion because a four mile stretch of the main turnpike "was in a state of Macadamization" and traffic had been diverted.

The key to road improvement in the latter part of the 18th and early 19th century was law-based rather than engineering-based. The famous Scottish road building pioneer, John McAdam (1756-1836), did not begin his second career until he returned from the United States in 1783 to become a trustee of the Ayrshire turnpike. He had previously been a financier and it was to be a little while before his new "macadamised" road construction techniques were to have a significant effect in England. The first Act was the Highways Act 1662 but it was not until the latter part of the 18th century that they were to come into their own. It was the general Turnpike Roads Act of 1773 that was to do for turnpikes what seventy-two years later the Railways Clauses Consolidation Act 1845 was to do for railways – provide a code which would simplify the passing of legislation dealing with the establishment of a particular turnpike or railway undertaking. The basic idea behind the legislation was to encourage private trusts to be responsible for the financing, construction and management of a particular stretch of public highway for which they would be remunerated by the collection of tolls, except that the collection aspect was let for a period to the highest bidder. For 18th century governments the arrangement had the same attraction as Private Finance Initiatives have for those of our own day: keeping unwelcome capital costs off the Treasury's balance sheet. By all accounts the levels of efficiency achieved by such financial legerdemain then and now were not significantly different but at least in the case of turnpike trusts they were an improvement on what had gone before. Under previous arrangements public highways had been the responsibility of the parishes through which each section happened to pass – hardly a recipe for joined-up governance, let alone joined-up transport.

Yet even under the turnpike system most trusts were only responsible for stretches of about 20-30 miles and no attempt was made at any unified system of management over the entirety of key "trunk" routes but at least there were slightly more joined-up than they had been under the old parish system. However, there were still problems: many trusts raised excessive mortgages and became overwhelmed by the interest payments and thus unable to spend the necessary funds in keeping their stretch of road in repair. Also, there were many exemptions from the tolls, most obviously foot passengers, ie the poor and, more significantly, the mail coaches. From 1840 onwards, with the rapid expansion of railways,[3] there was a marked decline in the long distance carriage trade upon which turnpikes depended for most of their profit. They effectively disappeared entirely with the creation of county councils by the Local Government Act 1888 with power to declare "main" roads and take over responsibility for their maintenance. Parliament, however, is still struggling even today to lay the ghosts of turnpikes past. Really sharp-eyed members of the Society may have noticed, for example, that Part 10 of Schedule 1 of the Statute Law (Repeals) Act 2008 disposed of no less than 50 Turnpike Acts, ranging in time from the London to Harwich Roads Act 1695 to the Norwich and Swaffham Road Act 1835.

Turnpike trusts in their heyday must have proved a useful source of income for solicitors. One of the Society's founder members, William Gray, was clerk to the Tadcaster-York turnpike (part of the present A64). The following advertisement appeared above his name in the *Leeds Intelligencer* in 1798:

Turnpike-Road from York to Tadcaſter

TOLLS to be LETT

NOTICE is hereby given , That the Tolls ariſing from the Toll-Gate and Weighing Engine upon the Turnpike-Road leading from Tadcaſter Bridge , in the County of York , to a Place , near the ſaid City , called Hobmoor-Lane End , will be Lett by Auction , to the beſt Bidder , at the Guildhall of the City of York , on Tueſday the Eleventh Day of December next , at the Hour of Twelve o'Clock , in the manner directed by the Act paſſed in the Thirteenth Year of the Reign of His preſent Majeſty King George the Third , " for regulating the Turnpike-Roads ; " which Tolls produced the laſt Year the Sum of Six Hundred and Eight Pounds , above the Expences of collecting the ſame reſpectively , and will be put up at ſuch Sum as the Truſtees preſent at the Meeting ſhall , from the Attendance of Bidders and other Circumſtances , judge expedient : The Letting to take Place from the Twenty-fifth Day of March next .

Whoever happens to be the beſt Bidder , muſt , at the ſame Time give Security , with sufficient Sureties , to the Satisfaction of the Truſtees of the ſaid Turnpike Road , for Payment of the Rent agreed for , and at ſuch Time as they ſhall direct .

Dated this Sixth Day of November, 1798

WILLIAM GRAY
Clerk of the ſaid Truſtees

The same edition of the *Leeds Intelligencer* contained four other similar advertisements for turnpike franchises. Traffic between Tadcaster and York on the A64 in 1798 seems comparatively modest in raising a net income of only £608. The tariff on this particular stretch of highway at the time was a shilling for a six horse coach and one penny for a single horse and rider. The Wakefield and Austerlands (Saddleworth) Turnpike Road over the same period raised £2,755 but perhaps this is not entirely surprising as anyone making this journey today would spend much of their time on the M62. The clergy also had an interest in turnpikes as trustees since not only were they local residents, they could read and write[4] as can be seen from a charming letter of resignation as trustee of the York to Oswaldkirk Turnpike (the present B1363) from the Rev Sydney Smith to William Gray's son Jonathan. Smith had been a trustee of this particular turnpike when he had been rector of Foston but had forgotten to resign on moving to Combe Florey in Somerset. It was to prove an expensive oversight as the letter reveals.

The White Bear at Stillington, to which the letter's postscript refers, still exists. Most trusts had many trustees, often 40 to 50 – hence the reference to the trustees being "jammed together", "crushed into a mass" or "perspiring intensely". The clerk was almost invariably a local lawyer but there would also be a treasurer and a surveyor as well as representatives of the local gentry, tradesmen and clergy.

To Jonathan Gray Esq, York

Combe Florey, Taunton Oct 10th 1829

My dear Sir,

Nobody can more sincerely wish the prosperity of the road from York to Oswaldkirk than I do. I wish to you hard materials, diligent trustees, gentle convexity, fruitful tolls, cleanly gutters, obedient parishes, favouring justices, and every combination of fortunate circumstances which can fall to the lot of any human highway. These are my wishes, but I can only wish. I cannot, from the bottom of Somersetshire, attend in person, as a letter (2s.6d. postage) yesterday invited me to do. Perhaps you will have the goodness to scratch my name out of the list of trustees.

You will be glad to hear that I am extremely pleased with this place. Friendships and acquaintances are not speedily replaced; but as far as outward circumstances, I am quite satisfied. If ever you come into this country I shall be very glad to see you; and I remain, dear Sir, with sincere respect and goodwill, yours truly,

SYDNEY SMITH

PS I shall think on the 15th of my friends at the White Bear, Stillington. How honourable to English gentlemen, that, once or twice every month, half the men of fortune in England are jammed together at the White Bear, crushed into a mass at the Three Pigeons, or perspiring intensely at the Green Dragon.

The reference to "2s.6d" postage (roughly £12.50 in today's money) may need some explanation for the modern reader. The high cost of postage (charged as much by distance rather than just weight) and the fact that before the introduction of stamps and the "penny post" by Sir Rowland Hill in 1840, postage was generally payable by the recipient, made for great inefficiency.[5] Fraud was commonplace – the sender could include coded messages in the address which the intended recipient could examine and then simply refuse to accept delivery.[6]

Such chicanery was by no means confined to the general population. The year 1786 which saw the establishment of the Society and the *Edinbro' Mail*, equally witnessed the 27 year old Prime Minister William Pitt struggling to end the scandal of MPs abusing one of their perks in the form of an entitlement to free postage by posting letters for family and friends as their own. This "free postage" was estimated at the time to be costing the taxpayers, and there were far fewer of them then, about £40,000 a year – possibly £4M or so in terms of today's money although, as we have seen, before the advent of the railways and the penny post the relative cost of postage was significantly higher than it was later to become. Pitt's efforts to control abuse of the postal system by parliamentarians was wholly effective. They were clearly keen to protect their perks. In 1800 Lord Petre, whose descendants still occupy Ingatestone Hall near Chelmsford, was in dispute with the Postmaster-General on the subject of free postage for peers (as parliamentarians). They were still entitled at the time to frank their correspondence by the simple expedient of signing it. The problem was that Lord Petre was a Catholic and although, as a peer, he was entitled to turn up at the House of Lords, his faith made it impossible to take the oath required at the time. In legal terms, was the entitlement based on the mere fact of being a peer of the realm, or was it necessary to have been as it were "sworn in"? He brought a test case against the Postmaster-General for the recovery of 7d which he had been obliged to pay on one of his letters. He lost.[7]

It so happens that both Jonathan Gray and Sydney Smith left ample records of their activities in the form of letters which have been preserved.[8] Despite the cost of postage, both were prolific letter writers. In addition, by the standards of the age, Jonathan Gray travelled extensively both within Britain and on the continent. Even Sydney Smith as a clergyman certainly got around but his visits to Edinburgh were essentially work-related although he did manage to visit Paris, Belgium and the Netherlands in 1837. Jonathan, however, was a passionate traveller to places which had nothing to do with his legal practice: Scotland, the Isle of Man, France, Germany and Switzerland. He even made it to Blackpool, which he compared unfavourably to Scarborough, and to Waterloo which he visited on 25 August 1815, just ten weeks or so after the battle. Of his spur-of-the-moment visit to France the previous year (during the temporary peace after the original defeat of Napoleon but before his escape from Elba) he has left an account which serves as a graphic reminder of some of the difficulties and hazards of travel in those days as well as illustrating his close involvement of promoting a bill in parliament relating to the York – Tadcaster turnpike of which his father William was the clerk to the trustees. This is in the form of letters to his wife from Boulogne (23 May 1814) and from Calais the following day.

Boulogne, May 23, 1814

My Dear Mary,

You will be surprized to hear from me here; but need not be alarmed as I never intended to proceed further into France than I am at present; I am to be in London again on Wednesday morning; and hope to finish my business so as to be in York by Saturday night. Finding there would be an interval of 3 or 4 days after I had got my Tadcaster road bill through the Commons before I should be wanted in the Lords I preferred a short ramble to remaining in London, and left the opening of any letters on business to Brodrick [his London agent]. On Saturday I left London in company with D. Tuke and Mr Atkinson of Ouse Bridge.

He goes on to describe the journey to Dover along the Old Kent Road, through "Shooters Hill 8 miles from London" through Dartford, Gravesend, Rochester, Chatham and Canterbury. But at first the rambling tourists from York are not hopeful of achieving their ambition of a brief cross-channel break. Jonathan's letter continues:

> Finding that there would be no packet for Calais before Wednesday,[9] we had given up all thoughts of visiting this country. We saw about noon 100 French prisoners embark for Boulogne to revisit their homes; an interesting sight; but I for one did not wish to break the Sunday by joining their party: immediately after afternoon service however an unexpected circumstance occurred; a Russian messenger arrived with despatches from London to sail immediately. D. Tuke, who did not go along with us to church was so eager, that he had sent a person to fetch us out of church on the occasion but we missed him. Not a moment was to be lost. The officer pd. 20£ for the packet boat and we and two other passengers a guinea each; our luggage (2 small parcels) was smuggled into the packet without the knowledge of the Customhouse officers, which had it been of weight it could not have been. The packet was a compact elegantly furnished vessel; with several clean beds in it: it was carpeted and neatly furnished. The wind was strong from the N.E. and it being impossible to make Calais we were to sail for Boulogne.

Dover Harbour with Dover Castle in the background. Precise date unknown but doubtless more recognisable to Jonathan Gray in 1814 than it would be to the modern traveller on a cross-channel ferry.
(Image supplied by the Dover Museum and Bronze Age Boat Trust)

After describing the crossing when all the passengers were sick, particularly the Russian officer who had chartered the packet, Jonathan describes their arrival at Boulogne:

> It now became necessary to take in our sails (it being low water) and to take soundings for fear of striking the shore. We had been only 3 hours in performing about 30 miles, but this operation was tedious, and occupied about 40 minutes. At length we anchored about 1½ a mile from the harbour, and let down our small boat; the getting into which from the swell in the sea was attended with difficulty. We now rowed away for the shore; the sea was quite out of the pier, and a number of women came running down to the pier end to assist. When they saw our boat could not reach dry ground from the flatness of the beach sands, they came wading about a hundred yards to take us on their backs to the shore. Their foreign appearance and their gabble were very singular. All of them had large pendant gold earrings; most of them several handsome finger rings, and some of them large gold crosses. Their dress was loose and slovenly; their countenances very lively and animated. When Daniel presented himself, the woman in waiting called out "Non, non!" wishing to avoid such a burden; but Dan persisted & she very soon deposited her burden in the sea. I contrive to get one of the boatmen to carry me out. Our difficulties were not over; It was necessary either to walk 2 miles or ford the river which runs through the harbour, a rapid stream of about 2½ feet deep; but much broader than the Ouse. About 100 women were standing on the other side of the river: several now came to help. Each woman took a man on her back, & other two women assisted her, & each took half a leg of the man to keep it out of the water. Thus I was carried over; & the women carefully wrung out my coat laps, which had drabbled in the stream. But the grandest spectacle remained, Daniel was unwilling to cross, but was besought by a multitude of women to venture. At length he consented, & was brought over by nine women; each of whom laid hold of an arm, a leg, a rump, a shoulder, or anything they could catch. You may conceive the laughter which this occasioned to the females ashore amongst whom we stood. We could not understand their observations, but one of them exclaimed groupe! groupe!" and indeed it was a group which Hogarth might have painted. We now proceeded at a little before 8 o'clock into the town followed by about 100 people; chiefly women. The countenances of the women sparkle with animation. They were from 25 to 40 years of age. About 60 of them claimed to be remunerated for assistance, we desired them to attend at the hotel; and gave them 12 livres to "divide as they

thought best". They were completely satisfied & happy. We understand they are chiefly the wives of poor fishermen and extremely poor.

Later he describes the hotel where the waiter, somewhat surprisingly, was English. The following day, 24 May, Jonathan writes again to his wife, this time from Calais. After describing various sights the letter continues:

> The landlord of our inn, *Parker*, is an Englishman, and has lived in France a great many years and kept this Inn. During the short peace he married a young English wife from Canterbury; probably with a view of managing the Inn in the English fashion; she and her relation Miss Davis have lived here ever since and managed the Inn; Parker is paralytic and bedridden. The war ruined the fortunes of him and his wife, who were in good circumstances; and they have now, she says, to begin the world anew. It is surprising how awkwardly she now expresses herself in English. The head waiter who is a Yorkshire man has only been here 3 or 4 days, and knows not a word of French. The other waiters are equally ignorant of English, and we had some ludicrous blunders and difficulties.

Jonathan Gray's letters give a vivid account of the "blunders and difficulties", both practical and linguistic experienced in his time attendant upon a relatively modest cross-channel journey. Also, it is fair to note that even land-based journeys were not always trouble free. In 1758 VJ Peyton published a combined English grammar and phrase book for the benefit of the French *Les Élémens de la Langue Angloise*. New editions were published in 1776, 1787 and 1794. It was the Berlitz phrase book of the age. As so often with contemporary documents, it casts an instructive light on the social conventions of the age. We can also see the difficulties, then as now, that French speakers had with both pronunciation and tonic accent in English, to say nothing of the usual difficulties of the road. A brief extract will suffice to illustrate:

English English

Maid, make my bed, and give me clean sheets. – Bring me other sheets. Why, Sir? These are not clean. They were washed yesterday. Excuse me, they have been already lain in. I'll give you something if you give me clean ones.

English – as spoken by the French

Maide, maique mai bédde, ann guive mi clíne chítze. – Brínng mi o-ther chítze. Houai Sorr? Thize aire natte cline. Thai ouaire ouâchte yiss-terdai. Es-quiouze mi, thai haive binn âll-ré-dy laine inn. – aille guive iou somme-thinng, iffe iou guive mi cline ouonnze.

French

Servante, faites mon lit, & Donnez-moi des draps blancs. – Donnez m'en d'autres. Pourquoi, Monsieur? Ceux-ci ne sont pas nets. Ils furent blanchis hier. Pardonnez-moi, ils ont déjà servi. – Je vous donnerez quelque chose, si vous m'en donnez de blancs & de nets.

It is interesting to note that in 1814 there were English staff working in both hotels (Boulogne and Calais) in which Jonathan stayed in France and the one in Calais was actually owned by an Englishman and had been throughout the war. He had suffered only financially – in the loss of cross-channel traffic and hence trade – due to the hostilities. Although the French revolutionary and Napoleonic wars are considered by historians to be the first wars in modern European history which engaged the entire "nation" there was seemingly no concept of any general need for internment.[10]

Another member of the Society to attest to the newfound middle class taste and opportunity for travel for pleasure rather than from necessity was Richard Garland (1775-1827). He was originally a York man but on joining the Society in 1808 he had seemingly been practising in Hull since 1802. Before moving to Hull in that year he had lived at Barnard Castle. There he had published anonymously one or two pamphlets suggesting a variety of improvements to the town which were subsequently adopted. Whilst living at Barnard Castle he had several letters published in the *York Herald* extolling the tourist attractions of Teesdale which were subsequently published in York in 1813 under the title *Tour in Teesdale*. It was to go through several editions.

This ability to get about as the result of improved road transport had social and economic implications for York as will be seen in the next chapter. For most of the 18th century leisure travel was largely the preserve of the aristocracy or the very dedicated and determined. But if some of the physical difficulties had been removed, the cost of travel and indeed postage remained high and would continue to be so until the advent of the railway age. This high cost was an economic fact of life for the legal profession and equally, of course, for their clients. The York firm of Grays has in its possession a conveyancing bill dating from 1801 where they were acting for the purchasers. The total invoice was for £6.19s.10d. Of this £2.4s.10d. represented stamp duty and the cost of parchment – the latter would not nowadays be regarded as a disbursement – and a further 3s.8d. represented the fee payable to the North Riding Deeds Registry at Northallerton. However, there was a further disbursement of 15s.0d. for a proportion of "horsehire and expenses" of the journey to Northallerton to register the deed. This meant that only £3.16s.4d. was what we would now call "profit costs", so the cost of horsehire and expenses amounted to roughly 20% of the former. If leisure travel was no longer the exclusive preserve of the aristocracy it was still in practice confined to the monied classes. This was to remain so until the advent of the railway age. When Thomas Cook (1808-1892) organised what is thought to be the first railway excursion (for temperance supporters) from Leicester to Loughborough in 1841 it truly marked the beginning of the transition from the age of travelling to the age of tourism. This transition did not always meet with universal favour: the Duke of Wellington, for one, is said to have objected to railways on the grounds that they would only "encourage the lower orders to move about". However, even the pioneering Thomas Cook could hardly have foreseen that in 1886, less than fifty years later, when the Society was celebrating its centenary, the occasion would be marked by no less than three railway excursions from York to Ripon (for Fountains Abbey), Scarborough and Whitby (the latter with an optional add-on between Whitby and Scarborough by the newly opened coast line). Further, that the (London) Law Society's National Conference would be held in York likewise to mark the occasion, drawing solicitors from all over England and Wales – something which would hardly have been possible but for the extraordinary way in which rail travel was to revolutionise travel for all.[11]

NOTES

1. See Tom Bradley *The Old Coaching Days in Yorkshire* Yorkshire Conservative Newspaper Co (The Yorkshire Post) Leeds 1889

2. *William Pitt the Younger* by William Hague – Harper Collins 2005

3. From the moment the railway arrived in York in 1839 improvement was rapid. A rail connection with London was available from 1840 when the journey took 14 hours via the York and North Midland connection to Normanton. By 1841 this had reduced to 10 hours 20 minutes and by 1848 to 6 hours 10 minutes.

4. The gentry were not always as well educated as the clergy. Sydney Smith himself, whilst living in Heslington pending the construction of his new vicarage at Foston, wrote of his neighbour the local squire, Henry Yarburgh of Heslington Hall "At first, he heard I was a Jacobin and a dangerous fellow, and turned aside as I passed: but at length when he found the peace of the village undisturbed … he first bowed, then called, and at last reached such a pitch of confidence that he used to bring the papers that I might explain the difficult words to him … and ended by inviting me to see his dogs." – Lady Holland *A Memoir of the Reverend Sydney Smith*, Longman, Brown, Green and Longmans 1855.

5. The public was beginning to appreciate the general inconvenience of postage being normally payable by the recipient and facilities were available for pre-payment by the sender. At a general meeting of the Society held on 28 March 1828 it was resolved "that all circular Letters sent by the Treasurer or Secretary to the Members shall be Post paid and the expense thereof paid out of the Funds of this Society".

6. At least Jonathan Gray's letter (2s.6d. postage) had been accepted by its intended recipient. Dick Turpin in an earlier age had not been so lucky with these curious postal arrangements. Whilst operating under the alias of "John Palmer" the infamous highwayman had got himself arrested in 1739 at Brough where he had unwisely, in a fit of drunken frustration, shot a game-cock belonging to the landlord of the *Ferry Inn* where he was lodging at the time. He had then threatened to shoot an innocent bystander who had objected to this rather anti-social behaviour. The local magistrate was minded to bind him over to keep the peace but Turpin aka Palmer was penniless at the time and unable to provide the necessary sureties. Accordingly he found himself in the House of Correction at Beverley. But he had a cunning plan and wrote to his brother-in-law in Essex in an appeal for help. This proved to be his undoing as Turpin was estranged from his wife and the brother-in-law declined to pay the sixpence postage. As a result the letter came into the hands of the village post-master, John Smith. Unfortunately for Turpin, Smith was not only the village post-master he

was also the village schoolmaster who had taught him to read and write. Smith recognised his former pupil's handwriting and decided to travel to York from Essex to report the matter to the authorities as there was by this time a substantial reward of £200 for Turpin's apprehension. Palmer's true identity was thus revealed and in due course he found himself in the Debtor's Prison in York (now the Castle Museum) where his cell can still be seen, although not the one that was previously thought to be his until the museum's previous error came to light in 2009. In due course he was tried, convicted and hanged on the Knavesmire.

7. Robert Edward 9th Baron Petre (1742-1801) may have missed a useful vocation as a member of the law's awkward squad. During his lifetime two papal bulls in 1738 and 1751 had been issued in condemnation of freemasonry but as they had never been promulgated in England, he did not consider himself bound by them. He accordingly had no compunction about serving as Grand Master from 1772 to 1776.

8. For members of the Gray family see *Papers and Diaries of a York Family* by Mrs Edwin (Almyra) Gray – Sheldon Press 1927 and *A History of Grays of York 1695-1988* by William Cobb – William Sessions Ltd 1989. For Sydney Smith, see Lady Holland – op. cit.

9. Before the days of steam, cross-channel traffic was of course always at the mercy of the wind and, until deep water ports were established at Dover and Calais in the middle of the 19th century, at the mercy of the tide also. It was not until 1821 that the French government purchased a Glasgow-built paddle steamer, the *Rob Roy* to transport mail between Calais and Dover. It was still tiny by today's standards – 88 tons with only a 30 horsepower engine. It managed the crossing in about 2¾ hours – only a little faster than Johnathan Gray's three hour crossing by sail but still dependant on the state of the tide for entering the harbour. And it was not until 1928 that the first cross-channel car-ferry service was established – with space for 15 cars that had to be craned on and off and the first roll-on, roll-off car ferry did not make its appearance until 1953.

10. Compared with much present day practice the attitudes of both the French and British governments towards "enemy aliens" could be surprisingly relaxed. In 1813 at the height of the war with France Sir Humphry Davy (who had received his knighthood only the previous year), accompanied by his assistant Michael Faraday, travelled to Paris at Napoleon's invitation to receive a medal bestowed on him by the Emperor for his electro-chemical work. Even attitudes to prisoners of war were often just as relaxed. Over the

period 1793-1815 the are estimated to have been about 200,000 POWs in Britain altogether of whom about 120,000 were French. Prisoner exchange was common, particularly during the earlier period and most officers were eligible for release on parole unless they had acquired a reputation as troublemakers when under actual confinement or broke their parole conditions. Civilians on the whole tended to be left in peace unless they were men of military age although the French had a system for those they described as *détenus*. One of the principal locations for both POWs on parole and *détenus* was the fortress town of Verdun. In 1812 the town contained a total of 840 UK citizens on conditional liberty, roughly half of each category. Their numbers were sufficient to support a number of flourishing clubs. Such was the economic benefit to the town that Metz itself petitioned the French government to become a parole centre. On the British side, the relaxed attitude to the officer class was much the same; some were able to arrange for their wives to join them in "captivity" and one senior French officer spent the latter part of the war at Chatsworth as the personal guest of the Duke of Devonshire. In his later years this particular POW described his time there as one of the most enjoyable periods of his life. French tolerance in such matters, however, could vary according to time and place and the régime in power. One Yorkshire woman Maria Crathorne, later to become the wife of Michael Tasburgh-Anne, the squire of Burghwallis Hall, near Doncaster, had found herself in France at the beginning of the war in the charge of some Augustinian nuns but had only managed to escape back to England in a coffin labelled as containing the body of one of the dead sisters.

11. For details of the centenary celebrations, see Chapter 7. In just ten years, between 1840 and 1850, the total route mileage of Britain's railways increased by about 4,750 miles from 1,850 miles to 6,600 miles, roughly 66% of its current network of 10,000 miles or so. It was to reach its greatest extent in 1927 at about 20,400 route miles. This rapid railway development was linked to the equally rapid (and symbiotic) development of the telegraph. The railway companies had a close interest in telegraphic technology for their own purposes and the construction of new railways provided convenient routes for the laying of cables. The Electric Telegraph Company was founded in England in 1846 and by 1855 had become the Electric and International Telegraph Company. It was thanks to the astonishingly rapid spread of the international telegraph network that senior commanders, both British and French (many of whom had seen service under Wellington and Napoleon respectively) found to their dismay

during the Crimean War (1854-1856) that they were subject to political interference from London and Paris of a kind that would have been impossible in any earlier age.

Chapter Five

THE DOLDRUMS
1815 – 1849

"York ambled along sociably and complacently with barely a tolerant smile for its reckless neighbours"

Patrick Nuttgens

The years between the founding of the Society in 1786 and 1815 had been stirring ones that had seen the immense upheavals across the Channel of the French Revolution, war with France around the globe from the Iberian peninsular, the Mediterranean, India and the West Indies, the rise of Napoleon, rebellion in Ireland, followed by the abolition of the Irish parliament and the incorporation of the country itself into the United Kingdom and war with the United States at the same time as the increasing tempo of the Industrial Revolution and canal transport at home.

In the autumn of 1823 a young Frenchman, Jérôme-Adolphe Blanqui (1798-1854) decided he would visit Britain. He was later to become a distinguished and well-travelled economist, advocate of free trade and a prolific author. He was just twenty-five years old on this, his first visit to Britain. The final defeat of Napoleon on the battlefield of Waterloo in 1815 was a recent memory. Blanqui was just sixteen at the time of that historic French defeat – an impressionable age – and only twenty-four on the occasion of his first visit here. It is clear from the introduction to his account of his adventures, *Voyage d'un Jeune Français en Angleterre et en Écosse*, published in Paris the following year, that he arrived imbued with the familiar French prejudices against *le perfide Albion*, not least in respect of our food on which he has some amusing comments. But he had a lively and perceptive mind and his account of his grand tour sheds an interesting light on the state of the post-war Britain. After an uncomfortable Channel crossing from Le Havre to Southampton his tour took him as far north as Glasgow and Edinburgh but for our purpose its particular interest is his description of York.[1]

> Woe betide the stranger who arrives in an English town on the occasion of a boxing match, a race meeting or an important music festival! Unless he has already booked his accommodation he runs a serious risk of finding himself on the street. It was gone nine when we got to York, after enduring a frightful and continuous downpour from the moment we left Durham. It was a very dark night and the city, which was poorly lit, was completely unfamiliar to us. No bed was available at the coaching inn; neither was there anyone to act as our guide nor any means of procuring one. However, following the usual English practice, the coach had been cleared at breakneck speed and our baggage dumped unceremoniously at the coach office, which was heaving with travellers. After a long wait and a tedious journey through twisting streets streaming with water, we eventually found an inn which deigned to admit us. Two ancient women conducted us to the attic with alacrity – the reason for which only became apparent the following morning: our garret was going to cost us two guineas!
>
> I couldn't leave our lodgings quickly enough in order to visit the city, which was very unprepossessing, and the minster which goes beyond and above anything you have ever seen in the gothic style …

He was ecstatic about the minster, although retaining his critical faculties. The central tower he described as being "somewhat heavy", suggesting that it would be a good idea if each passing day reduced it slightly in size, reckoning that its size and crenellations rendered it more suitable for a military fort than a cathedral. "But as for the rest", he continued, "what majestic harmony invests the whole of this august metropolitan church! What captivating grace in every detail!" The minster of course has not much changed in its essentials since the young Frenchman's visit in the autumn of 1823 although he does comment that "the portraits of the kings of England arranged around the choir add an element of sovereign majesty to that of the sanctuary".

The two other features of York which seem to have seized Blanqui's imagination were the York Music Festival and the Retreat. It was the former, the Music Festival of 1823, rather than a boxing match or race meeting which had occasioned his accommodation problems on the night of his arrival in the dark and under the pouring rain.

This was not the first time that York had hosted a music festival. A previous one had been held in 1791 but the receipts on that occasion had only totalled £1,700 or so and as Madame Gertrud Mara, one of the most celebrated German operatic sopranos of the day, received 50 guineas for each performance and about a hundred other musicians were involved, the surplus (if any) cannot have been very great. The 1823 Festival, however, was clearly a major event. The city boasts the oldest musical society in England, founded in 1765, and York solicitor Jonathan Gray (1779-1837) was an enthusiastic member. He and a group of fellow enthusiasts had been closely involved in its promotion. Gray was equally involved in the following festivals in 1825 and 1828 and was one of the secretaries of the organising committee in 1823 and 1825. Festivals were to become a distinguishing feature of York life in the years to come but "tourism" as a word and a concept was in its infancy at the beginning of the 19th century and we have to accept that by the 1820s York was entering a period of decline as a centre of economic and social importance. The truth is that the industrial revolution which was to make the modern world was gradually but relentlessly passing it by. Professor Nuttgens summed the period up succinctly when he observed "York ambled along sociably and complacently with barely a tolerant smile for its reckless neighbours."[2] At the beginning of the 19th century York was reckoned to be the 16th largest city in England but by the end of the century it had fallen to 41st place.

Perhaps the word which best describes York in this period was "genteel". It was a world of the established church, the legal and medical professions, "respectable" shopkeepers and of entrenched and inward -looking city governance, determined to preserve the status quo. The status of York itself was little disturbed by the passing of the Representation of the People Act of 1832, better known to history as "the Great Reform Act". York was certainly not a "rotten borough" in the classic mould of Old Sarum which had only 13 voters or Dunwich, once a flourishing mediæval east coast port, most of which by 1832 was to be found under the North Sea.

There was, however, one significant development during this period. On 21 January 1828 a meeting took place at Ettridge's Hotel[3] of various members of the legal profession in York to discuss the establishment of a law library. This initial discussion was followed by a further meeting on 7 February when certain rules and regulations were adopted. At a third meeting, on 1 September later that year, the original rules were amended and thereafter formed the basis of a subscription library for which certain books had in fact already been acquired. Looking back 188 or so years later it does seem slightly curious that this was not something undertaken by the Yorkshire Law Society itself. The contemporary records do not suggest that such an idea even occurred to anyone although it is clear that there were disagreements as to policy and, as always on such occasions, one can only speculate as to what was not minuted. The only reference to the subject is to be found in the minutes of a general meeting of the Society on 28 March 1828 which does not really shed much light on the matter:

> Resolved, That it is the opinion of this meeting that the Rules of the York Law Book Society do not in their present form offer any adequate inducement to Professional Gentlemen residing more than 3 miles from York to become Members of that Society, although it is evidently for the interest of the Society to increase the number of its members and particularly of Proprietary Members.
>
> That it appears to this meet that the rules of the Society might be advantageously altered in the following respects (viz)
>
> That the Society should be called the "York and Yorkshire Law Book Society"
>
> That Proprietary Members residing in or within 3 miles of York should pay an annual subscription of 10/- per annum and that annual Subscribers beyond that distance should pay 15/- per annum and Proprietary Members beyond that distance nothing.
>
> That Members not residing in York should not be excluded as at present by Rules 9 and 10 from offices in the Society.

That a discretionary power be given to the Committee either originally or on appeal with respect to the Penalty imposed by Rule 18.

That the time of holding the General Meetings be altered so as to make two of such meetings fall in the Assize Weeks.

That the penalty of 1/- per day imposed by Rule 17 be increased to 5/- at least per day during the Assizes.

That the President of this Society be requested to use his best endeavours to get the rules altered in the instances before mentioned.

It is clear from the rules as amended on 1 September that some but not all of the Yorkshire Law Society's objections had been met. In particular, the suggested name of the "York and Yorkshire Law Book Society" was not adopted, the members preferring to be known simply as the "Yorkshire Law Library" – a decision with which one can perhaps sympathise. On the other hand, the suggestion that two of the general meetings be held during the Summer and Lent Assize weeks was adopted, as was the suggestion of a penalty of 5/- per day during the assizes for failure to return books borrowed on the appointed day, as opposed to 1/- per day at other times. Retention of books for any significant period was not encouraged – if borrowed, they were supposed to be returned by the following day at the latest.

The arrangements relating to proprietary members were curious and, as was eventually realised, defective.[4] The rules provided that the proprietary members, who were of course the founders of the Yorkshire Law Library, should hold the assets of the library not as trustees but beneficially, granting to the subscribing members the use of the library in return for an annual payment. They also provided that the interest of the proprietary members in the assets should be in proportion to the amount of their several shares. This was all very well but it meant that the annual subscribers had no interest in the property of the library, merely the right to use that property on payment of their annual subscription. Unfortunately, the rules made no provision which enabled the proprietary members to terminate the membership of any annual subscriber as long as he adhered to the rules and paid his subscription. This meant that such a subscriber had a vested interest (in the technical legal sense) in the use of the books, renewable annually as of right on those conditions. To complicate matters further, the rules conferred on the annual subscribers an equal share with the proprietary members in the management of the library.

More than half a century, however, was to elapse before the essential incoherence of these arrangements was to prompt an amalgamation of the Yorkshire Law Library with the Yorkshire Law Society and a transfer of the library to the latter, by which time it had become a valuable and important asset.[5] The legal complexities were considerable and it eventually required a lengthy deed dated 20 August 1885, comprising 19 parties of the first part, 16 of the second part and 12 of the third part, with three lengthy schedules to effect the transfer. Preparing and executing the (handwritten) engrossment must have been a considerable labour. The third schedule comprised the entire library catalogue and all the signatories, ostensibly at least, executed the deed in the presence of F Hugh Munby, clerk to FJ Munby, solicitor, York. What is notable is that of the 19 proprietary members of the first part, 18 were members of the Yorkshire Law Society. Furthermore, throughout its 57 years of existence the great majority of its officers were members of the Yorkshire Law Society, including William Gray who was President of the Yorkshire Law Library from 1852 to 1880. All this, however, was in the future.

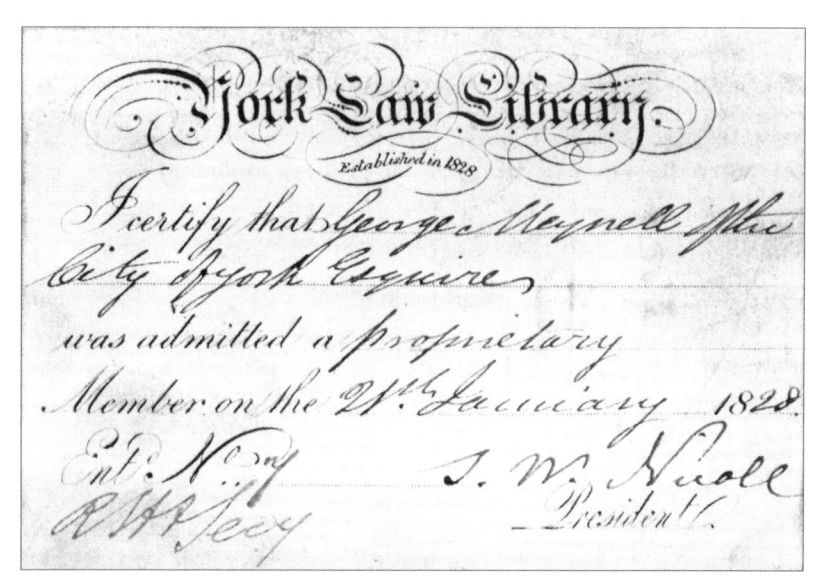

An early proprietary member's certificate dated 21 January 1828 in favour of George Meynell of the City of York Esquire

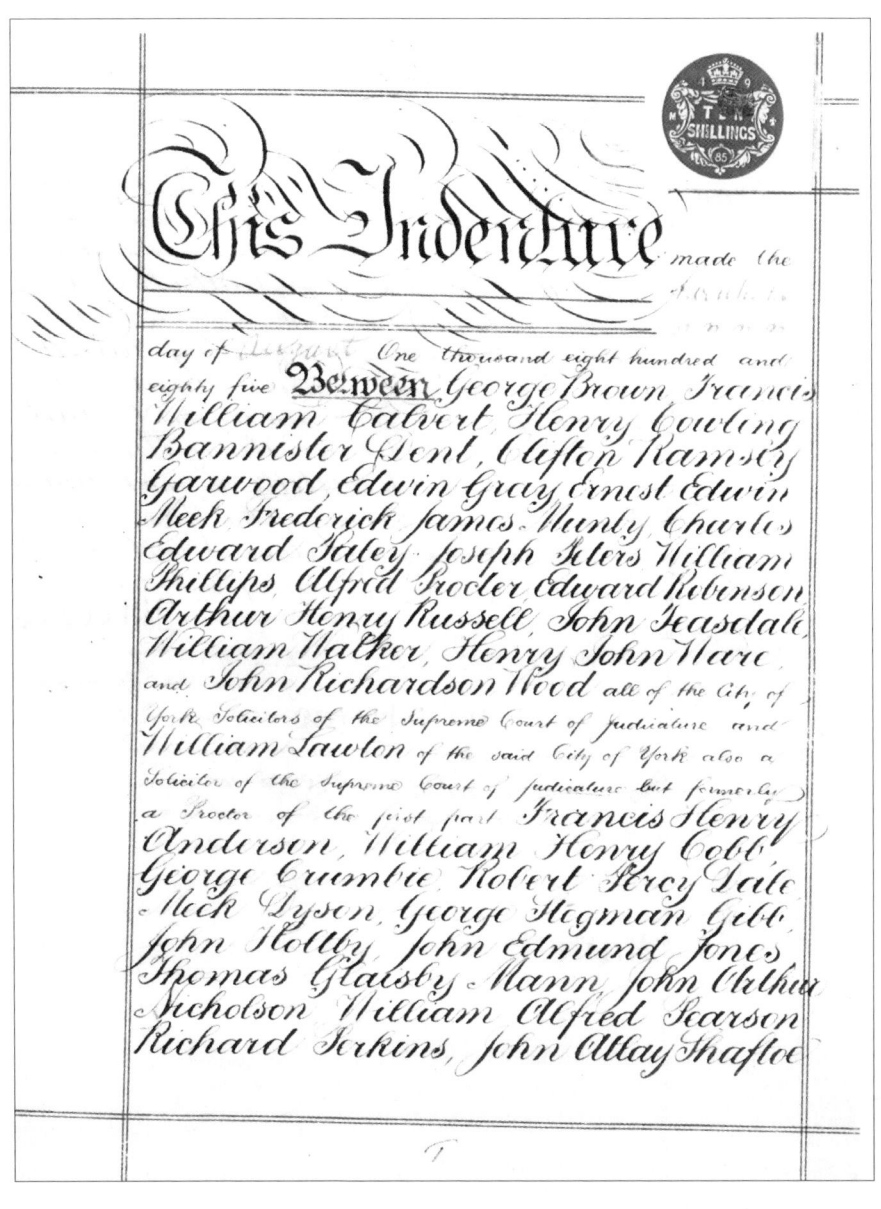

Sorting out a fine lawyers' mess of their own creation – The first page of the assignment dated 20 August 1885 by the proprietary members and annual members of the York Law Library to the Yorkshire Law Society. Altogether 47 signatures were required in order to bring about the desired result. As a result of lack of forethought and incautious drafting when the library was established in 1828 fifty-seven years of confusion were to elapse before coherence was re-established.

Notwithstanding its somewhat convoluted constitutional arrangements, the Yorkshire Law Library was evidently a success during the period of its independent existence. The original 1828 rules provided for a reduced annual subscription for proctors (30/-) those admitted for less than three years (£1) and those residing more than three miles from York (10/-). In addition, there was provision for "Clerks to Attorneys and Proctors, resident in York ... on the proposal of their masters, being Members, and on payment of an annual subscription of 10/-; but they shall not be entitled to attend the meetings of the Society, or to have a share in its management." Although never formally provided for in the rules, it seems to have been the practice to permit the use the library facilities to barristers on circuit subject to conditions. Indeed, at one time there was a published subscription rate of 10/- for members of the Bar which put them on the same level as attorneys' clerks. The position of judges was even less formal. A note dated 14 January 1847 but with later addenda records without explanation "Donations from Judges". Among the judicial donors whose names it is possible to decipher are Bayley J (1829) £2, Alderson B (1833) £10, Wightman J (no date) £2.2.0. and Platt B and Cresswell J[6] (1851) £2.2.0. each. It is not clear whether these "donations" were originally intended to cover judicial use of the library or simply a disinterested (or possibly interested) desire on the part of the judges for lawyers to be better legally informed. It is also clear that these donations from the judges were solicited. Among the miscellaneous documents which have survived is a draft or copy letter dated 9 March 1860 which reads as follows:

> The Secretary of the Yorkshire Law Society (W Phillips Solicitor, 9 Lendal) presents his compts to the Honble Mr Justice Blackburn[7] and begs his acceptance of a Copy of the Catalogue of the Library with the privilege of the use of the Books whenever his Lordship is holding the Assizes in York.
>
> As the yearly income of the Institution is inadequate for the purchase of many valuable new Works and some of the Reports a donation to its funds is respectfully solicited which may be paid to the President (Wm Gray Esqre Undersheriff of Yorkshire) to the Secretary, Lendal or to the Librarian, Wm Marsh, Minster Gates.

The slightly curious feature of this letter is that it refers to the Yorkshire Law Society but this was clearly inaccurate as Mr W Phillips was never the Society's Secretary in 1860 or at any other time and William Gray was its President for one year only in 1850. The latter, however, was the President of the Yorkshire Law Library from 1852-1880. William Phillips, like many other solicitors was a member both of the Society and the Yorkshire Law Library and clearly forgot, when drafting his letter soliciting a donation, on whose behalf he was soliciting. This suggests a fairly large common membership and the possibility of some confusion generally between the two bodies and their ultimate amalgamation in 1885 was doubtless inevitable.

Apart from Music Festivals and the establishment of the Yorkshire Law Library, life in York in the 1820s, 1830s and 1840s seemed to continue without high drama unless one includes the great Minster fire of 1829.

Towards the end of this period one professional matter at least did receive close attention. At a general meeting of the Society held on 16 March 1841 it was resolved "that a Petition be presented to the House of Commons on the subject of the County Courts Bill now before Parliament and that the following Petition be adopted 'That Sir Edward B Sugden be requested to present the Petition and that a printed Copy of it be sent to each of the Yorkshire Members [of Parliament] with a request that he will support the prayer.'" The Bill in question eventually became the County Courts Act 1846, an early Victorian attempt to deal with the problem of small claims. Until then such claims were dealt with, if dealt with at all, either in what we would now call the High Court (ie at Westminster or the county assizes) or by the old common law "county courts" or courts of request. The system, if it could be described as such, was local, haphazard and inefficient and had defied any attempt at reform from the 1820s onwards. Much of the opposition, it has to be said, came from lawyers. On the other hand having mundane claims for the price of goods sold and delivered by a judge of assize was equally inefficient and ridiculous. The petition is worth reproducing in full as it is quite revealing about the reality of such litigation in the early Victorian period and of attitudes to law reform at the time and by way of comparison with current practice. It also reflects the care and attention given by the Society to questions of law reform. Petitions to parliament were commonly used by the Society throughout the 19th century and this example is not untypical.

To the Honourable the Commons of the United Kingdom of Great Britain and Ireland in Parliament assembled.

The Humble Petition of the undersigned Members of the Yorkshire Law Society Sheweth That your Petitioners in perusing the Bill introduced into your Honourable House in this Session of Parliament to improve the Practice and extend the Jurisdiction of County Courts have pleasure in observing the improvements that are made therein upon the Bill of 1839 and with the exception of a few clauses to which they entertain objections, they are willing for the sake of the advantages which the Bill promises to the public, to submit to the trial of the experiment, and to the injury which they must unavoidable sustain in their professional emoluments on its being passed into Law.

Your Petitioners consider Clause 38 which it is proposed to be enacted that all Suits should be brought in the County Court of the District where the Defendant resides at the time of the entry of the plaint to be highly objectionable. Thus a person, after contracting a large number of Debts, may remove to a great distance from the place where the Plaintiffs witnesses reside and effectually deprive his creditors of all remedy against him on account of the expence of taking their Witnesses to the Court of the District to which he has removed. The ancient rule in all local Courts is much more consonant with justice and is more economical to both parties namely that the Suit should be brought in the District where the cause of action arose.

It is difficult to discover any reason why the service of process should be confined to the Bailiffs of the Court who must often be overburdened with the multiplicity of processes requiring their attention. A plaintiff might often be able to procure the service of a process gratuitously by a Friend or a Servant and thus save the Bailiff's expenses.

If the process be served on any other person than the Defendant it may be desirable to provide that it should be read over to that person, but your Petitioners know from practical experience that if it be required that the process should be read over to the Defendant himself, it would be frequently in the power of a Defendant to avoid the effectual service of a process.

Your Petitioners cannot but think that a sufficient invasion is made by this Bill upon the ancient system of Trial by Jury without abolishing it altogether as the Bill proposes to do in all cases under £5, and they consider that no sufficient reason has been shewn for altering the ancient mode of Trial by Jury at all, and that, the proposed enactment respecting it, would be highly unconstitutional.

It is extremely objectionable that the rules of evidence should be different in various Courts and the constant endeavour of the Judges in the Courts of Law and Equity for many years past has been to remove any variations that exist and to effect a perfect assimilation on this subject amongst all the Courts. Your Petitioners therefore object to the Clause dispensing with the Rules of Evidence and they think that allowing Parties to a Suit to be examined will unnecessarily offer an inducement to the Commission of Perjury.[8]

With respect to Clause 63 your Petitioners submit that in the great majority of instances, parties will not be disposed to conduct their own Cases, Merchants, Tradesmen, and others are usually too much occupied with their own Businesses to attend to the recovery of their Debts in Courts of Law. Persons of Integrity unused to public Business, or of retired habits, would have no chance with shrewd and cunning parties opposed to them, the Services of an Attorney are therefore indispensable, and it will be a great hardship if the expense of such Services, which are necessary to the attainment of the just rights of parties, should be a burthen upon the persons requiring them, instead of being made costs in the cause. The proposed fees to be paid to Attorneys are miserable and inadequate and it is absurd to suppose that any respectable practitioner will accept the remuneration offered by this Clause which is to be the same in all instances, whether the Cases be complicated, or clear, and whether the Services rendered be great, or little, and the whole practice of the Courts must therefore fall into the hands of the lowest Members of the Profession or more probably into the Hands of Bailiff's followers and Debt Collectors; and your petitioners protest most strongly against the proposed enactment, that, no person, except by leave of the Court, shall be entitled to argue any question in any summary proceeding in the County Courts, as it is impossible for an Advocate to do his Duty to his Client, unless he be heard as of right and not as a favor, and your petitioners are surprised to find that after the late Act giving power to Attorneys to be heard as of right before Magistrates, any attempt should be made to return to the antiquated system.

The expense of the Bailiff travelling into another jurisdiction when a Defendant removes from that in which judgment is obtained to get the signature of a Magistrate on the back of the Warrant on his making oath of the same being duly issued will often amount to more than the Sum recovered in the Action.

If the Seal of the Court were made evidence, the process might be transmitted from one Court to another to be executed by an Officer of the Court where the Defendant resides & it would in that case be done at little expense.

The 89th Clause is highly objectionable for its effect will be that if any party to a suit, in going to, or returning from the Court House shall consider himself insulted, the supposed aggressor may be taken into Custody & fined £5 at the will of a single Judge, without any written evidence, any record of conviction, or any power of Appeal.

The impunity given to the Bailiffs by Clause 92 would enable them to make use of the process of the Court as an Instrument of the most vexatious aggression, so long as they take care to inflict a greater amount of injury than may be estimated at the sum of £19.19.0.

Your Petitioners therefore, although highly approving of the Objects of the Bill for improving County Courts in affording a cheaper and easier means of recovering small Debts, Humbly Pray that your Honourable House will only support such alterations in the Law as will be practically beneficial to the Public and that in so doing the fair and just rights of the Profession to which your Petitioners belong may be considered.

And your Petitioners will ever pray &c.

Notwithstanding the emollient opening and closing paragraphs of the petition, it seems fairly clear that the Society's members found quite a lot to criticise. Some of their objections seem quaint and curious today. To the modern practitioner the notion that an everyday claim for the price of goods sold and delivered should be tried before a *jury* seems wholly fanciful even if it were in excess of £5 (say £220 in today's money). In fact, when the Bill finally became law as the County Courts Act 1846, it was followed by a marked increase in the number of small claims and equally marked increase in the number of solicitors. The increase in claims was doubtless foreseen; the increase in the number of solicitors perhaps less so. What was *not* foreseen but which perhaps should have been, was a vast increase in the indebtedness of the ordinary working man. In the days when debt recovery was difficult and expensive on account of the need to bring claims in the traditional common law courts, tradesmen were reluctant to give credit to those whom they did not consider creditworthy – the ordinary labourer or artisan. The facility to bring "small claims" in the new county courts had an immediate effect on the outlook of the previously cautious tradesmen. The effect was not dissimilar to the ready availability of hire-purchase and latterly plastic credit in our own time. It was a shattering example of the law of unintended consequences.

On the First Reading of the County Courts Act Amendment Bill in the House of Lords on 6 May 1864 the Lord Chancellor, Lord Westbury, provided a veritable litany of what he perceived as the 1846 Act's shortcomings.[9] Among the more plangent items on his list was the astonishing contribution which the Act had made to civil imprisonment for debt. In the period of two years to 31 December 1863 no fewer than 17,979 persons had been committed to prison pursuant to its provisions. The overwhelming majority of those imprisoned,17,850, had been so for one reason only: they had failed to satisfy a judgment and costs after having been adjudged to have had the means to do so. As the Lord Chancellor pointed out, a judgment debtor in the County Court was in a less favourable position than a bankrupt in the Bankruptcy Court except where a creditor could prove that the bankrupt had obtained credit by fraud. He gave examples of the ridiculously small amounts which regularly resulted in the imprisonment of the judgment creditor, 1/6, 3/1, 1/10, 2/9 and even mentioned one case where a man had been imprisoned for several days for the sum of 9d. Another cause of grave concern was that the Act had spawned a wholly novel species of huckster or loan-shark who specialised in providing credit to the poor, a problem familiar enough in our own day. These and other defects resulted in due course in the passing of the County Courts Act 1866.

Two objections which the Society had raised in their petition in 1841 but which proved to have been totally misplaced were those relating to trial by jury and giving parties the right to give evidence on their own behalf. Less than ten years after the passing of the 1846 Act the practical convenience of dispensing with the jury in civil cases in the County Court had come to be widely recognised. By the Common Law Procedure Act 1854 litigants in the Court of Queen's Bench were permitted to elect trial by judge alone and this was an option which was increasingly exercised.[10]

Whatever its failings, the County Courts Act 1846 was but an early part of a serious and sustained effort to reform English law and English legal procedure in a way which had at least some semblance of logic and consistency. It was to be a lengthy exercise but it had received a notable impetus by the passing of the Representation of the People Act 1832, better known to historians as the Great Reform Act. But it was really from the middle of the 19th century onwards that English legal life began to assume a form which we could at least recognise as bearing some relation to our modern world. For the most part law and practice in the first half of the century would still appear both weird and harsh to our way of thinking. For example, despite the tentative reforms of the criminal law in the early part of the 19th century, much remained to be done and the law's approach to offenders still remained astonishingly casual, harsh and dismissive to modern eyes. In his memoirs Serjeant Ballantine[11] gives an alarming insight into the casualness that prevailed at the Old Bailey:

> The sittings of the court commenced at nine o'clock in the morning, and continued until nine at night. There were relays of judges. Two luxurious dinners were provided, one at three o'clock, the other at five. The Ordinary of Newgate dined at both. The scenes in the evening may be imagined, the actors in them having generally dined at the first dinner. There was much genial hospitality exercised towards the bar ... one cannot but look back with a feeling of disgust to the mode in which eating and drinking, transporting and hanging were shuffled together. The City judges rushing from the table to take their seats upon the bench, the leading counsel scurrying after them, the jokes of the table scarcely out of their lips, and the amount of wine drunk, not rendered less apparent from having been drunk quickly – that is now all changed. The early dinners and evening sittings have been interred with other barbarisms ...

Some idea of the prevailing attitude towards prisoners can also be gauged from an account by Ballantine's near contemporary, Henry Hawkins.[12] He confirms Ballantine's account of the conviviality of the "early dinners" but goes on to describe how the general atmosphere which they engendered was wont to affect judges' attitudes towards the accused who had the misfortune to appear before them. Their "trial" went something like this:

Prosecuting counsel to first witness:

I think you were walking up Ludgate Hill on Thursday, 25th, about half-past-two in the afternoon and suddenly felt a tug at your pocket and missed your handkerchief, which the constable now produces. Is that it?

Witness:

Yes, sir.

Judge:

I suppose you have nothing to ask him? Next witness!

Constable stands up

Were you following the prosecutor on the occasion when he was robbed on Ludgate Hill? And did you see the prisoner put his hand into the prosecutor's pocket and take his handkerchief out of it?

Constable:

Yes, sir.

Judge to prisoner:

Nothing to say, I suppose?

Then to the jury:

Gentlemen, I suppose you have no doubt?

Jury:

Guilty, my Lord (as though to oblige his Lordship)

Judge to prisoner:

Jones, we have met before, we shall not meet again for some time, seven years transportation. Next case.

Time Two minutes, fifty-three seconds. (And, he might have added, no issues about leading questions, prisoners being allowed to give evidence on their own behalf or legal aid.)

It cannot be said, however, that the Society was only concerned with the daily grind of professional preoccupations and neglected the literary and artistic aspects of life. On 17 July 1840 it was resolved "That this Society subscribe for 10 copies of a Translation of Ovid's Epistles by Miss Emma Garland daughter of the late Mr Garland[13] of Hull, Solicitor, formerly a Member of this Society". Emma's translation was published two years later in 1842. What became of the ten copies to which the Society subscribed is not known; neither is it known for that matter what ambition prompted the daughter of a Hull solicitor to undertake a task that had previously attracted some rather better-known literary figures such as John Dryden.

NOTES

1. Author's translation. Blanqui's account never seems to have been published in English – a pity as it is a lively and often humorous read.

2. Quoted by Leonard Robinson in *William Etty – The Life and Art* – McFarland & Co Ltd, Jefferson North Carolina 2007.

3. This was the same establishment in what is now known as Museum Street York and previously known as "Mr Ringrose's House" or "Bluitt's Inn" where the first meeting of the Society was held on 21 March 1786.

4. It is surprising how often lawyers fall into error when dealing with their own affairs. RE Megarry in his entertaining book *Miscellany-at-Law* (Stevens & Sons Ltd – London 1955) mentions an impressive list of judges taken from the 17th edition of Hayes & Jarman's *Concise Forms of Wills* whose testamentary efforts have given rise to Chancery litigation over the years: Thompson CB, Holt CJ, Eyre CJ, Wood B, Vaughan J, Lord Westbury LC, Lord Cottenham LC and Cleasby B. Megarry himself goes on to cite two whole pages of testamentary disasters suffered by eminent lawyers, including Dr TH Tristram (of Tristram and Coote's *Probate Practice*) whose will was imperfectly executed and the above mentioned Thomas Jarman, the eminent author of *Jarman on Wills*, who contrived to die intestate.

5. In 1933 the Society commissioned a report by George Laycock Brown, a respected President of the Society, to prepare a report on some of the antiquarian items in the library and their condition. See generally Appendix C.

6. Sir Cresswell Cresswell (1794-1863) formerly a Northern Circuiteer and latterly its leader, became a judge of the Common Pleas and subsequently in 1858 the first judge of the newly established Probate Divorce and Admiralty Courts on which he set his mark. His reputation in the Court of Common Pleas had not been very high but in exercising the former ecclesiastical jurisdiction he was much more successful, deciding over 1,000 case in six years, only one of which seems to have been reversed on appeal.

7. Sir Colin Blackburn (later Baron) (1813-1896) was a member of the Northern Circuit before becoming a judge of the Queen's Bench. Raised to the peerage in 1876, he served on several royal commissions and wrote on a number of legal topics. He was one of the judges sitting in the Court of Exchequer Chamber in the case well-known to lawyers of *Rylands v Fletcher* (1866) LR 1 Ex 265 which eventually made its way to the House of Lords (1868) 3 HL 330. It concerned strict legal liability for the escape of substances deliberately accumulated on land (ie not naturally there). In this particular case the substance was water.

8. Readers of *Pickwick Papers* by Charles Dickens, first published in 1836, will recall the fictional case of *Bardell v Pickwick*, a claim for breach of promise of marriage. The jury's verdict against the unfortunate Mr Pickwick would never have arisen if the parties had been able to give evidence on their own behalf and clear up what had been nothing more than a tragic misunderstanding. Despite the certainty of the Society's members that any change in the law would encourage perjury, no doubt justified, S2 of the Evidence Act 1851 finally allowed it.

9. Hansard – House of Lords Debates 6 May 1864 Vol 175 cc 85-98

10. Trial by jury ceased to be the norm in civil cases in England and Wales by virtue of the Administration of Justice (Miscellaneous Provisions) Act 1933. This guaranteed the right to trial by jury in all cases of alleged fraud, libel, slander, malicious prosecution, false imprisonment, seduction, and breach of promise of marriage. However, as the late Sir Jack Jacob observed "After the Second World War, there arose a marked disenchantment with [civil] jury trials, and there began a conscious move to avoid trial by jury. This was largely because of the fundamental changes in the character of civil litigation due to the enormous increase in claims and actions for damages for personal injury and death. As these came to dominate the case-load of the Queen's Bench Division, both trades unions and insurance companies, who were respectively supporting the receiving and paying parties in these classes of cases, adopted a policy of shunning jury trials. Their desire was

to have speedy, simple and inexpensive procedures and above all a measure of certainty and uniformity on the question of damages for different kinds of personal injuries so that they could arrive at what they conceived to be fair settlements and avoid trials or even proceedings." *The Fabric of English Civil Justice* (The Hamlyn Lectures 38) Stevens and Sons Ltd 1987. Curiously, there has been no real corresponding trend in Scotland where jury trials in the Court of Session are still relatively common even for cases of "delinquency or quasi-delinquency" (ie delict or tort) including personal injury and fatal accident cases. Indeed, in June 2012 two fatal accident cases came on as conjoined appeals before the First Division of the Inner House of the Court of Session, *Hamilton v Fergus Transport (Spean Bridge) Ltd* and *Thomson v Dennis Thomson Builders Ltd* [2012] CSIH 52. In his opinion Lord Hamilton, the Lord President observed that the current absence of guidance from the presiding judge at civil jury trials over the level of damages was "an unsatisfactory feature of our practice. It should, in my view, now be changed." He concluded that the trial judge, after hearing submissions in the absence of the jury, would subsequently in addressing them "suggest ... a spectrum within which their award might lie. " There is a hint here, perhaps that the Scots may be moving in our direction.

Our own faith in juries for criminal trials seems more deeply rooted but even here there has been nibbling at the edges. Lord Roskill's Fraud Trials Committee was among the first to suggest other options for the more sophisticated cases of fraud (See Chapter 14) although it was not unanimous. More recently S43 of the Criminal Justice Act 2003 provides for the prosecution to apply for trial by judge alone in serious or complex cases of fraud. S44 also makes similar provision where there is a "real and present danger" of jury tampering, albeit subject to fairly stringent conditions. Both provisions have been fairly controversial and there is little doubt that there would be strong objection to any further curtailment.

11. Serjeant Ballantine (1812-1887) *Some Experiences of a Barrister's Life* – Richard Bentley & Son London 1882

12. Richard Harris KC (ed) *Reminiscences of Sir Henry Hawkins* 1906. Henry Hawkins (1817-1907) son of a country solicitor, started his legal career articled to his uncle but "hating the drudgery of an attorney's office" went to London, joined the Middle Temple and had a distinguished legal career at the Bar, taking silk in 1859 and appointed to the bench in 1876. At the Bar his cross-examinations in the Tichbourne case, one of the *causes célèbres* of Victorian England, brought him much notoriety and a very substantial income – a fact that was well-known to his fellow barristers.

One day Serjeant Ballantine said to him "Look here, Hawkins, why do you take so much care of your money?" – Hawkins was a bachelor at the time – "It can't be much use to you in this world, and you can't take it with you to the next. Even if you could, it would only melt." Retiring from the bench in 1898 at the age of 81, Hawkins was raised to the peerage as Baron Brampton the following year. On the bench he had the reputation of being a hanging judge but seems to have mellowed in his old age. In the year of his retirement he had became a Catholic and in 1903 he and his wife provided the funds to establish the chapel of SS Gregory and Augustine in the newly erected Westminster Cathedral. He was evidently a devout man but equally a very hard working one. He admitted once "I am generally so dead beat by the time I kneel down to pray that I begin out of habit 'Gentlemen of the jury'".

13. Richard Garland, Emma's father, had joined the Society in 1808 and in fact had served as President in 1818. In 1814 he had been appointed to the sub-committee, along with Charles Frost and Jonathan Gray, charged with the task of going down to London to lobby the common law judges about costs and allowances to witnesses. See Chapter 3.

Chapter Six

THE LAST DAYS OF THE ANCIEN RÉGIME
1850 – 1886

*"The thing was canva/s'd, and it feem'd paft doubt
Much we adher'd to we could do without"*

Ronald A Knox
Ab/olute and Abitofhell

It was not for nothing that the previous decade had come to be known as "the hungry forties". Increasing urbanisation following the trade recession of 1839, the protectionism which had preceded the repeal of the Corn Laws in 1846, famine in Ireland, the political upheaval of Chartism at home and revolution on the continent had a decidedly unsettling effect on all sections of English society. A combination of the railway revolution,[1] mechanisation of printing and the penny post all meant that the country had undergone a radical change that could not be undone. In 1837 *The Northern Star*, a Chartist newspaper, had been established in Leeds. For the first time ordinary working men in different parts of the country could be in touch with one another and the rapid dissemination of new social and political ideas became possible in a way that had previously been impossible. The Great Exhibition of 1851, it is true, had a calming effect but if anyone imagined that everything would settle down again in the old routines they were mistaken. The Crimean War (1854-1856) had come as a considerable shock to British complacency. The country had not been involved in a war with another European power since the defeat of Napoleon in 1815. In military terms Britain had slumbered for nearly forty years and was substantially unprepared for the waging of a serious war extending over a large area from the Crimea itself to the Baltic. Military and naval technology had changed since the days of Wellington and Nelson but not that much. Commissions in the army were still acquired by purchase and the navy still put to sea in wooden sailing ships even if some of them had the benefit of auxiliary steam power. One aspect of war, however, had changed for ever: the way in which it was reported – and this had an effect on the way it was perceived back home.

The man largely responsible for this was William Howard Russell of *The Times*. His graphic reports of the suffering, the muddle and the early administrative incompetence of the army's senior command had a dramatic effect on public opinion. Russell's journalistic skills combined with the new technology of telegraph and photography and the printing and distribution of newspapers (by rail) brought the reality of war to "the home front" with a hitherto unknown immediacy. And to underline the point there was Florence Nightingale whose exploits equally struck a chord with public opinion.

The old way of doing things was simply not working. Reform was in the air. The army was more conservative perhaps than the legal profession. They, for example, had to wait until the Cardwell reforms of 1870 and 1871 for the abolition of such 18th century relics as flogging as a form of punishment and the sale of commissions as well as much-needed administrative reforms. Even then there was widespread resistance from the die-hards in the military establishment.

Legal reform, however, raised more complex issues. Often the inertia was just as great and the vested interests more extensive. In 1852-3 Dickens had published his novel *Bleak House* in monthly parts. It is the novel which contains the celebrated critique of the abuses in the Court of Chancery elaborated in the fictional case of *Jarndyce v Jarndyce*. In fact the abuses were well-known to those in authority and to any wretched litigant who had the misfortune to experience them. It was equally well-known to their lawyers. Dickens memorably described the scene in the first chapter:

> … with bills, cross-bills, answers, rejoinders, injunctions, affidavits, issues, references to masters, master's reports, mountains of costly nonsense … which so exhausts finances, patience, courage, hope, so overthrows the brain and breaks the heart, that there is not an honourable man among its practitioners who would not give – who does not often give – the warning, "Suffer any wrong that can be done you rather than come here!"

Some modern commentators have questioned whether Dickens actually led public opinion or merely reflected it. Parliament had in fact been attempting to get to grips with chancery reform, not altogether successfully, for some years, well before the first appearance of *Bleak House*. In the previous century the great Lord Mansfield had been embarrassingly confronted with the problems of chancery litigation, to which Dickens had alluded, whilst trying a dispute about a parish boundary. A farmer was giving evidence and had hinted at the misuse of parish money. Mansfield, unwisely in the circumstances, decided to intervene:

Q   In the course of your evidence I think you noticed that the parish money was very often improperly applied … but as you mentioned that you were once churchwarden, if you have no objection I should wish to hear what was done with the money at that time.

A   Why, my lord, the money was worse applied while I was churchwarden than ever I knew it in my life.

Q   Indeed! I should be glad to know how.

A   Well, my lord, I'll tell you. A gentleman who had lived some time among us went into Yorkshire where he died. In his will he bequeathed about £120 to the poor of our parish. We applied for it often but could not get it; the executors and the lawyers were determined to keep the money in their hands; for you know, my lord, 'tis an old saying, that "might can overcome right." Well, we did not know what to do, and I came to your lordship for advice. You were then Chancellor Murray. I remember, my lord, you advised us to file a bill in Chancery. We did so, and after throwing a great deal of good money after bad, we got I think they call it a decree and such decree it was that, when all expenses were paid, I reckon we were about £175 out of pocket, through acting on your lordship's advice. Now, my lord, I leave you to judge whether the parish money was not likely to be worse employed while I was churchwarden than even I knew it before.[2]

On 12 March 1850 the Committee of the Society reported to members that they had been considering "the necessity for a thorough and effective reform of the Court of Chancery" and had "joined other Societies in endeavouring to effect that object". A petition had been prepared to the

House of Commons on the subject which was submitted for members' approval which was duly obtained. The petition opened as follows:

> To the Honorable the Commons of the United Kingdom of Great Britain and Ireland in Parliament assembled
>
> The Humble Petition of the Yorkshire Law Society Sheweth
>
> That the Members of this Society and they believe nearly the whole profession of the Law are of Opinion that the present system of proceedings in the Court of Chancery, and the mode of conducting business in its Offices, is injurious to the Suitors and to the whole community and requires thorough and speedy Reform.
>
> That the delay and expense at present attendant on proceedings in the Court of Chancery are so great as effectively to close its doors against all except the richer classes of the Community.
>
> That the expense is so serious as to render it imperative on the profession to prevent as far as possible the institution of suits except for great amounts.
>
> That therefore, whilst at common law rights of small amount can without impropriety be submitted to legal decision, a very large and important section of the community viz persons interested in small matters requiring the interference of a Court of Equity, are left without the protection of the Law and for them there is absolutely no Equity Court in operation.
>
> That owing to this defect in our Judicial Institutions not only is individual wrong inflicted, without redress, on this class of Society, but frauds as to trust property, offences against the most confidential relations are actually encouraged by Law, because permitted to pass with entire impunity.
>
> That your petitioners hope that in the representations which they have made of the importance of rendering the proceedings in Equity more expeditious and cheap, it will be felt by Your Honorable House that they are advocating improvements of the greatest importance to the interests of the Suitors and of the Community, whilst at the same time Your Petitioners freely admit that they believe these improvements will also, in the end, be advantageous to their own body, from the conviction that the interests of the Solicitor is in these questions is identified with that of his client.

The petition then proceeded to deal with procedural specifics and noted with regret that attempts to deal with many such issues by judges' rules authorised under previous legislation had been ineffective and that delays had become even worse than they were previously. There was also a plea for arrangements to be made for *viva voce* evidence to be taken elsewhere than in London. The document goes on to observe that the petitioners have had an opportunity of perusing the government Bill then before the Commons relating to Chancery reform in Ireland and "cordially approves" of its provisions. The Petitioners conclude by saying that "all the arguments which shew that the said Bill would be an advantage in Ireland equally shew that it would be so in England where as an experiment its provisions could as your Petitioners confidently believe be more conveniently and satisfactorily tested."

In the event it was not until two years later that *two* Court of Chancery Acts were passed and ten years later the Chancery Regulation Act 1862. The problems to be addressed were indeed long-standing and grievous and need to be considered under two broad headings: firstly fees and secondly the linked question of procedures and jurisdiction. The biggest scandal had been the archaic, not to say corrupt, basis of fees payable personally to officials *virtute officii*. Such fees were payable at every procedural twist and turn. As the Lord Chancellor himself put it when later commenting on the Act in the House of Lords on 16 November 1852 "A great burden was imposed upon the suitors in having to pay a great many fees upon every occasion at many offices".[3] These fees were not perhaps particularly exorbitant when reckoned individually but collectively they were overwhelming and of course gave the officials concerned a strong financial interest in preserving the complexity and discouraged any temptation to pro-activity on their part. It was only by the Suitors in Chancery Relief Act 1852 that all Chancery Officials were provided with salaries and the payment of fees to individuals abolished. The Act even went as far as to make the receipt of "gratuities" (perhaps more accurately described as bribes) illegal.[4] Unfortunately the cost of doing so was to be a financial clog on reform for many years as the officials concerned had purchased their respective offices and had to be compensated. The scale of the problem can be judged from the fact that by 1853 one of them, George Gatty (a Taxing Master) had already received almost £69,000 –

say about £4,000,000 in today's values.[5] Throughout the 1850s and 1860s compensation was still being paid for offices abolished in 1842 and 1852.

Further, the Chancery procedures themselves were of astonishing complexity and bedevilled by issues of jurisdiction. The Court of Chancery was not supposed to be a suitable forum for determining questions of fact. If in the course of proceedings any disputed question of fact were to arise the issue had to be referred to one of the common law courts for determination – by a jury. The traditional English obsession with juries in purely civil matters and their reluctance to entrust factual issues to judges continued to flourish and was to remain for another eighty years.[6] Even now it has not totally expired. Another cause of complexity was that Chancery procedure required everyone who had an interest in the proceedings, however slight, to be joined as a party. These two requirements naturally gave anyone who wished to delay (and had the financial means to do so) a golden opportunity to stay proceedings simply by raising a question of "fact", however, tenuous, or insisting that some other allegedly interested party be added. This shuttling of a case between Chancery and the common law courts was matched by internal shuttling between the Chancery judges and the Masters. The former had no means of conducting any form of administrative enquiries and the latter had no jurisdiction to decide anything; even their administrative enquiries were grossly hampered by the fact that there were no continuous hearings *de die in diem*, merely hourly appointments. Even then the allotted hour was often spent in the Master having to be reminded of what had happened on the previous appointment.

What was really required, as seems obvious with the benefit of hindsight, was a total fusion of law and equity[7] coupled with a rationalisation of the court system. This was eventually achieved – up to a point – with the Judicature Acts in the 1870s but it was a long time in coming. One reason for this was the traditional English reluctance to grapple with first principles and our penchant for ad hocery. Revolutionary France in 1789 had faced, in legal terms at least, a not dissimilar task and, under Napoleon, had achieved logically coherent goals in the form of the *Code Civil* (1804) and the codes which followed it – the *Code de Procedure Civile* (1806), the *Code Commerciale* (1807) and the *Code d'Instruction Criminelle* (1810). But such revolutionary zeal was not the English way.

Doctors Commons, Knightrider Street, London – Ackermann 1808

It has to be admitted that English lawyers can sometimes be slightly sniffy about the whole concept of the *Code Napoléon* as it has collectively come to be known, but it was a remarkable achievement in which Napoleon himself took a close interest. Sure, as originally enacted it reflected the social attitudes of the time, especially as regards the status of women, but it survived largely intact in the Prussian Rhineland until 1900 and likewise in Belgium, Luxembourg, Monaco and of course France itself until the present day – and parts of it even survive in such disparate territories as Japan, Egypt, Quebec and Louisiana.

It was not merely the reform of the Court of Chancery that called for detailed attention in the 1850s. Parliament also decided to turn its attention to matters ecclesiastical. The eventual outcome was the Court of Probate Act 1857 and the Matrimonial Causes Act 1857 followed by the High Court of Admiralty Act 1859. The link connecting these seemingly disparate topics is that wills, matrimonial law and ships were all governed by ecclesiastical or civil law, not common law. That law was administered by a different system of courts where the lawyers were quite differently qualified. Their equivalent of barristers were known as advocates[8] and the work of attorneys or solicitors was undertaken by proctors. To understand why this should have been so requires an even more profound delve into history than in the case of the Court of Chancery. In pre-reformation times the one body that exercised jurisdiction throughout Europe was the church, that is to say the universal or "Catholic" Church based in Rome and headed by the Pope. The church's administrative infrastructure had inherited much from that of the Roman Empire, including Roman or "civil" law. Dr Arthur Duck (1580-1648), Fellow of All Souls and one of the leading civil lawyers of his day, published a treatise *On the Authority of the Civil Law in the Kingdom of England*. After demonstrating the historical link between the civil or Roman law and international law and the law of the sea, he continues:

> In the Ecclesiastical Courts, the Archbishops, Bishops, Archdeacons or Vicars General, Commissiaries or Officials appointed by them, are Judges; whose distinct Power is deriv'd from [William] the Conqueror, who separated the Episcopal from the Secular jurisdiction: These, by the indulgence of our Kings and Custom of England have the cognizance of many Causes both Criminal and Civil; as Blasphemy, Apostacy, Heresie, Schism, Simony, Incest, Adultery, Whoredom, Fornication, Chastity attempted, Sacred Orders, Institutions to Ecclesiastical Benefices, or Relinquishment of the same; Performance of Divine Service, Matrimony, Divorce, Tithes, Offerings, Mortuaries, repairing of Churches, Dilapidation of Parsonage Houses, Pensions, Procurations, Wills, Codicils, Legacies, Succession to Intestates by Administration, and several other Matters … All these are exactly taken notice of by our Lawyers: All these are determined in this Court by the Civil and Canon Law, together with the Provincial Constitutions of Canterbury, and those of the Pope's Legates sent hither to our Kings; from all which our Ecclesiastical Law is taken, and by which it is allowed, all these Causes are to be decided.

Duck, of course, was writing in the 17th century and, two hundred years on, the scope of the ecclesiastical courts was not in practice quite as extensive it was in his day. But even the mid-Victorians had come to the conclusion that wills and succession, matrimonial causes and admiralty matters really ought to be outwith the jurisdiction of the church and a matter for the secular courts. Nevertheless, although the royal courts took over jurisdiction, much of the substantive law remained except where specifically amended by statute. For example, modern practitioners dealing with wills will know that the usual requirements as to form are relaxed for those who are either on, or about to embark on, active service, whether it be in the Crimea, Iraq, Afghanistan or Syria. What they may possibly not know is that this is a Roman relic in our law to be found in Justinian's Institutes:

> ... videlicet cum in expeditionibus occupati sunt ... (De Militari testamento – Lib.ii Tit.xi)

Another jurisdictional relic which has survived is the office of notary public – the *notarius* or *scriba* of the Roman Empire. In England the office is not the exact counterpart of the notary known throughout the countries of the world which have adopted the civil law – where much of their work is what we would call conveyancing – but rather the attesting of what the civil lawyers would call "authentic documents". In practice for us this means documents for use abroad, especially in civil law jurisdictions. The church's involvement, even today, is due to the fact that originally notaries were appointed by the Pope but in 1279 this power was delegated to the Papal Legate who exercised it until Henry VIII decided to confiscate it through the Ecclesiastical Licenses Act 1533 – "An Acte for the exonaracion frome exaccions payable to the See of Rome". He then delegated it to the Archbishop of Canterbury who still has it – as those members of the Society who are notaries will be well-aware. The 1533 Act, whose preamble claims that the authority of the King's "imperial crown" is diminished by the "unreasonable and uncharitable usurpations and exactions" of the Pope, is still in force.

The last of these reforming acts abolishing the civil law jurisdiction of the ecclesiastical courts was the Act of 1859 dealing with admiralty matters. As we shall see, this led in due course to the creation of the Probate, Divorce and Admiralty Division of the High Court under the Judicature Acts. To those unacquainted with its origins in the civil law, this curious combination of subject matters was waggishly justified on the basis that they were all concerned with wrecks – wrecks of wills, wrecks of marriages and wrecks of ships. However, their common heritage was to sink beneath the waves under the provisions of the Administration of

Justice Act 1970. This assigned marriage and family matters, as well as non-contentious probate to a newly created Family Division; contentious probate was allocated to the Chancery Division and admiralty matters to the Queen's Bench Division. *Sic transit gloria Romae.*

The first inkling that the Society received of the proposed creation of a Court of Probate seems to have been at a general meeting on 14 March 1854 when the Committee reported the introduction by the Lord Chancellor in the House of Lords of a Bill "to transfer to the Court of Chancery the testamentary jurisdiction of the Ecclesiastical Courts and to alter and amend the law in relation to matters of Testacy and Intestacy". The Committee noted that it was proposed that all wills be sent to London and that contested probate business be assigned to the Court of Chancery. The only sop to provincials under the Bill was a proposal to establish certain district courts but their jurisdiction would be limited to cases where the deceased's effects were sworn at under £1,500. On this occasion the Committee was "glad to find that a Petition from the Merchants, Bankers and other Inhabitants of York against the centralizing part of the Bill and in favor of Courts in the Country being established having Jurisdiction unrestricted in Amount has been forwarded for presentation to the House of Lords."

Sixteen months later, on 17 July 1855, the Committee was to report in greater detail to the effect that in accordance with their previously expressed intention at an earlier general meeting, they had prepared and forwarded to the House of Commons a Petition objecting to that part of the Bill centralising the entire business of the Ecclesiastical Courts in London. The Petition had been signed on behalf of the Society by the President, the Vice-President and the Secretary. It had been published in the *Law Times* and apparently given rise "to considerable comment and controversy". Their report went on "The Committee regret to find that several Country Solicitors appear to be in favour of this Bill. The Committee think that a thorough Reform of the Ecclesiastical Courts may be effected by the establishment of Testamentary Offices for the Deposit and Proof of Wills in Districts of suitable extent." The Society, like "the Merchants, Bankers and other Inhabitants of York", clearly objected to the "centralizing" tendency of governments and their protest echoes their plea five years earlier that provision be made for viva voce examinations in Chancery to be held "elsewhere than in London".

Another aspect of the *ancien régime* to receive close attention at this period was the legal status of women – particularly married women. Although parliament had tinkered with the issue over the years and the development of equity had produced some improvement to the property rights of married women, their fundamental status was governed by the common law and its doctrine of "coverture" as developed by case law. There were three aspects altogether which affected not only her person but equally her property and her contracts and other transactions. As to her person, this was deemed by right to belong to her husband to the point that under some older authorities this gave him the right of "moderate correction" as was the case with a child. By the end of the 17th century this view was no longer tenable but as Blackstone had observed "Yet the lower rank of people , who were always fond of the old common law, still claim and exert their antient privilege; and the courts of law will still permit a husband to restrain his wife of her liberty, in case of any gross misbehaviour." His point was that a husband still had a right to the custody of his wife's person.

In 1870 parliament passed the Married Women's Property Act of that year and although one of its purposes was to enable married women to retain control over their own earnings it had the unintended effect on the one hand of enabling women to repudiate contractual obligations entered into prior to marriage and on the other to absolve the new husband of any obligations for them either, with the result that creditors were entirely without remedy. To rectify this parliamentary oversight a bill – immediately baptised "the Creditors' Bill" was introduced which in due course became the Married Women's Property Act (1870) Amendment Act 1874. Another bill, however, had been introduced which was clearly a precursor of what eight years later was to become the Married Women's Property Act 1882. It was this bill which came to be considered by the Committee of the Society and their report, which appeared in the minutes of a general meeting held on 24 March 1873, makes interesting reading:

> It is proposed that a married woman shall be capable of holding, acquiring, alienating devising and bequeathing real and personal property, of contracting and of suing and being sued as if she were a feme sole.

> That every woman shall notwithstanding her coverture (but as regards women married prior to the Act, subject to any marriage settlement)

have and hold all real and personal property, free from the debts and obligations of her husband and from his control and disposition in all respects whatsoever as if she had continued unmarried.

And full and ample privilege is given to each party to the marriage contract to sue the other, and if the remedy is sought for in the County Court, unlimited jurisdiction as to amount is given, and either party is permitted to require that the question may be debated in the Judge's private room.

Your Committee believe that the passing of this Measure would be productive of serious injury to both man and wife, and therefore recommend that a Petition should be presented against the Bill.

The minute then continues "A second Bill to amend the Married Women's Property Act (1870) has been introduced. It is not, however, so objectionable as the one to which your Committee have invited special attention."

The bill which was "so objectionable" was the result of campaigning by the Married Women's Property Committee of which Elizabeth Wolstenholme[9] was to become a leading member. The Committee, however, was originally established in 1855 and when eventually the 1882 Act was passed by Gladstone's government following a pledge given in the Liberal election campaign in 1880, it followed twenty-seven years of campaigning on the subject. By the time of its eventual enactment in 1882 passions among the members of the Committee of the Yorkshire Law Society seem to have subsided, or perhaps they were just resigned to the inevitable. Their report presented to the members' meeting on 27 January 1883 was seemingly short and uncontroversial. Under the heading "Married Women's Property Act 1882 – 45 & 46 Vict. c.76" it simply noted: "This is another consolidation Act. It clearly defines the rights of married women, whether married before or after the passing of the Act, to such property, real or personal, as is according to its provisions, to be treated as separate property."

But if parliament seems to have been somewhat tardy in affording justice to married women who might have property (if the law allowed) it was even tardier in doing so where they had been deserted by their husbands. It was not until the enactment of the Married Women (Maintenance in Case of Desertion) Act 1886-49 & 50 Vict. c.52 that this glaring lacuna was rectified. The problem was that although at common law a husband had a generalised duty to provide for his wife, direct enforcement of that duty was another matter entirely. In practice a deserted wife was without remedy unless and until she was in receipt of poor relief, or in other words, destitute. Even then it was only the poor law authorities who could take direct action against the husband (to protect the ratepayers!) not the impecunious and deserted wife; furthermore there was a cap of £2 per week on what could be awarded coupled with an express provision under S1(2) "that no order for payment of any such sum shall be made in favour of a wife who shall be proved to have committed adultery, unless such adultery has been condoned…" Although eventually passed, even this modest enough reform was not without controversy, an earlier bill having failed at the second reading, one MP objecting that it constituted "meddling interference with …the domestic concerns of life".

But even as regards women's property rights there was still some way to go before English law reached its present state of virtual equilibrium on the subject. The Act of 1882 was to be followed by the Married Women's Property Act 1893, and the Married Women (Restraint upon Anticipation) Act 1949 which dealt with a rather more mundane aspect of women's affairs than its somewhat enigmatic title might suggest.[10] There were also, of course, various technical amending and repealing acts over this period. However, questions of property are inevitably linked to questions of taxation and it was not until 1990 that the tax affairs of husband and wife were to be finally disentangled although whether they are destined ever to remain so may be a more open question given recent controversies regarding child allowances.

Another great reform in this period was the abolition of public executions by the Capital Punishment (Amendment) Act 1868. If the Treason Act 1790 had at least abolished the appalling public spectacle of burning women to death for high or petty treason[11] this act at last removed all executions from public gaze – or almost. On 26 February 1879 *The Times* reported on the execution at Armley Gaol of Charles (Charlie) Peace for the murder of Arthur Dyson of Sheffield on 29 November 1876. By the time of his final apprehension, trial and execution he had acquired considerable notoriety as a burglar as well as a murderer. In the former capacity he seems to have been at least moderately successful – successful enough to summon a solicitor, William Warren of the firm eventually to become Ford & Warren, to make his last will just two days before his final demise. Apparently after Peace had signed the document Warren, in response to an enquiry from his client, assured him that there would be no fee. "Well", said the condemned man, "you are about as honest as any lawyer could be!" After it was all over *The Times* gave a detailed – not to say glowing account – of the entire proceedings, including the fact that the condemned man "partook very heartily of a breakfast which consisted of toast, bacon, eggs and tea". The procession to the gallows which had been erected at the western side of the prison was equally described in detail: "First came the Governor of the prison, Mr. Keene, and the Under-Sheriff, Mr W. Gray; then came the chaplain, attired in his surplice and reading the service customary on such occasions; and immediately behind was the convict with his arms pinioned to his side and supported by a couple of warders … ". The executioner, Marwood, was about to put the white cap over his head, when Peace said rather sharply,

> "Don't, I want to look." Then, as the chaplain came to a certain portion of the service, he said with much fervency, "God have mercy upon me, Christ have mercy upon me." Thinking that he had finished, Marwood again was in the act of putting the cap over his face, when he said "Don't; stop a bit, if you please." Then, turning to the four reporters who were standing by, he said in a loud tone, – "You gentlemen reporters, I wish you to notice the few words I am going to say to you. I know that my life has been base and bad. I wish you to ask the world after you have seen my death what man could die as I die if he did not die in the fear of the Lord. Tell all my friends that I feel sure they have sincerely forgiven me, and that I am going into the Kingdom of Heaven at last. Amen. Say that my last wishes and my last respects are to my dear children and to their dear mother. I hope no person will disgrace them by taunting them or jeering at them on my account, but will have mercy upon them. God bless you, my children! My children, each Good-bye. Amen. Oh, my Lord God, have mercy upon me!" Then Marwood placed the cap over his face, and as he was doing it, Peace, in a quite different tone from that in which he had been speaking, said, "I should like a drink; have you a drink to give me?" Taking no notice of the request, the chaplain continued his prayers, but Peace again interrupted, and asked "for a drink". The service was now near its close, and just as the chaplain came to the words, "Lord Jesus receive his spirit," Marwood pulled the bolt, and the wretched man disappeared from view. Death was instantaneous.

William Gray, the Under-Sheriff, responsible on behalf of the High Sheriff for executing the judgments of the court, was a member of the Society and the grandson of the first William Gray mentioned in an earlier chapter. He was the third Gray in the York firm which still bears the "Gray" name. For many years successive partners in the firm held the appointment of under-sheriff for Yorkshire and responsibility for executions was one of their less palatable duties. It often required the cultivation of what is still termed "gallows" humour. William Gray had arrived at Armley Gaol early in the morning and had come across Mr William Marwood the executioner splicing the rope. Asked why he was doing this, Marwood replied "Well sir, I've heard that this fellow (Peace) has escaped justice several times, and I don't mean to let him do it again." "Oh," said Gray, "I see; piece at the top, Peace in the middle; may there be Peace at the end." A feeble pun, perhaps, but at Armley Gaol in the early hours of a February morning with such a gruesome duty to oversee, any member of the Society might be forgiven for attempting to lighten the atmosphere.

Peace had indeed escaped justice on a number of occasions, once having being on the run for over two years. Marwood would have known, of course that just two years earlier, on 3 April 1877, at the very same gaol, another executioner, Thomas Askern, was to suffer the unnerving experience of a botched execution – the rope broke. Botched executions were by no means unknown at this period. To Marwood's credit he was largely responsible for the introduction of "the long drop" – a method which was designed to ensure that the condemned man died instantly of asphyxia when unconscious. It was one of the scandals of the previous use of "the short drop" that death was frequently long drawn out. Gray himself, as the under-sheriff in attendance in 1864 at Armley Goal fifteen years earlier, would have recalled the double *public* execution of James Sargisson and Joseph Myers. On that occasion, according to the *Leeds Mercury*, Myers appeared to die immediately when a wound to his throat – the result of an earlier suicide attempt – opened, but Sargisson struggled for some minutes. According to the same source, a crowd of between 80,000 and 100,000 had gathered to watch the spectacle on that occasion. It is difficult for the modern mind to accept the enthusiasm for viewing public executions that gripped the British public well into the second half of the 19th century and which doubtless would have continued had not parliament chosen to intervene. Such was the enthusiasm, indeed, that railway companies would lay on special trains to cover newsworthy hangings. In accordance with the entrepreneurial spirit of the age, they always had a keen eye for additional business. One of the oldest railway companies in the land, the *Bodmin & Wadebridge*, used to run excursion trains to the local assizes and on 13 April 1840 it ran no less than *three* special trains to Bodmin:

> ... so that Wadebridge people might see the hanging of William and James Lightfoot. convicted of the murder of a Mr. Norway, one of their townspeople.
>
> No fewer than 1,100 travelled on this occasion, almost exactly half of the population of the town! As the jail adjoined the railway depot at Bodmin, passengers were able to see the spectacle in comfort from their carriages.[12]

Cornwall, of course, was a sparsely populated part of the country and an execution there was easily out-trumped by Norfolk. At Norwich the execution of Samuel Yarham on Tombland Fair Day, 11 April 1845, for the murder of Harriet Chandler, attracted an estimated crowd of 30,000 assembled on Castle Hill with 800 coming in a single train from Wymondham. All business for the day was suspended.

> After the execution gongs, drums and other instruments commenced their uproar, mountebanks and clowns their antics, the vendors of wares and exhibitors of prodigies, their cries, while the whirligigs and up-and-downs were soon in full swing. The public-houses round the Hill were crowded, and hundreds finished the day in riot and intoxication.[13]

To the credit of the more responsible citizens of Norwich, and owing to the scandalous nature of the proceedings, a public meeting was held the following month presided over by the Mayor at which it was resolved to petition parliament for the abolition of capital punishment. The petitioners, however, were well in advance of their time. Eventual parliamentary intervention in 1868 to abolish public executions appears to have been prompted more by concern over the potential for public disorder than any thought that there might be a issue of principle involved.

Even after "public" executions ceased the practice of inviting the press to attend continued well into the 20th century – a practice still followed in a number of states in the US, with the added intrusion of television. But it is clear that at this period the serious press at least affected to take seriously their responsibility to edify their readers. After all, the whole case for executing prisoners in public had been the need to frighten malefactors into good behaviour and to edify the more law-abiding spectators – this despite clear evidence that it had no such effect. At public executions pickpockets had a field day[14] even in the days when that itself was a capital offence. For the majority of spectators, it was generally taken as an excuse for what we would today call binge drinking and general disorder. Charles Dickens, after mixing with the crowd at an execution outside Horsemonger Lane Gaol, Southwark, wrote a letter to *The Times* which was published on 13 November 1849 to protest at the spectacle, billed by the tabloids of the day as the "Hanging of the Century". The condemned couple were Frederich George Manning and his Swiss wife Marie who had murdered a friend for his money and buried him under the kitchen floor. It was the first husband and wife execution for 150 years. Dickens had arrived at the scene at about midnight and had observed "the shrillness of the cries and howls that were raised from time to time denoting that they came from a concourse of boys and girls assembled in the best places" which made his blood run cold. "I believe" he wrote, "that a sight so inconceivably awful as the wickedness and levity of the immense crowd collected at that execution this morning could be imagined by no man, and could be presented in no heathen land under the sun". He went on to describe the "thieves, low prostitutes, ruffians and vagabonds of every kind" and "swooning women [who] were dragged out of the crowd by the police with their dresses disordered [which] gave a new zest to the general entertainment".

The notion that public executions were somehow edifying had been a persistent one, all evidence to the contrary notwithstanding. On 13 April 1793 William Atkinson, Richard Watson and Thomas Jewett had been executed on the Knavesmire in York. Atkinson was a Whitby carpenter, over sixty years of age, and had allegedly been involved in a riot in the course of which a house in the town belonging to a Mr William Cooper had been destroyed. The local paper was determined to set the tone from the beginning: "By the execution of this culprit" it intoned in the second paragraph, "we may learn a very useful and important lesson" but it was later apparent that the unfortunate Atkinson claimed not to have been involved in the riot in any way but had simply approached to see what was going on and to check that his sons were not involved. His quoted words were "I have no malice to the Constables who seized me, but I must let the world know that they dragged me from my poor habitation, and as the real offenders could not be secured, it has now so happened that I must suffer for others, having done nothing myself to deserve so shameful a death."

Richard Watson, bookbinder of Newcastle, had been convicted of grand larceny of a mahogany desk, seven or eight guineas in gold and some silver, three gold rings, one pair of gilt earings, two or three gilt seals, a quantity of silver thimbles and "other articles to a considerable amount". He had confessed, though whether before or after conviction is not clear. "I, Richard Watson, aged 30 years, confess that I was guilty of the crime for which I am condemned to die a shameful and ignominious death; but at the same time I must solemnly declare, that it was necessity alone that prompted me to commit so atrocious a deed, which has caused me to leave a virtuous, loving and affectionate wife, with her helpless infants, to lament the loss of a husband and father. I now resign my soul to God, in whom I hope to meet forgiveness, and hope at the same time, that the liberal hand of Charity will be extended towards my poor little helpless orphans."

The third condemned man, Thomas Jewitt was 40 years old and left a widow and four children. He had been "convicted of stealing eleven heifers out of the open fields at Askham Bryan and Copmanthorpe, near York". The report described it as

> A crime of such magnitude as … is seldom to be met with. The day before the executions a most excellent and applicable discourse, was preached … to Atkinson and Watson by the Rev. James Richardson, from the following text: And he said unto Jesus, "Lord, remember me when thou comest into thy kingdom." Luke XXIII. 42. The concluding part of the Clergyman's discourse was delivered with a truly christian concern for his unhappy fellow-creatures, and the general exhortation was marked with every expression of tender regard for his hearers.

All very edifying, to be sure, but one cannot help wondering if "the very great concourse of people" who had accompanied the three felons to the

Knavesmire had gone there for the express purpose of being edified or even to be deterred from committing crimes "of such magnitude as are seldom to be met with". At least with the abolition of public executions by the Capital Punishment (Amendment) Act 1868 "great concourses" of spectators had been eliminated and the public at large were reduced to reading all about it in the sedate pages of *The Times*. If it all seems unspeakably barbaric and referable to "a far-away country" of which we know nothing, we should not be too complacent. Capital punishment for murder in this country was only finally abolished on 18 December 1969[15] when a motion was finally carried in parliament making permanent the five year temporary suspension under the Murder (Abolition of the Death Penalty) Act 1965. But even that did not apply to Northern Ireland where it was not finally abolished until the Northern Ireland (Emergency Provisions) Act 1973. The death penalty still remained on the statute book, however, at least in peace time, for the much rarer offences of treason and piracy until the Crime and Disorder Act 1998, S36 of which amended various acts ranging from the Treason Act (Ireland) 1537 to the Piracy Act 1837. That still left open the possibility of the death penalty being imposed for service personnel in time of war but on 1 February 2004 the United Kingdom ratified the 13th Protocol of the European Convention on Human Rights which prohibits the imposition of the death penalty in all circumstances. Final *legal* abolition is therefore quite recent. It is perhaps salutary to recall, too, that as recently as the 1950s the colonial government of Kenya was seriously considering public hanging as a deterrent during the emergency when a total of 1,090 Kikuyu were convicted of offences in connection with the Mau Mau rebellion and sent to the gallows. The total number of European settlers who met their deaths during the emergency was thirty-two[16] but this is hardly the impression one would have gained from reading the English newspapers at the time.

Another controversial topic to appear on the horizon during this period was land registration – one that was destined to rumble on for the next 150 years or so – almost until the present day in fact – so much so that in order to describe it coherently it is dealt with as a separate topic in Appendix D. This was in marked contrast to most legal reforms of the mid Victorian era which quickly gained acceptance even among the die-hards of the *ancien régime*.

But perhaps the greatest reform of all which really marked the beginning of the modern legal world was the creation of the Supreme Court of Judicature under the Judicature Acts of 1873 and 1875 and various amending acts which followed and given practical form by the building of the Royal Courts of Justice in the Strand – a fascinating, if somewhat inconvenient Victorian edifice, completed in 1882 which is with us still and stands as a monument to a very remarkable, if overdue, achievement in law reform. One of the key figures in bringing about the first of the Judicature Acts, that of 1873 which created the Supreme Court, was Sir William Harcourt (1827-1904), born in York and a grandson of Edward Harcourt who had been Archbishop of York from 1807 to 1847. It would be a shame to end the chapter without recording the unsuccessful attempt by Bowen LJ to amend the terms of the loyal address which the judges presented to HM the Queen on this auspicious occasion. The draft contained the words "Conscious as we are of our shortcomings … ". One judge objected on the grounds that it indicated excessive humility and was hypocritical. Bowen immediately suggested a simple amendment: "Conscious as we are of *one another's* shortcomings … ". Sadly, the hypocrites won the day.

NOTES

1. See Chapter 4 p. 76 note 3.

2. Cyrus Jay *The Law: What I Have Seen, What I Have Heard and What I Have Known* – Tinsley Brothers London 1868

3. Hansard HL debates vol 123 col 170

4. Cf Hale CJ's *Things Necessary to be Continually had in Rembrance* viz "to charge my servants not to take more than their known fees" – See Appendix C item 14 p. 401.

5. Government largesse with taxpayers' money in favour of individuals can sometimes be truly eye-watering. Perhaps the nearest modern parallel is the equally eye-watering bonuses received by certain favoured individuals – only possible as the result of the government's recent bank bailouts. At least in the case of our Victorian forebears it may have been the only way of getting desperately needed reform through parliament.

6. Trial by jury in civil cases only ceased to be the norm following the Administration of Justice (Miscellaneous Provisions) Act 1933 – see Chapter 5 p. 97 note 10.

7. The whole issue of Chancery reform was a major preoccupation of lawyers, politicians and the increasingly important mercantile class in the early and middle years of the 19th century. The latter in particular were not prepared to put up with Dickens's "mountains of costly nonsense" and, with the extension of the franchise, were in a position to make their voices heard. Professor Michael Lobban, Professor of Legal History at Queen Mary's College, University of London, has carried out a detailed and authoritative study of the subject: *Preparing for Fusion: Reforming the Nineteenth Century Court of Chancery* – Law and History Review 22 (2004).

8. In Scotland, whose legal system is based on civil or Roman law principles albeit subject to later common law influences, a barrister is usually known as an "advocate" governed by the Faculty of Advocates based in Edinburgh. The term "counsel" is also used.

9. Elizabeth Wolstenholme (1834-1913) daughter of a Methodist minister from Eccles and a leading feminist was involved with most of the other right-on issues of the day. Amongst others, she campaigned for women's education, and against the Contagious Diseases Act 1864 (which obliged women suspected of being prostitutes to undergo a medical examination and if found to be suffering from a venereal disease, to be forcibly detained in a secure unit until cured; there was no equivalent imposition on men). In 1889 she joined Emmeline Pankhurst to form the Women's Franchise League and was also a member of the Manchester branch of the Independent Labour Party. She was equally an atheist and although she married Benjamin Elmy, a poet from Congleton in 1874 when six months pregnant, it was a civil ceremony and only entered into under pressure from her friends. In short, almost nothing about her was calculated to engage the sympathies of the "respectable" and conservative members of the Society.

10. The "restraint on anticipation" affecting married women was a curious device, invented by chancery lawyers, which prevented married women who were beneficiaries of a settlement from freely disposing of the settled property *but only while they were married*. It pre-dated the Married Women's Property Act 1882 and was designed to protect married women on whom property had been settled for their separate use – itself an equitable device to protect them from the common law rule which vested their entire property in their husbands. By the mid 20th century an arrangement originally intended to protect women's property interests had merely become a tiresome nuisance.

11. See Chapter 1 pp. 20-21. The pace of law reform could be very slow at times. In a great fit of abhorrence occasioned by a poisoning case in Kent, parliament had been moved to enact "An Acte for Poysonyng" 1530 (22 Hen. 8 c. 9). It recited how "One Richarde Roose late of Rouchester in the Countie of Kent coke … of his moste wyked and dampnable dysposicyon etc, etc," – eventually enacting that "the said poysonyng be adjuged and deemed as high treason," and as it "requyreth condigñe punysshemente for the same" the Act then provided "that the said Richarde Roose shal be therefore boyled to deathe withoute havynge any advauntage of his clargie." Richarde Roose was in fact the Bishop of Rochester's cook although the bishop himself did not succumb to whatever it was that the unfortunate Roose was adjudged to have done. No matter – five years later he was to die the same martyr's death on Tower Hill as Thomas More, the former Lord Chancellor. By the Repeal of Statutes as to Treasons, Felonies etc Act 1547 1 Edw. 6 c.12, poisoning was assimilated to murder as regards penalty but the original Poisoning Act 1530 was only formally repealed by the Statute Law Revision Act 1863.

12. The *Railway Magazine* November 1909 p.435

13. *Norfolk Annals* March 1846

14. Charles Dickens, on a visit to Rome in 1846, attended a public execution and tells how "My empty pockets were tried several times, in the crowd immediately below the scaffold, as the corpse was being put into its coffin. It was an ugly, filthy, careless, sickening spectacle." – *Pictures from Italy* Chapter 10, Bradbury & Evans London 1846.

15. The year 1969 also saw the formal abolition of capital punishment by the Vatican although in fact no such penalty had been inflicted since the de facto incorporation of the Papal States into the Kingdom of Italy in 1870.

16. David Anderson *Histories of the Hanged – Britain's Dirty War in Kenya and the End of Empire* Weidenfeld & Nicholson 2005. Any reader who is unsettled by the thought that all UK executions were conducted in public until 1868 should be aware that in France they continued to be conducted in this way until 1939. The last such execution was of a 31 year old German, Eugen Weidmann, on 17 June of that year in Versailles, attended by some 200-300 members of the public. The resulting media circus (which included an unlawfully-taken ciné film) so scandalised the French President that he banned all future executions in public with immediate effect.

Chapter Seven

A CENTENARY INTERLUDE 1886

"I hope and believe ... that there are men in every branch of the legal profession prepared to do their duty to the public and help forward the great cause of law reform."

Lord Ripon at the Yorkshire Law Society's Centenary Banquet at the Guildhall, York on 12 October 1886

With the benefit of hindsight we can see that the Society's centenary celebrations in 1886 happened to coincide with the high point of the country's power and prestige in the world and, as we shall see, the Society's members were happy to share in the reflected glory of that prestige. It is also a good point at which to take stock. Momentous changes had taken place in English society over the previous century. The industrial revolution and the coming of the railways had altered much of the English landscape, and more particularly the great cities, in a way in which the Society's founding fathers could scarcely have imagined. But much else had occurred during this period which is right to keep in mind.

After more than a century of two world wars and vast and unsettling political, social and economic upheavals on the world stage, we can only wonder at the sheer self-confidence of the late Victorian age. So much had been accomplished in the previous hundred years. That self-confidence of course was fully shared by solicitors and the rest of the legal profession. For the nation as a whole it was general and based in part on politics and in part on economics. Throughout the 18th century Britain had been engaged in a mighty struggle with her arch-rival France

– *the* great European land power of the period. Between 1700 and 1815 Britain and France had been at war on seven occasions covering a period altogether of over 50 years. This had finally been brought to a conclusion on 18 June 1815 just outside Brussels on the battlefield of Waterloo but in reality this victory had been the triumph of sea power – something to which Napoleon had aspired[1] but never understood. From 1815 onwards, for a further period of a hundred years, the British navy had been able to preserve the *Pax Britannica*. With the exception of the Crimean War (1854-1856) the British army was not to be involved again in hostilities against another European power until 1914. The defeat of France in the Franco-Prussian war of 1870 was viewed here with some satisfaction. The new Emperor of Germany and seventh King of Prussia, Wilhelm I (1797-1888), had after all entered Paris with the allies as a young officer in 1814 and had formed a close friendship with Queen Victoria and Prince Albert when he first visited Britain in the 1840s. Furthermore, his son, Frederick III, whose tragically short reign lasted only three months (March to June 1888), was married to Queen Victoria's eldest daughter, the Princess Royal. In the Society's centenary year, however, the accession in June 1888 of the Kaiser Wilhelm II had yet to cast its shadow over Europe.

But the political and economic development which we see on the surface of the Victorian age is only part of the story. Something else was happening too. Towards the end of his book *The Politics of Hope* the former Chief Rabbi, Jonathan Sacks, reflects on the possibility of rescuing our present-day society from its current crime-based dysfunction. After quoting from Disraeli's *Sybil* and earlier 18th century writers and commentators, Daniel Defoe, Henry Fielding, Horace Walpole and Middlesex magistrate Patrick Colquhoun,[2] he makes the point that although in the 1840s, when *Sybil* was published, crime was still endemic in England and a major problem, the Victorians managed to reverse the trend:

> Where we have drug addiction, the Victorians had drunkenness. Where we have broken families, they had neglected and often brutalised children. By the end of the nineteenth century crime rates were down. In a remarkable and well-documented transformation, the mid-nineteenth century witnessed a reversal in historical patterns of criminal behaviour. Law-breaking and violence, which had risen steadily until 1850, then began, and continued, to fall. Ted Robert Gurr found that in London

"the number of murders, assaults, and thefts of almost all kinds which came to police attention declined irregularly, but consistently, for half a century or more" as did the numbers of persons arrested and convicted for such offences. So too did illegitimacy, one of the indicators of the strength or weakness of the family as an institution. By the end of the century, the rate of births outside wedlock was down to half of what it had been in 1845. Most strikingly, in East London, the poorest section of the city, it was below the national average. These changes defy conventional wisdom. They took place in a period of urbanisation, industrialisation, and widespread immigration, the very factors which are associated with a breakdown of social order. There were ample reasons for, and occasional manifestations of, unrest. We know them: they are a continuing theme of Victorian literature. Nevertheless, families were strengthened, law-abidingness increased, alcoholism declined and schools improved. Nor was this confined to England. The same trends, during the same period, can be documented for the United States as well, and they were brought about in the same way. How did it happen?

Well it did, and we should be grateful to our Victorian forebears for what they achieved. It is all too easy nowadays to decry "Victorian values" and in modern times the attempts by some politicians to misappropriate them for their own purposes tell us rather more about the politicians than they do about the Victorians. Hypocrisy, for example, is no less rampant in many areas of life among the former than it was among the latter. But nevertheless in October 1886 Members of the Yorkshire Law Society, celebrating their centenary, could look back with pride over what had been achieved over the previous hundred years.

Contemporary records illustrate their sentiments and their self-confidence very clearly. and, just as clearly, how seriously they took themselves. The earnest debates on the legal issues of the day included further reform[3] of the law of real property, bankruptcy, maintenance for deserted wives, county court procedure and much else. There was even a paper entitled *The Profession – What it is, and what it should be* – an ongoing topic already considered in Chapter 2, by a Mr AH Hastie. He was concerned about the status of solicitors as *gentlemen*. As a period piece, it is instructive:

> Among the many anomalies which crowd our Statute Book there is none more startling to the man of the world of today than that which grants to

every solicitor the right to subscribe himself a gentleman. There are still in the profession men of birth, education and breeding; there are also, it cannot be denied, men who have travelled up the gutter from Fleet-street to the Law Institution, and who are fast travelling back by the same route. Doubtful h's and dirty linen pass freely through the examination hall of our society and come out with gentleman written after him ... we must commence by raising the standard of the preliminary examination to such a height as shall ensure that none shall step across our threshold but those rendered capable, by clear intellect and sound education, of thoroughly understanding the intricacies of the law, and advising their fellow men in all their social and business difficulties.

When we have done this, we may, I think, work out some scheme for ensuring that the integrity in pecuniary matters of every solicitor shall be vouched for by substantial sureties. If, in the elaboration of these reforms, we should fortunately or unfortunately, limit our numbers and increase our worldly prosperity, the public will be the gainers, for instead of having to choose a good adviser from a shoal of bad ones, they will be sure that every solicitor is intelligent, capable and solvent. Possibly, when these reforms have been accomplished, we may no longer have to invoke the statute law to prove that we are gentlemen ... The fight has begun, intellect against inertia, legislation against laissez-faire. The issue lies in your hands.

And here, for example, is how *The Times* described the Lord Lieutenant's speech at the Lord Mayor's banquet in the Guildhall on 12 October in honour of the Yorkshire Law Society's centenary and the visit of the Incorporated Law Society:

The Marquess of Ripon[4] responded, and in doing so said he confessed he was perhaps a little alarmed at the magnitude of the duties which were described as those which fell to the lot of the Houses of Parliament by the gentleman who had just sat down. But all he could say was that the Parliament of England [sic] in these days, as in the past, would always he trusted desire faithfully to discharge those duties which were entrusted to its members by the constitution and by the people, and would labour so to discharge its duties as to promote the general interest of the public in all respects ...

Speaking for himself, he was glad to be present on that occasion, and to ... offer a cordial welcome to the Incorporated Law Society upon its visit to that ancient city, and to have the opportunity of marking the unfeigned respect which he entertained for the members of the profession of which these law societies were composed, and his strong conviction of the great services which they were constantly rendering to the public of this country. (*hear, hear*) It seemed to him that it must be a great advantage to any profession to have established amongst its societies such as the Incorporated Law Society – societies which made it one of their important duties to maintain the reputation and to uphold the character of the great profession to which their members belong. (*hear, hear.*) He need not remind those who were assembled that night how much the public owed to the solicitors of this country – (*hear, hear*), – how much they were dependent upon them for their comfort and welfare, and how much their honour and their reputation were often in their hands – (*hear, hear*) …

That night they celebrated not only the visit of the Incorporated Law Society of the United Kingdom to that city but they celebrated also the centenary of the Yorkshire Law Society (*applause*), and if they carried back their minds for a hundred years into the past, and remembered how much during that century had been done for the reform and for the improvement of their legal arrangements and for the law of this country, have good reason to be proud of the progress that had been made. At the commencement of this hundred years, when nothing had been heard of the labours of Romilly and Brougham and other great law reformers, who had done so much to place the jurisprudence of this country upon a solid and righteous basis … their criminal law had been reformed, their courts had been improved and multiplied, their civic procedure had been simplified and cheapened. He did not think the work of law reform had been brought to a conclusion, there were yet many departments in which much might be done …

It used to be often supposed that those connected to the legal profession were not friendly to law reform. He hoped and believed that that notion no longer existed, and that there were men in every branch of the legal profession prepared to do their duty to the public and help forward the great cause of law reform. For these reasons he had been rejoiced to come forward, in his capacity as Lord Lieutenant, to offer his congratulations on their having attained their centenary, and also to offer a warm welcome to the Incorporated Law Society on their visit to this ancient city. (*cheers.*)

It is natural, of course, that a politician's after-dinner speech on such an occasion should tend more to eulogy than critique, but it does serve to convey the sheer optimism of the period.

> **➤ PROGRAMME ➤**
>
> OF THE
>
> EXCURSION TO WHITBY,
>
> ON THURSDAY THE 14TH OCTOBER, 1886.
>
> A SPECIAL TRAIN will leave YORK STATION at 9-45 a.m., and, proceeding via Malton and Pickering, will arrive at Whitby (Town Station) at 11-20 a.m.
>
> From Pickering the Railway to Whitby, one of the earliest efforts of the late George Stephenson, and worked originally by Horse power, runs up the Glen of the Pickering Beck into the heart of some of the most beautiful scenery of this part of Yorkshire.

A somewhat more relaxed tone had been set on the eve of the combined four day centenary celebrations and national Conference when Mrs Emma Walker, wife of the Society's President and Lord Mayor William Walker, was 'At Home' at the Mansion House where no effort had been spared to welcome members and visitors alike. And likewise the last day was devoted entirely to showing off the attractions of Yorkshire involving no less than three special trains to Whitby, Scarborough and Ripon. The first left York at 9.45 am and proceeded to Whitby via Malton and Pickering and to due to arrive there at 11.20 am. It was to be quite a day. The official programme above the name of the Hon Excursion Secretary, Mr R Percy Dale, was nothing if not enthusiastic. After describing the route beyond Pickering "one of the earliest efforts of the late George Stephenson, and worked originally by Horse power" members were informed that "On arrival at Whitby the Visitors will be received and welcomed at the Railway Station by a Committee of Gentlemen representing the Solicitors of that Town." The rest of the morning was occupied with a visit to the Abbey (described in detail) and the Museum on the West Pier which members were assured had "one of the best collections of Lias Fossils[5] in the Kingdom". Before all this could happen, however, members were informed that "they will be conducted to the Crown Hotel" before being conducted "after a short interval" to the abbey itself. Victorian reticence doubtless precluded this from being described as a "comfort stop" – reticence with a different label, but reticence nonetheless. Luncheon at the Crown Hotel was scheduled for 2 pm. By four o'clock members were due to leave Whitby by another "Special Train from the West Cliffe Station by the new Coast Line,[6] to Scarboro', arriving at 4.45 pm". Arrival in Scarborough was to be followed by tea and coffee at the Grand Hotel.

At 6.45 pm yet a third special train was scheduled to leave Scarborough for the return journey to York, arriving 7.50 pm. But here is the amazing detail: the Whitby excursionists at this point met the Scarborough excursionists who had arrived there by yet a third special train that had left York at the same time of 9.45 am that morning. On arrival at Scarborough they had been greeted at the station by another committee of gentlemen, this time representing the Scarborough solicitors before they too proceeded this time to the Grand Hotel "for a few minutes". There followed a welcome at the Spa Saloon of the Cliff Bridge Company "by the Mayor of Scarbro', MR ALDERMAN WOODALL, J.P." All this was to be accompanied by "the Band of HERR MEYER LUTE" who would play "A CHOICE SELECTION OF MUSIC on the SPA PROMENADE between the hours of 11 a.m. and 1 p.m." In addition to the more familiar delights of Scarborough in October (described in detail in the notice), visitors were assured that the spa contained "two Springs, containing carbonates of lime and magnesia". Lunch at the Grand Hotel was at 1.30 pm "on the invitation of the Yorkshire and Scarbro' Law Societies". In the afternoon visitors were received between 4 and 5.30 pm by the Mayor "at an AFTERNOON RECEPTION at his residence, St. Nicholas House." Altogether it must have been quite a day, particularly for the Hon Excursion Secretary, Mr Dale. Since he could not be in both Scarborough and Whitby (or as we shall see in Ripon) at the same time, it is safe to assume that he appointed a deputy. Those members who might have felt unable to stay the whole course – mayoral receptions, lunches, more receptions and exposure to Lias fossils, and carbonates of lime and magnesia, in addition to two hours of Herr Lute's merry teutonic music-making on the Spa Promenade – were reassured by a note in the programme: "The Railway Company have kindly consented to allow Visitors on this Excursion to return to York by any Ordinary Train on the same day, if desired."

The Centenary Celebrations – the lighter side ...

INCORPORATED LAW SOCIETY

ANNUAL MEETING IN YORK
CIVIC RECEPTION

The business in connection with the centenary of the Yorkshire Law Society and the annual provincial meeting of the Incorporated Law Society of the United Kingdom will be commenced this morning. The centenary of the York Law Society was regarded as a fitting opportunity on which to hold the conference of the larger though very much younger society, and the invitation was accepted two years ago when the society met at Birmingham. Mr. W Walker, J.P., chairman, and Mr. F.J. Munby, hon.sec., have used every effort to make the gathering a success, and they have received valuable assistance from Mr. R. Perkins, hon. treasurer, who is unfortunately absent owing to indisposition, Mr. A. Procter, Mr. W.H. Badger, and Mr. R.P Dale; and Mr. F. Arey's services were secured as secretary. Excellent arrangements have been made for the convenience of the numerous members of the society, who hail from all parts of the country, and there is every prospect that this reunion will be one of the most successful as well as the most enjoyable that the society has held.

The Lord Mayor, with that regard for the welfare and honour of the city over which he presides which has always distinguished him, at once came forward with his characteristic generosity and offered his assistance, and the hospitality of the Mansion House. It was, therefore, arranged that on the eve of the business meeting, the Lady Mayoress should be "At Home" to receive the members of the Society and friends. Accordingly this initiatory and pleasing event in connection with the visit of so large a number of distinguished legal and other gentlemen to York took place yesterday evening, when over 500 guests were entertained. The Mansion House was connected to the Guildhall by a temporary staircase from the reception room in the former building and by an awning, the steps and floor of which were carpeted with crimson cloth, bordered on each side with conifers in pots. The Guildhall had undergone considerable adornment at the hands of Messrs. Hartley and Son, but the decorations were of so judicious a description that the ancient appearance of the building was preserved.

as reported in the Yorkshire Gazette – 16th October 1886

The high pew-like erections which give accommodation to witnesses, spectators, and others on the holding of Assize, Sessional, and County Courts, had been removed, and the slightly raised platform covered, like the floor of the hall, with crimson cloth. Here and on the judges bench were placed the city charters, books, and various ancient documents, which will doubtless afford great interest to visitors. Beautiful palms and ferns adorned this portion of the hall, and conspicuous on either side were the arms of the See of York and the See of Ripon. Immediately over the judges seat was a shield bearing the city arms, backed by a trophy of flags, and on a temporary gallery, raised several feet above the jurors' box, and at a corresponding height on the opposite side were placed many fine ferns, palms and other handsome plants. The crossed muskets and stars of bayonets, which have occupied a position on the side walls, were very properly allowed to remain, and underneath the windows were arranged plants relieved by banners. The octagonal oak pillars were draped with crimson repp for about eight feet, the covering being terminated with a gilt band, upon which was inscribed the name of a town, among those mentioned being Dewsbury, Bradford, Leeds, Hull and Sheffield. The lower part of the pillars were adorned with creeping and other plants of delicate foliage, and the effect was of a very pleasing nature. The plants for decorative purposes were supplied by Messrs. Backhouse. The orchestra was erected over the entrance door, and occupied by the band of the 9th Lancers, who during the evening played a choice selection of music. The Guildhall, in which refreshments were served, presented a handsome appearance when lighted up, and afforded a pleasant retreat for distinguished company during intervals between dancing. The guests began to arrive at nine o'clock and were received in the dining-room by the Lord Mayor and Lady Mayoress. The State Room was used as a ball room, and during the dancing the spectacle was of a brilliant character. Thrush's band supplied the music for the ball, which was kept up until midnight. The following was the programme:– Valse, *Maid of the Mill*; Valse, *Queenie*; Lancers *Varsity*; Valse, *Ivy*; Polka, *Crosspatch*; Lancers, *Princess Ida*; Valse, *Only Once More*; Polka, *Cinderella*; Lancers, *Iolanthe*; Valse, *Fairie Voices*; Polka, *P and O.*, Valse, *Sweet Seventeen*. At intervals in the evening's proceedings Dr. Naylor and Herr Padel played a duet on the pianoforte in the dining-room to the great gratification of the company present.

The "Reception" was a great success in every way, and was enjoyed alike by the strangers visiting the city, and those residents who had the privilege of being present.

Incredibly, on the same day, 14 October, yet a *third* excursion by special train, this time to Ripon and Fountains Abbey, with similar pomp and circumstance had been organised by the indomitable Mr Dale. This time there was the option of dinner at the Unicorn Hotel at 4.15 pm or leaving Ripon by ordinary train for York at 4.47 pm arriving at York at 6.05 pm "in time to catch the Express trains for London and the West of England; and also in Time for the Train to the North, at Thirsk Junction." These arrangements, remarkable in themselves, also mark the near culmination of the remarkable Victorian railway achievement.[7]

It is clear that the Society's centenary celebrations were understandably regarded by its members as a great success. At their first general meeting after the event, held on 13 November 1886 the report of the organising sub-committee was read and approved. The celebrations had evidently gone slightly over budget as the first part of the report was a recommendation that the members approve a further contribution of £215 "to enable the Treasurer to close the Centenary Account" which was readily agreed. The sub-committee's report continued:

> The Committee in making this recommendation need scarcely allude to the success of the gathering which this brought about, and which has attracted so much public attention. The assurance of those most actively concerned in this matter that the Society's money has been well spent may be relied on by those who have been unable to attend this gathering. For the present, the fact that the President of our Society has been voted to a seat on the Council of the Incorporated Law Society of the United Kingdom may be referred to as one proof, among many, that the Yorkshire Law Society is entering on a new century in which, though it may not as of old, take the lead in the Kingdom, it will secure a due acknowledgment of its position in London, in the provinces and particularly in the County of York.

The sub-committee's report was dated 8 November and signed by the President, William Walker.

The minutes of the general meeting on 13 November include detailed resolutions of thanks in connection with the celebrations, proposed by WH Cobb Esq and seconded by JW Mann Esq, the first of these to the effect

That the best thanks of the Society be conveyed to William Walker Esq JP, the President for his handsome reception of their guests in October last and to Mrs Walker for her gracious attention as hostess at the Ball in the Assembly Rooms.

This was followed by a veritable litany of thanks to the Lord and Lady Mayoress, Lord and Lady Wenlock "for their very courteous reception of the guests of this Society at Escrick Park on 13th October last", the Very Reverend Dean of York, the Yorkshire Philosophical Society, the solicitors of Whitby, the Scarborough Law Society, the Dean of Ripon and the Ripon solicitors, the Vicar and Churchwardens of St Martin Coney Street, the Rector and Churchwardens of Holy Trinity Goodramgate, the Rector and Churchwardens of St Dennis Walmgate, the Rector and Churchwardens of St Margaret Walmgate "for their attention to guests of the Society". And, of course, the home team was not forgotten: "FJ Munby, the Hon Secretary for the unwearied zeal shewn by him in promoting the success of the meeting to celebrate the Centenary of the Society". And finally it was resolved "that the thanks of the Society be conveyed to Messrs HW Badger, RP Dale and A Procter and the members of the several special Committees of which they were the active and efficient Honorary Secretaries for their successful efforts".

However satisfied members might have been in November 1886 at the outcome of these "successful efforts", there was already a clear understanding and acknowledgment that the Society would not "as of old, take the lead in the Kingdom". The records show very clearly that the centre of legal gravity had been moving away from York for some time and that after the first hundred years of its existence it would continue to do so. From then on the Society would be following events rather than initiating them. The same was true of Britain as a whole: much was happening in the final years of the 19th century and the early years of the 20th century. Few observers realised at the time (and some have not realised it even now) but these events were to presage a fundamental change in Britain's status in the world and a very different way of looking at it.

NOTES

1. In 1783 Napoleon, son of a Corsican lawyer and an Italian mother, as a young teenager in Corsica had dreamt of a career as a naval officer. The Royal Navy was the most prestigious navy in the world at the time. He had written with the help of his schoolmaster to the Admiralty in London seeking a post as a midshipman. Seemingly the letter duly arrived but the Admiralty never replied – arguably prompting one of the greatest "what ifs" of modern European history. See *Nelson: The Immortal Memory* by David & Stephen Howarth – JW Dent & Sons 1988.

2. Patrick Colquhoun (1745-1820), like Fielding, was a magistrate. Before settling in London he had been a tobacco merchant in Glasgow. See also p. 12 n. 8.

3. The Conveyancing Acts of 1881 and 1882 seem merely to have whetted the appetites of some practitioners although not everyone was clamouring for more law reform now. Land registration had been in the air for some time – see Chapter 6 and Appendix D– and already there were dissenting voices. The Married Women's Property Act 1882 had likewise been hotly contested by many.

4. George Frederick Samuel Robinson, first Marquess of Ripon (1827- 1909). A pillar of the establishment, he had been born in Downing Street at a time when his father, Viscount Goderich, had been Prime Minister. By 1886 he himself had become First Lord of the Admiralty. *The Times* had clearly chosen to forgive the noble Marquess and forget its own outrage when it had learnt twelve years earlier that the one-time MP for Huddersfield and subsequently the West Riding of Yorkshire had become a Catholic. "A statesman who becomes a convert to Roman Catholicism" it thundered, "forfeits at once the confidence of the English people. Such a move … can only be regarded as betraying an irreparable weakness of character."

5. The Victorians were fascinated by natural history and there was much modish enthusiasm for all aspects of the subject – botany, shells, ferns, geology – all had their amateur followers at various times. Many more of the Society's members than now would have been well aware that geologically speaking, the Scarborough area is among the most interesting in the country where the complete sequence of strata can be readily studied. The Lias group of fossils were formed during the late triassic and early jurassic periods.

6. The construction of this line by the Scarborough and Whitby Railway Company had only been completed the year before, although the first sod had been cut in 1872. Financial difficulties had arisen in 1878 which had held up the work. The line was always financially precarious. The total cost of construction was £649,813 but a few years later it was purchased by the North Eastern Railway company for only £261,633.

7. Apart from the diversion of the East Coast Main Line in the 1980s made necessary by the development of the Selby coal field, and the building of the high speed Channel Tunnel link, an Anglo-French undertaking, and the current (uncompleted) London Crossrail project, the last significant new railway building in Britain was the construction of the West Highland Line, authorised in 1889, the Mallaig extension being finally completed in 1901 – the year of Queen Victoria's death. Her reign neatly covered the age of railway development in Britain. The Society's centenary excursions vividly illustrate the subsequent decline in rural railway services. It is no longer possible to travel by rail between York and Whitby via Malton and Pickering, nor for that matter "by the new Coast Line" between Whitby and Scarborough. Also, there is now no rail connection between York and Ripon and Thirsk is no longer a junction. All were the victims of the Beeching closures in the 1960s and although efforts have since been made to restore a rail link to Ripon, the problems would seem to be insurmountable.

Chapter Eight

THE DAWN OF THE MODERN AGE
1886 – 1914

"The interests of the Profession and indeed the interests of their clients, the public, demand that Solicitors should be able to resist the tendency to place on the public by the creation of public officials a burden which may become intolerable."

Committee report to members 23 July 1894

Two years before the Society's celebration of its centenary, parliament had enacted the Representation of the People Act 1884 – often referred to as the Third Reform Act. The political complexion of Britain was in a stage of major transition. The Liberal party which had emerged in the middle years of the 19th century owed its origins to an inherently unstable alliance of aristocratic Whigs in the House of Lords and reforming radicals in the House of Commons. Until his death in 1898 the party's radical tendency had been best exemplified by William Gladstone[1] who had been responsible for the passing of the 1884 Act which had the effect of extending the vote previously granted to the urban working classes to those in the countryside. It was a continuation of the process of democratisation which had begun with the Great Reform Act of 1832, followed by the Representation of the People Act 1867 (the Second Reform Act). The latter had roughly doubled the number of adult males entitled to vote, broadly by enfranchising much of the urban working class. The effect of the 1884 Act, however, was to extend the franchise to male members of the working class in the countryside. But, as always, the law of unintended consequences lurks there in the undergrowth to confound political calculations. The unintended consequence of extending the franchise to the rural working class, desirable in itself though it might be, had the practical effect of bringing the Irish peasantry directly into Westminster politics and the Irish Parliamentary Party increased its number of seats from 63 to 86. Another intruder into the seeming tranquillity of British politics during this period was the rise of strident German nationalism following the country's unification in 1870 at the conclusion of the Franco-Prussian war of that year and which British public opinion had welcomed at the time.

However, before either Ireland or Germany were to become really major headaches, the war in South Africa (1899-1902) or the "Boer War" as it came to be more generally known, was to serve as an unnerving prelude. Its ostensible justification was that the Dutch Afrikaner or "Boer" settlers in their own territories were refusing to give civic rights to the large number of roistering gold prospectors who had appeared from all over the world following the discovery in 1886 of gold at Witwatersrand in the Transvaal (now part of the Greater Johannesburg Metropolitan Area and said to be the source of 40% of the gold ever mined on earth). These new arrivals had caused an immediate and potent source of friction for the Boers who were predominantly farmers – which is what the word "Boer" means in Dutch – and ultra-strict Calvinists in religion. In 1895 a Scottish doctor and son of an Edinburgh lawyer, Leander Starr Jameson had become commercially involved with Cecil Rhodes, Prime Minister of Cape Colony and the founder of De Beers and the British South Africa Company. Between them they had decided that it would be a good wheeze for Jameson, with 500 or so supporters, to carry out a raid into Transvaal with a view to provoking an uprising against the authorities there. Rhodes himself was Prime Minister of Cape Colony at the time, so he needed to distance himself from the plot but its real object was to give the British authorities an excuse to intervene. The raid was a fiasco and Jameson and his followers surrendered to the Boers who handed them over to the British authorities with a view to punishment. The British had little option but to prosecute and after a seven day trial Jameson was sentenced to 15 months imprisonment although released after six months, thereafter becoming something of a national hero.

By 1899 the British, having decided that it was their mission in life to protect the human rights of the prospectors, whether British or not, sought to negotiate on their behalf. This, needless to say, had nothing to do with the fact that the rapidly expanding city of Johannesburg was, quite literally "sitting on a gold mine". To back up the British negotiating position troops had been dispatched to the Cape – originally a Dutch colony which we had "acquired" in 1806 to prevent any risk of it falling into the hands of the French during the Napoleonic wars. It was this acquisition which had prompted many of the Boers to migrate northwards across the Vaal River to set up their own republics in the first place. The Boers, however, were not impressed by the strong-arm negotiating tactics of their neighbours to the south and demanded that the troops be withdrawn.

The British chose to treat this as a declaration of war and the Boers for their part retaliated by invading the British colony of Natal to their east. The whole British approach had not endeared itself to international opinion, neither did our subsequent frustrated adoption of a "scorched earth" policy in Afrikaner territory. The latter involved the burning of crops and farm buildings and the salting of the land to render it infertile, together with the rounding up of women and children and "concentrating" them in mismanaged "camps" in the open veld. Such was the level of mismanagement and neglect in these "concentration camps" that a total of 26,370 Boer women and children perished, together with a somewhat smaller number of black Africans. This compares with estimated Boer combat losses of about 4,000. We lost 7,792 troops killed in action or dying from their wounds plus a further 13,250 who died from disease. Understandably, opinion in the country was deeply divided and, although the British might had finally succeeded in defeating a rag-taggle army of Dutch "Afrikaners", the physical and financial cost was considerable. It was also a severe psychological blow to the easy optimism of the high Victorian age as manifested in the Society's centenary celebrations just thirteen years earlier.

As for Ireland, it had been an unwelcome distraction to London-based governments of all religious and ideological complexions for centuries but from now on the Irish question ceased to be a mere distraction or even a major distraction and in one form or another came to be a dominating factor in British politics. What made it so peculiarly difficult to resolve was the existence in Ireland of two increasingly powerful and strident interests with mutually exclusive ambitions: the nationalists and the unionists. Furthermore, mass Irish immigration into Britain following the great famine of the 1840s, the close affinity between the Presbyterian Protestants of Ulster and their co-religionists in Scotland and the existence of the traditional Anglo-Irish ascendancy (famously described by the Irish writer Brendan Behan as "the Anglo-Irish horse Protestants") which straddled almost all of Ireland and the southern half of Britain combined to guarantee that any polarisation in Ireland itself would be reflected over here.

Irish national sentiment in one shape or another had been a live issue in mainland politics throughout the Society's existence. Before 1829 it had been dominated by the campaign for Catholic Emancipation orchestrated in Ireland by Daniel O'Connell and his efforts to secure election to the House of Commons. That specific issue had been largely resolved by the passing of the Roman Catholic Relief Act in April of that year. This had been followed by the "Great Famine". Between 1845 and 1852 it is estimated that about a million people in Ireland died of starvation and a further million were forced to emigrate. The British government's handling of the crisis had been grotesquely inept to say the least and as a nation the Irish have never really recovered from the disaster; its impact was immediate but the psychological scars have yet to heal.

From the 1880s onwards the temperature of Anglo-Irish politics began to rise rapidly, largely fuelled by agrarian issues. The eviction of agricultural tenants, unable to pay their rents, had long been the cause of discontent among the Irish peasantry. The end of the American Civil War fifteen years earlier and the consequent opening up of the prairies coupled with rapid development of US railroads and the greater efficiency of transatlantic shipping had sharply increased competition from across the pond. Farmers in Britain suffered but the those in Ireland suffered more. The year 1880 was to bring the agricultural problems of Ireland to general public attention in a most dramatic and memorable way. In that year Lord Erne's land agent, Captain Charles Boycott, had taken over a farm on Erne's estate in County Mayo, following the eviction of its tenant. This had provoked the fury of the local population, encouraged by the Irish Land League, who refused to have anything to do with Boycott or his employer. It quickly became clear that the noble earl was not going to be able to get in his harvest that year for none of the local labourers were prepared to undertake the task – and harvesting at that

An original Spy cartoon of Captain Boycott, published in January 1881

time was a labour intensive undertaking. The resultant publicity attracted the attention of Orangemen from the neighbouring counties of Cavan and Monaghan who were totally opposed to the nationalist ambitions of the protestors. Fifty volunteers moved in to undertake the harvesting but that merely provoked the local population to even greater fury. The government was then obliged to deploy over a thousand troops and police in order to protect the volunteers. Inevitably the ensuing cost to the taxpayer exceeded the value of the crops "saved" by a large margin. One result of course was that the English language acquired a new word which is with us still: "boycott" – a word which promptly carried over into most western European languages and even into Hungarian and Russian. There too, the name of Captain Boycott is still in current use.

The events of 1880 had attracted much publicity, but it was only the beginning. In 1882 two senior figures had been assassinated whilst walking in Phoenix Park, Dublin. One was Lord Frederick Cavendish who had arrived there only hours earlier to take up his new appointment as Chief Secretary for Ireland. A protégé of Gladstone, he was the second son of the 7th Duke of Devonshire and had been Liberal MP for the Northern Division of the West Riding of Yorkshire since 1865. His companion on that fatal walk in Phoenix Park was TH Burke, the Permanent Under Secretary at Dublin Castle. In fact it was Burke who was the actual target of the assassins, an extremist off-shoot of the Irish Republican Brotherhood (IRB) who did not know Cavendish by sight; he was killed simply because of the company he was keeping. These assassinations occurred in the course of a prolonged IRB bombing campaign in Britain which had begun the previous year and which were to continue until 1885. A bomb exploded in London's Mansion House and another in the chamber of the House of Commons itself. One attempt which failed was to blow up London Bridge. On this occasion the only fatalities were the three IRB perpetrators who died when their bomb exploded prematurely. One of them, William Mackey Lomasney, was in fact a US citizen, having been born in Ohio to Irish immigrant parents. It all had a dramatic (and divisive) effect on public opinion in Ireland – and, of course, in Britain itself which by then had a sizeable population of Irish descent, but equally it alienated much working-class opinion in Britain which had previously been sympathetic to Irish political aspirations. Gladstone himself became a convert to the necessity of Irish Home Rule which he saw as the only possible solution to national aspirations but attitudes on both sides of this particular political divide were hardening and in Ireland nowhere more so than among the Protestant unionists of the north east.

The two general elections in 1910 both resulted in Liberal minority governments under Herbert Asquith, supported by Irish Nationalists. The Unionists of Ulster could see what lay ahead and they were not having it. By 28 September 1912 almost half a million Ulster Protestants had signed the Ulster Covenant and Declaration – the Covenant itself being for men and the Declaration for women. The terms of the Covenant were unambiguous. The signatories had undertaken " … using all means which may be found necessary to defeat the present conspiracy to set up a Home Rule parliament in Ireland … ". A corresponding British Covenant designed for signature by British unionists had acquired two million signatures by the summer of 1914 following a mass meeting in Hyde Park on 4 April. It was not a case of "the usual suspects" who go on demos nowadays, protesting about poll tax, the Iraq war, student fees or "globalisation" but fully paid-up members of the establishment tendency. The signatories included Field-Marshal Lord Roberts VC, KG, KP, GCB, OM, GCSI, KStJ, PC and Admiral of the Fleet Sir Edward Seymour GCB, OM, GCVO as well as Rudyard Kipling[2] and many other "establishment" figures of the day. Indeed, it would be hard to imagine a more illustrious pillar of the military establishment than Lord Roberts (Eton and Sandhurst). A veteran of the Indian Mutiny where he gained his VC, he equally found time to complete a successful occupation of Kabul in the course of the Second Afghan War and to lift the siege of Kimberley in the course of the Boer War.

Any perception there might have been that the dyed-in-the-wool Unionists and Ulster Protestants who had signed the covenant in the autumn of 1912 were bluffing was quickly dispelled by the events of the following eighteen months. In January 1913 the Ulster Unionist Council had raised the Ulster Volunteer Force – 100,000 men between the ages of seventeen and sixty-five. Their Commander-in-Chief was Lt-General Sir George Richardson KCB, like Roberts, a veteran of the Second Afghan war who had also led an assault on Peking in 1900 during the Boxer Rebellion. In the summer of that year they staged a march-past of 15,000 in Belfast's agricultural show-ground at Balmoral when FE Smith, the future Solicitor General, Attorney-General and Lord Chancellor was among those who took the salute in addition to Sir George Richardson. By March 1914 the government was deeply concerned by this Ulster unionist militancy and General Sir Arthur Paget, the British Commander-in-Chief Ireland, was ordered to start preparations to move troops to Ulster in order to forestall any UVF violence that might arise. Paget's orders also included what must be one of the most extraordinary set of instructions ever issued by government to a British commander in peacetime. They came from Colonel John Seely,[3] Secretary of State for War in Asquith's government and were in the following terms:

1. Officers whose houses are actually in the province of Ulster who wish to do so may apply for permission to be absent from duty during the period of operations and will be allowed to disappear from Ireland. Such officers will, subsequently, be reinstated, and will suffer no loss in their career.

2. Any officer who from conscientious or other motives is not prepared to carry out his duties as ordered should say so at once. Such officers will, at once, be dismissed from the service.

No doubt Seely, who was an honourable man, was concerned to avoid the nightmare possibility of an actual mutiny in law: if serving officers refused to obey orders the government would have felt obliged, if in practice able to do so, to ensure prosecution under military law. If on the other hand the officers concerned were to be dismissed before the orders were actually issued, they would not technically have been guilty of mutiny. Whatever Seely's intentions, his political position became untenable and by the end of March he was obliged to resign.

In the event, Paget had seemingly misinterpreted his orders: he had not been instructed to proceed directly against the recalcitrant Unionists in the north but merely to prepare a precautionary deployment. Following this order Paget felt obliged to send the following telegram to the War Office:

```
OFFICER COMMANDING 5TH LANCERS STATES THAT
ALL OFFICERS EXCEPT TWO AND ONE DOUBTFUL ARE
RESIGNING THEIR COMMISSIONS TODAY. I MUCH FEAR THE
SAME CONDITIONS IN THE 16TH LANCERS. FEAR MEN WILL
REFUSE TO MOVE. REGRET BRIGADIER-GENERAL GOUGH
AND FIFTY-SEVEN OFFICERS 3RD CAVALRY BRIGADE
PREFER TO ACCEPT DISMISSAL IF ORDERED NORTH.
```

The government was forced to back down,[4] claiming an "honest misunderstanding". By the following month matters had become even more critical. On the night of 24-25 April the UVF, in a brilliant feat of organisation involving much subterfuge and deception, had succeeded in landing and distributing an estimated 24,000 rifles at Larne, Donaghadee and Bangor together with a vast supply of ammunition.[5] The authorities either could not or would not intervene. This and the so-called "Curragh Mutiny" inevitably persuaded the Irish nationalists that even if the British government succeeded in getting the Home Rule bill onto the statute book, they would in practice be unable to enforce it and resulted in the "tit-for-tat" gun-running into Howth on 26 July of 900 German Mausers dating from the Franco-Prussian war of 1870 and 29,000 rounds of ammunition. Alerted by the harbour-master at Howth, a detachment of the King's Own Scottish Borderers from Kilmainham Barracks managed to make contact with the Irish Citizen's Army, led by Countess Markiewicz,[6] which was responsible for the unloading and distribution of the arms but the government troops were hindered by a hostile crowd and only managed to retrieve three rifles. The soldiers opened fire and two men and a woman were killed instantly and thirty-two others were injured.

Despite the rapidly deteriorating situation in Ireland in the spring and summer of 1914, the Liberal government was still doggedly determined to get its Home Rule Bill through parliament. Twice it had been rejected by the House of Lords but when it passed the Commons for the third time on 27 May 1914, the government relied on the Parliament Act 1911 to gain royal assent and the act finally passed into law on 18 September 1914. By then, of course, the country was at war with Germany and in no position to get bogged down in a highly contested constitutional upheaval. Accordingly the government had rushed through the Suspensory Act 1914 which by a strange irony also received the royal assent on 18 September. The Government of Ireland Act 1914 therefore had the distinction (together with that other highly contested measure, the Welsh Church Act 1914) of being passed and suspended on the same day.

The assassination of the Austrian Archduke Franz Ferdinand in Sarajevo on 28 June had set in train the events which were to bring Britain into war with the German and Austro-Hungarian empires. This traumatic event which had put both Irish and Welsh Church affairs on hold for its duration was to accelerate a change in the ground rules of British society which was both sudden and dramatic but in reality that change had begun a generation earlier and would take several more generations to work itself out – if indeed it has yet done so. The events of the spring and summer of 1914 have led some commentators to suggest that they were one factor at least which prompted the British government to declare war on 4 August on the basis that it would "unite the country" – and so it did, but only up to a point as the Easter Rising in 1916 and the subsequent Anglo-Irish war of 1920-1921 were to clearly demonstrate. There was to be a temporary truce of sorts from the outbreak of war in August 1914 until Easter 1916 but political life in these islands was never to be quite the same again. Indeed, during the last years of "peace" Irish issues had brought not just

Ireland but mainland Britain itself perilously close to civil war – a fact which is not always fully appreciated in our own day.

If the complex Anglo-Irish relationship has been the seemingly permanent distraction of virtually every government in England from mediæval times to the present day, one factor has been its sheer ambivalence – a factor which makes it peculiarly difficult to explain to outsiders and even native British unfamiliar with the detailed background. In the 20th century at least, this ambivalence has been exemplified by the Comyn family and the appointment of James Comyn QC (1921-1997) as one of Her Majesty's Justices of the Supreme Court in 1978 at the height of the second round of IRA troubles. Not only was Comyn an Irishman, (born Dublin, died Navan Co. Meath, buried Ballyvaughan Co. Clare) who never gave up his Irish passport, but an Irishman of impeccable republican stock. His father, James Comyn, and his uncle Michael Comyn KC were both members of the Irish Bar and both staunch republicans. Indeed Michael Comyn KC had had the unusual task for an advocate of having to inform the Court of Appeal in Dublin in late 1922 that his client Erskine Childers had been executed by the Free State authorities on 24 November while the appeal against sentence was still pending.[7] Both brothers had been legal advisers to the IRA in the first round of troubles in the 1920s and de Valera sought sanctuary for a time in James Comyn senior's house when he was on the run during the Irish civil war which followed the 1922 Anglo-Irish treaty. However, when de Valera eventually came to power in 1933 the family expected Michael Comyn to be appointed Attorney-General. When he was passed over there was a falling-out and James Comyn junior was taken away from Belvedere, the Jesuit college in Dublin, and sent to the Oratory School in Birmingham where he flourished, went up to Oxford (defeating Roy Jenkins for presidency of the Union), went to the English Bar and ended up on the High Court Bench. Doubtless for the sake of good order and legal discipline the listing officers were given strict instructions to keep any "inappropriate" Irish cases well away from Comyn J but otherwise the judicial career of this scion of Irish republicanism proceeded with due normality. Nevertheless, in order to show their disapprobation, the latter-day IRA burnt his house at Tara outside Dublin to the ground, thus achieving a spectacular own goal as it contained a significant IRA archive of the republican movement of earlier times.

If the Irish Question was of long standing to British governments, the problem of Germany and its military, naval and colonial and expansionist ambitions during the closing years of the 19th and the first half of the 20th centuries was a relative novelty. The unification of Germany and the creation of the German Empire under the Kaiser (formerly the King of Prussia prior to the Franco-Prussian war of 1870) had not been an immediate cause of concern. Unlike our relationship with the French (or for that matter, the Irish) there was no historical tradition of hostility to the Germans – rather the contrary. Our monarchs since the time of George I had been Hanoverians and the German connection had been reinforced with the Queen's marriage to Prince Albert of Saxe-Coburg (her first cousin) in 1840. Indeed, at the outbreak of war in 1914 the Kaiser and our own King George V were equally first cousins – a family connection with Germany which continues to this day through the present Queen's consort, Prince Philip Duke of Edinburgh, her third cousin. In the end this was to count for nothing: Kaiser Wilhelm was determined to assert German naval and military superiority come what may and if what came was war, then so be it. With hindsight it may be that the political classes in Britain just couldn't bring themselves to recognise the appalling threat posed by German nationalism and the Kaiser's ambitions until it was too late – at least this was the view of Viscount Grey, the Foreign Secretary at the outbreak of war: "… the whole policy of the years from 1886 to 1904 [might] be criticised as having played into the hands of Germany…"[8]

Contention in the late Victorian and Edwardian era across the Irish sea, the North Sea (or German Ocean as it was then known) and in South Africa was to be compounded by serious domestic issues which were rapidly coming to the fore: the suffragette movement, labour and resulting trades union disputes, rows over educational reform and "faith" schools connected with the Education Act 1902 and rows over economic and social policy. This culminated in the constitutional crisis from 1909 to 1911 when the House of Lords, in its legislative capacity, was using its powers to block the Liberal government's budget. The House of Lords eventually backed down and the crisis was resolved by the passing of the Parliament Act 1911 but only under the government's threat to advise the King to create sufficient additional peers – 249 to be precise, the list including Gilbert Murray, JM Barrie, Thomas Hardy, and Bertrand Russell – to ensure the bill's passage into law.

In the light of all that was actually happening during the last years of the 19th and the first years of the 20th century it seems strange that the period should somehow be regarded in retrospect as a golden age. Perhaps we are too much conditioned by an awareness of the catastrophe that was about to engulf almost the whole of Europe and much of the rest of the world which was never to be the same again. For the most part, however, our forebears truly had little idea of what that war was going to mean for all those involved. In the nationalistic euphoria of the late summer of 1914 they imagined that the war would be "over by Christmas". They were to be cruelly deceived. Professional soldiers and politicians on both sides had totally failed to appreciate the extent to which technology, in particular the development of the machine gun and artillery, together with the industrial capacity to manufacture them and the ammunition which they required in vast quantities, had completely overtaken the development of strategic and tactical military thinking.

It is a sobering fact that the British Army saw fit to re-adopt the lance for its six Lancer regiments in 1908, having abandoned them just a few years earlier as a result of experiencing their total ineffectiveness against Boer irregulars in South Africa. Indeed, they were not finally to lose their lances – a weapon which would have been instantly recognisable to a mediæval knight – until 1928, ten years after the First World War; and it was not until 1942, during the Second World War, that the Army finally lost its last mounted cavalry regiment, the Queen's Own Yorkshire Dragoons. As Lloyd George rather unkindly put it in his *War Memoirs* "The military mind makes up in retentiveness what it lacks in agility." Yet the better-informed had a foreboding about what to expect. On 3 August 1914 Germany had finally declared war on France, and Viscount Grey the Foreign Secretary, knew that this would inevitably take the UK into war with Germany the following day. Looking out at the lights of London that evening from a window of the Foreign Office, he sadly and famously observed, "The lamps are going out all over Europe. We shall not see them lit again in out time".[8] He was perhaps more right than he realised: he lived to see the advent of Hitler as Chancellor of Germany in 1933.

Neither the minutes of the general meetings, nor the minutes of the committee between 1886 and the outbreak of war in 1914 give the impression that all these turbulent events were impinging on the Society and its members in any way. Obviously they were concerned about technical issues which affected the profession in a technical way as they always had been. Nevertheless, there are clues of an awareness that in some respects society was moving in a direction which was cause for concern. At a general meeting on 5 March 1891, for example, the committee commented on the proposed creation of a Public Trustee Office:

> Officialism has so far been kept out of family affairs, and the introduction of it would result in the erection of an executive department of the State, practically beyond the control either of the courts or public opinion, and worked so as to be a source of profit to the state. It would tend to make the administration of trusts more expensive, cumbrous and inelastic and the objects of the Bill, so far as they are legitimate, can be better secured by granting to private trustees the right to remuneration and immunities proposed to be conferred upon a public trustee and by giving statutory powers, under proper restrictions, to duly constituted public companies to perform the office of trustee or executor.

One can detect here the classic voice of 19th century liberalism with its instinctive distrust of officialdom and big government. The same distrust can be seen in the constant and long-running battle throughout this period against any proposal for compulsory registration of title – so constant and long-running in fact, as well as being technical, that detailed treatment of the whole subject has been relegated to Appendix D. It is, however, worth noting at this point some comments in the committee's report to members at the Society's general meeting on 23 July 1894:

> Those members of the House of Lords who have voted in favour of compulsion [of registration] are not familiar, as Solicitors are, with the small transactions in buying, selling and mortgaging land and houses; and they have not had the experience of Lord Cairns who, in 1875, arrived at the conclusion that "a system of Compulsory Registration was undesirable because of the great obstacles which it would throw in the way of these small transactions in land". The fact that the Bill would have the effect of repealing the Statute of Limitations, or that no one could acquire a title to land or any easement over it (in the district in which it is brought upon the Register), by possession, however, long, cannot be too widely known or too carefully considered.

The technical objections about the Statute of Limitations were ultimately of course resolved but the substantive objection to compulsory registration of title was much the same as that to the creation of a Public Trustee – it was a manifestation of "big government", or what nowadays would be labelled "the nanny state'.[9] This is clear from a concluding paragraph of the committee's report on the Land Transfer Bill and is linked with an encouragement to membership of the Incorporated Law Society:

> The interests of the Profession and indeed the interests of their clients, the public, demand that Solicitors should be united and able to resist the tendency to place on the public by the creation of public officials, a burden which may become intolerable; and this Society will therefore welcome an addition to the number of its members who may also become members of the Incorporated Law Society (UK).

Apart from the customary protests about compulsion in the Land Transfer Bill, the following year, 1895 marked two small items of domestic interest. The first was an announcement to members:

> ... that the President had presented to the Society a beautiful work of art as a badge to be worn by the President on public occasions during his year of office. The badge consisted of a circular gold plate with a White Rose of York in silver upon it. On the back it bears the following inscription "Presented to the Yorkshire Law Society by JT Atkinson, President, March 1895. Floreat Eboriensis."

The badge of office of course is still in regular use. The second item, however, may raise a wry smile among members: a sub-committee appointed earlier in the year was

> ... instructed to revise the Rules of the Society in such a way that the revised rules could either be embodied in the trust deed or utilised for Memorandum and Articles of Association and to report with regard to such proposed revision of rules to a subsequent meeting and that the question of incorporation be left in abeyance for the present.

In the event the question of incorporation was left in abeyance for 90 years and the Society did not finally abandon its trust status and become a company limited by guarantee until 4 April 1985 – a long period of gestation by any standards. Precisely why such a straightforward decision should have taken so long is not altogether clear. One is tempted to echo the words of Comyn J, the Irish judge (already mentioned above in another context) "This case bristles with simplicity". [10]

Another domestic matter was reported by the committee to the Society's meeting on 28 January 1897, to the effect that it had made "a large purchase of useful books, at a cost of about £80, which, it is hoped, will prove a valuable and much needed addition to the library".[11] This was evidently prompted by the move from the library's former premises in Spurriergate "to the beautiful and commodious room below the old Council Chamber in the Guildhall" – coupled with the hope that "the Society may prove to be such satisfactory tenants that the York Corporation will have no wish to disturb them in their occupancy."

But then on 22 January 1901 Queen Victoria died. Her passing had a profound effect on the entire nation. She had come to the throne on 20 June 1837 when she was still a teenager and less than a month after celebrating her coming of age, eighteen, not twenty-one, being the age of majority for royalty at that time. Anyone under the age of seventy would hardly have remembered a time when she was not on the throne. Her death must have seemed like the end of an era but in reality it was more than half way through the first chapter of modern times.

The Society's first meeting following the Queen's death was on 31 January 1901 when the following resolution was passed:

> The Yorkshire Law Society desires to record an expression of their sense of the great loss which has befallen the legal profession in the death of Her Majesty Victoria, our late beloved Queen, and to acknowledge their loyalty to King Edward the Seventh, whom they pray God to preserve as the Fountain of Justice and Honour to a truly undivided and contented people.

Whether in truth her people could be said to be "truly undivided and contented" must be a matter of some doubt in the light of the events of the previous twenty years – but of course the Society's members are never on oath on such occasions. The Queen's death also caused the postponement of the annual dinner, normally held in February at the time at the York Station Hotel, from 15 February to 7 May.

The euphoria in 1897 concerning "the beautiful and commodious room below the old Council Chamber in the Guildhall" does not long seem to have outlived the Queen herself. At a meeting of the Society on 26 January 1903 the minutes record:

> A discussion was raised as to the fitness of the present room provided by the Society for a Library and it was moved by Mr F Perkins, seconded by Mr RP Dale, that it be an instruction to the Committee to make inquiries and ascertain if a better room could not be obtained for the purpose. This was carried with some dissentients.

The instruction to the Committee was to bear fruit. The Society's meeting on 24 November 1904 was held at the two rooms forming its new premises at 14 Coney Street with a formal opening of the Library by the President, Mr RP Dale. Reading between the lines, it seems that the original move from Spurriergate had been the occasion of a sharp jolt to complacency about the running of the library, particularly as regards the condition of the books and the enforcement of the library rules, and members were becoming more demanding about available facilities. Two years later, in 1906, it was recorded that "the telephone has been added to the Library on the penny-in-the-slot system, so that anyone can communicate with the Library or from it to his own office which should prove a boon to country members".

Meanwhile the report of the Committee to the 118th meeting of the Society on 28 January 1904 makes mention of acts dealing with a number of activities with a clear indication of the way in which society was moving, including restrictions on child employment, extension of the county court jurisdiction from £50 to £100, the Housing of the Working Classes Act 1903 and the Poor Prisoners Defence Act 1903.[12] But the following two items in particular illustrate just how far society was still removed from the modern world.

MOTOR-CARS

> The Motor-Car Act [UK], which came into operation on 1st January, is limited to expire on December 31, 1906.
>
> The reckless, negligent, or too rapid driving (at whatever speed) on a public highway or roadway to which the public are granted access is an offence under the Act, and any police-constable may apprehend without warrant a driver who has offended within his view if he refuses to give his

name and address or produce the licence required by the Act, of if the car cannot be identified under the Act. Every car must be registered with the council of a county or county borough with a separate number and mark indicating it fixed on the car or vehicle drawn by it or both, and on payment of a fee of 5s. each for motor-cycles and 20s. each for other cars.

The enforcement of the maximum speed of 12 miles an hour is replaced by the enactment that: –

> A person shall not, under any circumstances, drive a motor-car on a public highway or roadway to which the public are granted access at a speed exceeding 20 miles an hour,[13] and within any limits or place referred to in regulations made by the Local Government Board with a view to the safety of the public, on the application of the local authority of the area in which the limits or place are situate, a person shall not drive a motor-car at a speed exceeding 10 miles an hour.

Contravention of this enactment is punishable by fine up to £10 for a first offence, £20 for a second, and £50 for any subsequent offence. The Local Government Board may also prohibit or restrict the driving of any motor-car on any highway which does not exceed 16 feet in width "or on which ordinary motor-car traffic would in their opinion be especially dangerous." In case of accident to any person or to a horse or vehicle in charge of any person owing to the presence of a motor-car on a road, the driver is directed to stop and to give his and the owner's name, if required, on pain of a fine of up to £10 for a first offence, £20 for a second, and £20 or imprisonment up to one month for any subsequent offence. All common law and statutory liabilities of owners are expressly left unaffected.

PISTOLS

The Pistols Act [E.S.] makes it unlawful to sell or let a pistol (except an antique sold for curiosity or ornament) to any person not producing a gun or game licence or proving that he is entitled to carry a gun without a gun or game licence for scaring birds or otherwise under the Gun Licence Act, or that, being a householder, he will either use the pistol only at home or is about to go abroad for not less than six months, and produces a vouched statement to that effect. An entry of each sale or letting must be made in a book to be produced for inspection on the request of any police or Inland Revenue Officer. Any person contravening any of these provisions may be fined up to £5, and a similar fine may be incurred by any person selling or delivering a pistol to any person under the age of 18 not legally liable for carrying a gun without a gun or game licence, the young person himself being liable up to £5 for buying, hiring, using or carrying the pistol, as to the forfeiture of which the Court inflicting the fine may make such order as may seem fit. Lastly. any person who knowingly sells a pistol to any person intoxicated or not of sound mind may be fined up to £5, or be imprisoned with or without hard labour up to three months.

The Pistols Act was the first real attempt to control firearms. The Gun Licence Act 1870 to which the Committee referred in their report was more of a revenue raising exercise than any attempt to exercise control in the modern manner. Indeed, the reference to "Inland Revenue Officer" in the above report makes it clear that as late as 1903 the raising of revenue was still just as much in parliament's mind as the actual control of firearms. For one thing, no licence was required merely to *purchase* a gun, nor was it required if its retention and use was confined to the purchaser's own premises. As a measure of control the 1903 Act was largely ineffective – as will be fairly evident to the modern eye from the above summary – and could readily be evaded by the criminally-minded or unscrupulous. The first modern statute did not appear until the Firearms Act 1920.

What we are beginning to see during this period is the increasing regulation of life prompted by the tendency of the modern state to involve itself in the affairs of its citizens in ways which simply would not have occurred to a earlier generation of Victorian reformers. The radical element in the Liberal party was beginning to predominate, its standard-bearer being of course David Lloyd George, the future wartime Prime Minister and President of the Board of Trade in 1905 in a Liberal minority government. The liberal landslide victory in the general election of 1906 had provided a significant boost to his career and by 1908 he had been appointed Chancellor of the Exchequer when Herbert Asquith took over the premiership on the resignation and death of Henry Campbell-Bannerman. His People's Budget of 1909 which was to raise such a political storm was still in the future but at the Society's general meeting held at the new library premises on 31 January 1907 the committee reported somewhat laconically to members "The new Government has been somewhat active in the matter of legislation, and several Acts of Parliament to which attention should be drawn have been passed." Various particulars follow which do not require comment here but they do include two matters concerning solicitors and a reference to the Workmen's Compensation Act 1906 which was due to come into force on 1 July 1907 "also of much importance" according to the committee.

The main matter of concern to solicitors as such was the abolition of the property qualification in the Justices of the Peace Act 1906 for appointment as a county magistrate, thus facilitating the appointment of solicitors to the county bench. One significant restriction remained, however: no solicitor so appointed, nor any partner of his could either appear or practise, directly or indirectly, before a justice for the county or any borough within the county. The committee clearly regarded this restriction as unnecessary and quixotic, pointing out that "With regard to a County so large as Yorkshire, this is [a] somewhat sweeping disqualification, and is also somewhat mechanical in its operation. For instance, a solicitor in Thornaby who was appointed a Justice of the Peace for the North Riding could not carry on a prosecution at Sheffield, but might do so at Stockton-on-Tees."

The other matter of concern was the Prevention of Corruption Act 1906. The problem for solicitors was that it raised a question mark over their long-established practice of sharing commissions relating to insurance policies and stock-exchange transactions undertaken on behalf of clients. The committee seemed to take a reassuringly commonsense view of the matter, observing that the Act "has caused an almost unnecessary amount of emotion in the breasts of Solicitors", and recommending simply with regard to insurance premiums, "that a note of the fact that these are paid and received should appear on the receipts and notices" and that "in all cases where brokerage is shared with broker, the fact should be brought to the knowledge of the client".

A domestic matter which seems to have given far greater satisfaction to the committee was the prospect of a more proactive régime for the regulation of solicitors' accounts – or rather *some* form of regulation. It is interesting to note that the initiative for this seems to have come from lawyers themselves, as will be seen from the following extract from the committee's report:

The Society will be aware that there is a proposal on foot, inaugurated by a number of influential members of the legal profession to appoint a committee to go into the question of solicitors' accounts with a view, if possible, to recommend some scheme of keeping such accounts. Your Committee heartily support the proposal to appoint such a committee and the proposal has now been carried, after an appeal for a Poll, by 1169 to 609.

It was, of course, under the Solicitors Act 1906 that the Law Society first acquired a statutory disciplinary committee, with power to investigate solicitors' accounts and to issue annual practising certificates although the first occasion on which it had instituted proceedings against a dishonest solicitor was in 1834. It was under the 1906 Act also that the provisions relating to the issue of practising certificates that the Law Society was able, in effect, to prevent solicitors who had become bankrupt from practising – a development which gives some indication as to the relative lack of regulation governing the profession compared to the present day. Equally, even after 1907 the rules governing solicitors' accounts were relatively relaxed. It was only in 1934 that solicitors were actually required for the first time to keep clients' monies completely separate from their own and many of the present rules have only come in comparatively recently.[14]

As far as the latest Workmen's Compensation Act was concerned, the committee was clearly right to draw members' attention to its importance. The Liberal government was beginning its serious challenge to many "Victorian" attitudes. That challenge was to cause more than ripples in the politics of the Edwardian period and was to culminate in the great constitutional struggle over the status and power of the House of Lords between 1909 and 1911. For the moment, however, the emphasis was on labour law. A hundred years on it requires a certain effort of the will to recall how the law and the courts regarded the relationship between employers and their "workmen". Their approach was well illustrated in the case of *Simpson v Ebbw Vale Steel, Iron & Coal Company* [1905] 1 KB 453 where the Court of Appeal had to consider a claim by the widow of a colliery manager killed in an underground explosion. It was held that the deceased was outside the (limited) provisions of the Workmen's Compensation Act 1897 because although the act extended to non-manual workers, the victim "must still be a workman". The act according to Lord Collins MR "presupposes a position of dependence; it treats the class of workmen as being in a sense *inopes consilii*,[15] and the legislation does for them what they cannot do for themselves; it gives them a sort of State insurance, it being assumed that they are either not sufficiently intelligent or not sufficiently in funds to insure themselves. In no sense can such a principle extend to those who are earning good salaries".

There was still at this period a traditional assumption among the educated classes that ordinary "workmen" must, by definition, be completely unlettered and ignorant – a failure to appreciate that Bradford MP William Foster's Elementary Education Act of 1870, which made elementary education compulsory, had had its effect on an entire generation and that if the teaching was good, which it often was, and the pupils reasonably bright, it could take them a long way. Arthur Balfour, former Conservative Prime Minister (Eton and Trinity), having been invited to attend discussions with the TUC in 1915 over wartime production, was "surprised to find the workmen's representatives talked so well".[16] Occasionally we may be tempted to wonder aloud whether we have moved on that far over the last hundred years.

What was actually happening during this period was a major shift in the political landscape. The Whig tradition dating from the 17th century had gradually given way in the latter part of the 19th century to radical liberalism. That in turn was to rise spectacularly in the first two decades of the 20th century only to fall away again in response to competition from the rising phenomenon of specifically Labour politics. Few can have foreseen, following the Liberal victory at the general election of 1906, that after 1922 there would never again be a Liberal government. Nature would no longer contrive in the words of *Iolanthe's* Private Willis,

That every boy and every gal
That's born into the world alive
Is either a little Liberal
Or else a little Conservative

That process of change, however, was to be both interrupted and accelerated by the disaster of the First World War.

NOTES

1. William Ewart Gladstone (1809-1898) was a pivotal figure in British politics in the second half of the 19th century. He began the gradual weaning of the Liberal party from the aristocratic *laissez-faire* tenets of traditional Whiggery.

2. Rudyard Kipling (1865-1936) whose literary achievements included the post of unofficial balladeer of empire, was a fervent unionist as one might expect. Following the Hyde Park meeting on 4 April he was moved to write a poem *Ulster 1912* which was published five days later in *The Morning Post*. It very much reflected the Ulster Protestant fear encapsulated in the slogan "Home Rule means Rome Rule!" One verse reads:

   We know the war prepared
   On every peaceful home,
   We know the hells declared
   For such as serve not Rome
   The terror, threats and bread
   In market, hearth and field –
   We know when all is said,
   We perish if we yield.

3. John Seely, later Lord Mottistone (1868-1947). Forced to resign on 30 March 1914 as a result of his perceived mishandling of the Curragh incident, he resumed his career as a cavalryman. By 11 August 1914 he and his horse *Warrior* were in France. By March 1918 after four years of very active service on the western front, Seely, by then a popular general who had earned himself the sobriquet "Galloping Jack", found himself commanding the thousand strong Canadian cavalry. There followed what was to be one of the last great cavalry charges in history at Moreuil Wood on the banks of the River Avre near Amiens. It was a significant contribution to halting General Ludendorff's Spring Offensive. Seely was no back-stage cavalry general. Mounted as always on *Warrior*, he took personal charge of the leading signal section consisting of his ADC Prince Antoine d'Orléans-Bragance (a great-grandson of France's last king, Louis Philippe) and eleven others. Seely, Prince Antoine and six others of the leading section survived. Five didn't. The whole cavalry engagement cost the Canadians a quarter of their men and half their horses but Moreuil Wood was taken and the German offensive checked. *Warrior* survived until 1941 and he and Galloping Jack were immortalised by Sir Alfred Munnings in a portrait now in the National Gallery of Canada in Ottawa.

4. In the modern democratic world it is very difficult for any government to deal with such situations. Harold Wilson's government was faced with a somewhat similar one in May 1974 at the time of the general strike organised by the Ulster Workers' Council against the Sunningdale agreement which

was intended to introduce power sharing with the Irish nationalists. During a two week period between 15 and 28 May loyalist paramilitaries effectively brought the entire province to a standstill and were responsible for the deaths of 39 civilians. Gerry Fitt, deputy chief executive of the short-lived power sharing executive and Liam Cosgrave. the Irish taoiseach were both calling for military intervention by the British government, the latter on the basis of "no matter what it costs". Until the last moment it seemed as if the British government might be prepared to do just that, but doubtless warned of the likely casualties by the newly-appointed GOC Northern Ireland, General Sir Frank King, the government backed down. This was the end of Sunningdale and any prospect of power-sharing for a generation. The distinguished journalist Robert Fisk described the event at the time as "a million British citizens, the Protestants of Northern Ireland, staged what amounted to a rebellion against the government and won.... During those fifteen days ... a section of the realm became totally ungovernable."

5. In the course of the second instalment of the "Troubles" from 1969 onwards the British army in Northern Ireland from time to time continued to turn up caches of carefully greased arms dating from this period, ready for immediate use subject only to de-greasing.

6. Countess (Constance) Markievicz, née Gore-Booth (1868-1927) Sinn Féin and Fianna Fail politician, revolutionary nationalist and suffragette, landscape painter and daughter of an Anglo-Irish baronet Sir Henry Gore-Booth. She was the first woman to be elected to the UK House of Commons in December 1918 although she never took her seat. Her title of countess derived from her Polish husband, Count Casimir Markievicz.

7. The comparative ruthlessness of the Free State authorities towards the anti-treaty republicans following the end of the Anglo-Irish war is often overlooked. Erskine Childers was among a total of 77 republicans executed during this period. By contrast the British had merely executed 24 of "the rebels" in the course of the Anglo-Irish war. Until his (accidental) death on 12 August 1922 the President of the Dáil Éireann (who had also been one of the principal treaty negotiators) was Arthur Griffith, the actual founder of Sinn Féin, and of Welsh descent – yet another ambiguity of Anglo-Irish relations.

8. *Twenty-five Years – 1892-1916* Viscount Grey of Falloden 1925

9. "Until August 1914 a sensible, law-abiding Englishman could pass through life and hardly notice the existence of the state, beyond the post office and the policeman" – the opening words of AJP Taylor's *English History 1914-1945* OUP 1965.

10. *The Lawyers' Quotation Book* edited by John Reay-Smith – Robert Hale London 1991. Like so many Irish lawyers who have practised in England, James Comyn had a way with words and used them to good effect, especially as a jury advocate. As one commentator said of him when he was still at the Bar "Jimmy can take the stink out of anything!"

11. It was only since 1885 that the Society had been responsible for the library – see Chapter Five.

12. As to the Poor Prisoners Defence Act 1903, see also Chapter Twelve The Post War Years 1945-1960 p. 241.

13. The overall limit of 20 mph was to remain until the coming into force of the Road Traffic Act 1930. Prior to 1903 the relevant law was contained in the Locomotives on Highways Act 1896 which had increased the speed limit for motor-cars to 14 mph. Before that they had been limited to 4 mph in rural areas and 2 mph in towns. The first recorded conviction of a motorist for exceeding the speed limit of 2 mph in a built-up area (ie before the 1896 Act came into force) was that of Walter Arnold. A constable in Kent was quietly having his dinner when he happened to look out of the window and saw Arnold speeding by at an estimated 8 mph. With an admirable devotion to duty, he abandoned his meal, grabbed his helmet, jumped on his bike and gave chase. Five miles later he was at last able to overtake the miscreant, flag him down and book him. The result was an appearance before the Tonbridge justices on 28 January 1896 which resulted in a fine of one shilling (5p) plus costs. If only…The presence of motorised vehicles on highways was a highly controversial subject at this period and parliamentary debates over speed limits were acrimonious.

14. By S.1 of the Solicitors Act 1933 the Law Society had been authorised for the first time to introduce practice rules (subject to the approval of the Master of the Rolls). The extraordinary scope and detail of what is effectively the statutory control of the minutiae of solicitors' practice is a fairly modern phenomenon. In an article in the Law Society Gazette on 1 April 2010 Andrew Hopper and Gregory Treverton-Jones, looking back on the changes since 1936 observed "The single most dramatic change was in the size of the rule book. The first set of rules, the Solicitors Practice Rules 1936, made by virtue of section 1 of the Solicitors Act 1933, comprised seven rules (in reality only four) and could be printed on one page. In summary this comprised – rule 1: no touting; rule 2: no charging under the published scale fees (!); rule 3: no fee sharing; rule 4: no association with ambulance chasers." Between 1936 and 1972 the rules had escalated

somewhat to 13 pages. Since 1972, however, as practitioners will be well-aware, the increase has accelerated exponentially.

15. The Latin phrase *inopes consilii* conveyed both the notion of being deprived of advice and of destitution. It was used in the past to justify a greater latitude to those deemed to be *inopes consilii* when construing their wills. One is inevitably reminded of Serjeant Sullivan's riposte to a questioning judge in the Court of Appeal when addressing them on behalf of a workman injured at work: "Has your client never heard of the maxim *volenti non fit injuria?*" To which the fearless Irish Serjeant had only one appropriate answer: "My Lord, it is the sole topic of conversation in the little village of Antrim from which my client comes".

16. AJP Taylor (ed) *Lloyd George*.

Chapter Nine

ARMAGEDDON – THE GREAT WAR 1914–1918

"Your Committee note with pride and gratitude the long roll of members of the Society and the clerks of members who have volunteered and are serving their King and Country."

Report to members 28 January 1916

To mark the beginning of the new century the London publishing house of George Allen had decided to bring out *The Living Rulers of Mankind* in twelve monthly parts – "A popular Biographical Account of all the living EMPERORS, KINGS and QUEENS of the WORLD and their Families, together with all the reigning PRINCES, PRESIDENTS, RAJAS, and SULTANS". Its author, the Rev HN Hutchinson, BA, FGS, FRGS, previously responsible for *"Extinct Monsters, Marriage Customs of Many Lands* ETC, ETC", clearly had broad interests. Nevertheless, the reverend polymath cannot have foreseen that within so few years of his panegyric the world of EMPERORS, KINGS and QUEENS to say nothing of PRINCES … RAJAS, and SULTANS would be seriously diminished. True, with the benefit of hindsight, his judgment does seem to have been somewhat open to question in certain respects – his verdict on Kaiser Wilhelm II for example: " … combining in himself several of the noblest types. He is, above all, brave, morally and physically, and honest" and commending him for "the purity of his motives and the loftiness of his ideals". In 1914 the German, Austrian and Russian empires between them accounted for by far the greater part of central and eastern Europe. The Ottoman empire still had a toe-hold in SE Europe – and their former territories in the Balkans, including Greece, were all independent kingdoms or principalities. The Scandinavian countries of Sweden, Norway and Denmark were all monarchies, as were the Netherlands and Belgium. Luxembourg was a Grand Duchy, Andorra, Monaco and Liechtenstein were Principalities and Italy and Spain were kingdoms, as of course was the United Kingdom of Great Britain and Ireland whose King Emperor equally ruled over India and much else besides. Before the war, therefore, there were only three European countries flying the flag of a republic: France, Switzerland and Portugal, or four if you include the minuscule Republic of San Marino. Even Portugal had only joined the republican club very recently – as the result of a coup against its monarchy in 1910.

On the face of it this was hardly a vote of confidence for republicanism[1] but sometimes in history a single event can precipitate momentous change. One such event was the assassination on 28 June 1914 in a small provincial town in Bosnia of the Archduke Franz Ferdinand, the Austrian Emperor's nephew and heir to his throne. In little over a month it proved to be the catalyst which brought about a world war and changed both face and fate of Europe for ever.

How precisely this came about has been the subject of endless analysis and debate by historians and politicians ever since. Was it somehow historically inevitable given the nature of European power politics in the second half of the 19th century or could it have been avoided if only the ruling classes of the day had been less insouciant? The more thoughtful and well-informed could see what was coming. In 1913 Pope Pius X had observed to a departing Brazilian ambassador[2] that Europe would not get through 1914 without a major war – and yet so many seem to have been caught completely off-guard. In some ways the most surprising element in this most extraordinary disaster is that at the outset at least three of the five principal belligerents, the United Kingdom, Russia and Germany, were headed by sovereigns who were closely related: our own King George V and his cousins Nicky (the Tsar) and Willy (the Kaiser) whose mother, Victoria (1840–1901) Empress of Germany and Queen of Prussia was equally the eldest daughter of Queen Victoria and Princess Royal. Indeed, she was generally referred to in Germany as *die Engländerin* and normally spoke English in her own household. And although Franz

Jozef, the Emperor of Austria-Hungary may have regarded the German Kaiser with considerable reservations, if not disdain – a sentiment shared by Nicky's English cousin King George – he was his ally, albeit somewhat reluctantly. At a purely personal level, Franz Jozef was on much more friendly terms with the British Royals and they with him. When the news of the assassination of Franz Ferdinand and his wife at Sarajevo first reached him on 28 June 1914 King George noted in his journal "Terrible shock for the dear old Emperor". "Poor Emperor, nothing is he spared" noted Queen Mary a few days later.[3]

In the light of subsequent events we can see that the post-war dismemberment of the Austro-Hungarian empire did not prove to be the solution to central European and Balkan problems that the optimists at the Versailles Peace Conference of 1919 had hoped. Equally, the assassination of the Tsar and his family and the overthrow of his empire did not do much for the Russian people either. Indeed, the whole titanic struggle produced no lasting settlement and merely stored up much worse problems for the future: the emergence of Hitlerite Germany which was to precipitate the second world war, the Stalinist terror in Russia and post-war Soviet expansionism from 1945 onwards, ethnic cleansing in the former Yugoslavia and the current Arab-Israeli conflict – all owe their origins in one way or another to that fateful assassination in Bosnia in the summer of 1914.

The battle casualties were truly appalling – for Britain between 700,000 and 800,000 altogether were killed either immediately on the field of battle or shortly afterwards. The figures are not precise because of problems of definition. The number of those severely and permanently wounded, was of course higher still and many of them were to die prematurely as a consequence of injuries or disease contracted as a result of war service.

There were also some civilian deaths due to air raids. The Zeppelin attacks in particular lingered in the popular imagination, but these only accounted for 498 deaths. More civilians, 619 altogether, were killed in conventional attacks by aircraft. The biggest number of fatalities in one day occurred on 13 June 1917 when a total of 158 civilians lost their lives in Margate, Essex and London. Some civilian deaths were the result of naval shelling; Scarborough, Whitby and Hartlepool all suffered in this way. But even the casualty figures do not really convey the sheer size of the armies involved in the conflict – numbered in millions. The shortage of labour was dire, notwithstanding a huge influx of women doing "men's work" as it had hitherto been regarded. In the latter stages of the war this was causing great difficulties for solicitors' firms everywhere.

There is comparatively little in the Society's minutes and committee reports of the 1914 -1918 period to give much clue as to the seismic events occurring across the channel and indeed across the world but the effect on the day-to-day lives of members, their families and their staff was incredibly disruptive. The first indication we have of this disruption appears in the committee's report to members at the 130th Annual Meeting on 28 January 1916:

> It will be noticed that your Committee has held very few meetings during the year, and as a matter of fact the war has dominated everything and it was felt that the early cry of business as usual was no longer suitable and that all extraneous business which could be avoided should be, so that your overburdened officials should not be distracted from the work which they had to carry on very shorthanded by work in connection with the Society, which might very fairly be left over to a more convenient season.

The report goes on to note that the finances of the Society were in a healthy condition and that although subscriptions were down due to the fact that those of members serving with HM Forces had been remitted, this was more than counterbalanced by the fact that no dinner had been held. The penultimate paragraph of the report headed simply "The War" does, however, make it clear that the committee knew well-enough the sacrifice that so many members were enduring and would endure for another three years almost:

> Your Committee note with pride and gratitude the long roll of members of the Society and the clerks of members who have volunteered and are serving their King and Country. It is suggested that after the war their names should be inscribed on a board to be put up in the Law Library.

Two years later, at the annual meeting of the Society held on 29 January 1918, when the Battle of the Somme had taken its appalling toll, the Battle of Passchendaele had just passed its climax and the country had over a year's experience of conscription, unlimited submarine warfare with its threat of starvation and the dreaded novelty of air-raids, it was clear that "business as usual" was but a distant memory and there was still little prospect of a return to anything approaching normality. The main problem was manpower:

> Increasing difficulty having been found with regard to depletion of Solicitors Offices by the War, your Committee, in the month of October, decided to appoint an Advisory Committee, consisting of the whole of the members of the Committee of the Yorkshire Law Society to act with regard to such places in the North and East Ridings of the County of York as have not already appointed local Advisory Committees, for the purpose of assisting the Military Authorities in coming to conclusion on claims for exemption[4] put in by Solicitors on behalf of themselves or their clerks. This Advisory Committee is now in working order.

By this stage members of the Society, along with everyone else in the country, would have had no illusions whatsoever about the truly appalling casualties inflicted by this war of attrition. The suggestion of erecting a memorial in the Society's library, first mooted two years earlier, was still very much in the committee's mind:

> Your Committee propose to place in the Law Library a permanent record in the shape of a War Shrine, of those members of the Society or Clerks of members who have made in the war the supreme sacrifice by death. They also propose to place there a roll of all members and articled clerks of members who have joined HM Forces, with a record of all distinctions, honours and mentions of those who have gained them.

On 11 November 1918 peace came at last following the failure of Ludendorff's spring offensives. It had indeed been a war of attrition and thanks to the arrival on the scene of the American "doughboys"[5] in sufficient numbers, 943,000 by the end of July, Germany's fate was sealed: they had run out of men first but it was a tragic way to run a war for all concerned and, as we now know beyond all doubt, the ensuing peace in fact settled nothing and unsettled just about everything. It only remained for the Society to redeem its pledge.

THE WAR MEMORIAL

In the 1930s the term "Thankful Village" was coined to designate those English villages – the survey only extended to England – which were reckoned to have lost no inhabitants, in other words those whose men (and women) had gone off to war from that particular location and had all returned safely. As for all war casualties, there is inevitably an element of inexactitude – for example, as to how precisely one defines "inhabitant". At most there were only 50 or so such villages and of these five were in Yorkshire, Catwick north of Beverley, Cundall near Thirsk, Helperthorpe in the Wolds, Norton-le-Clay near Ripon and Scruton near Northallerton. Author and journalist Arthur Mee, who coined the expression, said of the first, "thirty men went from Catwick to the Great War and thirty came back, though one left an arm behind." Members of the Yorkshire Law Society and those associated with it, that is to say articled clerks and staff, were not so lucky and had rather less reason to be thankful as sixty-four went and seventeen failed to return at all. When hostilities were at last concluded the Society decided to commission a war memorial to commemorate all those who had lost their lives or who had served in "the war to end wars". This was formally unveiled on 8 March 1922 by Mr Commissioner Ashton KC, acting as Judge of Assize and a large gathering of members. Originally Bray and McCardie JJ, the two judges of assize were proposing to attend but in the event neither was able to be present.

Brief biographical details of those who died are set out below, together with the names and regimental details of those who served but survived. The information is based on the Society's own War Memorial supplemented by the *Record of Service of Solicitors and Articles Clerks in His Majesty's Service 1914-1919* (originally published by the Solicitors War Memorial Fund in 1920) together with details from the Commonwealth War Graves Commission's own records and a few other miscellaneous sources. The information is believed to be substantially correct but the Society would be glad to receive particulars of any errors or omissions.

According to the Committee's report to the Annual General Meeting held on 28 January 1914 the Society at that time consisted of 122 members and four honorary members (His Honour Fossett Lock, His Honour Judge Templar, WA Meek Esq, the ex-Recorder of York and HT Kemp

Esq, the Recorder of York). A further six members were admitted at that AGM, bringing the total of ordinary members to 128. Ten members lost their lives on the battlefield – nearly 8% of the total membership at the outbreak of war. If one adds the seven articled clerks who equally lost their lives one begins to have some notion of the sheer scale of the casualties. Its devastating effect on a relatively small professional community can scarcely be imagined. But then one has to take into account the number of members and staff who served in the armed forces and survived – a total of 48 altogether, making a grand total of 65 including those who died.

The Committee minutes for 8 May 1922 record that the Hon Sec read out letters of thanks from relatives of those who had lost their lives for the photographs of the memorial which had been sent to them on behalf of the Society.

Members who died

Bushell, Horace — Admitted January 1913. Practised in York. Joined September 1914 as Private in 21st Bn. Royal Fusiliers. Commissioned in Machine Gun Corps September 1916. Promoted to Lieutenant June 1917 and Captain March 1918. Killed in action near Cherisy (Pas de Calais) 6 September 1918 and buried at Sun Quarry Cemetery 13km SE of Arras.

Dale, Alwynne Percy — Admitted October 1906. Member 1911. Practised in Knaresborough and York. mobilised August 1914 as Captain in 5th Bn. West Yorkshire Regiment and subsequently promoted to Major. Awarded OBE. Served in France and killed in action 1 March 1917 and buried at Queens Cemetery Bucquoy, Pas de Calais.

Edmundson, Charles Robert Ewbank — Admitted February 1914. Practised in Masham and Ripon. Joined as Private in Middlesex Regiment. Ten days later commissioned and attached to 8th Bn. Yorkshire and Lancashire Regiment. Promoted Lieutenant January 1915, Captain February 1915. Killed at the Battle of the Somme, 1 July 1916 and buried at Adanac Cemetery, Miraumont, Somme. Awarded posthumous MC.

Knowles, Frank Henry — Admitted November 1911. Practised in York. Joined August 1914 as Captain in 5th Bn. West Yorkshire Regiment. Served in France. Killed in action at Bullecourt (Pas de Calais) 3 May 1917. Grave unknown. Commemorated on the Arras Memorial along with 32,794 others with no known grave. The First and Second Battles of Bullecourt in April and May 1917 were part of the ill-fated Nivelle Offensive, and fairly typical of their type – ie little was gained and the losses horrific. Of the British troops attacking on the other flank of the village of Bullecourt, consisting of the 2/6th West Yorkshires, only 100 men made it back to their trenches in one piece; all the others having been killed, wounded or captured.

Mackay, Donald Paley — Admitted May 1909. Member of the firm Russell & Mackay of York. Mobilised August 1914 as Captain 1st/5th Bn. West Yorkshire Regiment and subsequently promoted Major. Served in France from April 1915 to October 1917. Killed in action at Passchendaele 9 October 1917. Grave unknown. Commemorated on the Tyne Cot Memorial 9km NE of Ypres.

Robson, Edward Moore Admitted October 1912. Managing Clerk with Messrs Rider Heaton & Co of 8, New Square, Lincoln's Inn. Joined 5th Bn. Yorkshire Regiment and subsequently promoted to Lieutenant and then Captain. Awarded MC. Served at home and in France and Belgium. Twice wounded. Killed in action 11 April 1918. Grave unknown. Commemorated on the Ploegsteert Memorial, Hainaut, 12km S of Ypres.

Robson, Frank William Brother of above. Admitted August 1909. Practised in Pocklington. Mobilised August 1914 as Captain in 5th Bn. Yorkshire Regiment. Went overseas in April 1915 and slightly wounded at Battle of St Julien the same month. Promoted to Lt-Colonel. Appointed to command 6th Bn. Durham Light Infantry in 1917. Three times mentioned in dispatches and awarded DSO. Served at home and in France and Belgium. Killed in action 28 March 1918. Grave unknown. Commemorated on the Poziers Memorial, 6km NE of Albert (Somme).

Turnbull, William Andrew Admitted 1902. Member, Turnbull & Sons, Scarborough. Joined 5th Bn. Yorkshire Regiment September 1914 and subsequently gazetted as 2nd Lieutenant in the same regiment. Wounded at Hooge in 1915. Killed in action 17 July 1916 and buried at La Laterie Cemetery, 7km S of Ypres.

Thompson, Frank Charles — Admitted April 1896. Practised in York. Mobilised as Captain in 5th Bn. West Yorkshire Regiment August 1914. Promoted Major 1915. Once mentioned in dispatches. Served in France from April 1915 to July 1916. Reported missing at the Battle of the Somme 2 July 1916 and presumed to have been killed that day. Grave unknown. Commemorated on the Thiepval Memorial, one of 72,194 commemorated there with no known grave.

Ward, Cecil Wellesley — Admitted 1906. Member of Cowling & Swift, York. Joined Royal Field Artillery as 2nd Lieutenant. Served in Flanders. Killed in action there 12 September 1917 and buried at Lindenhoek Chalet Cemetry 9km SW of Ypres.

Articled Clerks who died

Bromet, John Neville — Articled to GA Bromet of Tadcaster. Joined Middlesex Bn. Public Schools & University Corps as Private September 1914. Gazetted 2nd Lieutenant Royal Field Artillery October 1914. Promoted Lieutenant July 1915. Served in France. Killed in action Gouzeaucourt (Nord) 15km SW of Cambrai 30 November 1917. Grave unknown. Commemorated at Cambrai Memorial, Louverval, some 16km SW of Cambrai. Another officer 'missing, presumed killed' at Gouzeaucourt just two months earlier on 25 September that year was Mortimer Edward Harold Schiff, a Captain in the Suffolk Regiment and in civilian life a solicitor managing clerk at Stephenson Harwood & Co of Lombard Street.

Unusually for an officer in the British Army at that time, he was of German parentage, his father Herman Schiff being a stockbroker's agent in London, although Harold himself was born in London and a graduate of Jesus College Cambridge.

The village of Gouzeaucourt was one which had changed hands repeatedly in the course of the war. It had originally been occupied by the Germans in December 1914 who remained there until it was recaptured by the 8th Division in April 1917. Lost again seven months later in the German counter-offensive of 30 November (the day on which Lt Bromet died), it was recaptured once more by the Irish Guards later the same day. Lost yet again on 22 March 1918, it was attacked without success by the 38th Welsh Division on 18 September. It finally changed hands for the last time following an attack by the 21st Division on 8 October, just over a month before the war's end – only to be retaken by the Germans in May 1940 before finally falling to the Americans in September 1944. A Commonwealth War Grave Commission sign at Gouzeaucourt identifies a total of 1,296 burials, subsequently reduced to 1,295. Of these, 1,181 were identified as British, 3 as Canadians, 85 as New Zealanders, 24 as South Africans, 1 as Indian and 2 as Russians.

Dearden, Reginald Articled to HS Thompson, Harrogate. Joined 4th (University and Public Schools) Bn. September 1914, 21st Royal Fusiliers as Private. Went to France November 1915 as

Divisional Cyclist with 33rd Division and in May 1916 joined 1st Bn. Cameronians (Scottish Rifles). Killed in action at High Wood, Mametz at Battle of the Somme 16 July 1916. Grave unknown but commemorated on the Thiepval Monument.

Elmhirst, William — Articled to CE Elmhirst of York. Joined 9th Bn. East Yorkshire Regiment as 2nd Lieutenant. Promoted to Lieutenant and then Captain. Served at home and in France. Killed in action at Serre 13 November 1916 and buried at Serre Road Cemetery No. 1, 11km NNE of Albert (Pas de Calais).

Garbutt, Joseph Herbert — Articled to HE Harrowell, York. Joined 28th Bn. City of London Regiment (Artists Rifles) as Private. Promoted Sergeant October 1918. Served in France and Belgium. Killed in action at Harveng, Belgium 10 November 1918 and buried, with two other soldiers of his regiment killed on the same day, at Harveng Churchyard south of Mons.

Hutchinson Hanley — Admitted October 1913. Practised in Ripon. Joined 5th Bn. West Yorkshire Regiment as Lieutenant. Subsequently appointed Machine Gun Officer to Brigade. Served in France. Wounded 31 August 1917; died 1 September 1917 and buried at Grevillers British Cemetery 3km W of Bapaume (Pas de Calais).

The Thiepval Memorial, designed by Sir Edward Lutyens, commemorates the 72,194 members of the UK and South African forces who died in the Somme sector before 20 March 1918 and who have no known grave. Among them were Frederick Charles Thompson (missing, presumed killed on 2 July 1916) and Reginal Dearden (killed in action on 16 July 1916). Members of other allied forces are commemorated in other memorials in the area.

Thiepval Memorial © CWGC

Harveng Churchyard © CWGC

This tiny CWGC cemetery of just six graves forms part of the village churchyard at Harveng, near Mons. The grave of Sgt Joseph Garbutt (aged 24 and articled to HE Harrowell of York) is fourth from the left, buried here with two others of his regiment, all three killed in action on 10 November 1918. Mons was where the war's first serious engagement between British and German troops had occurred in August 1914. Just 7km to the north of Harveng is St Symphorien (mixed) military cemetery, the last resting place of both German and Commonwealth soldiers of the Battle of Mons where the slaughter had begun. Among those killed in that opening battle and who lie buried there are Lt Maurice Dease, also aged 24, of the 4th Bn. Royal Fusiliers and Musketier Oskar Niemeyer of the 84th (German) Infantry Division, the first recipients respectively of the Victoria Cross and the Iron Cross in that conflict.

Morley, David Articled to JW Mills, Beverley. Joined Argyll & Sutherland Highlanders as Private, December 1914 and subsequently promoted Corporal. Gazetted 2nd Lieutenant 4th Bn. East Yorkshire Regiment and attached to 13th Bn. December 1916. Served in France and Salonika and again in France. Killed near Arras 16 June 1917 and buried at Bailleul Road East Cemetery, St Laurent-Blagny (Pas de Calais).

Peters, Gerard Clerk with Collyer, Bristow & Co, 4, Bedford Row, London WC. Joined Inns of Court OTC as Private October 1915. Gazetted 2nd Lieutenant 6th Bn. Gloucestershire Regiment September 1916. Served in France. Died in action (heart failure through exhaustion) near Chaulnes 24 February 1917 and buried at Fouquercourt British Cemetery 35km E of Arras.

Perhaps the most poignant in many ways of all the deaths recorded on the Society's War Memorial is that of articled clerk, Sergeant David Garbutt, killed in action on 10 November 1918, the day before the armistice – see entry on page 174 and illustration on page 175. A surprising number of men lost their lives at this time, many on the very morning of Armistice Day prior to the 11am cease-fire. In some cases they were the victims of obsessive officers, anxious for their moment of glory before an armistice which everybody knew was imminent. My own grandfather who had miraculously survived both the Battles of the Somme and Passchendaele, being wounded only once, almost certainly escaped death on that same day, 10 November, but only by an uncharacteristic refusal to obey orders. He and his unit had refused an order to carry out a suicide mission from just such an officer, determined to make his mark by capturing a bridge over a canal in Belgium defended by a fiercely determined German machine-gunner. With the armistice the following day, this mini-mutiny was sensibly and quietly overlooked by someone higher up the chain of command. Had it occurred at any other time the mutineers would probably have been court-martialled, convicted and shot.

Solicitor Members who served

Anderson, Major HF	11th Sherwood Foresters
Dodsworth, Captain B OBE	General Staff
Green, Lt D, MC	Royal Garrison Artillery
Green, Major W	East Yorkshire Regiment
Haigh, Lt JJ, MC	5th Bn Yorkshire & Lancashire Regiment
Hewitt, Lt AE	Home Staff
Hall, Lt AH	Royal Army Flying Corps
Hill, Lt EH	Royal Garrison Artillery
Hunt, Capt J	4th Bn. North Lancashire Regiment
Hunton, Capt WB	3rd Bn. Yorkshire Regiment
Jones, Capt ES	York
Maughan, Lt GH	Royal Field Artillery
Pearson, Major HW	East Riding Yeomanry
Pearson, Capt RT, MC	Royal Army Flying Corps
Peters, Capt JC, MC	5th Bn. West Yorkshire Regiment
Petty, Bombadier RS	Royal Garrison Artillery
Proctor, Pte JN	Royal Army Medical Corps
Puckering, Pte WE	Officers Training Corps
Scott, Lt-Colonel HC	West Yorkshire Regiment
Snowball, Major JS, MC	Machine Gun Corps
Whitehead, Capt JL 3rd Bn.	Yorkshire Regiment
Wilberforce, Lt-Colonel HH, DSO	Royal Army Flying Corps
Green, 2nd Lt HS	East Riding Yeomanry

Solicitors with members

Munby, JD 2nd Lt	MTRA
Stewart, Capt DN	Welch Regiment
Shaftoe, Capt HI	5th Bn. West Yorkshire Regiment
Gaunt, Lt-Colonel A OBE	5th Bn. West Yorkshire Regiment

Articled Clerks who served

Brown, Lt HN	5th Bn. King's Regiment
Butterworth, Major J OBE	AP Corps
Dawson, 2nd Lt W	Royal Air Force
Dixon, Cpl M	Royal Garrison Artillery
Dickinson, L/Cpl J	Royal Army Service Corps
Gardner, Major GD, MC	IT Med 4th Bn. Yorkshire Regiment
Gill, Capt RS	Royal Army Service Corps
Hesketh, Sgt S	Royal Air Force
Hopkins, Air Mech H	Royal Air Force
Johnstone, Pte WR	Officer Training Corps
Kay, Lt W	5th Bn. West Yorkshire Regiment
Kay, Pte WA	Royal Air Force
Mackay, Capt K, MC	5th Bn. West Yorkshire Regiment
Millhouse, Lt G	8th Bn. Yorkshire Regiment
Procter, Capt AK	Royal Army Flying Corps
Raworth, Lt RG	Royal Engineers
Trundle, Capt AL, Croix de Guerre	RFA
Turner, Capt GM	Royal Air Force
Waddington, Capt HL	Royal Air Force
Ware, Capt IN	RGA

Wood, Major RM   5th Bn. West Yorkshire Regiment

The following report appeared in *The Yorkshire Herald* on Thursday 9 March 1922:

YORKSHIRE LAW SOCIETY MEMORIAL
Unveiled by Mr Commissioner Ashton
The Legal Profession's Proud Record

In the presence of a large gathering of members of the legal profession from all parts of the county, Mr Commissioner Ashton KC last evening unveiled the war memorial erected to the memory of the members of the Yorkshire Law Society who fought and fell in the Great War. The memorial, which is erected in a conspicuous position in the Law Society's Library in Coney Street, takes the form of an oak triptych, the work of Messrs WH Smith and Sons. In the centre panel in gold lettering are recorded the names of eleven solicitors and seven articled clerks who made the supreme sacrifice, and surmounting the panel is the inscription:–

THE YORKSHIRE LAW SOCIETY
To the Glory of God
AND IN GRATEFUL MEMORY OF OUR BROTHERS WHO FELL IN THE GREAT WAR, 1914 – 1919

The wing panels contain the names of the solicitors and articled clerks who served with the Forces.

The Yorkshire Herlad report continues with the various names and regiments of those who died and those who served as they appear on the Society's memorial.

A RECORD TO BE PROUD OF

Mr ER Dodsworth (President of the Yorkshire Law Society) presided at the unveiling at which the Commissioner was accompanied by his

Marshall, the High Sheriff of Yorkshire (Mr JL Dugdale) and the High Sheriff's Chaplain.

The President, before calling upon the Commissioner to perform the ceremony, said it seemed singularly appropriate that they should have the memorial unveiled by a direct representative of the King himself. The Yorkshire Law Society was celebrated for its antiquity, it approaching something like the 150th year of its reign. That there was considerable vigour and activity in the Society was shown by the fact that out of 124 members at the commencement of the war, 65 joined up and went to fight for their country. It had to be remembered that out of the total number of members a large number were disqualified by age and other infirmities from joining up, so that made the proportion who did go still larger. It was very sad to think that one out of every four of the members who did go never returned. That was a very large proportion indeed compared with the mortality in the rest of the country. The members of the Society thought that by setting up a memorial they would provide inspiration for those who came after them in their profession to do their duty in the same way if called upon to do so.

THE UNVEILING

Mr Commissioner Ashton after unveiling the memorial, said Mr Justice Bray regretted very much his inability to be present. Although speaking on behalf of the Judges of Assize, he would rather also speak in his natural character, as a member of that branch of their great profession to which he belonged. He was probably the only barrister present and he was glad to think on behalf of that branch of the profession he could express sympathy with their branch of the profession in the City of York. In his own profession, in his own circuit they had quite a different memorial. They had – or he should say they were going to have – a statuette upon a pedestal, on which would be the names of those members of the circuit who fell. The difference between the two memorials was that in the barristers' case, as they wandered around and were pilgrims on the circuit they would take the statuette with them. So just as the Law Society had erected a memorial in their own home to remind them with affection and pride of those who had fallen, they in his circuit took round with them their memorial of those whom they respected and loved.

The President thanked the Commissioner for unveiling the memorial and the ceremony concluded with the singing of the National Anthem.

(The Society's memorial is currently (2016) on display at the Castle Museum, York as part of its special exhibition *1914: When the World Changed for Ever* to mark the centenary of the First World War.)

NOTES

1. Norway, which was only to achieve its peaceful independence from Sweden in 1905, held a national referendum which expressed a preference for a monarchy rather than a republic. The throne was then offered to Prince Carl of Denmark who, as Haakon VII, became the first king of a fully independent Norway in 586 years.

2. At a formal international level the position of the Vatican (technically distinct from the Holy See) in 1914 was anomalous. The territory of the Papal States, formerly constituting a large part of central Italy, had been forcibly incorporated into the Kingdom of Italy in 1870. This *de facto* incorporation had never been accepted by the papacy and the resulting diplomatic stand-off came to be known as "the Roman Question". It was only resolved by the Lateran Treaty of 1929 which created the international territorial entity now known as the Vatican City. At one level this might be fairly described as a statelet but nevertheless the nature of its relationship with the Holy See is such that it is very well placed to know what is happening in the world. It is for this reason that whatever their confessional position or whatever their theoretical or ideological reservations might be, over 170 states, including the United Kingdom, deem it useful to have diplomatic relations with it.

3. This was a reference to the succession of family misfortunes which Franz Jozef had suffered over the years – the execution of his brother Maximilian, the ill-fated Emperor of Mexico, by Mexican revolutionaries in 1867, the suicide of his son Crown Prince Rudolf with his mistress at Mayerling in 1889, the death of his sister-in-law Sophie in Paris in a disastrous fire which killed 200 people attending a Charity Bazar in Paris in 1897 and the assassination of his wife, the Empress Elisabeth the following year, stabbed to death by an Italian anarchist whilst she was on holiday for her health in Geneva.

4. Questions of exemption or deferment were also to cause acute problems for solicitors during the Second World War – see Chapter 11 p. 213-214.

5. The origin of the term "doughboys" to describe American infantrymen, and by later extension, other members of the American military, is obscure but it certainly seems to have been in use at the time of the American-Mexican war of 1846-7. It was never used in a derogatory sense but did not survive into the Second World War when it was replaced by "GI" – "general issue", assumed to be a reference to every item of equipment which they carried which, with typical soldiers' irony, they then seem to have attached to themselves. Britain's "Tommies" had a much older origin which did survive into the Second World War and beyond. It is thought to have come into general use in 1815 when an official publication used the name "Thomas Atkins" when providing guidance as to how to fill in a soldier's pay book. It may have been in use much earlier.

Chapter Ten

BETWEEN THE WARS
1919 – 1939

"Curious! I seem to hear a child weeping"

Will Dyson

If the actual scale of the slaughter of "the war to end all wars" was largely due to the failure of the generals and their thinking, the failure of the peace settlement was largely due to the failure of the politicians and their thinking. One of the comparatively few contemporaries to grasp that failure *and* its implications, curiously enough, was an Australian illustrator, political cartoonist and poet, Will Dyson (1880-1938). In 1919 Dyson was working in London and on 17 May the *Daily Herald* published the iconic cartoon for which he is best known and which many regard as the most astonishingly prophetic political cartoon of all time. It shows Wilson, the US President, Lloyd George and Orlando, the UK and Italian Prime Ministers, leaving a meeting of the Peace Conference with Georges Clemenceau, the French Prime Minister, "the Tiger". It was Clemenceau, the President of the Conference, whose visceral hatred of Germany and the Germans and determination "to make Germany pay" set the tone – a tone which Lloyd George was more than ready to follow, as Cabinet Secretary Maurice Hankey's diary reveals:[1]

> Lloyd George, under the stimulus of our remarkable military success, showed a very hard attitude, talking of judgements and penalties. I fear he may over-rate our power and miss securing a good peace which will, as far as possible, remove bones of contention ... [He] is out for blood and wants to give Germany a thorough hiding. In fact he actually used the term "destroy Germany" as punishment for the atrocities by land and sea.

Will Dyson's prophetic cartoon which appeared in the Daily Herald on 13 May 1919.

Dyson's caption reads "Curious! I seem to hear a child weeping". The child represents the "call-up" class of 1940. Dyson was only one year out in his prediction although Hankey's diary reveals that the popular mood of the time notwithstanding, there were thoughtful and well-informed people who could see that humiliating Germany was merely storing up a great pack of political troubles for the future.[2] If Clausewitz was right and "Victory is the creation of a better political reality" then the allied "victory" was at best hollow.

Not the least of those troubles was the tremendous impetus it gave to an instinctive need among those who had endured such appalling suffering to find a scapegoat. In Britain this manifested itself in the relatively harmless anodyne of blaming the generals – more specifically "cavalry" generals. This was hardly a rational reaction but it was surprisingly widespread even among those who really should have known better. It suited the prejudices of the time: cavalry officers, so a popular notion went, were useless upper-class wastrels who had used their connections to acquire a stranglehold on senior military appointments; everyone knew that. Some may have been useless but the belief that they dominated senior ranks was complete nonsense and yet this absurd myth persisted. "The army chiefs were mostly horsemen ... " (Lloyd George, *War Memoirs*). " ... most British Generals were cavalry men." (AJP Taylor, *The First World War*). "All our generals were cavalrymen ... " (Robert Graves, *Promises of Greatness*). Lloyd George, of course, had been Prime Minister for the latter part of the war, AJP Taylor was an Oxford professor and a leading historian of the period and Robert Graves, a noted poet and classicist who had himself been a serving officer on the Western Front and seriously injured at the Battle of the Somme. Had any of them bothered to consult the Army List they would have discovered that the British Army in 1914 had altogether eight Field Marshals (excluding royalty) of whom two were cavalrymen, 18 full Generals, of whom one was a cavalryman, 27 Lieutenant-Generals, of whom three were cavalrymen and 114 Major-Generals of whom eight were cavalrymen.

But Germany had not only been impoverished by the terms of the Versailles Treaty. Under the Weimar Republic stratospheric inflation which by the middle of November 1923 had resulted in an exchange rate of 4.2 billion marks against the US dollar had a devastating effect on the German middle classes and indeed on anyone whose savings were not directly asset based. Perhaps more significant than the direct economic loss and disruption was the fact that she had been humiliated. And how was such a great nation as Germany going to react to that humiliation?

For complex historical reasons anti-semitism had had a long and tragic history in Europe but under the influence of the Enlightenment and as a result of increasing integration it had been of declining significance for most of the 19th century. In its last years, however, there had been a sudden resurgence which was to cast a terrible shadow over the whole of the 20th century. It reached its apogee with the advent of Hitler in Germany and the Second World War, and its effects are with us still. It all began by the arrival in Central and Western Europe of the flood of Jewish refugees from the pogroms of Tsarist Russia. France, for example, had experienced the extraordinary anti-semitic eruption both illustrated and exacerbated by the infamous *Dreyfus* affair.[3] Captain Dreyfus's cause had prompted energetic support from France's left-inclined intelligentsia which in turn had resulted an equally energetic reaction from their opponents – right wing traditionalist Catholic monarchists with their inherent tendency to anti-semitism.

Both Austria and Germany had equally experienced a rash of anti-semitism, albeit in a rather different form and without the catalyst of the unfortunate Captain Dreyfus. In Vienna an increasing Jewish presence in the city had prompted anti-Jewish antagonism from about 1890 onwards among the city's working and small shopkeeper classes who regarded the new arrivals as competing for jobs and trade respectively. This was articulated by the lawyer politician Karl Lueger who founded the *Christlichsoziale Partei* (Christian Social Party) in 1893 which quickly became a serious player in the politics of the time. Eventually he managed to become Mayor of Vienna in 1897 – a position which he held until his death in 1910. To his great credit, the Emperor Franz Jozef, would have no truck with the fashionable anti-semitism of the day; he managed to block Lueger's accession to the mayoralty on three occasions, although he eventually succumbed to pressure from the Vatican in Lueger's favour. One feature of the prevailing anti-Jewish mood which particularly baffled the deeply Catholic Emperor was its prevalence among the Austrian upper classes. "Among the highest social circles", he wrote to the Empress Elisabeth in December 1895 "anti-semitism is an extraordinarily widespread disease and the agitation is unbelievable". Much later, after the outbreak of war, Russian successes in Galicia were forcing thousands more Jewish refugees into Vienna, thereby causing acute difficulties for the city authorities. This prompted Richard Weiskirchner, Lueger's successor as mayor, to suggest that they be settled in camps in Moravia. The Emperor would have none of it: "If Vienna has no more room for refugees" he had observed testily to Weiskirchner, "I shall make Schönbrunn available for my Jewish subjects." No more was heard about concentrating them in camps in Moravia.

In fact, despite his subsequent eulogy by Hitler in *Mein Kampf*, Lueger himself was, by all accounts, a popular and genial man, very much in the Austrian tradition of *Gemütlichkeit* and his municipal authority in Vienna had been fairly efficient and liberal. Certainly, his anti-semitism seems to have been more of a veneer designed to achieve electoral support rather than based on any personal animosity towards Jews. Once, asked to explain why so many of his friends were Jews, he famously replied "I decide who is a Jew!"

Germany too, had earlier experienced a very similar phenomenon when the Protestant pastor Adolf Stoecker had formed the *Christlich-Soziale Arbeitpartei* which even changed its name in 1881 to the almost identical *Christlich-Soziale Partei*. In Germany, however, the party had less influence amongst the German, especially the Prussian, aristocratic landowners, as it was more overtly socialist in tone than its Austrian counterpart. Also, the German anti-semitism was rather more sinister. Franz Jozef's bewilderment and irritation at the phenomenon was definitely not shared by Kaiser Wilhelm. Notoriously "anti-Jewish" before the outbreak of war, the experience of defeat only served to convince him that Germany's disaster at the hand of the Allies and especially the Americans was all the fault of the Jews. On 2 December 1919 just over a year after his abdication whilst in exile in the Netherlands the former Kaiser wrote to Field Marshal von Mackensen "Germany had been egged on and misled by the tribe of Judah. Let no German ever forget this, nor rest until these parasites have been destroyed and exterminated from German soil ... the Jews are a nuisance that humanity must get rid of some way or other. I believe the best would be gas."

How did Britain fit into this picture? By 1911 its Jewish population had increased very significantly, the majority being fairly recent immigrants from Russia and Poland. Like all immigrants everywhere these newcomers tended to settle where there were existing Jewish communities, with their own Jewish shops and synagogues. This in practice meant major cities such as London, Manchester, Leeds and Glasgow. Somewhat surprisingly the main source of friction in that year was in Cardiff, where the Jewish population of Wales was quite tiny – about 1,800. There were, however, local aggravating factors, including an eleven-month strike in the mining industry, combined with a railway strike, resulting in trouble which the authorities had sought to contain by dispatching a contingent of Metropolitan Police to the city to patrol strike areas. Members of the Cardiff Jewish community were generally neither miners nor railwaymen but were fairly well-represented among the small local shopkeepers whose prices had risen as a result of the strikes. With the lack of logic that is so often characteristic of such situations, this had resulted in what Home Secretary Winston Churchill had described as a "pogrom". Pogrom or not, he felt obliged to dispatch the Worcestershire Regiment to restore order. In January of that same year London's *Evening*

Standard had begun to publish a series of articles on the "alien problem" (For "alien" read "Jewish"). The first, which appeared on 25 January, was headlined: PROBLEM OF THE ALIEN – LONDON OVERRUN BY UNDESIRABLES – VAST FOREIGN AREAS – A GROWING MENACE.

The middle and upper classes on the whole were inclined to distance themselves from the cruder aspects of anti-semitism as manifested by rioting in working-class areas. For them it took a more subdued form: non-acceptance of applications for membership of golf clubs and such like.

The outbreak of war three years later had of course given Home Secretaries, police, army and headline writers more pressing worries but the so-called "Jewish question" was not one that was going to go away. Indeed, the pre-war experience in trying to resolve it led to the well-intentioned but incautious "Balfour Declaration" which lies at the very heart of the seemingly insoluble problems of the Middle East in our own day. In one sense, of course, the "Jewish Question" hardly impinged on the City of York at all since its Jewish population was negligible. This was due to the infamous massacre of Jews at Clifford's Tower in 1190. The York Hebrew Congregation had been formed in 1892 and a room at 9 Aldwark had been rented for services. When first established there had been about 20 families but by 1956 there were no more than eight and there was no resident Rabbi by this date. The Aldwark synagogue finally closed in 1975, although recently a newly established Liberal Jewish Community has been recognised by the Liberal Judaism Council and it is hoped to appoint a part-time Rabbi in the not too distance future. Nevertheless the "Jewish Question" was to become a leitmotiv of events on the continent of Europe which were to have a profound effect on the lives of all of us over the following years. To these events we shall have to return.

The first general meeting of the Society following the end of hostilities was held on 7 February 1919. Members could at last contemplate the return of some form of normality although demobilisation was clearly going to take some time. The committee noted "the great and useful work" of the Advisory Committee set up to advise the military authorities on claims for exemption raised by solicitors. After expressing their thanks to Mr AE Walster who had supervised the work, they noted that the Advisory Committee had met on thirteen occasions. Their advice had clearly been persuasive since out of a total of 56 cases, not one had been rejected by the military.

Before turning to their nomination of Vice-President for 1919 and the award of the Society's Prize, the committee turned to the subject which must have been very much on the minds of the entire membership:

> Your Committee feel that some reference must be made to the ending of hostilities in the great war. They congratulate the members of the Society on the manner in which the legal business of the City and the neighbourhood has been conducted throughout the trying time of the war, with depleted staffs and in the absence of many younger members of the profession and would fain hope that in the near future the difficulties which have arisen in the past will be much alleviated. They have had under consideration the resumption of the Annual Dinner, but have decided that this should be deferred until "Peace" has actually been declared and the food restrictions are somewhat modified. It is hoped, however, that a special dinner in celebration of Peace may be held during the current year.

A dinner was certainly held on 3 February 1920 attended by 46 members and seven guests, including the Dean of York, the Lord Mayor and Lt-General Ivor Maxse, GOC Northern Command although it is not described in the Society's records as being a special dinner. At the general meeting held earlier in the day the committee noted that in the course of the past year many solicitors, articled clerks and other clerks had returned from the war, thus enabling members to carry on their business more normally, the pressure of work had still been very considerable "owing to the large quantity of property which has been put into the market from one cause and another" and that most solicitors had found it difficult to carry on their normal business "and well nigh impossible to cope with arrears which in many cases had accumulated during the war". There was also a stark reference to the housing problem:

> The greatest difficulty which has confronted the Profession and the public during the past year has undoubtedly been the housing question and the acuteness of this difficulty is shown by the fact that during the year two Acts of Parliament have been passed restricting the ordinary rights of ownership of property. This, however, is only a palliative and merely

transfers the difficulty of the Government, to provide accommodation, from their own shoulders to those of the owners of houses, and it is open to argument whether the real evil would not have been better dealt with and the manifest inconvenience have been less, if the Government had set to work in the provision of houses and accommodation and allowed the Law to remain as it was or only amended it to the extent necessary to prevent manifest hardship and injustice. Unfortunately the difficulty appears to be increasing rather than diminishing at present.

The reality of the problem to which the committee alluded is vividly illustrated by a report that appeared in the *Yorkshire Herald* on 5 February 1920. Under the headline "A House to Let!" the paper continued:

> A York Gentleman who advertised a house to sell or let "with prompt possession" in Tuesday's "Yorkshire Evening Press" had his house besieged with applicants and altogether spent a rather uncomfortable evening.
>
> The first arrivals reached his house about 5.30 p.m, and from that time onwards there was an almost endless procession of would-be tenants many of whom had left home without hats and coats in their haste. A long queue was formed outside the advertiser's garden gate and on one occasion when the door was opened to admit an applicant the entrance was almost rushed by others frantically pressing behind.
>
> It is estimated that there were close on fifty applicants for the house on Tuesday night alone, and the advertiser's first concern as soon as he had breathing space, was to send an urgent telephone message to the "Yorkshire Evening Press" office requesting that the advertisement should not be repeated!

A striking feature of the committee's report is that it illustrates the remarkable shift in perception that had occurred as the result of war-induced "big government".[4] It is unlikely that it would have occurred to any member of the Society in 1914 that "the provision of houses and accommodation" was somehow the direct responsibility of *government* but it is clear from public debates and press reports of the time that the presumed responsibilities of "the government" had been much extended by experience of war. Another striking feature is that it marks the beginning of the housing problem in England in its modern form. In its original form it had been essentially concerned with urban slums – the product of the industrial revolution particularly in London and in the manufacturing conurbations of the north. That is not to say that rural slums did not exist, simply that they were not so concentrated. Seebohm Rowntree's report *Poverty – A Study of Town Life* published in 1901 had served as a vivid reminder of the true condition of working class housing, where one in four infants died during the first year of life and successive governments were beginning to deal with it. The war, however, had brought about a rather different problem: a serious overall shortage. With so many men fighting for King and Country and so many women working in munitions factories, transport and other essential occupations, house building had virtually ceased. That, together with significant movements of population due to the exigencies of war had produced a crisis. [5] Parliament's response had been to pass the Increase of Rent and Mortgage Interest (War Restrictions) Act 1915. This was followed by a series of amending acts in 1917, 1918 and 1919 but the original act of 1915 proved to be the first of many more under the general rubric of "the Rent Acts" which survived in one form or another into the 1930s and every subsequent decade until the 1980s. The key features of all of them were to control rents and provide a very large measure of security of tenure. Over time the practical effect of this well-meaning legislation was to bring about the disappearance of the private landlord, since the first reaction of any landlord subject to a Rent Act tenancy was to sell immediately if he were lucky enough to obtain vacant possession and nobody, of course, would deliberately seek to create such a tenancy. The unintended effect was to prompt the beginning of Britain's long term obsession with house ownership, and ultimately encourage over-borrowing which has made a significant contribution to our recent economic woes.

Of much less general significance than national housing policy was the confirmation of the decision taken by the Society at the previous general meeting in 1921 that remains current policy to this day:

> It will be remembered that at the Annual Dinner last year each Member paid for his own dinner instead of the cost being defrayed by the Society. The condition of your Society's finances renders it necessary that the same practice should be followed this year and your Committee hope that there may be as good an attendance this year as there was on the last occasion.

War always has its casualties, major and minor. The loss of "free dinners" for the Society's members must be counted a very minor one.

Of more significance during the immediate post-war period was the matter of clerks' salaries. At a meeting of the Society on 9 April 1920 it was reported that an application had been received from the York and District Law Clerks Association on the subject of remuneration. This was read and discussed and resulted in the appointment of a sub-committee consisting of the President, Secretary and three other members, G Crombie, A Procter and B Dodsworth. This sub-committee duly reported on 7 May 1920, concluding that the law clerks had made "an unanswerable case for a considerable rise in the scale of salaries at present prevailing", their recommendation to members being a scale of 40/- per week at age 21, 60/- per week at age 25 and 80/- per week at age 30. Thereafter the sub-committee felt that remuneration should be a matter of arrangement "consideration being given to ability, length of service &c". These recommendations included a proviso that to enable solicitors "to meet the extra charges thrown upon them" the scale fixed by the Solicitors Remuneration Act [1881] in conveyancing matters should be strictly adhered to in all cases and in all offices".

These recommendations were accepted as regards the remuneration proposed, subject to the proviso "that in country places, as for instance Tadcaster, Richmond, Scarborough &c, some latitude should be allowed". There were two further provisos, firstly as to a provision in the clerks' scale regarding "typists and copyists over 21 having salaries according to age and ability from £100 to £160 per annum" to be included and secondly that it be "left to the committee to take all steps in their power to bring this before the whole of the members of the Society and to get the written assent of all members thereto". The sub-committee was asked to meet the clerks again "and to lay the proposals before them with a view to settlement of the whole matter". The requested further meeting with the clerks took place on 1 June 1920 and whilst the proposed scale up to age 30 seems to have been accepted without demur, there was clearly an issue between the parties concerning senior clerks. An exchange of correspondence followed from which it seems that the parties agreed to disagree on the question of chief clerks and others over 30 "doing important work with slight supervision". A month or so later, on 5 July, the Society resolved "after a very long discussion":

> That having dealt with the question of minimum wages, the Society cannot see their way to pass any recommendation with regard to Clerks over 30 as they consider that the question of their remuneration should be a matter of negotiation between each solicitor and his Clerk but that it be a recommendation to all members of the Society periodically to consider the matter of the wages of the Clerks over 30.

The question of early closing on Saturdays had also been raised by the Clerks and here the Society seems to have been more emollient: "The question of 1 o'clock closing on Saturday was considered and it was decided that Offices should close at 1 o'clock on one day in the week Saturday if possible."

It is very clear from the minutes of this and earlier meetings that the question of clerks' remuneration was closely linked in members' minds to scale fees for conveyancing. The same meeting also passed another resolution on that issue:

> That the making of a Charge for Conveyancing Work under any circumstances at a rate below the Scale under the Solicitors Remuneration Act (exclusive of out of pocket expenses) except under such circumstances as shall be previously approved by the Committee be condemned; that any Member of the Society in contravention of this Resolution be regarded as guilty of conduct unbecoming a member of this Society. Provided that this Resolution shall not apply to Building Land or Friendly Societies scales of charges for mortgage work.

What is interesting about the Society's dealings with the York & District Law Clerks Association is that it seems to have been its first and last encounter with anything resembling a trade union or collective bargaining. Unions and unionism were a controversial topic at the time. Trade Unions were nothing new but parliament had always traditionally viewed them and any attempt at what we would call "collective bargaining" with grave suspicion ever since the Labourers, Artificers etc Act 1349 had attempted to deal (quite ineffectually) with labour problems resulting from the effects of the Black Death. There had been a further flurry of parliamentary concern about Jacobinism at the time of the French Revolutionary wars at the very end of the 18th century. Two "Combination" Acts passed at that time had been repealed and replaced by the Combinations of

Workmen Act 1825 which had grudgingly accepted the existence of trade unions but had severely restricted their activities. Further recognition had been granted by the Trade Union Act 1871. Early in the 20th century, however, the legal equilibrium was brutally shattered by a decision of the House of Lords in *Taff Vale Railway Company v Amalgamated Society of Railway Servants* [1901] AC 426 usually referred to simply as "the Taff Vale Railway case".

The litigation had been provoked by an acrimonious union-organised strike on the Taff Vale Railway in South Wales. The strike itself had been marred by various acts of sabotage, greasing rails, uncoupling waggons and the like. Such conduct would not have endeared the strikers to the judiciary of any period, and certainly not that of the early 20th century. The strike settled as strikes usually do, but to the union's astonishment the railway company then brought proceedings against the union, claiming £23,000 for economic loss arising from the strike. The plaintiffs succeeded at first instance but the judgment was overturned on appeal. The case then went to the House of Lords who restored the original judgment. It was not only the union that was astonished by the outcome. Even lawyers had assumed up to that point that such a claim was impossible. The effect of the judgment was immediate, profound and long-lasting, not least by the impetus it gave to the fledgling Labour Party. In 1901 the number of affiliations from Trades Unions to the Labour Representative Committee was about 350,000. By the following year there were about 450,000 and by 1903 this had risen to 850,000 or so. Politically, and despite the enactment of the Trades Disputes Act 1906 by the Liberal government following their landslide victory of that year, the judgment also had a significant effect on the development of the Labour party in its 20th century form and, from the 1920s onwards, its supplanting of the Liberal Party as the principal left-of-centre party in British politics.

But whatever their political prejudices may have been, the sub-committee appointed to negotiate with the York & District Law Clerks Association seem to have reacted with sympathy to the problems of their junior members at least. No other construction is possible in the light of their unambiguous statement that the Association had made "an unanswerable case for a considerable rise in the scale of salaries at present prevailing". One can also sympathise with their conclusion that the remuneration of more senior clerks "should be a matter of negotiation between each solicitor" and the person concerned. Members of the Society would have been well-aware of the financial and other difficulties, such as housing, resulting from over four years of war.

Anti-semitism, housing and labour relations were not to be the only troubles to burden British society during the inter-war years. Another was the great financial crisis of 1929 and the ensuing great depression. Its effect on most of the western world was disastrous. Its effect on defeated Germany, following so soon after "the great inflation" was not only another financial catastrophe but combined with pre-existing anti-semitic tendencies with results now long familiar to the entire world. Outside Germany, however, the 1920s had been a period of increasing financial confidence. Perhaps the writing was on the wall but most people did not see it and those who did chose to ignore what they saw. Commenting about their own bank (Barclays) in the period from 1926 onwards, AW Tuke and RGH Gillman[6] stressed the continuing pre-eminence of London as a world financial centre:

> In the beginning of this period the country was on the gold standard, the post war boom was continuing and the confidence in sterling was strong. Because it was the major world currency, a large proportion of international trade was settled in sterling and the bill on London was the accepted method of finance and payment for goods whether or not they touched the UK. The sterling documentary acceptance credit enjoyed its heyday ... Exchange dealing was unrestricted up to 1939 and the London exchange market was the world centre for foreign currency dealings ... At this time it was very rare for any of the Chief Foreign Branch management to travel overseas as funds and business flowed to London almost automatically because of the special position of sterling as a means of settling international debts. Foreign bankers came to London to ask for lines of credit and when we opened an account abroad we did so on our own terms.

However, the buoyant economic euphoria of the 1920s was to come to an abrupt end with the 1929 Wall Street crash and subsequent depression. One effect of this was to prompt a growing public concern over defaulting solicitors. Fifty years earlier Anthony Trollope[7] had put into the mouth of his fictional character, senator Gotobed, the words which sum up an inherent problem with legal practice: "It is a noble profession, that of the law; the finest perhaps that the work of the world affords; but it gives scope and temptation to roguery." That temptation becomes all the greater in times of economic stress although as often as not it is fuelled simply by greed and lack of moral scruple; also, because of the way in which the legal profession is organised in this country, the scope is increased for solicitors because they handle client monies.

In the minutes of a meeting of the committee held on 23 April 1929 (which was actually some months before the great crash) appears the following:

> Defaulting Solicitors – The Law Society's proposals and a subsequent letter from the Law Society were considered. They stated that at a joint meeting with the Associated Provincial Law Societies there was an almost unanimous wish that the subject should be dealt with. It was proposed by Mr ER Dodsworth Seconded by Mr HL Swift and resolved that this Society is not prepared to support any scheme for indemnifying Defaulting Solicitors' clients.

Less than a year later, at a meeting on 13 March 1930 the matter was once more before the Committee. Under the same rubric of "Defaulting Solicitors" appears the following minute:

> A memorandum issued by the Law Society dealing with the two proposals (a) compulsory membership of the Law Society and (b) Insurance was read but deferred until the Committee had had an opportunity of dealing with it.

At the next meeting of the Committee on 11 June 1930 its members had rather more to go on and they seem to have gone on it:

> The recommendation of the Law Society including the draft of the Solicitors Act 1930 and the recommendation of the Staffordshire Law Society were considered.
>
> The approval of the Law Society's bill was proposed and seconded but after some discussion this Resolution was withdrawn.
>
> Mr ER Dodsworth then proposed and Mr JL Whitehead seconded That we do not support any bill containing any provisions for making a relief fund for objects of defaulting solicitors (sic). This was carried 11 votes for it and 4 against.

> Mr ER Dodsworth then proposed and Mr E Stanley Jones seconded That membership of the Law Society be compulsory. This was carried with one dissentient.
>
> Mr E Stanley Jones proposed and Mr HC Scott seconded That the Society approve the proposals of the North Staffordshire Law Society with the exception of clause 7(D) (relating to the provision of a fund to make up defalcations). This was carried with two dissentients.
>
> Mr HL Swift then proposed and Mr NT Crombie seconded That separate accounts be kept of clients' monies. This was carried.
>
> Mr CC Lucas proposed and Mr KET Wilkinson seconded That a Solicitor must keep accounts containing such particulars and information as to money received, held or paid for or on account of clients as may be prescribed by the Rules made by the Law Society with the concurrence of the Master of the Rolls. This was carried.

Reading between the lines it must have been quite a lively meeting.[8] The "draft" Act considered by the Committee eventually came into effect on 1 October 1932 as the Solicitors Act of that year but the establishment of the Statutory Compensation Fund had to await the enactment of Section 2 of the Solicitors Act 1941. Despite the fact that parliament doubtless had more immediately pressing problems on its mind in that year, it still found time to enact S.2(1):

> A fund to be called "the Compensation Fund" shall be established, maintained and administered by the [Law] Society for enabling the Society to make grants thereout in any case which the Council thinks suitable for such treatment ... for the purposes of relieving or mitigating losses sustained by any person in consequence of the dishonesty of any solicitor ... in connection with such solicitor's practice ... or any trust of which such solicitor was a trustee ...

In later years the existence of that statutory Compensation Fund was to prove a useful marketing tool for the profession but the Society seems not to have appreciated its potential at the time.

In Britain the resurgent anti-semitism of pre-war days remained under the surface but was yet to become fulminating at a political level. On 24 April 1932, just two years after the Society had declined to give its approval to any creation of a compensation fund, a group of 500 or so ramblers led by a campaigning young Manchester communist, Benny Rothman, set out from Hayfield and Edale on a mass trespass to Kinder Scout, the highest peak in the Derbyshire Peak District, owned by the Duke of Devonshire and forming part of his grouse moor. They were confronted by armed gamekeepers specially engaged for the occasion for His Grace was determined not to have his grouse moor disturbed by these interlopers. The confrontation made the national headlines and was followed by the prosecution of Rothman and five other supposed ringleaders on various charges including riotous assembly, assault and incitement. In fact, by comparison with riots of more recent times, the actual damage was relatively minor. According to a contemporary newspaper report[9] "There will be plenty of bruises carefully nursed in the Gorton and other parts of Manchester tonight, but no-one was at all seriously hurt except one keeper, Mr. E. Beaver, who was knocked unconscious and damaged his ankle." The absence of serious hurt notwithstanding, the case still came on for trial at Derby assizes the following July. One of the accused was acquitted but the remaining five received sentences of imprisonment between two and six months. In his summing up Acton J observed that liberties could not be exercised in such a way as to amount to riot or unlawful assembly or to disturb the public peace and strike terror and alarm into the hearts of the King's subjects. In the course of it he had also made a slightly ambiguous remark: "I am sure", he said, that "the jury would not be prejudiced by the foreign sounding names of two or three of the defendants".

Apart from Benny Rothman himself, the other "foreign sounding" defendants he had in mind were clearly David Nussbaum and Julius Clyne. Was this a genuine attempt to warn the jury about prejudice against "foreign sounding" (aka Jewish) defendants or was it more in the tradition of Shakespeare's Mark Antony ("for Brutus is an *honourable* man")? Perhaps the learned judge should be given the benefit of any doubt. However, casual anti-Jewish prejudice among all classes was notoriously prevalent at the time, but perhaps more ominously among the upper classes, as they had influence. The Great Depression was to act as the catalyst in this country for something rather more sinister than "casual anti-Jewish prejudice" – it was responsible for the phenomenon of Mosleyite fascism in the following years leading up to the Second World

War. In Germany, of course, the effect was to be infinitely more sinister and bring about the meteoric rise of Adolf Hitler and within a few years the Holocaust.

Sir Oswald Ernald Mosley, 6th Baronet of Ancoats (1896-1980) was in many ways one of the most curious, sinister and chameleon-like figures of British public and political life of the 20th century but his real period of prominence was in the troubled decade of the 1930s when he was never out of the public eye. His early career had been typical of that background and that period. Educated at Winchester, he was commissioned in the 16th Queen's Lancers with whom he saw action on the Western Front before transferring to the Royal Flying Corps where at one period of the war the average life expectancy of young officers was just 23 days, although six weeks seems to have been more typical. Injured in a flying accident which left him with a permanent limp, he returned to the trenches before he had fully recovered but had to end the war in various desk jobs at the Ministry of Munitions and the Foreign Office. At the end of the war Mosley decided to enter politics and in the General Election held in December 1918 he was returned as Conservative Member of Parliament for Harrow to become the youngest member to take his seat. He was just 22.

In May 1920 Mosley married Lady Cynthia Curzon, the daughter of Lord Curzon of Kedleston, former Viceroy of India and Foreign Secretary. In addition to HM King George and Queen Mary, the wedding guests included other European royalty. So far, so predictable; like so many of his background, his future in Conservative politics seemed assured, but it was not to be. Mosley, although having quickly attracted attention as a speaker in the House of Commons, equally quickly found himself at odds with the coalition government over Irish policy, in particular with regard to the use of police auxiliaries, the "Black and Tans". It was not long before he "crossed the floor", sitting as an Independent and retaining his seat in the general elections of 1922 and 1923. In 1924 he joined the Independent Labour Party. Later that year he was to oppose Neville Chamberlain in the Birmingham Ladywood constituency when he was only narrowly defeated but later returned to parliament as Labour member for the Smethwick constituency in the general election in December 1926. Thereafter Mosley and his wife became committed Fabians. Following the general election of 1929 and the premiership of Ramsay MacDonald he found himself Chancellor of the Duchy of Lancaster. However, it was not long before he fell out with the Labour Party just as he had fallen out with the Conservatives in the early 1920s but this time it was over their policy (or lack of policy as he saw it) for dealing with the dire economic situation and the crisis of unemployment.

From this period onwards he turned more and more to the fascist philosophy of the corporate state, mainly exemplified at the time by the Italians under Mussolini who had come to power there in 1922. One of the problems, of course, for any discussion of politics at this period is that "fascism" has ceased to be simply descriptive of a particular political philosophy and become a vulgar term of abuse, having been hijacked by continental dictators with their own pernicious agenda. Endowed with uncritical 21st century retrospection, it is easy to forget that in the 1920s and 30s many perfectly reasonable people, in despair over the economic and social problems of the day, were prepared at least to give it a try as a possible solution. After all, early supporters of Mosley's corporatist ideas included not only the future Conservative Prime Minister Harold Macmillan but equally that doyen of the left and future architect of the National Health Service and deputy leader of the Labour Party, Aneurin Bevan. And even 30 years later, in 1961, another doyen of the left, Richard Crossman, was to describe Mosley's proposals for a programme of public works to tackle unemployment and tariffs to protect British industry in lyrical terms: " … this brilliant memorandum was a whole generation ahead of Labour thinking." Roy Jenkins in his biography of Stanley Baldwin[10] was harsher and more succinct about Mosley: "He was a charismatic vulgarian, a visionary who organised thugs, and an improbable Wykehamist."

The euphoria was short-lived. Mosley went on to form the New Party which later metamorphasised into the British Union of Fascists which then quickly began to adopt the aggressively anti-Jewish policies being followed in Germany after the appointment of Hitler as Chancellor in 1933. The latter's subversion of the German state from then on was to have a mesmerising effect on political opinion in Britain. There was a growing realisation for many that perhaps after all the punitive political and economic restrictions imposed on Germany by the Treaty of Versailles had been unreasonable. Unfortunately this realisation had come too late. The damage had been done and no policy of appeasement was going to undo it, it was merely going to encourage Hitler's increasingly hysterical ambitions. From the re-occupation of the Rhineland in 1936, the *Anschluss* with Austria and the occupation of the Sudetenland in 1938, to the final invasion of Poland in 1939, the whole process had a tragic inevitability about it.

The latter of course made a declaration of war by France and Britain inevitable but the infamous Munich Agreement of 29 September 1938 had permitted Hitler to annex the Sudetenland, a part of Czechoslovakia with a large ethnic German population. In a gross act of appeasement the French and UK governments had acceded to Hitler's demands. The Prime Minister, Neville Chamberlain, had returned from his negotiations with Hitler in Munich, declaring that he had come to an agreement with him and that there would be "peace for our time". The audience cheered. What they did not know was that Hitler was furious at having been seen to depend on any "agreement" whatsoever and in any event held Chamberlain in utter contempt, viewing him as "an impertinent busybody who spoke the ridiculous language of an outmoded democracy". The umbrella, which to the ordinary German was a symbol of peace, was in Hitler's view only a subject of derision. Indeed, Hitler had been heard to say that "If that silly old man comes interfering here again with his umbrella, I'll kick him downstairs and jump on his stomach in front of the photographers." As Lloyd George perceptively remarked on the outbreak of war in September 1939, "The worst thing Neville Chamberlain ever did was to meet Hitler and let Hitler see him." But perhaps this was being wise after the event: Lloyd George himself in an article in the *Daily Express* on 17 September 1936 had grievously misjudged the situation in Germany following a visit to the *Reichskanzler* himself:

> Those who imagine that Germany has swung back to its old imperialist temper cannot have any understanding of the character of the change. The idea of a Germany intimidating Europe with a threat that its irresistible army might march across frontiers forms no part in the new vision …

The radical French Prime Minister at the time, Édouard Daladier, had his feet far more firmly on the ground than Chamberlain. Pushed by the latter into doing a deal with Hitler at Munich, he had few illusions: six months previously, in April 1938, he had told the British that Hitler's real aim was to secure

> ... a domination of the continent in comparison with which the ambitions of Napoleon were feeble ... Today it is the turn of Czechoslovakia. Tomorrow it will be the turn of Poland and Romania. When Germany has obtained the oil and wheat it needs, she will turn on the West. Certainly we must multiply our efforts to avoid war. But that will not be obtained unless Great Britain and France stick together, intervening in Prague for new concessions but declaring at the same time that they will safeguard the independence of Czechoslovakia. If, on the contrary, the Western Powers capitulate again they will only precipitate the war they wish to avoid.

Indeed, throughout the summer of 1938 Whitehall received a series of intelligence reports warning that Hitler had decided to seize the Sudetenland by force. Some of this information came from an aristocratic anti-Nazi German diplomat, Wolfgang Putlitz via Peter Ustinov's father, Klop Ustinov, who was working at the time with British Intelligence. Daladier and Putlitz's warnings however fell on deaf ears.

The Nazi deception was calculated and deliberate – as we know all too clearly from a remarkable transcript of a confidential briefing to selected journalists given by Joseph Goebbels on 5 April 1940, just four days before the invasion of Norway:

> Up to now we have succeeded in leaving the enemy in the dark concerning Germany's real goals, just as before 1932 our domestic foes never saw where we were going ... That's exactly how it was in foreign policy ... In 1933 a French premier ought to have said (and if I had been the French premier I would have said it): 'The new Reich Chancellor is the man who wrote *Mein Kampf*, which says this and that. This man cannot be tolerated in our vicinity. Either he disappears or we march!' But they didn't do it. They left us alone and let us slip through the risky zone, and we were able to sail around all dangerous reefs. And when we were done, and well armed, better than they, then they started the war![11]

On his return to Paris from Munich, Daladier was expecting a hostile reaction, unlike Chamberlain who was feeling very pleased with himself. When the French crowds cheered his arrival, he simply turned to his aide, Alexis Léger, and observed "Ah, les cons!" – which just about sums it all up. It was subsequently argued on behalf of the appeasers that neither France nor Britain was ready for war in 1938. This was perfectly true but it was equally true of Germany. Not everything was state-of-the-art in the German army even after the war had begun. At the time of Munich the position was far worse. When Hitler's relatively peaceful *Anschluss* or union with Austria (forbidden by the Treaty of Versailles) had taken place in March of that year the route of the German forces entering Austria was littered with broken-down army vehicles, and there had been no resistance!

Throughout this period of European political turmoil the only hint of what was to come in the Society's records was a brief reference in the minutes of the Committee's meeting on 25 February 1937:

> It was resolved that a circular be sent out to members pointing out the desirability of encouraging Recruiting for the Territorial Forces and asking members to grant a week's holiday with pay in addition to the fortnight's training.

What effect this resolution may have had on the Society's members is difficult to gauge but certainly the real surge in recruiting did not come until two years later with Hitler's final move against Czechoslovakia. From that moment onwards most people in Britain, after the euphoria of Munich, realised that any prospect of doing business with "Mr Hitler" was a chimera and that war was inevitable.

As a final epitaph on this extraordinary period I can only add the experiences of my own family. On the afternoon of Friday 30 September 1938 my father was on his own in London. Convinced that war was going to break out any day, he had just taken my mother down to Cornwall where she had family and friends. At a loose end, he had gone to the Stoll cinema in Kingsway. In the middle of the film a news flash appeared on the screen announcing that Neville Chamberlain had returned from Munich following his agreement with Hitler in Munich, and had announced "Peace for our time". The audience cheered and the following day my father set off to Cornwall to bring my mother back to London. However, in the spring of 1939 he did finally decide to join the *London Irish*, a territorial regiment, as did his brother-in-law, my maternal uncle, although my father was subsequently posted to a regular battalion of the *Royal Ulster Rifles*.

> Lincoln's Inn. Easter Term 1938 181
>
> PROPOSED by *The Hon. Mr. Justice Macnaghten, K.B.E., Treasurer*
> PUBLISHED to the BAR by *The Hon. Mr. Justice Macnaghten, K.B.E., Treasurer* on the 11th day of May 1938 in the presence of
>
> No. *14*
>
> £5
>
> PURSUANT to an ORDER OF COUNCIL of *10th day of May 1938*
>
> *H. Lietzmann*

An extract from page 181 of the Lincoln's Inn Call Register for Easter Term 1938 whereby Dr Heinrich Lietzmann, alraedy a fully qualified German and French barrister duly became a fully fledged member of the Bar in England on 11 May 1938.

(Reproduced by kind permission of the Treasurer and Benchers of Lincoln's Inn)

Then in August 1939 my parents received a lunch invitation from a German friend, Heinrich Lietzmann, a former pupil of my father and member of Lincoln's Inn who practised at the German Bar and who was on a professional visit to London. My father was unable to accept as he was on his first TA camp in the New Forest but my mother accepted and she and Heinrich duly met. Over lunch the conversation inevitably turned to the international situation and the possibility of war between Britain and Germany. Heinrich thought this unlikely but my mother was not in doubt: "If Germany invades Poland", she told him "Britain will go to war." I never thought to ask my mother whether Heinrich thought it unlikely that Germany would invade Poland, or if she did that Britain would go to war and now I shall never know. Heinrich and my parents had been close friends to the point of having gone on holiday together before the war – a practice that was resumed afterwards when my parents visited Germany in 1948, the first year in which civilian visits were possible. A curious aspect of this story is that at the time of that lunch meeting in

August 1939 the anglophile Lietzmann had not only a double but a triple professional qualification: *Rechtsanwalt* in Germany, barrister-at-law in England and *avocat à la cour* in France and had already established an international practice in Essen. It is surprising, therefore, that he had such an over-sanguine view about the likelihood of a European war a mere month before it began.

NOTES

1. Quoted by Roy Hattersley in *David Lloyd George The Great Outsider* Little, Brown – London 2010.

2. Maurice Hankey (1877-1963), a former Royal Marine officer, was the first person to hold the post of Cabinet Secretary. As an alumnus of Rugby, he would no doubt have received the classical education of the day (unlike Lloyd George) and been aware of the cardinal error made by the Samnite general, Gaius Pontius, following the Battle of the Caudine Forks in 321 BC. Pontius had sought his father's advice as to what he should do with his captured Roman enemies when he had them in his power. The old man advised that he should release them unharmed and thus gain Rome's enduring friendship. Reluctant to accept this advice, Pontius asked his father to reconsider and was then advised to slaughter the entire captured army, thus ensuring that Rome would cease to be a threat for generations. Faced with this conflicting advice, Pontius wanted to know if there was not a middle way. "No" was the unequivocal answer. Humiliating without destroying the Romans would merely ensure that they would sooner or later seek revenge. Pontius ignored his father's advice and humiliated his captured enemies by requiring them to march under a symbolic yoke. For Pontius the resulting "peace" only lasted seven years – until 316 BC. The allied powers in 1919 did not do much better – their "peace" lasted twenty years.

3. The name "Dreyfus" is still familiar to many throughout the world whom one would hardly expect to be familiar with the name of a fairly junior French artillery officer sentenced over a century ago to life imprisonment for allegedly passing on military secrets to Germany. Certainly at the time, as a perceived gross miscarriage of justice, it raised an international fire-storm – so much so that at the specific request of Queen Victoria the formidable Lord Chief Justice, Lord Russell of Killowen had gone over to Brittany to attend Dreyfus's second court-martial at Rennes in 1899 and report back. The first conviction in 1894 had been set aside but only after the accused

had suffered almost five years of solitary confinement on Devil's Island in the French South American colony of Guiana. His supposed guilt had been highly dubious from the very start and it was quickly obvious to any impartial observer that his conviction was unsafe and likely to have been procured on the basis of false testimony, forgery and anti-Jewish prejudice. By the time of his second court-martial his innocence was hardly in doubt. Nevertheless he was found guilty once again. The Lord Chief Justice, present throughout as an observer, expressed himself as "appalled" by the patent bias of the judges. Although "pardoned" and released following his second conviction, it was not until 1906 that Dreyfus was finally exonerated and reinstated with the rank of major in the French Army. He served in the First World War, attaining the rank of Lieutenant-Colonel. He died in 1935 having been awarded the *Légion d'Honneur* and the *Croix de Guerre*. His granddaughter, Madeleine Levy was rounded up by the Gestapo in Paris in 1943 and transferred first to Drancy and subsequently to Auschwitz where she died of typhus the following year. The whole story is an unhappy memorial to the extraordinary vein of anti-semitism in French society so prevalent at the time and which is still to be found in certain quarters even today.

4. Total war of the kind experienced in the 20th century does seem to have had the effect of extending the reach of the state which never seems to revert to the *status quo ante* once hostilities have ceased. This certainly seems to have been the experience in Britain in two world wars. The economist John A Hobson (1858-1940) reckoned that "The war [of 1914] has advanced state socialism by half a century" – Hattersley *op cit*.

5. The victims of this chaos included my paternal grandparents. My grandfather had been demobilised in February 1919 and returned to duty as a prison officer at Parkhurst on the Isle of Wight where he had the use of a house provided by the Prison Commissioners. In November of that year, however, he was transferred to Winson Green Prison in Birmingham where there was no available staff accommodation. He was entitled to a married man's rent allowance if staff accommodation was not available except that there was no suitable accommodation available for a family to rent. My grandmother was reluctant to stay on her own with my eight year old father on the Isle of Wight as she had no relatives within easy and inexpensive travelling distance and so moved up to Yorkshire to stay with family there. But either way, she and my grandfather were forced to live apart for eighteen months. There were many thousands who shared similar difficulties.

6. *Barclays Bank Ltd* – London 1972

7. *The American Senator* – Chapman & Hall London 1877

8. We can see here once again in this lively discussion the clash between classical liberalism, deeply distrustful of any interference by or at the behest of the state and the modern regulatory world. Unfortunately the economic woes of the inter-war years had exacerbated the traditional temptations to which a profession handling other peoples's money has always been exposed. In 1934, just four years after this debate, a well-known member of the Society had died and Mr CH Cobb, the Society's then President, had dutifully attended his funeral. In the customary eulogy the Vicar of Clifton had referred in particular to the deceased's integrity. A few days later it was revealed that for years he had been living on his clients' monies, leaving an insolvent estate. Sam Holtby, the Clifton joiner and undertaker and one of the President's clients, at least had the foresight to cut his losses: "I thought there were summat wrong", he said "so I buried 'im in helm instead o' hoak". Even now, in the most fiercely regulated legal environment, local intelligence is often well ahead of any faraway regulator.

9. *Manchester Guardian* 25 April 1932

10. *Baldwin* Harper Collins Publishing London 1987

11. HA Jacobsen *Der Zweite Weltkreig: Grundzüge der Politik und Strategie in Dokumenten* Frankfürt 1965 quoted in Andreas Hillgruber's *Germany and the Two World Wars* (tr.Harvard 1981)

Chapter Eleven

THE SECOND WORLD WAR
1939 – 1945

"A player whose stroke is affected by the simultaneous explosion of a bomb may play another ball from the same place. Penalty one stroke."

Richmond Golf Club (From *Temporary Rules 1942*)

To those who lived through it, the simple phrase "before the war" conveyed a reality of which the real significance is largely lost to later generations. To the young or even the not so young the very words themselves may at best be unfamiliar or even provoke a puzzled look of incomprehension: "Which war … ?" It is difficult for them to comprehend the trauma, upheaval and often stark tragedy which afflicted the entire generation that somehow struggled through those years between 1939 and 1945. They were marked for ever by the experience. And some of course did not survive although only one member of the Society was to lose his life as a direct result of enemy action – in an air raid and not on the battlefield. This was in marked contrast to the astonishing number who had given their lives in the first world war. In the country as a whole those who had served in that earlier conflict suffered far greater fatalities – about 700,000 died or killed but British military deaths in the second world war were still very high – about 326,000.[1] The number of those wounded, often very severely, was, of course higher still in both wars. What is significant about the second world war was the number of civilian fatalities, about 62,000 or roughly one fifth of those killed in action. These were in addition to the deaths of servicemen. The large number of civilian deaths compared with those of the first world war was due to air raids.

However, neither the authorities nor the general public were under any illusions as to what they could expect at the outbreak of war as they had seen from afar the events of the Spanish Civil War and some had even taken part in it themselves. Indeed, the potential horrors of an air war had helped fuel pacifist sentiment in the run-up to hostilities. But sentiment changed as the inevitable conflict approached: many, even those of the most unmilitary and peaceable disposition, joined TA units or the Royal Naval or Royal Air Force Volunteer Reserves.

Regardless of fatalities, however, the war years were enormously disruptive of all work and domestic routines: conscription, blackouts, rationing (food, clothing and fuel), requisitioning, family separation, colossal disruption to travelling and colossal interference too with the minutest details of everyday life.

War was not declared until 3 September 1939 but already in May of that year there had been a hint in the committee minutes of the coming conflict. Under the heading "National Service" there is a reference to "arrangements which might be made in the case of National Emergency". These were approved and it was decided to have copies printed and sent to all solicitors "whether they are Members of our Society or not and to send a copy to the Law Society and the Bradford Society." When the committee met on 27 September 1939 "the case of National Emergency" had occurred and it was recorded without further comment that

> In accordance with the recommendations of the Society with regard to Practices of Solicitors absent on National Service the following were appointed a Bureau to consider such cases:
>
> The President R Teasdale Esq Mr B Dodsworth and Mr KET Wilkinson
>
> It was decided that all applications be sent to Mr Wilkinson and Mr Wilkinson promised to obtain a full set of Emergency Forms from the Law Society.

The so-called phoney war did not become serious until May 1940 with the invasion of France and the disaster of Dunkirk, immediately followed by the Battle of Britain – a period of some six months when the whole nation held its breath. At their meeting on 15 November 1940 the committee recorded their first and only reference to a war casualty amongst the Society's members:

A resolution of sympathy with the family of the late Mr AE Young of Pocklington on his sudden death by enemy action was passed and the Secretary was asked to convey this to his son.

Albert Edwin Young (1875-1940) of the firm of Powell & Young had been admitted as a solicitor in 1924, moving to Pocklington and joining Mr HS Powell the following year. The family home in Garths End had been bombed on or about 9 November 1940. His wife Mabel and son Peter survived but he himself died in hospital a day or so later on 11 November. His daughter Joan Lesley equally perished in the disaster. As in the first world war, many of the Society's members served in the forces but Young, as a civilian, appears to have been the only one to have been a direct war casualty.

Pocklington of course was to become home to one of the RAF's principal bomber bases but it was still under construction at the time of the raid. York for its part on 29 April 1942 suffered one of the Luftwaffe's infamous Baedeker air-raids, so-called because they were supposed to target historic centres featured in the Baedeker Guides although the city was a major railway junction and in addition was home to an RAF airfield at Clifton Moor. One York solicitor's firm which experienced a near disaster and massive disruption that night was the old-established one of Munby & Scott. Their office, until they merged with Langleys in 2008, was at 18 Blake Street, just two hundred yards or so from the Minster. True, their office was left standing, which is more than can be said of the building next door, now McDonalds, which did not survive.

Blake Street York "ankle-deep in glass and rubble" following the Baedeker raid on 29 April 1942 (Photo © York Press)

One wonders how many of the present generation of children, or their parents for that matter, tucking into their Big Macs realise that they are doing so on a second world war bomb site. Munby & Scott's office merely had their front door blown off and were left without a pane of glass in the whole building. Blake Street the following morning was ankle-deep in glass and rubble. With the exception of one office window which was replaced, the remaining windows in the building were boarded up for more than a year.[2] The bomb which caused such havoc in Blake Street was doubtless the one responsible for blowing the serpent weather vane off its mounting over the old dispensary (now part of Grays' offices) in Duncombe Place. Its disappearance from view seems to have been overlooked in the upheavals of war and only came to light when some roofing work was being carried out a few years ago and the wreckage was found in a gully. It has now been restored and replaced. York Civic Trust under the chairmanship of the late John Shannon made a welcome contribution to the cost of the restoration. As he himself was a former partner of Munby & Scott at the time of the restoration it must have served as a reminder of those dark days.

A former member, former President of the Society and former partner in Grays, the late Charlie Dodsworth, had a very clear recollection of that fateful night. He was living at home with his parents in Bishopthorpe at the time and at about half-past five in the morning he went into town and saw the devastation in the city centre. Miraculously the office of Gray & Dodsworth (as Grays were then known) was virtually unscathed but he was fully aware of the massive damage sustained by much of the city, including the railway station. On returning home his father Ben Dodsworth, undersheriff of Yorkshire at the time, confirmed his intention of taking the train to Leeds that day where he was due to be on shrievalty duty at the assizes. Charlie protested that any such attempt would be pointless, given the chaos at York station but his father was adamant and insisted on being driven there. He eventually abandoned his efforts and took the bus but only after one of the porters, who recognised him clambering over the still burning debris on the bridge over the platforms, called out in alarm "Mr Dodsworth, your trousers are on fire!" He looked down and saw that this was indeed the case. As a result of having to take the bus he was two hours late at court in Leeds and in a high dudgeon.

York suffered badly that night although overall it suffered much less during the war from the attention of the Luftwaffe than did more significant military targets in the north such as Hull, and of course London itself. Nevertheless, York's Guildhall was destroyed as was St Martin's Church in Coney Street. The railway station, as we have seen, was severely damaged together with the telephone exchange in Lendal. There was also severe damage to many residential areas of the city. Altogether 72 York civilians perished in that raid, 19 men, 39 women and 14 children, in addition to four civil defence workers and five soldiers. The civilian fatalities included five sisters at the Bar Convent in Blossom Street which received a direct hit. A quarter of the fatalities were accounted for by the bombs that fell in Chatsworth Terrace and Amberley Street off Poppleton Road. Although York suffered far less than many other cities, the minutes of the committee's meeting on 3 June 1942 record the receipt of a letter from the President of the Law Society in London expressing his sympathy with the York members who had suffered damage in this raid. With the passage of time a tinge of rosy nostalgia has tended to settle over the period and people forget General Sherman's famous aphorism "War is hell".

Air raids apart, questions of deferment and call up were to pose considerable headaches to many solicitors. Firms were very much smaller then than they are now and there were far more sole practitioners. It is perhaps salutary to recall that the great city firm of Freshfields, solicitors then as now to the Bank of England, had only seven partners at this period and Linklaters & Paines and Slaughter & May only had twelve. At one stage in the course of the war there were only four partners and two qualified staff at Freshfields left to deal with the work.[3] It was not only men who were to be involved in these matters of call-up and deferment; women too were concerned. On 27 August 1942 the Secretary of the Law Society TG (Tommy) Lund[4] found it necessary to write to the secretaries of all local law societies with a copy of a lengthy and detailed two page letter which he had written to the press two days earlier explaining how "unmarried women born in the years 1918-1921 who come under the National Service (No 2) Act 1941" were to be considered for deferment. It must have been a bureaucratic nightmare. It all depended on whether they were employed on 1 May 1940 or were not employed on 1 May 1940 but employed prior to first January 1941 and whether they held "pivotal positions". Further, where a District Manpower Board "was unable to agree that a woman so employed was in a pivotal position the case was to be referred to the Council of the Law Society who would make a recommendation to the Lord Chancellor's Department with regard to the matter." All this, apparently was due "to the increasingly urgent demands for women". But never let it be thought that even in the middle of a world war Britain lost its taste for the *minutiae* of due process. The Secretary's letter continued with a formidable 180 word sentence:

> The Council wish to direct the attention of the profession to the fact that where an existing deferment is cancelled or an application for deferment is refused in respect of a single woman in the 1920-1921 age groups or born in the first six months of 1922 the solicitor will receive Form 247 which states, inter alia, that (a) the District Man-Power Board cannot receive any representations from the employer against the decision taken, (b) if in an exceptional case an employer is of the opinion that as a result of the decision urgent work in which a Government Department is interested would be seriously curtailed, it is open to him to submit particulars to the Government Department concerned, which may, if it thinks fit, approach the District Man-power Board with a view to the reconsideration of the case and (c) such representations by a Government Department must be received by the District Man-Power Board not later than one week from the date at which the notification of the cancellation or rejection of the deferment application was sent to the employer.

The day before that letter of 27 August was written in 1942, half a million German and Romanian troops had launched their land attack on Stalingrad. It is unlikely that either side in that notorious engagement would have been agonising about the call-up or its deferment for women, whether they were born in the first or second six months of 1922, whether they were single or married and whether their position was pivotal or otherwise.

A year later, on 24 August 1943, Mr Lund again had occasion to write to the secretaries of all local law societies, this time on the subject of solicitors and articled clerks who were prisoners of war in Germany. The letter was concerned to support "in every possible way" the work being done by the Educational Books Section of the Prisoners of War Department of the Red Cross and the St John's War Organisation. It recalled that it had been "possible to hold the Society's examinations at Prisoner of War Camps in Germany, and there are many solicitors and articled clerks who are indebted to the War Organisation for Law books which have been purchased out of Red Cross Funds." The letter continued "The cost of law books is, I need scarcely say, very heavy, and owing to shortage of paper and printing difficulties, the supply is barely adequate." Lund was therefore appealing to solicitors to send any books particularly in demand and which they felt they could spare to the Educational Books Section of the two charities concerned which was based at the New Bodleian Library at Oxford. The books particularly in demand were various student works by Gibson, *Criminal and Magisterial Law, Probate, Conveyancing, Practice of the High Court and Divorce, Snell's Equity, Wilshere's Common Law, Kenny's Outlines of Criminal Law, Hart & Hart's Introduction to Local Government Law* and *Stevens' Mercantile Law*. There was also a request for "any recent editions of the standard text books on Torts, Contract, and Real Property".

Peter Knowles   *Kenneth Bloor*

Members of the Braunschweig-Querum Law Society, Oflag 79 Lower Saxony. A distinguished, albeit shortlived, local law society which flourished between December 1943 and April 1945 and which served as alma mater to two future Presidents of the Yorkshire Law Society, Peter Knowles (left) and Kenneth Bloor (right). (Photo courtesy of Peter Knowles)

Among the many young men at the time who were reluctant guests of the *Wehrmacht* were Kenneth Bloor and Peter Knowles both of whom were subsequently to become members and indeed Presidents of the Society. They were both able to benefit from these arrangements and prepare for their Law Society's finals in a German POW camp – the same one by a strange coincidence *Oflag 79* which was situated at Waggum near Brunswick in Lower Saxony. Kenneth died in 2005 but his fellow prisoner, Peter Knowles, is still one of the Society's honorary members. A young officer in the 2nd Indian Field Regiment RA, he was taken prisoner in the course of the North African campaign and after a brief period in Italy eventually arrived in Germany in 1943. There he was able to join what became known as the Braunschweig-Querum Law Society.

These efforts by the British Red Cross Society and the Order of St John of Jerusalem to mitigate the educational lot of British prisoners of war in Germany were remarkably successful. By the end of May 1943 over 24,000 requests for books had been received and over 150,000 books had been dispatched and the number of courses issued was over 6,000. The two charities' book scheme based on the New Bodleian in Oxford worked in close co-operation with the *International Red Cross* based in Geneva and with other bodies represented on the *Comité Consultatif*, the *YMCA*, the *European Student Relief Fund*, the *Bureau International d'Education* and the *Commission Oecumenique pour l'Aide Spirituelle des Prisonniers de Guerre*.

Classes at some camps were able to offer a wide field of instruction by qualified lecturers and teachers. For instance *Oflag VIIB* had a "university" with six faculties, agriculture, arts, commerce and industry, engineering, languages and law. In the language faculty 22 languages were being taught, including Albanian and Tamil. In another camp, *Stalag VIIIB* a Company Quarter-Master Sergeant (a headmaster in civilian life) reported "There are forty-one tutors, all qualified men. The syllabus, which comprises sixty-three subjects, includes electrical engineering, Diesel engineering, auto engineering, accountancy, shorthand, English, mathematics, geography, advertising, music, German, French, Spanish, Greek, Latin, anatomy, physiology and first aid." All things considered, a fairly comprehensive education.

For a later generation brought up on war films such as *The Colditz Story* and *The Great Escape*, the sheer boredom factor of POW life, together with its dreariness and hunger is not always appreciated.[5] But the fact remains that with the war generally the earlier generation managed in a way that has now largely been lost. The veteran TV reporter Kate Adie put it very succinctly once in an interview: "Over the years it's become more fashionable to talk about emotional effects, whereas I come from a generation whose parents went through six years of war and they didn't go around talking about how they coped." But coped they did. It is not easy to convey to a post-war generation how they did it. It required a particular mind-set which may now have been lost. A golfing client once sent me a document[6] which perhaps conveys the flavour of that lost world more effectively than the earnest writings of historians:

RICHMOND GOLF CLUB
TEMPORARY RULES 1940

1. Players are asked to collect Bomb and Shrapnel splinters to save these causing damage to the Mowing Machines.

2. In Competitions, during gunfire or while bombs are falling, players may take cover without penalty for ceasing play.

3. The positions of known delayed action bombs are marked by red flags at reasonably, but not guaranteed, safe distance therefrom.

4. Shrapnel and/or bomb splinters on the Fairways, or in Bunkers within a club's length of a ball, may be moved without penalty, and no penalty shall be incurred if a ball is thereby caused to move accidentally.

5. A ball moved by enemy action may be replaced, or if lost or destroyed, a ball may be dropped not nearer the hole without penalty.

6. A ball lying in a crater may be lifted and dropped not nearer the hole, preserving the line to the hole, without penalty.

7. A player whose stroke is affected by the simultaneous explosion of a bomb may play another ball from the same place. Penalty one stroke.

The whole tenor of the Rules, particularly the wording of Rule 3, strongly suggests that a solicitor member of the committee had a hand in the drafting. Golfers were clearly expected to adopt the same calm, measured and law-abiding approach to their game as the employers of women in "pivotal positions" – even if trying for a birdie on the thirteenth and competing with a simultaneously exploding bomb on the fourteenth.

Fiat iustitia, ruat cœlum – Let justice be done though the heavens fall.

The procession into a fire blackened and roofless Guildhall for the reading of the Assize Commission following the Baedeker air-raid of 29 April 1942.

Leading the procession is Harry Herman, Chief Constable of York, followed by Tom Benfield, Town Clerk (in wig and bands) who later served as President of the Society.

(Photo courtesy of David Wilson)

All things considered, the law and the lawyers coped remarkably well with the upheavals of war but there were occasional wobbles. For example, there was the hysteria induced by the events of Dunkirk and the fall of France in May 1940. One particular case which conveys very vividly the legal atmosphere of the time is *Liversidge v Anderson* [1942] AC 206. To my own post-war generation this was a leading and much-discussed case in constitutional law but with the passing of the years its impact seems to have diminished. Now, however, when once again the dogs of war are roaming the streets, we should perhaps revisit it. The appellant, Robert Liversidge, otherwise known as Jack Perlzweig, had been detained on 29 May 1940 at the height of the Dunkirk crisis and taken to Brixton Prison. His detention had been ordered by the Home Secretary, Sir John Anderson, under the notorious Regulation 18b of the Defence (General) Regulations 1939 under the Emergency Powers (Defence) Act of that year (popularly known at the time as the "Everything and Everybody Act") which came into force on 1 September. Many such detentions had been ordered. The issue before the court was a deceptively simple one of construction: did the phrase "if the Secretary of State has reasonable cause to believe" [that the detention of the appellant was necessary] mean that viewed objectively the belief of the Secretary of State was reasonable or was the test a subjective one? The distinction was important because if the former view were correct, any decision by the Secretary of State could be subject to judicial control.

There is little doubt that the tradition of English law favoured the former interpretation but perhaps overwrought by the exigencies of the times, the majority of the law lords found in favour of the Home Secretary. Had the decision been unanimous it might very well have disappeared below the legal horizon following the end of hostilities in 1945. That this did not happen was entirely due to the dissenting judgment of Lord Atkin. Some of his observations were not calculated to make him popular at the time, particularly among his fellow law lords: eg in describing his colleagues on the bench (by implication) as "more executive-minded than the executive". Perhaps his Welsh-Australian roots made him less inclined to be deferential towards authority than his brethren. The Lord Chancellor, Lord Simon, having read the speeches in advance, had written to Lord Atkin asking him to delete the reference to Alice and Humpty Dumpty quoted below as he felt it ridiculed his colleagues and lowered the dignity of the court. Atkin politely refused. Afterwards the distinguished jurist CK Allen[7] also wrote to Atkin remarking "Such cries in the wilderness have strong and loud echoes". Indeed they do. The key passages of the judgment were memorable:

> I view with apprehension the attitude of judges who, on a mere question of construction, when face to face with claims involving the liberty of the subject, show themselves more executive-minded than the executive. Their function is to give words their natural meaning …
>
> In this country, amid the clash of arms, the laws are not silent. They may be changed, but they speak the same language in war as in peace. It has always been one of the pillars of freedom, one of the principles of liberty for which on recent authority, we are now fighting, that judges are no respecters of persons, and stand between the subject and any attempted encroachments on his liberty by the executive, alert to see that coercive action is justified in law. In this case I have listened to arguments which might have been addressed acceptably to the Court of King's Bench in the time of Charles I.
>
> I protest, even if I do it alone, against a strained construction put on words, with the effect of giving an uncontrolled power of imprisonment to the minister. To recapitulate: the words have only one meaning. They are used with that meaning in statements of the common law and in statutes. They have never been used in the sense now imputed to them. They are used in the Defence Regulations in the natural meaning, and, when it is intended to express the meaning now imputed to them, different and apt words are used in the regulations generally and in this regulation in particular. Even if it were relevant, which it is not, there is no absurdity or no such degree of public mischief as would lead to a non-natural construction.
>
> I know of only one authority which might justify the suggested method of construction: "When I use a word," Humpty Dumpty said in rather a scornful tone, "it means just what I choose it to mean, neither more nor less." "The question is," said Alice, "whether you can make words mean different things." "The question is," said Humpty Dumpty, "which is to be master – that's all.'" ("Through the Looking Glass," c.vi.) After all this long discussion the question is whether the words "If a man has" can mean "If a man thinks he has," I am of the opinion that they cannot, and that the case should be decided accordingly …

In an unprecedented departure from judicial etiquette the presiding law lord, Viscount Maugham, wrote a letter to *The Times* two days later entitled *War and Habeas Corpus*, in which he sharply criticised Atkin for his dissenting judgment. Judicial and indeed public opinion was divided. From the Judges' Lodgings in Leicester Stable J who had decided an earlier case (not cited in the House of Lords) wrote to him and said: "I venture to think the decision of the House of Lords has reduced the stature of the Judiciary with consequences that the nation will one day bitterly regret. Bacon. I think, said the judges were the lions under the Throne, but the House of Lords has reduced us to mice squeaking under a chair in the Home Office". [8]

The case of *Liversidge v Anderson* had its counterpart during the first world war in the lesser-known case of R (*at the prosecution of Arthur Zadig*) *v Halliday* [1917] AC 260 with the Scottish judge, Lord Shaw of Dunfermline, mirroring the dissenting rôle of Lord Atkin when the matter came before the House of Lords. Arthur Zadig was a naturalised British subject of German parentage and had been detained under Regulation 14b made under the Defence of the Realm Consolidation Act 1914. All the other judges considered the detention lawful but not Lord Shaw. Not for him Lord Atkin's mockery with his reference to Humpty Dumpty; Lord Shaw preferred a Caledonian frontal assault: "Under this the Government becomes a Committee of Public Safety" he thundered, "But its powers as such are far more arbitrary than those of the most famous Committee of Public Safety known to history." Short of directly comparing the Home Secretary to Robespierre, he could hardly have been more scathing. This approach seems to have unsettled the authorities. Despite having an overwhelming majority of the law lords on his side, the Home Secretary released the unfortunate Zadig just two weeks later. And on his retirement from the House of Lords in 1929 Shaw was given an hereditary peerage and became Lord Craigmyle.

However, once the dust had settled from the more recent conflict which produced Regulation 18b and its legal fall-out, the more traditional and sober opinion came to prevail and Humpty Dumpty was overruled. In *IRC v Rossminster Ltd* [1980] 1 All ER 80 at 92 Lord Diplock observed:

> I think the time has come to acknowledge openly that the majority of this House in Liversidge v Anderson was expediently and at that time perhaps excusably wrong; and the dissenting speech by Lord Atkin was right.

The sad fact is that in the febrile atmosphere of the 1940s the government, engaged then as now in what it perceived as a "war against terror", had come perilously close to losing all sense of proportion and the dissenting voices of the Shaws and Atkins went unheeded. Serious-minded contemporaries accepted that the exceptional circumstances of the time called for exceptional measures but then, as now, governments are indeed liable to over-react. CK Allen records that a total of 1,829 supposedly dangerous persons were detained under the regulations but tartly comments that of these, it subsequently proved possible to release 1,603 adding "The facility with which some releases have been made can only be explained by the recklessness of the arrests". He supported this charge by quoting the Labour MP for Kingston-upon-Hull East,[9] Mr George Muff, speaking in the House of Commons on 10 February 1943 (Hansard, Vol 386 Col 1397)

> I found in prison an Italian boy, aged 16. I asked the Home Office, "What right have you to keep this boy in prison? He should be in school." They admitted that they had made a mistake, and he went back to school. I found a Member of Parliament in my favourite prison – not a British Member of Parliament, but one of the Hon. Members for Prague. The Home Office said they had sent him to Leeds Prison to cure his rheumatism. I thought that was rather far-fetched. I possess a certain nuisance value, and I pressed my right hon. friend to let him out, which he did.

An even more notable detainee than the honourable and rheumatic member for Prague was the distinguished German economist Ernst Schumacher (1911-1977) – albeit as an enemy alien[10] rather than someone who was merely displeasing to the Home Secretary of the day. Schumacher had been a Rhodes Scholar at Oxford in the 1930s and a protégé of Maynard Keynes. At the outbreak of war he found himself in England as an ex-Lutheran marxist who couldn't face life in Nazi Germany (although, he did become a Catholic much later), rather than the more usual Jewish, refugee from his native Germany. That of course did not prevent him from being interned. Fortunately Maynard Keynes was eventually able to do for Schumacher what Muff had been able to do for the Italian schoolboy and the rheumatic Czech MP – secure his release – and by the end of the war Schumacher was advising the British government on economic matters; indeed he continued to advise them in connection with post-war German reconstruction through the Allied Control Commission.

Schumacher was lucky in having the support of Maynard Keynes – and perhaps too in being a gentile. In his recent book[11] *The Secret History of the Blitz* author and former member of the Bar, Joshua Levine, gives a striking example of just how tragic the consequences could be:

> Eleanor Rathbone, independent member for Combined Universities, cited the case of a sixty-two-year-old chemistry professor. The man had been imprisoned and tortured in a German concentration camp. On his release he had fled to Britain, where, after a year of research work, he had developed a process for utilising sisal waste for use in submarines. This, said Rathbone, was work of national importance. The professor's firm had recently applied to the Home Office for his exemption from internment – but in early July, two police officers arrived at his flat to take him away. He showed them his Home Office application, and asked them to wait until his case had been investigated before arresting him. They refused, and told him that they would return shortly. By the time they returned, two hours later, he had taken his own life. At the subsequent inquest, one of the policemen asked his widow whether he had been Jewish. She said that he was of Jewish origin, but had been baptised a Christian. "What a pity ... if we had only known before," said the officer – who believed that being a Christian was a reason for exempting him from internment. With these levels of bureaucracy and stupidity at work, "it is about as easy to get a man out of an internment camp," said Rathbone, "as it is to pull a camel out of the eye of the needle."

These two hours can hardly be counted among Britain's finest.

More than seventy years on it is curious from a rather different perspective to see the identities of some of the UK citizens who were detained since by all normal criteria some of them were very much from the heart of the British establishment. One such was Admiral Sir Barry Domvile KBE, CB, CMG. He had actually served as head of Naval Intelligence from 1927 to 1930 and President of the Royal Naval College at Greenwich from 1932 to 1934.

Another detainee at the time was the Scottish Unionist MP, Archibald Ramsay (Eton and Sandhurst) a descendant of the Earls of Dalhousie and the only member of parliament to be interned during the war. By the late 1930s he and his wife Ismay (the daughter of an Irish peer, and widow of a Scottish peer) had both became noted for their virulent anti-semitism. By May 1929 this had prompted Ramsay to form the notorious "Right Club". The proclaimed object of this 'club' was "to oppose and expose the activities of organised Jewry" and it became a hub for those with similar views for Ramsay, who was well-connected with certain strata of British society, had met Domvile at a party at the German Embassy in November 1938 together with a number of other prominent sympathisers. Once his 'club' had been established therefore, recruitment was not difficult. Members at one time included the Duke of Wellington who chaired its early meetings, the eccentric Lord Redesdale (best known as father of the six Mitford sisters), John Stourton (younger brother of William Stourton, 25th Baron Mowbray) and a number of others with aristocratic or high profile connections.

Of these, perhaps the most astonishing, although hardly a household name nowadays, was Lord Sempill (the 19th Baron Sempill) who was not only never prosecuted, let alone detained but given a job at the Admiralty in the Department of Air Material at the outbreak of war despite having had definite treasonable form going back to the 1920s when the authorities had incontrovertible evidence that he had been passing classified information (for money) to the Japanese. Although the matter had been considered at the highest level, a prosecution was deemed not to be in the public interest for two reasons: firstly it would have revealed that British Intelligence had cracked the Japanese cypher codes and perhaps even more compellingly, Sempill's father was ADC at the time to King George V, so Sempill merely received a warning. That, however, does not seem to have been a deterrent. By June 1941 MI5 once again had definite evidence that Sempill was receiving payments from Tokyo and were convinced that he was passing on secret information about Fleet Air Arm aircraft. Even these suspicions were seemingly insufficient to prompt action by the authorities who were concerned but prevaricating. It was only on 13 December 1941, six days after Japan's attack on Pearl Harbor when the United Kingdom had already been at war with Japan since 8 December that Sempill's office was raided and further incriminating evidence emerged and two days later he was detected making telephone calls to the Japanese Embassy. Even if the hard evidence was not sufficient to sustain a prosecution under the Treachery Act 1940 he was never detained but merely obliged to resign from the Admiralty and these details were not declassified until 2002.

What had spurred the authorities into action back in May 1940 was when it was discovered that one of the leading lights of the Right Club, Anna Wolkoff, had been receiving highly classified information from a cipher clerk in the US embassy, Tyler Kent, including cables exchanged between Churchill, when he was First Lord of the Admiralty, and President Roosevelt which she had passed on to the Italians who in turn were passing them on to Berlin. Both the Americans and Churchill were appalled when MI5 (which had managed to penetrate the *Right Club*) revealed this particular discovery to them. "Nothing like this has ever happened in American history", wrote the shocked US Assistant Secretary of State, Breckinridge Long. "It means not only that our codes are cracked ... But that our every diplomatic maneuver was exposed to Germany and Russia ... It is a terrible blow – almost a major catastrophe".[12]

All this, of course, occurred in May 1940, at the height of the Dunkirk crisis, and Churchill must have been under the most intense pressure. Perhaps, therefore some over-reaction was understandable in human terms. Also, the natural concern about treachery and fifth-columnists had affected official attitudes to enemy aliens generally, including, of course, the harmless and the innocent. Nevertheless the positive lack of reaction in respect of Lord Sempill does raise some awkward questions. Were the authorities applying different criteria as between "enemy aliens" and aristocrat members of the establishment and old Etonians? By August, when the initial panic had subsided somewhat, a government spokesman had admitted that due to official blunders, many innocent peopled had been interned and later in the month Churchill told the Commons, with what one historian has called "an impressive display of amnesia" that he had always thought the fifth-column danger exaggerated.[13] His actual instructions at the time, however, had been to "collar the lot".

York did not entirely escape the consequences of the application of extreme security measures. In all the confusion over internment, one of the selected locations was York Racecourse where an emergency camp was set up in the main grandstand and administrative buildings, surrounded by barbed wire and patrolling armed guards. One of its temporary guests, albeit only for six weeks, was the internationally recognised *avant garde*

German artist Kurt Schwitters (1887-1948). Himself a refugee from Nazi Germany who had fled to Norway to escape persecution in his native land, he had been forced to flee again to Scotland following the German invasion of his first country of sanctuary. Nevertheless, he was an "enemy alien" and so he was held for a short time in York before passing on, first to Bury in Lancashire and ultimately to the Isle of Man before his ultimate release. Unfortunately it took the authorities two years or so to decide that he posed no threat to national security. No matter – in 2010 the Isle of Man government did eventually make amends, albeit somewhat posthumously, by issuing a stamp showing his fine portrait of an equally harmless fellow internee, Dr Klaus E Hinrichsen.

There were no annual reports for the years 1942 to 1946, the Society having seemingly resolved at one point to suspend their publication due to the disruption of the war, although the minutes do refer to their being printed. Certainly the committee continued to meet during this period and their minutes have survived. During the whole period of the war there were a total of 21 such meetings but they were much less regular than under peacetime conditions. There were no meetings, for example between 8 February 1943 and 10 February 1944. Nevertheless day-to-day business was able to continue but with difficulty. It is clear, however, that even at the height of a world war some subjects of legal controversy were unwilling to submit to even a temporary truce. At a committee meeting on 11 January 1943 the question of compulsory registration of title was once again on the agenda.[14] Two months later at the Annual General meeting on 16 March 1943 the twelve members present were at least able to learn that a "Mr Catlow of Leeds had given evidence before the Commission [on Land Registration] upon the lines approved by our Committee on behalf of the Yorkshire Union of Law Societies".

Another topic was equally under discussion: the subject of "touting" and "ambulance chasing" – topics that had always been prone to raise members' blood pressure ever since the foundation of the Society. The AGM minutes record that Mr CG Bailey had raised the question of "legal aid societies" approaching persons injured in accidents, saying that they would deal with their claims on a commission basis. Apparently the matter had been drawn to the attention of the Law Society but they were powerless to act unless some solicitor was involved – they had no jurisdiction over touting by others.

A year later, on 9 March 1944, the subject of scale fees for conveyancing was under discussion – a subject inextricably linked at the time and in the minds of most solicitors to touting. Sixteen members were able to attend the AGM on that occasion. The specific issue was whether an authorised increase of 12% to the statutory scale should be adopted. It is clear that opinion was divided and it was left that members "should if possible charge the increased amount but there was no resolution to make it compulsory". Some members had noted that "owing to the increased prices at which property was being sold, the Solicitors were thereby obtaining a considerable increase in costs".

On 18 April 1944 the committee had to consider the first signs of a far more significant and far-reaching development: the Beveridge Report.[15]

> A memo on Social and Allied Services in Sir William Beveridge's Report was considered at the request of the Law Society. It was decided to write to the Society stating that we were in sympathy with their attitude to this question but thought that the time was not opportune for action and would like to hear if possible what action the Trade Unions were adopting towards it. Subject to this it was decided that a letter should be written to the members [of parliament] for York, Thirsk, Malton, Scarborough, Barkston Ash and Howden asking them to watch the Common Law principles which would be infringed by some of the proposals in the Report and to ask the Law Society if they could supply a draft of a suitable letter.

At their next meeting on 10 August 1944 the Committee noted that they had received replies from the Members of Parliament for York, Richmond, Howden, Scarborough and Thirsk and Malton concerning the Beveridge Report. The first four mentioned had agreed to watch the Society's interests when the bill before parliament. The member for Thirsk and Malton had said that he thought the suggestions were, on the whole, very necessary improvements to the existing law but he would be willing to consider specific objections from the Society, and, if necessary, meet the Society's members do discuss the questions with them.

On the domestic front it was reported that York Medical Society was prepared to provide rooms at their premises at 17 Stonegate for £70 p.a. plus part of the expenses of the caretaker. It was decided to try to negotiate a rent of £50 p.a. plus 5/- a week towards the cost of the caretaker. The negotiations with York Medical Society were eventually concluded at a rent of £70 p.a. inclusive of the caretaker. This was to be the library's last location as a separate law library before finally merging in 1989 with the library of the College of Law.[16]

The last wartime committee meeting took place on 16 July 1945. The war in Europe had come to an end two months earlier and at last the committee could at least consider the possibility once again of holding an annual dinner. But they were taking no chances: it was agreed to await the end of the war with Japan and thereupon the sub-committee could immediately proceed with the necessary arrangements. No doubt "peace for our time" – at least as far as Europe was concerned – had provided the committee with a burst of optimism. However, if the members of the Society were under the impression that it was soon once again to be "business as usual", they were mistaken. The upheavals of war had produced seismic changes in British Society and the country was about to face, for the first time, a Labour government with a working majority which was dedicated to reflecting those changes.

NOTES

1. Figures are not exact and can vary quite significantly – often depending on how they are defined. These figures are taken from the BBC's website.

2. My own family was luckier in one respect. At the time when our home near Richmond Park in London lost all its windows from a similar near miss we had a live-in maid, a lovely Irish girl named Mary Carter of whom I have fond childhood memories. Her boyfriend, to whom she naturally mentioned this disaster at the first opportunity, was an American GI. Days later a US army truck turned up on the doorstep with almost enough glass to re-glaze the Crystal Palace.

3. Judy Slinn *A History of Freshfields* Vanessa Charles. Freshfields 1984

4. Sir Thomas Lund (1906-1981) as he later became was one of the best known secretaries of the Law Society. He achieved the distinction of having his portrait in the National Portrait Gallery.

5. There were occasional moments of light relief but they were generally few and far between. The late Airey Neave MP claimed that a certain scene in *The Colditz Story* was authentic – and he was there. Following one particularly irritating escape, a furious German officer whose mastery of

colloquial English was not quite as good as he seemed to think it was, shouts at the assembled prisoners on parade "You British – you think I know damn nothing but I tell you I know DAMN ALL!". The Germans were quite often defeated by English slang and colloquialisms. Camp guards were usually nicknamed "Goons" – a name they accepted quite cheerfully when informed that it stood for G-O-O-Ns: "German Officers or Non-Coms".

6. I thought at first that these temporary rules had a slight hint of Ben Trovato's authorship about them but they do feature in Tom Brennand's *Richmond Golf Club, A Centenary History 1891-1991*. They were apparently a response to an occasion in the autumn of 1940 when bombs did fall on the course.

7. Sir Carleton Kemp Allen MC, KC (1887-1966) Sir Carleton (or "CK" as he was generally known) was Australian born and educated. As in the case of Lord Atkin himself, his Australian roots doubtless made him less inclined to be deferential to authority.

8. Quoted by Tom Bingham in *The Business of Judging* p. 217 – Oxford University Press 2000

9. A seat subsequently to be held by The Rt Hon John Prescott MP.

10. The decision of the UK to intern virtually all enemy aliens almost as a matter of course in both world wars was somewhat controversial at the time and subsequently. The initial panic with which the policy was introduced in 1939 inevitably meant that at first conditions for detainees were often quite unsuitable – in tented camps or in premises without beds – alleviated only by the general kindliness of those actually in charge. It is interesting to note that the French authorities at the time of the Napoleonic wars seem to have taken a much more relaxed attitude to Mr Parker, the owner of the hotel in Calais from which Jonathan Gray wrote to his wife on the occasion of his visit in 1814. Neither Parker nor his wife from Canterbury seem to have been troubled in this way throughout the much longer period of the war with France – see Chapter 4 note 10.

11. Joshua Levine *The Secret History of the Blitz* Simon & Schuster UK Ltd, London 2015

12. Quoted in Professor Christopher Andrew's *The Defence of the Realm – The Authorized History of MI5* p.226 – Allen Lane 2009

13. ibid p. 230

14. For a detailed account of this long-running controversy see Appendix D

15. The Report, commissioned by the wartime coalition government, identified five "giant evils in society: squalor, ignorance, want, idleness and disease" and went on to propose a wide-ranging reform to our system of social welfare which eventually provided the foundation for the modern welfare state. It received fairly widespread public approval, the main debate turning on whether it was more prudent to await the end of the war so that a better assessment might be made of the country's financial position. Interestingly, the "Tory Reform Committee" consisting of 45 backbench Conservative MPs demanded the immediate formation of a Ministry of Social Security. Equally interestingly, the reaction of many Labour MPs was more ambivalent. Some wanted a fully-fledged "state" system of National Health Service rather than one run through local health centres and regional hospital administrations. Ernest Bevin himself, with his Trade Union background, was more concerned with wage bargaining than social insurance. He followed the coalition government in believing that any action should await the end of the war.

16. See Appendix C p. 408.

Chapter Twelve

THE POST WAR YEARS
1945 – 1960

Death of His late Majesty King George VI
The Secretary was asked to write to the Law Society to enquire whether it was recommended that solicitors should wear any form of mourning.

Committee Minute 12 February 1952

The war years, as we have seen, had been extraordinarily disruptive and the immediate post-war period was hardly less so. Aerial warfare had caused immense material damage quite apart from the direct cost of the war itself. In 1946 the government was obliged to borrow a total of $4.34 billion (certainly well over $100 billion at today's values) from the US and Canada, not so much to pay for the conflict as to avoid national insolvency. The last repayment instalment was not made until 29 December 2006. For years bomb sites were part of the natural landscape in much of urban Britain. In York, for example, it was not until 1960 that the rebuilding of the Guildhall, shattered on the night of the Baedeker raid of 29 April 1942 was completed, being officially re-opened by Her late Majesty, Queen Elizabeth the Queen Mother on 21 June 1960. St Martin's Church in Coney Street, which also suffered on the same night, has never been completely rebuilt. Hull, as a major east coast port, had suffered particularly badly at the hands of the Luftwaffe and the visible effects were to last for years.

However, it was not just the material consequences of the war which were to affect people's lives in the immediate post-war years. Rationing was a major worry, particularly in urban areas, and did not apply just to food but to clothing and fuel as well. Many other resources, such as building materials, were scarce. For this reason no building could take place without a licence and priority was given to the rebuilding of bomb sites and public sector housing – restrictions which were not finally lifted until 1954, nine years after the war's end. Food and clothing also continued to be a major problem for some years. The rationing of flour which ended in 1948, began the slow return to normality, followed by clothes (1949) canned and dried fruit and petrol (1950) tea (1952) sugar and sweets (1953) and bananas in 1954 which finally saw the whole system dismantled. Before then, however, the whole country had to get through the winter of 1947; only that of 1963 even began to approach its severity. For much of the three months of January, February and March there was widespread snow cover with massive dislocation of rail and road transport. To add to the misery, coal was in short supply. This prompted many to acquire and use electric fires which in turn exacerbated the problems of electricity generation from power stations (almost wholly dependant on coal). The government was soon obliged to restrict electricity supply to 19 hours a day – in addition to the unplanned power cuts directly attributable to weather conditions.

In the middle of all this misery it was not altogether surprising that only fifteen members (out of a total membership of eighty) were able to attend the Annual General Meeting held on 11 February 1947. Of these, only two were not from York, Mr FSH Ward (Malton) and Mr WR Johnston (Pocklington). Nevertheless, this still represented over 18% of the membership, which is higher than the 12% or so of members who normally attend in more recent and clement times with no petrol rationing. The 1947 minutes remark somewhat laconically "Apologies for non-attendance were reported from a number of Members and Honorary Members". It was doubtless, too, that the weather prompted a letter from one of the non-attenders, Mr Stanley Jones of Malton, with a heartfelt plea to the effect that "February was the worst time of the year for country members attending the Annual Meeting and dinner" and suggesting that some change might be made. After some discussion it was agreed that the dinner would in future be held in "during the November Assize". Nothing was minuted about a change to the date of the AGM but the records show that it was never again held earlier than March.

Three other matters of record were reported to the 1947 AGM. Firstly, that the Society was returning to the custom of issuing an annual report which had been in abeyance since 1942 due to the war – something that the Kaiser had been unable to achieve in the First World War. Secondly, it appeared that only one member of the Society had been killed in the course of the war – a very different state of affairs from the previous conflict. Nevertheless, the Society seems to have escaped lightly. Although no specific record seems to exist as to the number who served in the armed forces, most members of military age would have been called up. Conscription was in force throughout whereas in the First World War it did not begin until 1916 and then in a fairly limited form; universal conscription had not been introduced until the following year. In practice a combination of keenness and social pressure made it unnecessary in the early stages of that war. Finally, the Committee thought it prudent to remind members before their next practising certificate could be renewed they would have to provide an accountant's certificate. "The Council of the Law Society" members were informed "had issued a booklet entitled 'Solicitors' Accounts" which is being sent to every member of the Law Society, and can be obtained from the Law Society by non-members at the price of 2/-."

The year 1947 was, however, marked by one notable, indeed unprecedented event. For the first time in its 161 year history the Society acquired its first woman member, Mrs GL Moore from Harrogate. Her proposer and seconder respectively were Henry Scott and Lumley Dodsworth. Mrs Moore was seemingly admitted without there being any comment or debate (or at least if there was, it was not minuted). One cannot help speculating what the reaction might have been but for the fact that so few members were able to attend. Another seven years were to pass before she was joined by two further women, Miss AMI Ware and Miss V Wayper. This may seem somewhat surprising, given that there had been women solicitors since 1922 when Corrie Morrison became the first one to be admitted to practise, this having become legally possible as a result of the Sex Disqualification (Removal) Act 1919. Before the first world war, in 1913, four women had applied to sit the Law Society's examinations but had been refused permission to do so. The matter eventually went to court in the case of *Bebb v The Law Society* [1914] 1 Ch 286 but Joyce J ruled that women were not "persons" for the purposes of the Solicitors Act 1843, so that was that. But such an outcome could hardly survive the experiences of the war where, for the first time, women had been undertaking all manner of tasks for which they had previously been considered (by men) as unsuitable. However, society changed more slowly than the letter of the law. Ten years after Corrie Morrison's pioneering achievement there were still hardly a hundred women solicitors in practice. Many solicitors who were in practice for some years before the second world war had never encountered a woman solicitor in their professional lives until after it and even then they were a rarity. In 1957, ten years after Mrs Moore's admission as a member of the Yorkshire Law Society, women comprised only 1.94% of practising solicitors in the country as a whole. When I joined the Society in 1967 there were no women members at all and that remained the position for a further two years until 1969 when one was admitted. In 1967 the total number of women in the profession as a whole comprised only 2.7%, rising to 7.33% in 1977, 16% in 1987 and 32.75% in 1997 and 48% in 2014.[1]

Those first pioneering women cannot have found legal life very easy.[2] On 30 September 1949 there was a meeting of the Dinner Sub-Committee consisting of the President, Mr JC Peters, together with Mr RB Holden, Mr CNP Crombie, Mr NB Kay and Hon Secretary Mr John Shannon. After recording an inspection of the Merchant Adventurers' Hall "and on receiving satisfactory assurances from Mr GNR Crombie, as the Governor, as to the cooking, heating and sanitary facilities to be provided, it was unanimously agreed that the hall would be a most suitable place to hold the Dinner". It is clear from the minutes that item 2 on the agenda was more controversial than any mere change of venue: "The Secretary reported that Mrs GL Moore wished to know whether it would be in order for her to bring a lady guest (Dr Thwaites) to the Dinner. It was decided to refer the question to the full committee with a recommendation that the request be not approved "as a precedent might otherwise be created". The minutes of the following full committee meeting make no mention of Mrs Moore's request and as the cash-book does not include items relating to the dinner, I have been unable to determine whether Mrs Moore attended, either with or without her "lady guest". Probably not, I imagine.

The same meeting agreed that the following drinks should be supplied: "two glasses of sherry in the Ante-Room, one glass of sherry with the soup, two of red or white, with one glass of port". This was followed by a discussion on the supply of cigars and cigarettes: "It was decided that the cost os supplying cigars to all those present would be prohibitive". However, the President then intervened, expressing a desire "to provide personally cigars for the top table and cigarettes for the remainder of those attending the dinner at his own expense and this offer was gratefully accepted". Incidentally, the direct per capita cost of the dinner was 12/6 and the cost of tickets 27/6.

It was not until its Annual General Meeting in 1981 that the Society formally resolved that members be permitted to invite women guests to its annual dinner. According to the minutes of that meeting the discussion relating to the annual dinner was "long" although in fairness two other issues were involved, namely venue and balloting for guests. The fact remains that between the admission of Mrs Moore in 1947 and 1981 (a period of 34 years) women members were in a most ambivalent position: whilst it eventually became tacitly accepted that they could invite other women as guests, there was certainly an assumption that they would not invite men as guests and I am not sure that they ever did.

At least as regards the admission of women as members, the Society was ahead of the House of Lords. In was only by the Life Peerage Act 1958, ten years after Mrs Moore's admission and four hundred years after John Knox's diatribe,[3] that women peers were first admitted to the House of Lords. Their lordships' debate over their own reform had prompted a notable contribution from James Patrick Boyle, Earl of Glasgow, the eighth of that ilk, whose forebears came over with the Conqueror:

> Women, ... are not suited to politics, for the following reasons. They are often moved by their hearts more than they are by their heads, and the emotional urge which exists in a woman's make up does not help towards good judgement ... Many of us do not want to sit beside them on these benches, nor do we want to meet them in the library. This is a house of men, a House of Lords. We do not wish this to become a House of Lords and Ladies.

The noble earl was but one of a total of thirty refuseniks. Fortunately for the reputation of Scottish peers, the Earl of Home was able to redress the balance "... taking women into parliamentary embrace" he reminded their lordships, "would seem to be only a modest extension of the normal function and privileges of a peer". Eventually normality carried the day, the Life Peerages Bill passed into law, peers embraced women and Baroness Wooton took her place on the benches and in the library of that particular house of men. But she was only a life peer; the women hereditaries, of whom there were twelve, had to wait until the Peerage Act 1963 before they were able to join her and others on whom life peerages had been conferred.

As far as women solicitors were concerned, there were of course economic and social reasons for the slow take-off. Even for middle class families (from which the profession was largely drawn at the time) assisting daughters to qualify as solicitors was an onerous undertaking. Degrees of any kind did not become the norm even for men until years later, which of course meant five years of articles which were not only unpaid but could involve a substantial premium.[4] And then there was stamp duty of £80 on the articles themselves. The latter had not been abolished until 1947. The practice of demanding premiums took much longer to disappear. The late Michael Dryland, a member of the Society for many years, recalled that when he began his articles in 1949, his father had paid a premium of £300 for the privilege; moreover, he received no wages, merely a Christmas Box of £5. The practice of paying premiums lingered on into the 1960s but by 1968 only 5% of firms would admit to be still taking them. Minute 12 of the Society's AGM held on 21 March 1967 – the year of my own admission to the Society – reads as follows:

> The recommendations of the Committee that in future no specific amount for remuneration should be recommended to members but that instead it should be recommended that no premium be asked for and that an articled clerk should be adequately remunerated by his principal, was approved and that any previous recommendation should be rescinded.

Still, qualifying as a solicitor was expensive and the cost had to be met by the candidate's family. At a time, when there was still a widely held assumption that women should and would cease to work on marriage[5] and certainly after starting a family, it was a bold and prosperous father who was prepared to invest in his daughter qualifying as a solicitor.

If women did not appear to preoccupy the Society unduly in those post-war years, other topics certainly did. One of them was the advent of "legal aid" in the context of the Poor Man's Lawyer Scheme. This scheme, for which the Law Society had originally assumed responsibility in 1926, was struggling to mitigate the enormously increased difficulties faced by the poor in dealing with the numerous legal issues for which the war had served as a catalyst. The old saw that justice was "open to all; like the Ritz Hotel"[6] was still very much the reality in immediate post-war Britain but gradually it was coming to be seen that a modern society could not function effectively, let alone fairly, unless the ordinary citizen was in a position to obtain proper and effective legal aid and advice when required. This notion had had a long and difficult gestation which it is necessary to examine in some detail in order to understand the circumstances which eventually gave birth to the Legal Aid and Advice Act 1949. In a lecture at Gresham College on 20 June 2007 Michael Napier, senior partner of Irwin Mitchell,[7] traced its origins to Moses and the Book of Exodus.[8] As far as our jurisdiction was concerned, he recalled that the problem of access to justice specifically for the poor was first formally recognised by the Suing in Forma Pauperis Act 1495 which instituted a form of proceeding by providing relief from court fees and access to lawyers acting *pro bono*:

> Be it ordeyned and enacted by youre Highnes and by the Lordes Spirituall and temporall and the Comens in this present parliament assembled and by the auctorite of the same, that every pouer person or persones within the realme shall have by the discrecion of the Chaunceller of this realme ... writte or writtes originall and writtes of Sub pena according to the nature of their causes therefor nothing paieng to youre Highnes ... nor to any persone for the making of the same ... And the seid Chaunceller ... shall assigne such of the Clerkis which shall doo and use the making and writing of the same ... and also lerned Councell and attorneys for the same without any reward taking therefor ...[9]

To modern eyes one obvious omission was that there was no provision for poor defendants, only poor plaintiffs. This was no doubt due to the fact that under the social conditions of 1495 a poor defendant would hardly have been worth suing. In fact the Act of that year merely codified in statutory form a number of earlier ordinances. But, as Napier pointed out, the the plaintiff suing *in forma pauperis* had another hurdle to overcome if he lost: by the later Costs Act 1531 it was provided that although an

> ### Affidavits
>
> *Of a Pauper that he is not worth 5 l. to profecute in* Forma Pauperis.
>
> _____ That faid _____ maketh Oath, that he this Deponent is not worth in all the World the fum of 5 l. in Lands, Tenements, Goods or Chattels, his Wearing Apparel, and the Matters of the Suit only excepted.
>
> *To defend* in Forma Pauperis.
>
> _____ The faid Defendant maketh Oath, that his Debt being paid, he is not worth 5 l. in the whole World.

Legal Aid in forma pauperis from The Attorney's Compleat Pocket Book 1743. The procedure was not finally repealed until 1949 by the Legal Aid and Advice Act of that year.

unsuccessful plaintiff was not liable for his opponent's costs, he *was* liable to such other punishment as might be thought reasonable. This typically meant "being whipped or pilloried" although Blackstone comments that unsuccessful plaintiffs were later given the option of being whipped or paying the defendant's costs – hardly a realistic option if they were suing *in forma pauperis* since to qualify they had to swear that they had no property exceeding £5 in value, save for their wearing apparel and the subject matter of their claim. The 1531 Act also, for the first time, allowed successful defendants to recover their costs from the other side provided of course that the other side were not themselves suing in *forma pauperis*. Without the whipping or pillorying, this remained more or less the position until almost the end of the 19th century. When, however, the Rules of the new Supreme Court were promulgated in 1883 it was decided to discourage the unmeritorious claims of paupers by insisting on a certificate from counsel as to their merit. Whether this was as effective in discouraging unmeritorious claims as the prospect of being whipped or pilloried is perhaps debatable.

Slowly by fits and starts over the first part of the 20th century there was a movement away from the notion that the poor (however defined) could only look to a haphazard combination of Rules of Court and the charity of solicitors and counsel to assist them with their legal problems on a *pro bono* basis. The Law Society had been running the Poor Persons Scheme since 1926 but it was the confluence of two wholly unconnected events which in the end was to bring about the most significant change in approach. The two events in question were the Matrimonial Causes Act 1937 and the dramatic family disruption which had been brought about between 1939 and 1945 by the war.

Assistance in criminal cases was another matter entirely. For most of its existence the English legal system had not been overly sympathetic either to criminals or those suspected of crime, although over time judges developed rules of evidence to protect the accused from the worst excesses of over-zealous prosecutors. Even so, little enough distinction seems to have been made between the two. As the late Lord Bingham observed,[10]

> If the position of the poor man needing advice or assistance in the civil field was dire, the position of the criminal defendant was even worse. In the 18th century, the criminal trial was a very amateurish affair. Most prosecutions were brought by private individuals in the hope of reward. There were no professional prosecutors. The majority of trials were conducted without lawyers. The defendant had no right to give evidence. And one suspects that many of the judges were extremely arbitrary.

Despite procedural changes introduced in the 19th century Bingham goes on to quote from Sir James Stephen's *History of the Criminal Law* published in 1883:

> It must be remembered that most persons accused of crime are poor, stupid and helpless. They are often defended by solicitors who confine their exertions to getting a copy of the depositions and endorsing it with the name of some counsel to whom they pay a very small fee, so that even when prisoners are defended by counsel the defence is often extremely imperfect, and consists rather of what occurs at the moment to the solicitor and counsel than of what the man himself would say if he knew how to say it. When a prisoner is undefended his position is often pitiable, even if he has a good case. An ignorant uneducated man has the greatest possible difficulty in collecting his ideas, and seeing the bearing of facts

alleged. He is utterly unaccustomed to sustained attention or systematic thought, and it often appears to me as if the proceedings on a trial which to any experienced person appear plain and simple, must pass before the eyes and mind of the prisoner like a dream he cannot grasp.

During the first few decades of the Society's existence the principal function of the law had been to protect property. Parliament represented almost exclusively the interests of property owners and its members did not believe in half measures. The late Sir Leon Radzinowicz, first Woolfson Professor of Criminology at Cambridge, reckoned that between the "Glorious Revolution" of 1688 and 1820 the number of capital statutes increased from about 50 to over 200.[11] Of these most were concerned with property and ranged from such matters as injury to growing hops and obstructing law enforcement, to picking pockets and being found in the company of gypsies. One of the most notorious was the so-called Waltham Black Act (more properly the Criminal Law Act) 1723. Originally enacted as a reaction to a specific event in Essex – or possibly Hampshire, there is some confusion on the point – it was extended in 1725 for five years by 12 Geo. 1 c.30, amended in 1754 by 27 Geo 2 c.15 and made permanent in 1758 by 31 Geo. 3 c.42. It made it a felony without benefit of clergy (ie punishable by death) to go abroad into woods in any form of disguise or with a blackened face. It remained on the statute book for over a hundred years until repealed together with many other obsolete acts by Sir Robert Peel in the 1830s.

The fact is that before the Legal Aid and Advice Act 1949 any assistance to defendants in criminal cases was very limited. It was only with the coming into force of the Prisoners' Counsel Act 1836 that counsel had been permitted to summarise the case and address the jury on a defendant's behalf and even that concession to the accused had been highly controversial and subject to considerable opposition at the time from a significant number of judges and, perhaps more surprisingly, an equally significant number of counsel. As the century progressed the tradition of the "dock brief", previously a matter of discretion for the trial judge, became formalised. For a fixed fee of £1.3.6 (a guinea for counsel and 2/6 for the clerk) a defendant was permitted to choose any member of the Bar actually robed and in court and, having been chosen, counsel then became professionally obliged to represent the accused . But even this seemingly nominal sum was beyond the means of many defendants in Victorian times and of course there was no provision of any kind for investigation. The position of a poor defendant remained extremely precarious as he was not even allowed to give sworn evidence on his own behalf until the passing of the Criminal Evidence Act 1898. In practice the right to give evidence could prove to be something of a mixed blessing since, by doing so, the defendant became liable to be cross-examined. Even the Poor Prisoners Defence Act 1903 was not much more help. Firstly, it was never designed to ascertain whether the defendant had a defence, merely to ensure that if he did appear to have an arguable defence, it was properly presented. Secondly, many defendants were unaware of the Act's existence and indeed, so were many magistrates. And even those magistrates who were aware of it were reluctant to make the necessary orders as the cost burden would fall on the local ratepayers. It seems to have been used very sparingly.

So matters remained as regards the criminal law until the Poor Prisoners' Defence Act 1930 removed some of the deficiencies of the 1903 Act. In particular defendants were no longer required to disclose their defence at the committal stage and magistrates were given a wide discretion to grant legal aid where the defendant's means were insufficient and the interests of justice appeared to require it but the system was still far from satisfactory.

The problems which could arise are well illustrated by a case which occurred in 1946 where a foreign defendant, displaced as a result of the upheaval of war, had been convicted of the murder of his newborn baby daughter by drowning her in a bucket of water. He and the mother had made no attempt to conceal what they had done. The father was convicted of murder at the Old Bailey and sentenced to hang. All he had by way of representation was counsel assigned on a "dock brief". Unfortunately the defendant spoke no language that anyone, including counsel, understood and there was in consequence no interpretation. He was duly convicted. Whilst he was awaiting execution at Pentonville Prison, the warders appointed to supervise him became convinced that he did not actually know that he was going to be executed. They reported their concern to the governor who made his own enquiries and he too became suspicious. The condemned man was thought to originate from the Iberian peninsular (he had no papers) but the governor's enquiries (through the Catholic chaplain and a Basque priest friend) established that his language was neither Spanish nor Portuguese, Catalan nor Basque. It was thought it might be an obscure Spanish gypsy dialect. The Governor reported his concerns to the Home Office and the man was ultimately reprieved. The Governor was my paternal grandfather William John Lawton.

By the 1950s the Poor Man's Lawyer's Scheme, operated under the aegis of the Law Society and a number of provincial law societies, was creaking. The Society's archives contain the certificates in use at the time which were in the following form:

I HERBY CERTIFY that, in my opinion..
is qualified to be advised by the Poor Man's Lawyer, his average income being not more than £4 a week and his total possessions (excluding wearing apparel) being less than £100.
Signed..
~~*Probation Officer.*~~
YORK COMMUNITY COUNCIL, LTD.
Dated..

It will be seen that for legal purposes at least the upper limit of "poverty" in the intervening four and a half centuries since 1495 had inflated from £5 to £100 (always excluding wearing apparel) but on the other hand, income was taken into consideration if it exceeded £4pw. The scheme was operated by local law societies whose members volunteered on an essentially *pro bono* basis. Its limitations can be judged from the letter opposite (with names etc. omitted) from the Society's archives which is fairly typical of its type:

THE YORKSHIRE LAW SOCIETY

>Poor Man's Lawyer Service,
>Law Library
>17 Stonegate,
>York.

>25th. June 1952

Dear Mr.-------

    Since seeing you last night I have been in touch with the York Community Council who say that you were permitted to consult the Poor Man's Lawyer on the basis that it was advice you wanted only, and not action to be taken.

    Accordingly I can only repeat the advice which I gave you last night, namely that before any proceedings can be effective commenced, you should obtain good evidence of the statements which are being made and by whom. If it can then be proved that these statements are untrue and that as a result thereof you have suffered damage, you may have a good cause of action. At the moment however the matter is one for an enquiry agent rather than a Solicitor.

We return the letters which you left with us and have retained and two shillings and sixpence fee in view of the advice which has been given.

>Yours faithfully.
>(signed)
>Poor Man's Lawyer

(Address)
Enclosures

By 1959 S7 of the Legal Aid and Advice Act 1949 had come into effect and accordingly the Committee recommended that the Poor Man's Lawyer Scheme should cease to operate with effect from 2 March of that year. The 1959 Annual Report contained the following obituary:

> The Scheme has been operated by a rota of Members of the Society for many years and there is no doubt that it has satisfied a need in the City. The Committee tenders its most grateful thanks to those Members who have given of their time and services and also is greatly indebted to the Probation Officers and the Community Council for their invaluable assistance in helping the Scheme to run and to prevent its abuse.
>
> It is interesting to note that during the year under review no fewer than 104 cases, being one of the highest numbers ever recorded , were passed to the Honorary Secretary, Mr I Witcombe, for allocation to solicitors as follows:–
>
> 1. Custody, Maintenance, Separation and Divorce 68
> 2. Affiliation 15
> 3. Claims re Accidents, Insurance, Wages and Damages 8
> 4. Probate 3
> 5. Miscellaneous 10
>
> It will be seen that the number of cases dealt with under headings 1 and 2 are again higher than those reported last year when 61 and 13 cases respectively were attended to.
>
> Your Committee would like to tender their most sincere thanks to Mr Witcombe for acting as Secretary to this Scheme for so long and so well.

It was indeed the end of an era. Just nine years earlier the Committee had agreed that in future a nominal fee of half-a-crown (12½p) should be payable by those people seeking advice from the Poor Man's Lawyer and that the Probation Office and Citizens' Advice Bureau be informed accordingly. The availability of public money for legal aid and advice was to transform the legal scene over the next decades but perhaps the basis on which it was established contained a flaw which would eventually lead to its ultimate demise. Nobody could have foreseen the tsunami of marriage breakdown and cognate issues, employment law and personal injury litigation, to say nothing of crime, which was to overwhelm our own generation, and the unwillingness of government to pay for it.

More mundane matters equally attracted the attention of the Committee in those difficult post-war years. Although still well within living memory, the Committee minutes for this period convey an impression of a very different world from the present day with very different professional preoccupations. It represents a world which in some ways is as different from our own as that of the Society's founding fathers.

3 February 1950

President's Tea

The question was discussed as to whether the tea which it was customary for the outgoing President to give to members and their ladies should be borne by the Society. Lt-Colonel HJ Shaftoe, the President-Elect indicated his desire to meet the expense of this function and it was decided by the Committee that in future years the incoming President should be the host and that the Society should not take over the expense of the function.

Secretaries' Honorarium

The question was discussed of the payment of an honorarium to the Secretaries. [There were two joint Hon Secretaries at this time] This was approved and the Treasurer was instructed to agree an amount with the Secretaries and bring this before the next meeting of the Committee.

Law Courts, Solicitors and Barristers Room

As the accommodation at the Law Courts, Clifford Street, York is now quite inadequate for barristers, solicitors and witnesses attending the courts (particularly female witnesses) it was resolved that the York Corporation be approached through the Town Clerk with a request that the barristers' and solicitors' room which was in use before the war be furnished and made available for barristers and solicitors and that the room at present being used by barristers, solicitors and female witnesses be made available for female witnesses as was the case before the war.

28 March 1950

Secretaries' Honorarium

It was agreed that the Society should pay an honorarium of £25 to the Secretaries, this to be retrospective for a year.

27 February 1951

Vice Presidency

Letters from Mr LLS Dodsworth to the Secretaries and to the President were read where he expressed the opinion that some explanation should be forthcoming as to why the name of another member of the profession had not been considered for the office and further that he felt that by accepting it would be an act of discourtesy towards such fellow member who appeared to be as well qualified as Mr Dodsworth, and further, that the appointment had gone by seniority in the past.

> The Committee, after a full discussion of the matter, and being of the opinion that they were not in any way governed in the matter of custom or precedent, Resolved with only one dissentient, that the invitation should again be extended to Mr Dodsworth.

As always on these occasions, one cannot but speculate as to what was not minuted. Either "such fellow member" being passed over had done something to upset members of the Committee or there was some particular reason why they were keen to elect Mr Dodsworth. We shall never know but, whatever his scruples over possible "discourtesy", Mr Dodsworth duly took his place as Vice-President.

Following the death in his sleep of HM King George VI on 6 February 1952, the Committee was concerned with a matter of protocol.

12 February 1952

Death of His late Majesty King George VI

The Secretary was asked to write to the Law Society to enquire as to whether it was recommended that solicitors should wear any form of mourning. It was agreed that no action be taken on a suggestion that offices should close on the afternoon of the King's funeral.

On a rather different note, it is interesting to see the arrangements for the first annual dinner of the new Elizabethan reign:

9 September 1952

… that the following guests should be invited:

All the Honorary Members (of whom it was anticipated that only four would accept) and

> Mr Justice Cassels
> Mr Justice Gorman
> The Judge's Marshal
> Mr HB Hylton-Foster QC MP
> The High Sheriff of Yorkshire
> The High Sheriff of Yorkshire's Chaplain
> The President of the Bankers' Institute (York Centre)
> The President of the York Medical Society
> The President of the Land Agents' Society
> The President of the Law Society
> The Lord Mayor of York
> The Sheriff of York
> The Clerk of Assize
> HC Scott Junior
> The York County Court judge
> The Governor of the Merchant Adventurers' Company
> 3 Press Representatives

It was also agreed that Terry's "overhead" charge would be £34 and that they would provide dinner as per an approved menu for 18/6 per head. It was further agreed that the following wines would be served:

Cloister Sherry at 17/- per bottle

Louis Roederer Champagne (non vintage) at 24/6 per bottle and

1927 Vintage Port at 25/- per bottle

Agreed that the price of the annual dinner should be 45/- inclusive of all wine and cocktails.

Curiously there is no mention of claret or burgundy. In gastronomic terms Australia was best known in those days for tinned peaches and apricot jam and New Zealand for butter and lamb. For the English at least, the Balkans, California, South Africa and South America had not yet taken their place in the oenological firmament and Germany would probably have been excluded for ideological reasons. The guest list is certainly extensive and no doubt contributed to the difference between the actual cost of food (18/6 per head exclusive of of the overhead charge) and the cost to members of 45/-. The event, incidentally, incurred a deficit of £31.10s.9d.

The overall impression one gets from the Society's records and deliberations during the years of post-war reconstruction up until the beginning of the 1960s is one of a gradual return to "business as usual". But whatever usual business members of the Society may have thought that they were returning to in 1960 the reality was to be very different indeed – as we shall see in the next two chapters.

NOTES

1. The opening of the professions to women is of course a feature of all developed societies but the advance has not been achieved by any means over a united front – either as regards specific professions or in different countries, even in Europe. Elizabeth Garrett Anderson, the first woman doctor to have practised medicine in the UK, had to take her MD degree in Paris in 1870 and effectively got onto the medical register here by clever manipulation of the rules. In both France and Germany also women doctors were ahead of women lawyers. Although the first woman, Jeanne Chauvin, qualified to practise as an *avocat* at the French Bar in 1900, it was not until 1949 that France had its first woman *notaire*. By contrast the first woman to practise as a doctor in France was Madeleine Brès in 1875. The position was much the same in Germany. There the first woman allowed to practise as a lawyer was Margarete Berent – in 1925. During the Nazi period sporadic attempts were made to bar legal and medical practice to women on the classic *Kinder, Küche, Kirche* basis. Even today, although there are increasing numbers of women at the German Bar (ie as advocates), their earnings are well below that of their male counterparts and their influence in professional associations is said to be negligible. Angela Merkel notwithstanding, the Germans even have a word for women who

seek to venture too far outside the confines of *Kinder, Küche, und Kirche*: they are known as *Rabenmütter* – "ravenmothers".

2. The first women barristers didn't find life easy either. Not the least of the embarrassments that greeted their arrival was an unseemly row as to whether or not they should be permitted to wear wigs. The objectors claimed that wigs were male attire and the predictable "thin end of the wedge" arguments were trotted out: eg "They'll be wanting to wear trousers next!"

3. *The First Blast of the Trumpet Against the Monstrous Regiment of Women* by John Knox (1558): "For who can denie but it is repugneth to nature, that the blind shall be appointed to leade and conduct such as do see? That the weake, the sicke and impotent persons shal norishe and kepe the hole and strong? And finallie, that the foolishe, madde and phrenetike shal governe the discrete and give counsel to such as be sober of mind. And such be al women, compared unto man in bearing of authoritie. For their sight in civile regiment is but blindness; their strength, weaknes; their counsel, foolishnes; and judgment phrensie, if it be rightlie considered."

4. It is salutary to recall that as long ago as 1821 Isaac Disraeli, father of the future Prime Minister Benjamin, paid a premium of 400 guineas (over £20,000 in today's money – much more if calculated by reference to average earnings) for the privilege of having his son articled to a solicitor and Disraeli Senior was not one to throw money around. Some years earlier he had been elected Warden of the Bevis Marks synagogue but he was not prepared to pay the fee of £40 levied on those who declined such an honour. As a result he left the congregation and in 1817 and had his four children, including Benjamin, baptised into the Church of England – which is how Britain came to acquire its first ethnic Jewish Prime Minister.

5. As late as 1972 the Foreign and Commonwealth Office still required women to resign their posts on marriage.

6. The origin of the remark that "justice is open to all; like the Ritz Hotel" is obscure. It has been attributed at various times *inter alios* to Darling J, Mathew J, Lord Bowen and Lord Birkett.

7. Irwin Mitchell is now a major national law firm but the original founder was Walter Irwin Mitchell who established the practice in Sheffield in 1912. Michael Napier CBE, QC (Hon), LLB, LLD (Hon) became its senior partner in 1983. A member of the Legal Studies Board, he also became the Attorney-General's *Pro Bono* envoy.

8. Exodus c18 v21– Moses's father-in-law to Moses: "Moreover thou shalt provide out of all the people able men, such as fear God, men of truth … And let them judge the people at all seasons: and it shall be, that every great matter they shall bring unto thee, but every small matter they shall judge: so shall it be easier for thyself, and they shall bear the burden with thee." Napier did concede, however, that it might be "far fetched" to suggest that Moses was the architect of the first small claims court.

9. 11 Hen. 7 c.12. Parts of this act remained in force into modern times and were only finally repealed by S17(3)(a) of the Legal Aid and Advice Act 1949.

10. The Barnett Lecture at Toynbee Hall on the Centenary of its Legal Advice Centre on 11 June 1998, reproduced in *The Business of Judging – Selected Essays and Speeches* OUP Lord Bingham of Cornhill 2000

11. Sir Leon Radzinowicz *A History of English Criminal Law and its Administration from 1750* (4 vols) 1948 – 1968 Stevens & Sons.

Chapter Thirteen

MODERN TIMES – THE FIRST STIRINGS 1960 – 1986

"Sexual intercourse began
In nineteen sixty-three ...
Between the end of the 'Chatterley' ban
And the Beatles first LP."

Philip Larkin[1] *Annus Mirabilis*

All periods in historical narrative are essentially arbitrary but events happen in a regular sequence and, for anyone living through them, their long term significance is not always immediately apparent. Members who attended the 174th Annual General Meeting of the Society at the Institute of Advanced Architectural Studies (formerly the mediæval church of St John Micklegate) on 30 March 1960 are unlikely to have thought of themselves as entering on a new era even if they were joined on that occasion by Sir Thomas Lund, Secretary of the national Law Society, from Chancery Lane. The second world war had ended just fifteen years earlier and York's mediæval Guildhall, bombed in the infamous Baedeker raid in April 1942, had been effectively rebuilt but was not to be formally reopened by Queen Elizabeth the Queen Mother for another three months. Unless they were late vocations to the law the newly qualified would not have served in it, although as national servicemen they might well have seen active service in Korea, Kenya, Suez or Cyprus. This would not, of course, have applied to women members, except that there was only one. Of the 99 male members, more than half, 55, were admitted in

1939 or earlier and six were admitted before the first world war – one in 1896. At least this number, therefore, would have been liable to wartime conscription unless exempted on medical or other grounds. In practice this would have applied to quite a few others also who had reached military age before qualifying.

But let us return for a moment to sex. The Obscene Publications Act 1959 had provided for the first time a defence of "the public good" if it could be shown that a publication which might otherwise have been considered obscene was justified in the interests of scientific, literary, artistic, educational or other objects of general concern. Since the Act also provided for the consideration of expert evidence on any of these grounds, Penguin Books decided to put the new legislation to the test by publishing *Lady Chatterley's Lover* in paperback, price 3/6. The authorities were astonished and reacted swiftly. Criminal proceedings under the Act were quickly mounted and the case was duly heard at the Old Bailey in October 1960. On 2 November the jury announced their verdict: not guilty. As the *Oxford Companion to English Literature* has put it, it was "a victory which had a profound effect on both writing and publishing in subsequent decades". Yet all this, and much else besides, was in the future and it is doubtful if any of those present at that March afternoon's AGM in Micklegate could have foreseen the day when the very street in which they were assembled would be host not just to one but to two lap-dancing clubs.

Looking back, we can see that in so many ways the legal and social world of 1960 had far more in common with that of 1910 than our world of today. Two world wars had changed much, particularly in the international order, but the way in which solicitors went about their business was not that different from what it had been fifty years earlier. Mr WH Blakeston of Driffield (admitted 1896) would doubtless have conceded that the new-fangled electric telephone featured rather more in the conduct of business than it had when he started in practice. After all, that was just twenty years since Sir William Preece, Chief Engineer to the Post Office, in response to enquiries about Mr Graham Alexander Bell's new invention, had confidently observed "The Americans have need of the telephone, but we do not. We have plenty of messenger boys." And as for motor-cars, the Locomotives Act 1896 had only just increased their maximum speed limit from 4 mph (2 mph in built-up areas) to 14 mph.[2]

Also, most of the familiar legal landmarks were still *in situ* – assizes and quarter-sessions, local searches and enquiries costing £2 or less, old-style abstracts of title, physical exchange of contracts, personal attendance on completion, old-style managing clerks and copy typists – even if the latter were generally women rather than wimmin.

In many ways the social scene had not changed that much either. The first attempt to outlaw discrimination, the Race Relations Act 1965, was still five years away, did not apply to boarding houses or shops and created no criminal, merely civil offences and anyway did not apply to Northern Ireland where discrimination was a way of life. As for the United States, it was only in 1967 that the Supreme Court in *Loving et Uxor v Virgina* finally declared that paragraphs 20-58 of the Virginia penal code making interracial marriage a criminal offence were unconstitutional.[3] Even in England it was still common to see notices in windows "No coloureds or Irish" – that was to remain lawful until the Race Relations Act 1975 – and it was equally lawful to refuse to employ pregnant women or to terminate their employment if they became pregnant and there was no question of redundancy payments for anyone, pregnant or not – that too did not make its appearance until the Redundancy Payments Act 1965.

The Committee's Annual Report of 1960, in a format which had not changed for over sixty years (and which was not to change for another thirty), announced the nomination of William (Bill) Pinkney as President of the Society for the coming year: "Mr Pinkney, who was admitted in 1929, at the age of 21 has practised for thirty years in Bridlington and is particularly well known in the East Riding. He is a Joint Master of the Middleton Foxhounds, and has for many years been the President of the Flamborough Head Golf Club." The same report also contained the following paragraph headed "Lt. Col. RB Holden, DSO, TD, DL – Your Committee note with pleasure that Lt Col Holden, who has held the office of President with such distinction this year, was during the year appointed a Deputy Lieutenant for the West Riding of the County of York and of the City of York."

In retrospect we can see that the days of fox-hunting Presidents or even ones who were Deputy Lieutenants were beginning to draw to a close.[4] The Report contains other clues of an age so different from our own. The Committee was making recommendations about Schedule II costs.[5] The costs recommended by the Committee included a minimum of £1.11s.6d (one and a half guineas) for a simple will in the form of an "absolute gift of the property to one or more beneficiaries". For all other wills the recommendation was for a minimum fee of three guineas. A tenancy agreement attracted a recommended minimum fee of five guineas, a deed of gift ten guineas and a straightforward company formation thirty guineas. By way of comparison, the same report also contains details of the cost of the annual dinner between 1950 (price per head 12/6, ticket price 30/-) and 1959[6] (price per head 19/-, ticket price 52/6). It is perhaps fair to point out that the proportion of official guests was higher in those days (15 official guests to 152 members and private guests) and it was not the policy, as it is now, to pay for official guests from the general funds of the Society.

Scale fees for conveyancing had first been introduced in 1883 and were not abolished until 1972. Of the dozen or so current members of the Society who qualified before that date nearly all must have retired by now so there can only be very few of those in practice who have ever experienced the operation of "scale fees" as they existed between 1883 and 1972. Nevertheless, whilst they existed they were applied with considerable rigour. Just how rigorously can be judged from a committee minute of 13 June 1961:

13. Scale Fee Reduction

The Committee considered an application from Mr WD Pinkney [the Master of Foxhounds – see above] to make a reduction in the scale fee in a case in which he had acted for the Red Cross. It was agreed that he should be allowed to make a one-third reduction in this instance.

The attitude to scale fees needs to be understood in the context of the attitude at the time to any conduct which might constitute self-promotion or "touting" as it was generally and pejoratively known. It was reinforced by the Solicitors' Practice Rules 1936. In the Society's Annual Report for 1950 under the specific heading "Touting" the Committee had issued the following reminder:

Your Committee consider it appropriate to draw the attention of Members to the to the Solicitors' Practice Rules 1936.

Rule 1 states that a solicitor shall not directly or indirectly apply for or seek instructions for professional business or do or permit in the carrying out of his practice any act or thing which could reasonably be regarded as Touting or Advertising or is calculated to attract business unfairly.

Rule 2 lays down that a solicitor shall not hold himself out or allow himself to be held out directly or indirectly and whether or not by name as being prepared to do professional business ... at less than the Scale of Charges (if any) prevailing in the district in which the solicitor practises.

Rule 3 stipulates that a solicitor shall not share with any person not being a solicitor ... his profit costs in respect of any business either contentious or non-contentious.

Your Committee desire to point out that any arrangement whereby (a) a solicitor agrees with (say) an Estate Agent to allow him any proportion of his costs in consideration of the Agent introducing business to the solicitor or (b) an Agent shall recommend prospective Vendors or Purchasers to a particular solicitor in consideration of a reciprocal agreement on the part of the solicitor, constitutes an infraction of the Rules.

It is in the best interests of the profession and indeed of the public that the highest standards of professional etiquette shall be maintained and your Committee wish to assure Members that the fullest enquiry and immediate action will be taken in any case where the Committee is satisfied that an offence has been committed.

It is clear that the above warning was not altogether effective. In the Annual Reports for 1951 and 1952 the Committee felt obliged to repeat it. In their own words from the 1952 Report "during the year under review more complaints concerning breaches of professional etiquette reached them. One case in particular received the particular attention of the Committee."

In our own age of the cult of celebrity, where self-promotion is taken for granted, there is a temptation to be cynical about the profession's support of scale fees and its abhorrence of any conduct which might be regarded as advertising. Even when solicitors were first permitted to advertise at all in 1984, it was still regarded with considerable disfavour by many traditionalists. The reaction was partly cultural and cultures change over time. At its most positive the traditional attitude was prompted by a simple instinctive modesty coupled with a strong feeling that it was somehow unseemly for a professional man, who was concerned with providing a service, to advertise because to do so suggested that he was somehow superior to his colleagues with whom he was in personal contact on a daily basis. This hypersensitivity on the part of solicitors with any claim to respectability is well-illustrated by a Hitchin solicitor, antiquarian and author, Reginald L Hine (1883-1949). In his *Confessions of an Un-Common Attorney* (JM Dent & Sons Ltd 1945) he recalls how he had been giving a lecture on mediæval England to a village audience. In the course of his discourse he had given several examples of the somewhat whimsical provisions that had appeared over the years in the wills of testators of bye-gone ages – eg Mary Swain (1762) "To my niece Mary Swain my best stays and my worst, together with the nutmeg-grater and the jack and spit". He then observes:

> … a fine old country couple came up to me and said: "Muster 'Ine, we proper fancied what you said about them 'dieval wills, and if you dunt moind the missus and me 'ud loike to 'ave ouren dun arter ther same fashun". For a moment I was taken aback. It rather looked as if I had been touting for business.

In the event he overcomes his inhibitions and later visits the old couple's house to take instructions and it is clear that their testamentary ambitions were fulfilled to the letter.

A less pleasing aspect was that there may well have been for some an element of snobbery about it – a desire to distance themselves from "trade". This was sometimes coupled with a certain affectation of seeming "not to try too hard" – the object being to convey an aura of effortless superiority. This approach to practice, at least as manifested at the Bar, was the subject of Theo Mathew's gentle satire[7] *The Languid Leader and the Ducal Action* in one of his *Forensic Fables*. Though the subject of this particular fable was "both Learned and Industrious he Preferred to Pose as a Dilettante". Due to the indisposition of the learned Chancery silk who had originally been briefed, the "Languid Leader" is retained at the last moment on behalf of the Duke of Agincourt in a ferocious dispute with the Bogglesdale Rural District Council. The dispute concerns an alleged "Right of Way over his Grace's Best Grouse Moor". At the consultation on the eve of trial "The Languid Leader had Studied the

Brief with Care and Knew the Case Inside Out". However, he chooses to receive the duke, the ducal solicitor, his managing clerk and junior counsel with "Vague Cordiality", mistaking the duke for the managing clerk and opining that "the Case was about a Cargo of Chinese Pickled Eggs". This last misapprehension having been corrected, the conference then proceeds along similar lines, but it is not long before the subject of the fable casually announces that "he was Afraid he must be going to the House". His Grace is naturally speechless with rage but all is well on the morrow. The Bogglesdale Rural District Council receives a thorough forensic kicking by our hero who receives "the Congratulations of the Duke of Agincourt with Easy Nonchalance", explaining "that One Case was Much Like Another and that it was Quite Easy to Pick a Thing Up as You Went Along." Moral – Keep It Up. A solicitor's practice perhaps offered less scope for posing of this kind but it was by no means unknown.

The main objection to the ban on advertising was that there were plenty of less overt forms of self-promotion available to solicitors – from active membership of the local Rotary or Golf Club to a plethora of other charitable or social activities – "putting yourself about" was how it used to be described. Nowadays it would simply be known as "networking". This of course was not, and could not, be regulated in any way and proponents of advertising claimed that it was far better that such promotion should be open and transparent. Then at least any (unspoken) claims to legal virtue could be assessed on a more objective basis.

In addition to grappling with Schedule II costs, recommending minimum fees and authorising a MFH to reduce his fee to the Red Cross by one third "in this instance", the Committee did have other issues to consider. The annual dinner that year was held at the Merchant Adventurers" Hall on 3 November. For as long as anybody could remember it had been the Society's custom to invite the President of the York Medical Society but there was a problem: their President that year was Dr CB Crane – and she was a woman. The late John Shannon, the Hon Secretary, would doubtless have recalled the occasion just over ten years earlier when the Society's dinner sub-committee had been faced with a request by its first woman member, Mrs GL Moore, to invite another woman doctor (Dr Thwaites) as her personal guest. The dinner committee had not been favourably disposed to the request on that occasion "as a precedent might otherwise be created". But Dr Crane was different: she would be an official guest so any alleged precedent could presumably be distinguished. Clearly it was, because the 1961 Annual Report, after recording the attendance of "both Judges of Assize, Mr Justice Hinchcliffe and Mr Justice Davies", coyly added "The Society also had the unusual honour of the presence of a lady, Dr CB Crane, the President of the York Medical Society." Nevertheless, it was to be 50 years before the Society was able to follow York Medical Society's gallant example and elect a woman as their President in 2010 – Mrs Jenni Bartram.

Another portent in the 1960s of things to come was the abolition of maintenance and champerty by the Criminal Law Act 1967. Younger practitioners may even look blank at such baffling terminology. Maintenance was the financial or other support of a lawsuit by a third party having no interest in it. Champerty was an aggravated form of maintenance where there was an agreement between the plaintiff and the maintainor/champetor to share the proceeds of a successful claim. "Ah", the newly qualified solicitor's eyes light up "you mean a Conditional Fee Agreement or CFA!" Well, she would certainly be getting warm. Maintenance and champerty were both crimes and torts[8] but without their abolition the modern form of Conditional Fee Agreement would not have been possible.

Most people, however, were less concerned with champerty or maintenance or even Conditional Fee Agreements. In retrospect we can see that the biggest changes which were about to occur in the course of the ensuing decades were in family relationships – a subject which affects nearly everybody – and in the public perception of "marriage". Just over one hundred years earlier the Matrimonial Causes Act 1857 had removed from the ecclesiastical courts their longstanding jurisdiction over marriage and transferred it to the newly created Court of Divorce and Matrimonial Causes.[9] As the name of the new court implied, the act had introduced for the first time in England[10] the possibility of a valid marriage being dissolved otherwise than by private act of parliament – a procedure which managed to combine very considerable expense with the added deterrent of having the intimate details of one's marriage debated in public, often at considerable length. Although the term divorce had been used informally in the ecclesiastical courts it referred either to what we would now term "judicial separation" – *a mensa et thoro* (ie from board and lodging) or "a decree of nullity" – *a vinculo matrimonii* (from the bond of marriage). Even the latter was something of a misnomer because it amounted to a finding that there had never been a *vinculum* (bond) in the first place and therefore nothing to dissolve. To rub the point home any issue of such a divorce were deemed in law to be bastards. In the first year after the Act came into force a total of three hundred or so divorce petitions were presented – and there was to be no going back. By way of comparison, fewer than three hundred pre-1857 "parliamentary" divorces had ever been granted and of these, only four were to women.

Once the assumed link between English law and canon law – at least that of the Church of England – had been breached so had any notion of the perceived sacramental indissolubility of marriage. The logic was inescapable: parliament would have to work out its own theology of marriage and its financial implications. At first it was content to tinker. The Married Women's Property Act 1882 was followed by amending acts in 1884, 1893 and 1903. Its only real foray into what would previously have been regarded as the ecclesiastical domain was with the Deceased Wife's Sister's Marriage Act 1907 and Deceased Brother's Widow's Marriage Act 1921.[11] These had been subject to repeal and further amendment by the Law Reform (Married Women and Tortfeasors) Act 1935, the Matrimonial Causes Act 1937, the Married Women (Restraint upon Anticipation) Act 1949, the Matrimonial Causes (Property and Maintenance) Act 1958, the Law Reform (Husband and Wife) Act 1962 and the Matrimonial Proceedings and Property Act 1970. Unfortunately, as so often happens, all this legislative energy had been accompanied by the traditional English addiction to ad hocery and a somewhat cavalier disinclination to worry about first principles or even coherence. At a practical level, never mind theory, little thought seems to have been given for example as to how all this was to be integrated with the law relating to intestate succession under the Administration of Estates Act 1925 as amended in 1952, or with the provisions for maintenance of dependants in the Inheritance (Family Provision) Act 1938 as similarly amended. And how many of today's practitioners are aware, I wonder, that before 1962 husbands and wives could not sue each other in tort – a surprising relic of the old doctrine that a husband and wife were regarded for many purposes as one?

The interaction of law and public opinion is never entirely straightforward and often very subtle. The second half of the 19th century and the first half of the 20th century certainly witnessed a significant decline in traditional religious beliefs and observance but for most people marriage was essentially a matter of day-to-day practicality. In its simplest form, and leaving aside sexual attraction the intensity of which is apt to moderate over time, even if its depth may increase, men needed wives to keep house and see to the upbringing of children and women needed husbands to provide an income and a home. There were of course exceptions but that was the general, and generally accepted, pattern until the 1960s when quite suddenly it all began to unravel and public opinion began to exert pressure on parliament for radical change. Indeed, parliament faced not only the pressure of public opinion but equally of public behaviour. What was happening?

In 1951 the government had appointed Lord Morton of Henryton[12] to chair the Royal Commission on Marriage and Divorce. Its report was not finally published until 1955[13] – its members having proved to be hopelessly divided. On one point, however, they were all, bar one, in agreement: the "matrimonial offence" should continue to be the sole basis for divorce. They saw this as the only way of ensuring the stability of the institution of marriage. Public opinion, however, was becoming increasingly sceptical. The reality was that a consensual dissolution was available to any couple minded to end their marriage. All that was required was for one of them to commit, or at least appear to commit, a matrimonial offence involving an overnight hotel stay and a helpful chambermaid prepared to give evidence that when she came into the bedroom with the breakfast tray the following morning, she observed the respondent sharing a double bed with someone other than their spouse. Not only was such "evidence" bringing the law into disrepute, it was unfairly penalising honourable people unwilling to adopt such stratagems. However, it was not until the Divorce Reform Act 1969 that the state finally came to accept for the first time that the irretrievable breakdown of a marriage was sufficient grounds for its termination as far as the law was concerned. It was perhaps a recognition of a sociological fact but it seems also to have played its part in changing people's attitudes.

What is incontrovertible is that any concept of the Christian sacramental marriage recognised by law until 1857 and to some extent until 1969, is no longer so recognised. The law and society have both chosen to go their own way and society has done so more quickly but where precisely that way might eventually lead and the practical consequences of its arrival there is by no means clear even now. The one probable consequence is that both the courts and the family law specialists amongst the Society's members will be fully employed for the foreseeable future for "family problems", which used to be generally managed within families, now require a legal or at least a quasi-legal forum for their resolution. Whether the law is managing them any better is a very moot point indeed. One senior judge with considerable experience of the effect of our current epidemic of divorce was the Family Division judge, Sir Paul Coleridge.[14] Having specialised in the subject for thirty years whilst at the Bar and spent over twelve years as a judge in the that Division, he could reasonably claim to have an informed opinion on the subject. In 2011 he suggested that people needed to re-educate themselves about the value of stable relationships for the good of society, pointing out that getting a divorce was easier than getting a driving licence and that in any one year an estimated 500,000 children and adults are caught up in the family justice system and the estimated cost of family breakdown in the UK is £44 billion. The following year, and not without criticism from some quarters, he launched the Marriage Foundation with support from a number of high profile lawyers and judges and with the overall objective of increasing the rate of marriage and reducing the rate of divorce. More recently, in 2013, he has made the point that there has been no comprehensive look at family life and divorce for 60 years, claiming that no political party has the will or clout to reform divorce and family law because the changes would attract flak from one quarter or another.

Perhaps Sir Paul is right and that the law requires radical overhaul but isn't getting it so that "in the end we are doing the classic British thing of reform by inertia, stealth, common sense and the laws of cricket". In 1961 85% of marriages were first marriages, that is to say between a bachelor and a spinster. Only 10% involved the re-marriage of one of the partners and 5% the re-marriage of both partners. By 1996 only 58% were first marriages, 23% involved the re-marriage of one partner and 19% the re-marriage of both partners.[15] Another significant change has been the older age at which women marry for the first time. In 1970 among women marrying for the first time, 88% were under 25, whereas this had dropped to 57% by 1990. Many influences were at work to produce these sudden and unprecedented changes: more effective contraception, more women in higher education, more women working and changes in attitude to women working, especially after marriage, and increased mobility, both social and physical (the motor-car); it is reckoned that only one family in nine possessed a motor-car in 1960.

Even if they were not working, women had far more opportunity than they had in the past to meet people, including of course men, outside their immediate family and neighbourhood circle. For women at work there was much less segregation than in the past; they often found themselves in daily contact with male work colleagues. In short, the opportunities were there to form extra-marital relationships should they wish to take advantage of them. And the same of course applied to men, except that men had never been confined to the home in the way that women had been. Finally, there was a very significant change in many people's attitudes to their personal relationships: both men and women became distrustful of the old attitudes and to the very notion of commitment, which was a fundamental element in marriage as traditionally understood. One result has been that many choose not to marry at all. We have not yet seen the ultimate consequences of these changes, particularly their effect on tomorrow's children but one thing is certain: tomorrow's society will look and feel very different to any that has existed in the past.

But if Sir Paul Coleridge has been drawing attention to the importance of stable relationships in marriage and family, he might equally have concerned himself with their importance in the workplace. Here, too, there was the beginning of change from the 1960s onwards which accelerated markedly from the 1980s onwards and reaching supersonic speed in our own day. Until the war and the decade or so that followed distinctions of "class" broadly followed the division between manual and non-manual work, between the "working" class and the "middle" class, of which traditionally the former had made up by far the largest proportion of the population. The traditional grouping of the landed aristocracy and gentry, although still influential, constituted a much smaller class whose influence, in particular political influence, had been declining since the beginning of the 20th century. In the immediate post-war period the "middle" class, whose numbers, both absolutely and proportionately, had been increasing ever since the early years of the 19th century, had reached a state of apparent equilibrium. By and large its members had been educated beyond elementary level which meant that access to further education, via university or otherwise, was available to them if they chose to go in that direction. They might or might not have family money behind them but even if they did not, they had access to forms of employment largely denied to those of the traditional working class. The middle class of the mid-20th century had also tended to shed its former prejudice against trade and extended its boundaries, even if reluctantly, to embrace the superior echelons of business and even, if it were sufficiently respectable, of retail business. What distinguished its members from the traditional working class was that they were far more in control of their lives, particularly their future lives, than the latter; they could plan; they could embark on a career which conferred a recognised status, whether in the old established professions (law, medicine or the church) or the ever-expanding civil service. But all this was soon to change and the three main catalysts were firstly the great extension of secondary education as a result of the Education Act 1944, secondly, technological change in manufacturing industry, and thirdly, increased international competition. The sudden increase in the availability of secondary education also had the direct and inevitable effect of increasing the demand for teachers; this in turn was to lead in due course, albeit less directly, to an increased demand for higher and further education and consequently an expansion of the demand for teachers at all levels.

During the whole of this period of unprecedented social change one has to look quite hard for evidence of it in the Society's records. Such as there is seems to consist more of hints than clear indications of what was happening. Social revolutions tend to be prompted by the young whereas committees at that stage in the evolutionary process tend to be formed from the well-established – perhaps more so in the 1960s than in the 1980s. In 1960 the average post qualification experience for members of the committee was 23.6 years and all but five of them had been admitted for twenty years or more. In 1985 the average period of qualification was 19.45 years and twelve members had been admitted for less than twenty years, one of them, Mrs Barbara Jacobs (the only woman) for only five years. (Mrs Jacobs was not in fact the first woman to be elected to the committee – that honour fell to Mrs Sandra Keen in 1979, the year that Mrs Margaret Thatcher became Britain's first woman prime minister).

Neither event at the beginning of this period would have been foreseen by the Society's members, any more than they would have foreseen that Mrs Keen would have the honour of being the first woman to propose the toast of the Bench and the Bar at the Annual Dinner of the Society on 11 November 1982 – sharing the speeches with Lord Denning no less. Such was the speed at which British expectations and culture were changing over this 25 year period – and, as we shall see, that speed was accelerating.

The Society's annual report in 1961 recorded the election of Mr Thornton Kay as President for the coming year. The report also recorded that he was another foxhunting solicitor (with both the Ainsty and Bramham Moor packs) and also his athletic prowess as a young man – playing lawn tennis for Yorkshire in addition to keen involvement with football, hockey, squash and golf. More significant, perhaps was the new President's involvement with no less than five drainage boards of which he was clerk for 28 years and his claim that in the course of those years he had never missed a meeting. This record was all to his credit but by the 1980s it would have been almost impossible for any practitioner to equal it. Not only were the pressures of professional life rapidly increasing, but the institutional continuity known to Mr Kay's generation was becoming a thing of the past.

Two years later, in 1963, two items in the annual report might bring a smile to a modern practitioner. The first was a small technical matter headed "Carbon Copies":

> One of the Members of the Society has made the suggestion that when writing to another firm upon any matter which requires that firm to take their client's instructions, it is very helpful if a carbon copy of the letter and any relevant enclosure could be forwarded at the same time, and your Committee recommends this practice to Members.

The 1963 report was presented to members on 27 March. Earlier that month I had begun my articles with the Chief Solicitor to the British Railways Board – in its litigation department. Sharing a room with the solicitor in charge, my very first introduction to litigation practice was to observe him going through a file instructing his (shorthand) secretary as to which letters he required to be copy typed for the court bundles. It was a very large office as befitted an organisation where an average of 300 or so employees a year were killed in the course of their employment (to say nothing of those who were merely injured and of the deaths and injuries suffered by customers and other third parties). To support the level of legal activity required by such a department together with its associated property and parliamentary and general departments, there was one of the new-fangled Xerox photocopiers but although it was state-of-the-art at the time (and fascinated me) it had its drawbacks for actually getting stuff done; for one thing it was located at the other end of a very large office, it was always busy and time had to be booked. It was often quicker to use a reliable secretary who didn't think copy typing beneath her dignity. By the time I left British Rail in September 1966 "Xerographic" provision there had improved somewhat but it was something of a come-down to find myself confronted in York with a messy procedure that could only reproduce in purple ink or, as an alternative, with "Gestetner's Improved Cyclostyler"– a fearsome chain-driven contraption in wood and brass, and even more messy – to the point that it required the operator to wear protective clothing and was not worth setting up if only a small number of copies were required. My first secretary in York was the last person in the office who knew how to operate it and when she left it went into storage and was eventually donated to York's Castle Museum.

Producing copy documents in the early 1960s was certainly a chore but it did have the virtue of concentrating everyone's mind on what was actually relevant. One of the problems about the ease with which copies can be produced nowadays is that for some practitioners consideration of relevance has become almost a lost art, with a resulting clog on the whole litigation process. Judges fulminate about this from time to time and even threaten draconian penalties but it seems to have become endemic. A recent example was when Munby J in the case of *re L (A Child)* [2015] EWFC 15 listed over 200 pages of irrelevancy before demanding why they had been in the bundle at all and criticising lawyers for letting court bundles grow to the length of a novel.

At first technical developments in York may have been somewhat slow to intrude. The annual report for 1964 carried the following notice:

DUPLICATOR

Members are reminded that the Society own a Remington Duplicating machine which is available for use by Members of the Society on payment of the cost of the materials used. Members are free to use this at any time on prior application to the Honorary Secretary.

And yet just three years later, in 1967, we find the report's first reference to computers! Looking back, we can see that anyone starting out on a legal or any other career at this time was going to experience the most astonishing technical developments over a very short time span. In 1982 I recall using the Post Office's *Intel* fax service for the first time to send an urgent document to a solicitor in Harrogate. Neither of us had ever used such a facility before and my Harrogate correspondent from a well-known firm was not even aware that such a service existed. For both of us it involved a walk to the Post Office. A year or so later solicitors were beginning to ask each other "You don't happen to have a facsimile machine do you?" Six months later it was "Am I able to fax it to you?" A year later this had simply become "I'll fax it to you". Today it is almost regarded as the technology of the third world – all in less than thirty years.

Another change recorded in 1964 was the advent of Saturday closing:

The Committee noted the continued trend in Industry and Commerce towards the five-day week and its adoption by Local Government offices in the City. They felt that the trend would continue and that the time was approaching when a five-day week would be enjoyed by the majority of people. They also felt that one of the consequences of this would be that it would become increasingly difficult to attract staff to offices where the five-day week was not in operation.

The Committee, after considering carefully all the arguments for and against the proposals, came to the conclusion that the issue was one which would have to be faced sooner of later, and accordingly sought the views of all Members of the Society as to whether or not they were in favour of Saturday closing. It was clear from the response that firms in the City of York were predominantly in favour of the proposal, whereas in the Country the reverse was the case. The Committee therefore decided to recommend to Members in the City of York that as from the 10th August their offices should close on Saturday mornings and supplied printed notices to this effect to those Members who wished to display them.

The scheme has now been in operation for some six months and has been adopted by almost every office in the City. So fas as can be judged it is working very well and there would appear to be no indication of any desire to revert to the former practice.

The Committee's report has a curious period flavour, reflecting an age of well-regulated professional decorum in which it would be unseemly for some firms to be open on a Saturday morning and others not: the former might be seen as touting, don't you know! Also, it was an age which had yet to come to terms with computers, outsourcing, working from home, flexi-time, Sunday trading and, in the City of London at least, 24/24 hour working to accommodate the different time zones of North America and the Far East.

Another issue for the Society at the time was the position of articled clerks (trainees). The previous year "after discussing the matter fully" the members had decided to recommend that no premium should be demanded and a minimum scale of payment should be observed. This distinguished between the "ordinary five-year Articled Clerk" and those with a law degree who only had to serve three years. The recommended minimum scale of payment for the former was: in years 1 and 2 £2 p.w.; year 3 £5 p.w.; year 4 £7 p.w. and year 5 £8 p.w. For law graduates serving three years the recommendation was the same as for the last three years of non-law graduates. An articled clerk on £8 p.w. in his final year would be on an annual salary of £416 p.a. – not much over £7,000 p.a. today. By way of comparison the minimum required starting salary in 2014 for an a trainee outside central London was £16,650 p.a. and for central London, £18,590. In practice starting salaries for "magic circle" firms can be very much more– if you can get taken on, that is.

The year 1967 was significant for me personally as it was my first full year in practice in York, having only arrived from the south in the previous October. It was an unusual début in two respects. Firstly, I had been recruited the previous summer by Peter Whitfield, then the principal partner in a small firm then known as G Brown & Elmhirst based at 11 Lendal which at the time was semi-amalgamated with Gray Dodsworth & Cobb in Duncombe Place in which Peter was a partner. The three partners in Gray Dodsworth & Cobb were equally partners in G Brown & Elmhirst. Unfortunately between my arranging to join the latter as assistant solicitor and my arrival York after giving the required three months' notice to my former employers, Peter suffered a severe stroke and died the following January. Secondly, my articles had been served in the legal department of the British Railways Board, so I was entirely without experience in private practice. I found myself effectively in charge of a branch office, albeit with head office within two minutes walk. I need not have worried. The partners in Duncombe Place and the staff in both offices were enormously supportive but it was a slightly unnerving experience. More significantly perhaps for present purposes, everything which I relate from now on about the Society is more or less within my own personal knowledge rather than just "history" For me at least it is closer to current affairs. Also, from 1969 onwards I became Hon Treasurer of the Society, a post I was to hold until 1986. As the Hon Treasurer, like the Hon Secretary, was *ex officio* a member of the Committee/Council I did at least have the advantage of a continuous involvement with the Society's day-to-day affairs which again afforded me a slightly different perspective.

In the summer of 1966 the Lord Chancellor, Lord Gardiner, had announced in the House of Lords the government's intention to set up a Royal Commission on Assizes and Quarter Sessions. Its terms of reference were "To inquire into the present arrangements for the administration of justice at Assizes and Quarter Sessions outside Greater London, and to report what reforms should be made for the more convenient, economic and efficient disposal of the civil and criminal business at present dealt with by those courts". In due course its Chairman was to be Lord Beeching and as soon as this was announced I had a fair idea of what to expect as "Dr Beeching" as he was then known had been my former ultimate boss when I was employed at British Rail and his famous report on the railways had appeared in March 1963, the very month of the beginning of my articles. Whilst a research student at Imperial College London studying for his Ph.D, Beeching had been supervised by Sir George Thomson, the nuclear physicist who had subsequently been the Master of Corpus Christi College Cambridge during the whole of my time there. Neither the Master nor his pupil were of a character to be satisfied with half measures and this certainly proved to be the case as far as Doctor Beeching was concerned.

By 1970 the Royal Commission had made its report. At the Society's AGM on 25 March 1970 members of the Society were appraised of its likely consequences if their recommendations were implemented. The prognosis as far as York itself was not encouraging. It would cease to hold its own Quarter Sessions and in consequence there would cease to be a Recorder or a Clerk of the Peace. York would form part of the North

Eastern Circuit whose administrative headquarters would be in Leeds. Furthermore, until more courts were available at Leeds, York would continue to be a High Court and Crown Court centre; thereafter it would probably retain its Crown Court, presided over by a Circuit Judge, but as a venue for High Court cases, its days would seem to be numbered. In our heart of hearts we probably guessed as much. Speaking at the Society's annual dinner in November 1968 Mr Justice Cusack had warned that the city would have "to look to its privileges as an Assize Town". It was not long afterwards that my wife and I had been invited to dinner at the Judges' Lodgings in Lendal. Just as we were leaving our host expressed the expectation that York would continue to be a High Court Centre. I expressed my doubts. "They've just spent £20,000 on updating the kitchens in these lodgings", he observed "they're not going to waste all that money!" I looked at him carefully. "In that case, judge, I fear York's fate is definitely sealed!" "Tony, you're a dreadful cynic!" was his parting shot. Cynic or not, my fears proved to be well-founded. Centuries of tradition were about to come to an end.

In close co-operation with York City Council and its Clerk, Society member John Evans, a stout rearguard action was mounted. On 16 December 1969 Hon Secretary John Shannon wrote to the Secretary of the Law Society:

Dear Sir,

ROYAL COMMISSION ON ASSIZES AND QUARTER SESSIONS

Will you kindly note our Society's objections to the proposals contained in the Report of the Royal Commission in so far as it affects this City.

Our objections are based on the following reasons –

1. Historically this City is one of the oldest Assize centres in the country.

2. If the Commission's Report is adopted it will mean that in course of time York will not be a High Court and Crown Court Centre served by High Court Judges.

3. The present Assize Courts, comprising the Crown Court and Civil Court, have in recent years been extensively restored and must now

rank as amongst the finest in the country, with excellent facilities for Members of the Bar and solicitors and witnesses and others attending Court.

4. A tremendous amount of public money has been spent in the restoration of these Courts and it would seem to this Society to be the height of folly not to make the very fullest use of them.

5. The Report proposes that in due course when more Courts are available at Leeds, Civil and Criminal cases of the type now dealt with at York Assizes will have to go to Leeds for a hearing. This seems to us to be a very retrograde step. There are few cities in England more easily reached than York, and we believe it to be a mistake if people from the North and East Ridings have to travel to Leeds with all the congestion when the facilities already exist here in this City.

6. The extra travelling time involved for litigants, witnesses and others from this City will serve to increase costs very considerably.

7. There is in this City a very fine house which is used as the Judges' Lodgings and which has in the last few years been extensively restored at great cost in public money, and here again it would seem to be a mistake not to make use of this facility.

8. York is daily increasing in importance as an administrative centre and it would seem to be a most inappropriate time to reverse this trend.

Yours faithfully,

JOHN SHANNON

This and other lobbying was all to no avail. By 1972, as a result of the Courts Act 1971 the new arrangements were up if not necessarily running. Assizes and Quarter Sessions were no more.[16]

The upheavals in attitudes to sex and marriage, the role of women and technology and changes in the workings of the courts aside, the Society's own social programme continued much as it had before for most of the 20th century but the days when the attendance of at least one and often two High Court judges at its annual dinner could be taken for granted were about to end.

At the Society's annual dinner on 8 November 1979, the President Mr Ernest Smith, in responding to the toast of "The Yorkshire Law Society" made the bold decision to quote in full the following sub-paragraph from the Motor Vehicle (Construction and Use) Regulations 1968:

> (3) Where a motor vehicle to which paragraph (5) of either Regulation 59 or Regulation 64 applies, being a goods vehicle, is being used while drawing a trailer manufactured before 1st January 1968 (other than a trailer not required by these Regulations to be equipped with a braking system), whether or not that motor vehicle and trailer together form an articulated vehicle, then every part of every braking system with which that motor vehicle is equipped and every part of every braking system with which the trailer is equipped shall be so maintained that, when the brakes of any braking system of the motor vehicle (being a system to which the said paragraph (5) applies) are applied by their means of operation they produce (whether assisted by the brakes on the trailer or not) the same total braking efficiences as would be required of the brakes of such a motor vehicle when applied by that means of operation if that motor vehicle were not drawing a trailer and if it were treated as being a motor vehicle first used before 1st January 1968 and as having to comply with paragraph (7) of either Regulation 59 or Regulation 64 notwithstanding that the said paragraph does not apply to that motor vehicle.

Now as the President's response to that particular toast is the last of the formal speeches it has to be admitted that members' attention at that late hour is not necessarily at its most focussed. Nevertheless, as one present on that occasion, I have to record that his venture into the problems of statutory construction was well received. All lawyers have suffered from the all-too-frequent turgidities of the parliamentary draftsmen of which the above 209 word sentence is but an example.[17] At least, however, lawyers have been trained to struggle with them. As a magistrate, as well as a solicitor, the President was making the serious point that the Motor Vehicle (Construction and Use) Regulations and similar regulatory legislation is more usually dealt with in magistrates courts and most magistrates have not had the benefit of any formal legal training. I still have a copy of this regulation in my commonplace book. I found it a useful text for testing the capacity of actual and aspiring articled clerks. There were just two questions: could they explain what it meant and could they translate it into plain English. The pass rate was not encouraging.

Later in that presidential year, at the Society's Annual general Meeting on 2 April 1980, it also fell to Ernest Smith to fill the slot under the time-honoured rubric "President's Remarks". He began by observing that he was never quite sure just what it was that the President was supposed to remark about – a dilemma familiar to all us who have had to bear the burden of that office. A meticulous man who had noted the burgeoning influence of time recording in the profession, he had taken the trouble to log his presidential activities over the previous twelve months: one conference in London, six main committee meetings, five sub-committee meeting, 85 letters out (those in were not recorded), 100 telephone calls, three luncheons, nine professional dinners and listening to 41 speakers for an overall total of 12 hours 52 minutes – he does not seem to have recorded separately his own speaking time at the annual dinner noted above, nor of his time spent in preparation. Whilst expressly stating that he had no wish to deter anybody from undertaking the duties of President, he felt that the statistics would be of interest. Indeed. Practitioners will no doubt work out for themselves what a present-day costs draftsman would make of such a record.

The annual dinner on 6 November later that year was also notable for our having as a guest speaker not only a High Court judge (Mr Justice Smith) but the Attorney-General of the day, Sir Michael Havers, later to become Lord Chancellor. As far as I have been able to discover it was the only occasion on which the Society has had that particular honour. For the dinner sub-committee it presented a unique problem: the need to host Sir Michael's minder, an armed Special Branch officer. The 1970s had seen an appalling litany of IRA killings and the Attorney-General was thought to be at a particularly high risk. Such a thought was not without foundation. On 13 November 1981 Sir Michael's house in Wimbledon was bombed by the IRA although he was not there at the time. As the Society's Hon. Treasurer, and *ex officio* member of the dinner sub-committee, I found myself having to deal with some of the less familiar inner workings of government finance and ministerial security. I was told, for example, that it would be necessary to book two adjoining hotel bedrooms, one for our honoured guest and one for his minder; the Society would pay for the one but HMG would be financially responsible for the other. The minder would also need to attend the dinner, albeit incognito. As he could hardly be accommodated on the High Table on that basis, we had to consider where he should be seated. In addition, therefore, to the usual insoluble protocol issues relating to seating plans, members of the dinner sub-committee, for the first and possibly last time in the history of the Society, had to turn our collective minds to what the infantry term "fields of fire". Fortunately our somewhat amateurish solution to this last problem was never put to the test. Less fortunately, I also have to record that for seating plan purposes the uninvited guest was rather unimaginatively re-named "Smith" for the occasion which at least I suppose was a marginal improvement on "John Doe". I have often wondered what he found to talk about in the course of the evening with other members and their guests. Perhaps a repertoire of cover stories for such occasions is part of Special Branch training.

In the course of his speech Sir Michael did pass on one important message to the assembled lawyers in his audience. Little more than a month previously a very well-known and much loved television personality of the 1950s and 1960s, popularly but somewhat inaccurately known as Lady Isobel Barnett – it was not a courtesy title but her solicitor husband had been knighted – had taken her own life. The circumstances of her death were tragic. After schooling at The Mount in York and medical studies at Glasgow University, she had qualified as a doctor and later served as a magistrate for many years, but had never really come to terms with the ending of her television and radio career with the changing culture of the 1960s when a title of any kind and crystal clear diction were neither in demand nor even acceptable in broadcast media. By 1980 she had become eccentric and something of a recluse. Four days before her death she had been convicted of shoplifting – the theft of a tin of tuna and a carton of cream worth 87 pence for which she had been fined £75. The general feeling at the time was that she had not exactly been treated with sensitivity by the legal system. Sir Michael reminded his audience that prosecuting authorities had a discretion as to whether or not to prosecute in appropriate cases if it appeared not to be in the public interest to do so. They sometimes got it wrong and if we thought that such was the case with one of our clients we should feel perfectly free to contact his office and voice our concerns.

Some years later I was forcibly reminded of the Attorney-General's advice when I and my fellow trustees of a local charity were threatened with prosecution over a supposed infringement of planning rules in a conservation area. Our supposed offence was in cutting back an overgrown hedge. As it happened my co-trustees included a QC, a university professor and a well-known member of the Council for the Protection of Rural England. The local planning authority was refusing to accept that an overgrown hedge was an overgrown hedge and not a series of individual trees, each deemed to subject to a tree preservation order. Fortunately common sense eventually prevailed without the intervention of the Attorney-General. Quite apart from the absence of any conceivable public interest, we were able to persuade the planners at a late stage that they were wrong in law. We had consulted one of the leading authorities in the country on the matter whose opinion was short and to the point: any prosecution was bound to fail and the local planning authority would have to pay the costs. It struck me at the time as a fitting sequel to FE Smith's memorable one-liner: "There is no answer to this action and the damages must be enormous" – the end result apparently of an overnight reading of papers nearly four feet thick and the consumption of two dozen oysters and a bottle of Champagne. Perhaps common sense should be a compulsory paper in both the Bar and Law Society's finals although there might be some controversy over who was qualified to examine in the subject.

NOTES

1. Philip Larkin (1922-1985) *Annus Mirabilis*

2. See Chapter 8 page xxx.

3. *Loving et uxor v Virginia* 388 US 1. The facts shed a remarkable light on the state of American law and the American legal system of the period. In 1958 two residents of Virginia, Richard Loving, a white man and Mildred Jeter "a Negro woman" (or "black American" as she would now be described) were married in the District of Colombia in accordance with its laws. Shortly afterwards the couple returned to Caroline County Virginia (less than 100 miles from the federal capital of Washington where they had married) and established their matrimonial home there. Soon afterwards the newly-weds found themselves indicted by a grand jury of the local Circuit Court for violation of the state's ban on interracial marriages. They pleaded guilty and were sentenced to twelve months imprisonment, suspended for 25 years on condition that they left Virginia and did not return together for 25 years. The trial judge's opinion (judgment) contained the observation that

"Almighty God created the races white, black, yellow, malay and red, and he placed them on separate continents. And but for the interference with his arrangements there would be no cause for such marriages. The fact that he separated the races shows that he did not intend for the races to mix." At the time of the Supreme Court's judgment in 1967 Virginia was one of 16 states with similar legislation – in the case of Virginia such a prohibition had been part of its penal code since 1705.

4. The curtain had not quite come down in 1960. Kenneth Bloor (President 1977-78) certainly rode to hounds and Charlie Dodsworth (President 1981-82) was a Deputy Lieutenant of North Yorkshire.

5. Schedule II costs were costs not covered by the scale costs set out in Schedule I of the Solicitors' Remuneration Order.

6. Between 1951 and 1971 it was the practice to include in each year's annual report on a cumulative basis the cost of the dinner per head, the cost of the tickets, the number of members attending. the number of their guests and the number of official guests. The figures for the beginning and end of this period taken from the 1971 annual report are as follows:

Year	Price Per Head	Ticket Price	Members	Members' Guests	Official Guests
1951	18/6d	40/-	46	55	14
1970	41/-	75/-	94	92	22

7. Theobald Mathew was the author of *Forensic Fables* by O, first published between 1926 and 1932 and often republished since in various formats. Part of the charm of these fables is that on first reading they appear to reflect the foibles of the 1920s; however, on closer inspection they usually demonstrate eternal truths. As Lord Birkett observed many years later, "they defy the passage of time". They do indeed. One of the lesser objects of the author's satire was the traditional lawyer's Obsession with the Use of Capital Letters Contrary to the Standard Current Usage of English Grammar. Such obsession is still occasionally to be found to this day.

8. The practical and sometimes bizarre consequences of the old law are well illustrated by the case of *Kennedy v Broun* (1863) 13 CBNS 677; 143 ER 268. Charles Raun Kennedy became involved as counsel in what at first sight seems to have all the classic ingredients of high Victorian melodrama. Samuel Swinfen was the owner of Swinfen Hall, a stately Georgian pile (now a hotel) just outside Lichfield in Staffordshire. Sam's son, Henry John, had evidently married below him to the consternation of his family,

his inamorata being a former parlour-maid according to one account. No matter. On the death of Sam's wife father and son had been reconciled and Henry John and Patience thereupon took up residence at Swinfen Hall. Unfortunately not long afterwards Henry John died suddenly and as a result the widowed Patience became financially dependant on Sam who by that time had became very fond of her. Sam died in 1854 and by his will left £60,000 (more than £1M in today's money) to Patience. He also owned a large estate which was not mentioned in the will. Patience reckoned that she was entitled to that too. Sam's nephew, Henry Hay Swinfen, the heir-at-law, thought otherwise. The result was a contested probate action *Swinfen v Swinfen* (1856) 2 D & J 381 – the start of a series of trials between 1856 and 1864. Leading counsel for Patience was Sir Frederick Thesiger, later to become Lord Chelmsford LC; leading counsel for the nephew was Sir Alexander Cockburn, later to become Lord Chief Justice. The case opened at Stafford Assizes on a Saturday. After a day of evidence Thesiger was not happy at the way the plaintiff's case was going and was urging her to settle. Patience said she would sleep on it. The following day (Sunday) she telegraphed him to the effect that she would not settle. However, on arrival at court on the Monday morning she was dismayed to find that counsel had settled.

Although making no protest at the time, Patience subsequently declined to take any steps to give effect to the settlement, notwithstanding increasingly frantic solicitors' correspondence. What she did do was to engage a somewhat less exhalted member of the Bar, Charles Rann Kennedy whose only claim to legal notoriety at this stage was his authorship of *A Treatise on the New Rules of Pleading* – Butterworth, London 1841 and *A Treatise on Annuities: with an appendix, containing the statutes on the subject* – Benning, London 1846. His instructions: to sue his client's previous counsel for breach of contract in agreeing a settlement of her probate claim contrary to instructions. Unfortunately, as impecunious claimants are obliged to do nowadays, she entered into a conditional fee agreement. If successful, Kennedy was to receive £20,000. To reinforce this arrangement with her new adviser she also appears to have entered into what nowadays would be called "an intimate relationship". Just how intimate is not entirely clear, but certainly Kennedy was expecting to marry his new client.

Spurred on by these hopes, Kennedy duly launched proceedings on behalf of Patience against the somewhat imprudent Thesiger who rather more prudently decided that it "Would be a Good Idea to become Lord Chancellor" so those proceedings have come down to us as *Swinfen v Lord*

Chelmsford (1860) 5 H&N 890; 29 ER 382. The plaintiff succeeded at first instance but subsequently lost on appeal. Meanwhile our persistent ex-parlour-maid litigant had decided that she was enamoured of another, a Mr Charles Broun whom she proceeded to marry. She also decided not to pay the £20,000. This prompted yet another action, *Kennedy v Broun* 13 CB (NS) 648. There too, Kennedy was successful at first instance but lost on appeal, Erle CJ holding that there was no contract between counsel and litigant and that in any event such an agreement would have been champetous. This remained the law until modern times.

9. See Chapter 6 p. 107.

10. Until the Reformation took effect in Scotland in 1560 the position there had been the same as in England, and for the same reason: marriage was a matter for the church. In 1560 for the first time the Scots (or more precisely John Knox) permitted a valid marriage to be dissolved otherwise than by the death of one of the parties, namely in the case of adultery but it was perhaps a distinction without a difference as it was expressed in the following terms: "Mariage once lauchfullie contracted, may not be dissolved at manis pleasour, as oure maister Christ Jesus doeth witnesse, onles adulterie be committed; which being sufficientlie proven in presence of the Civil Magistrat, the innocent (yf thei so requyre) ought to be pronunced frie, and the offendar aught to suffer the death as God hath commanded."

11. It is very difficult from a 21st century perspective to understand the heat generated until almost within living memory by the seemingly innocuous question of whether a man could marry his deceased wife's sister or a woman her deceased husband's brother. The former restriction caused particular resentment as it was quite common in the 19th century for unmarried women to live in the same households as their married sisters and the rule precluded a widower, in obvious need of someone to look after any young children, from marrying the person already familiar to them as aunt. The Old Testament had indeed bequeathed to the Church an uncomfortable legacy – one which was to act as primer to the English Reformation at the time of Henry VIII and his "divorce". Henry and his supporters appealed to an uncertain and confusing prohibition in Leviticus Ch.18 v.18 to claim that his marriage to Catherine was unlawful and void. Catherine and her supporters appealed to Deuteronomy Ch.25 v. 5-6. The reality was that both texts were ambivalent and the cause of much argument over the centuries among theologians and others.

Shakespeare accurately summed up Henry's case as he summed up much else in life's rich tapestry:

Chamberlain	It seems this marriage with his brother's wife has crept too near his conscience.
Duke of Suffolk	No, his conscience has crept too near another lady.

Henry VIII Act II Scene 2

12. Fergus Morton Baron Morton of Henryton (1887-1973). Called to the Bar in 1912, KC 1929, judge of the Chancery Division 1938, Lord Justice of Appeal 1944 and Lord of Appeal in Ordinary 1947.

13. Cmnd 9678

14. Sir Paul Coleridge resigned from the High Court bench in 2013 after having been twice reprimanded by the Judicial Conduct and Investigations Office for allegedly bringing the judiciary into disrepute for airing his views on marriage breakdown.

15. These figures are extracted from the publications of the Office of Population, Censuses and Surveys – Marriage and Divorce Statistics England & Wales.

16. For a more detailed account of Assizes and Quarter Sessions see Appendix A pp. 332-347.

17. For Lord Roskill's comments on statutory drafting see Chapter 14 page 282. If the Gunning "Fog Index" on readability is applied to this sub-paragraph it gives a score of about 80. A score of about 12 indicates that a text should be readily intelligible to an 18 year old "A" Level student. If any readers are tempted to imagine that things have become easier since 1979 they may care to consult the updated Road Vehicles (Construction and Use) Regulations 1986 (SI 1986 No. 1078) as amended. We now have (for the time being at least) euro-directives to be taken into account.

Chapter 14

THE BICENTENARY AND BEYOND

I'm the Parliamentary draftsman,
I compose the country's laws
And of half the litigation
I'm undoubtedly the cause.

Anon

The Yorkshire Law Society's bicentenary celebrations in 1986 were much lower in profile than the Victorian high jinks in 1886 but a comparison is perhaps unfair as the latter included the National Conference. The two main components for the bicentenary were a banquet (rather than a mere dinner) in the Assembly Rooms and a public lecture at York University *What's Wrong with the Law?* by Lord Roskill.

The banquet at Lord Burlington's impressive Assembly Rooms in Blake Street, completed in 1735 and possibly the earliest neo-classical building in Europe, took place on Friday 21 March 1986. It was exactly two hundred years to the day from that first meeting of the Society at the house of Mr Ringrose; indeed, it

The Assembly Rooms, Blake Street, York. Reproduced courtesy of York Conservation Trust.

was within a few yards from its location in what was Little Blake Street or Lop Lane (now Museum Street/Duncombe Place) leading up to the west end of the Minster. Although impressive, the fare on this latter occasion could not hope to match in terms of gastronomic quantity and variety that provided at the Guildhall on 12 October 1886 on the occasion of the Society's centenary. Times and dietary requirements had changed fairly drastically over the intervening one hundred years. Nevertheless it was a grand occasion. The late Dr John Shannon, the highly respected and long-serving secretary of the Society, proposed the toast of the Bench and the Bar, to which the Honourable Mr Justice Kennedy and Mr Robin Stewart QC responded. The toast of The Yorkshire Law Society was proposed by the President of the Law Society, Mr CA Leslie, to which the Society's President, Mr RM Stanley, responded.

Later in the year, on 2 October, the Society was privileged to receive the Right Honourable Lord Roskill, one of the most eminent lawyers of his generation, who had recently retired as a law lord. He had accepted the Society's invitation to deliver an open lecture at the Lyons Concert Hall. It was well-attended by an audience of two hundred or so, including members of the Society, members of the Bar and magistrates, members of the general public and the University Vice-Chancellor, Professor Berwick Saul. For me, a most interesting and enjoyable evening got off to a rather disconcerting start. It had fallen to my lot to be responsible for collecting Lord Roskill and his wife from Middlethorpe Hall where they were staying and driving them to the University where the lecture was due to begin at 7.30 pm. I had arranged to collect them some time after six. Just before reaching Middlethrope I switched on the car radio to pick up the BBC's six o'clock news bulletin. I thus heard the announcement of the government's decision to reject Lord Roskill's recommendations in his report earlier that year on the conduct of serious fraud trials and in particular whether they were really suitable for trial by jury. I was relieved to some extent by the news as I thought it would at least give me an opening topic of conversation in the car on the way to the University. Arriving at the foot of the grand staircase at Middlethorpe Hall I was greeted warmly enough by Lord Roskill from the landing, only for him to add even before he reached the top of the stairs "I'm absolutely furious!" Just for a moment I had a near panic attack, wondering what on earth had gone wrong with the arrangements for the evening. I was reassured to discover that our guest's fury was not directed at me, the Society or even the staff at Middlethorpe Hall but at HM Government. It appeared that minutes earlier he had been listening in the hotel bedroom to the same 6 o'clock BBC news bulletin as I. The government's broadcast decision was news to me but it should not have been news to the author of the report. His fury was directed not at their rejection of his report but at the almost unbelievable discourtesy in their not having given him prior notice of their decision before it was released to the media. My anxiety at the possibility of entirely justified judicial ill-humour over-shadowing the rest of the evening was misplaced. The immediate fury quickly subsided and he and Lady Roskill proved to be the most amiable, courteous and easy-going companions, and genuinely delighted to be in York as the guests of the Society. Our speaker did confide, however, that he possessed what he believed to be the almost unique distinction when at the Bar of never having been briefed by any of the Society's members.

The lecture itself was a model of brevity and clarity. Over the years the Society has become fairly accustomed to hearing senior lawyers such as High Court judges, even the occasional Supreme Court Justice, Lord Justice of Appeal, Attorney-General or Law Society President, as after dinner speakers but such occasions are not really designed for serious detailed analysis and any attempts to use them as such are destined to fall if not on hostile ears, certainly on deaf ones. This, however, was a different occasion and it is worth considering his lecture in some detail, if only because, thirty years or so on, we know "what happened next". It was a sharp and effective riposte to those critics, especially in the media, who seem to have an unshakable conviction that a lifetime in the law and long experience on the bench leads to complacency, apathy, hardening of the arteries and a too-ready acceptance that nothing is wrong and that all changes in the law are for the worse. As the speaker himself put it:

> If you remain observant and have sensitive antennae you can often see the defects in the law from the Bench better than from elsewhere. If you remember that politicians too often will not help you to put right that which so often seems to be plainly wrong – for alas there are not and never have been any votes in law reform – you can sometimes within very strict limits yourself do something to remedy that wrong especially in appellate courts.

He went on to list examples where the courts had managed to run ahead of parliament in sensible law reform: killing the iniquitous doctrine of common employment before any statutory intervention, by evolving the doctrine of a safe system of work, development of the concept of judicial review to control the excesses of central and local government, making it possible, at a time of rapid depreciation in the value of sterling, to have first arbitrators' awards and then judgments expressed in a foreign currency, thus preventing a successful foreign creditor being deprived of the fruits of the award or judgment by having this debt discharged in devalued sterling – something that no politician had dared to address.

It is useful to reflect on these trenchant criticisms of the law as it was in 1986. Lord Roskill identified a number of shortcomings: "mystery" and avoidable complexity of much of our law, its slowness, its preoccupation with antique and technical rules of evidence,[1] particularly in the criminal law, designed to protect unrepresented defendants in a different age, and the drafting of statutes and statutory instruments. As to the latter, he asked a rhetorical question which will still resonate with all lawyers:

> Why should we all be afflicted by Finance Bills or Finance Acts which verge on the unintelligible? ... And why must there be this passion for legislation by reference of which there are some shattering examples in the most recent Finance Act? ... otherwise one of these days the House of Lords in its legislative capacity may be encouraged to throw out a major government bill and refuse to pass it into law unless and until it is re-written in intelligible and simple language.

The days of the dual functions of the House of Lords have, of course, passed into history but to hear such strictures on statutory drafting, from a former law lord and Chairman of the Joint Committee of both Houses of Parliament on the Consolidation of Statutes, was certainly not mere populism, but well-informed criticism from someone with a wealth of experience at the sharp end of the law. The problem, as he and other senior judges have reminded us time and time again, is that our legislators seem deaf to such criticism. That was true then and nothing has changed since – a point to which I shall refer again in more detail at the end of this chapter, especially with regard to the criminal law. However, before passing on and as an indication of the extent to which Lord Roskill's general strictures on the subject of statutory drafting were justified, I would refer to what should be the relatively uncontroversial but nevertheless important subject of road traffic in the relatively short three year period following his lecture on 2 October 1986.

The first Act to put in an appearance was the Motor Cycle Noise Act 1987 passed on 15 May 1987. There was, however, a more than elephantine period of gestation between conception and its coming to term almost ten years later on 1 August 1996 by the Motor Cycle Noise Act 1987 (Commencement) Order 1995 SI 11995/2367. Next to be conceived was the Motor Vehicles (Wearing of Rear Seat Belts by Children) Act 1988 on 28 June 1988. Sadly, however, S.1 together with S3(2) and (3) were were to suffer a neo-natal death, being repealed by S.3, Schedule 1, Part 1 of the Road Traffic (Consequential Provisions) Act 1988 passed less than five months later on 15 November 1988. Next in time came the Road Traffic Act 1988 likewise passed on 15 November. This was the big one, containing 197 sections and four schedules although the last schedule was repealed not long afterwards by S. 83 and Schedule 8 of the Road Traffic Act 1991. But 15 November had also seen the passing of the Road Traffic Offenders Act 1988. And although S.99(2) helpfully provides that it is to come into force "at the end of the period of six months beginning with the day on which it is passed", it less helpfully makes certain exceptions: S.59, for example, is only to come into force "on such day or days as the Secretary of State may by order made by statutory instrument appoint." Were it that simple. By S99(6) life on the road, at least in its legal manifestation, becomes even more complicated:

> An order under subsection (3) or (5) above may contain such transitional provisions and savings (whether or not involving the modification of any provisions contained in an Act or in subordinate legislation (within the meaning of the Interpretation Act 1978)) as appear to the Secretary of State necessary or expedient in connection with the provisions brought (wholly or partly) into force by the order, and different days may be appointed for different purposes.

As for S.59 itself, the Secretary of State had still failed to make any order bringing it into force by May 2001 over twelve years later!

Next we had the Road Traffic (Consequential Provisions) Act 1988, likewise passed on 15 November 1988. To ensure that all this legislation was suitably intelligible to all save those of the meanest intelligence,

S.4 enacted with pelucid clarity as follows under the helpful rubric "Prospective and consequential amendments":

> Schedule 2 to this Act (which re-enacts or makes consequential amendments of provisions which make prospective amendments of the repealed and other enactments, so that the re-enacted or amended provisions prospectively amend the Road Traffic Acts and other enactments) and Schedule 3 to this Act (which makes other consequential amendments) shall have effect.

It is clear that parliament was very preoccupied with road traffic in the late 1980s. Despite its herculean efforts already described it still managed to finish off the decade with the Parking Act 1989 and the Road Traffic (Driver Licensing and Information Systems) Act 1989.

James Scarlett,
1st Baron Abinger.
© National Portrait Gallery.

In his lecture Lord Roskill also turned his attention to the iniquitous doctrine of "common employment" – that is to say the rule that an employee could not sue his employer for the negligence of his fellow employee. Although fully justified in suggesting that its final abolition was due to judicial pressure for reform, he may have overlooked the fact that the doctrine itself did have a judicial origin. In *Priestly v Fowler* (1837) 3 M&W 1 Lord Abinger CB (who, as James Scarlett had advised the Society on costs in 1815)[2] was faced with the problem of a butcher's boy who was injured when his master's cart in which he was travelling collapsed seemingly as a result of having been overloaded by a fellow employee. It may have been the first case ever where an employee sought to make his employer responsible for negligence – or at least negligence which was independent of any breach of contract. Reviewing the case years later in *Radcliffe v Ribble Motor Services Ltd* [1939] AC 225 Lord Atkin observed:

> Lord Abinger felt that he had to decide the case on general principles, and that he was at liberty to look at the consequences ... surveying them he was alarmed, for he found that if the master was liable, he would be liable for the negligence of all his "inferior agents", eg to the footman for the negligence of his coachman ... to a domestic servant for the negligence of a chambermaid, the upholsterer, the cook the butcher and the builder ... faced with the absurdity of these consequences, the court concluded that the master is not bound to take more care of the servant than he may reasonably be expected to do for himself.

The doctrine of common employment was indeed formally abolished by S.1 of the Law Reform (Personal Injuries) Act 1948 but only after prolonged and strenuous attempts by the judiciary to "confess and avoid" – for example, by holding that the employer could not hide behind the doctrine if he had omitted to choose fellow employees of sufficient care and skill, nor for his own failure to avoid "unreasonable risks". But if the responsibility for establishing the doctrine in the first place was that of Lord Abinger, he would doubtless have agreed (with the benefit of hindsight) that his preoccupation in 1837 with footmen and chambermaids was to work intolerable injustice in the world of large industrial enterprises as they were to develop from the second half of the 19th century onwards. He was not suggesting that a master had no duty of care to his servant, merely that he could not be fixed with vicarious responsibility for the acts of a fellow servant, or, in modern terminology, to act as the servant's insurer. This is clear from a passage in his judgment:

> In truth the mere relation of master and servant can never imply an obligation on the part of the master to take more care of the servant than he may reasonably be expected to do for himself. *He is, no doubt, bound to provide for the safety of his servant in the course of his employment, to the best of his judgment, information and belief.* [my emphasis]

These last words were to act as the catalyst for the subsequent judicial development of the whole concept of a "safe system of work". However, the problem throughout the 19th century was that whilst parliament was quite prepared to intervene in the processes of the industrial revolution in the form of various statutes relating to factories, mines and shipping, it never seemed to concern itself with the practical consequences for a workman who was injured as a result of employers' failure to comply with their statutory obligations. The doctrine of common employment did not, of course, prevent the injured workman from suing the fellow worker directly responsible for his injuries but the development of large scale and complex industrial processes often made it impossible to identify the actual culprit and in any event, under the social conditions of the period any fellow worker would rarely, if ever, be worth suing even if the would-be plaintiff had the means to pursue an action at law. It was only with the passing of the Employers' Liability Act 1880 and the Workmen's Compensation Act 1897 that parliament had really begun to focus on the rights of employees as such rather than on the mere punishment of employers. It was indeed the judges who were prepared to fill the gaps where parliament imposed a statutory obligation on employers without bothering to consider the position of the workman who was injured as a result of that failure to comply. This they achieved by effectively creating a new cause of action: failure to comply with a statutory obligation.

The next aspect of the law which Lord Roskill raised was the interface between the judges and the politicians, with particular reference to judicial involvement in labour relations. Lord Roskill saw the danger:

> The powers of the courts in these matters of course depend on the legislation which the government have caused parliament to enact. The courts must apply that legislation according to its true interpretation whether they like it or not. But it is I think legitimate to point out that the more the legislation requires the court to interfere in industrial disputes and to interfere this way rather than that, the more the risk arises of the courts being accused of political motivation which is in truth wholly absent from particular decisions. Those decisions are necessitated by and only by the interpretation and application of the legislation in question. It is quite monstrous that these accusations of political motivation should be made, for it is a commonplace of judicial experience that particular decisions have to be reached without necessarily there being any great private enthusiasm for the result that the legislation compels.

These remarks of course were made in the context a long period of political turbulence dating back to the late 1960s, the three day week, and the

Thatcher government's battle of attrition with the unions culminating in the miners' strike of 1984-5. All this generated much media debate at the time on the lines of "Who governs Britain?" and a number of high profile cases where the courts were inevitably exposed to accusations of bias from left or right whatever they decided.

If an increasing involvement of the courts in labour law was liable to expose judges to the risk of being seen as "political" the same could equally be said of their increasing involvement in judicial review, itself a judge-made development of common law principles, described by Lord Diplock at the Fifth Commonwealth Law Conference in 1977 as having been "the great achievement of the twentieth century in the judicial development of the law".[3] That was the year in which Order 53 of the Rules of the Supreme Court finally gave modern procedural form to a jurisdiction which, in its mediæval form, had first been enunciated by Bracton[4] in the 13th century in his famous dictum *ipse autem rex non debet esse sub homine sed sub deo et sub lege, quia lex facit regem* – The king himself is not beholden to man but is subject to God and the law, because the law maketh the king. With certain hiccups during periods of Tudor and Stuart despotism which ended with the deposing of James II in 1688, it has always been a thread running through English legal history that no man is above the law, not even the King's ministers. Lord Denning often used to quote the well-known aphorism of the 17th century churchman and historian Thomas Fuller (1608-1661) "Be ye ever so high, the law is above you" and it even appeared in some of his judgments.[5] This did not endear him to some politicians. In its modern form the doctrine has been well described by Lord Bingham in a lecture delivered at King's College London on 14 February 1996.[6]

> In a democratic society governed by the rule of law no one – literally no one – is entrusted with unfettered power. The reason is obvious: unfettered power is tyranny or despotism, both of which are inconsistent with the rule of law. So, while the complexity of modern government leads to the conferment of wide powers and important discretions on particular bodies and office-holders, all such powers are conferred for a purpose which is either explicit or implicit and no discretion is so broad as to be the subject of no limit at all. Much the same is true of non-statutory prerogative powers. Whatever the source of the power in question, the judge's task when reduced to essentials is always the same: to examine whether the power

in question has been lawfully used. It will not have been lawfully used if it has been used for a purpose alien to that for which the power existed. It will not have been lawfully used if statutory conditions attaching to its exercise have not been observed. It will not have been lawfully exercised if the decision to exercise it has been swayed by irrelevant considerations or if the decision-maker has disregarded relevant considerations. It will not have been lawfully exercised if, in a situation where ordinary fairness required a certain procedure to be followed, and the decision was one calling for ordinary fairness, such a procedure has not been followed. It will not have been lawfully used if the decision to exercise the power was one which no one in his or her right mind could have made if properly advised in law … The judge's only role is to decide whether the challenged decision was lawful or not: if the challenge is upheld the consequence is not that the judge makes the decision, but almost invariably, that the decision is quashed, leaving the true decision-maker at liberty to make another decision, lawfully, whether to the same effect as the earlier decision or not. The only real exception is where a decision is condemned as perverse, such as no reasonable properly-directed person could have made, in a situation where there was an effective choice between two decisions; but the threshold of perversity is, rightly, very high.

Another trend in the law about which Lord Roskill expressed reservations was what he saw as the expansion of the current "claims culture" which of course has continued to expand over the last thirty years. He feared the law of unintended consequences – the increase in "defensive medicine" and "defensive lawyering" and pointed out the dilemma for doctors, lawyers or indeed any other professionals who have to make decisions, often on the spur of the moment, where *after the event* it is all too easy to say that the decision was "wrong". The same criticism might perhaps be made of the approach of some coroners towards the military hierarchy when dealing with inquests on soldiers killed in action in Iraq, Afghanistan or elsewhere. He also had misgivings about the delays and expense associated with personal injury claims and clearly favoured the national insurance solution recommended over thirty years ago by the Pearson Report.[7] This had been cooly received by the profession at the time and rejected by the Treasury on the grounds that it was too expensive. "I am no statistician or actuary" he added "but I strongly suspect that the cost to this country of doing nothing may in the end prove to be much greater than the cost of facing this problem and trying to solve it."

Finally, he reviewed what he described as the "really important changes in the last hundred years", many of which had been strenuously criticised at the time – legislation regarding trade union immunities, the passing of the Criminal Evidence Act in 1898 which enabled prisoners for the first time to give evidence in their own defence, the creation of the old Court of Criminal Appeal in 1907 and much else besides. "Some people may I think perhaps blush – yes they should blush – if they are reminded of what they said twenty years ago about the proposal to introduce majority verdicts yet where would one be in recent times without that change?" He concluded by reminding his audience that law and lawyers are not the solution to all life's issues, quoting some lines which he had come across in a scrap-book belonging to his mother:

> The law the lawyer knows about is property and land
> But why the leaves are on the trees
> And why the waves disturb the seas,
> Why honey is the food of bees,
> Why horses have such tender knees,
> Why winters come and rivers freeze,
> Why faith is more than what one sees,
> And hope survives the worst disease,
> And charity is more than these,
> They do not understand.

A salutary reminder perhaps to all of us.

What's Wrong with the Law? had been a title of Lord Roskill's own choosing but it accorded well with the *Zeitgeist* as did the follow-up which the Society organised some years later on 25 May 1995, a symposium *Can Citizens Abide the Law?* at the same venue. This time the format for the evening was rather different and based on the familiar BBC programme *Question Time* with Gilbert Gray QC, a leading member of the North Eastern Circuit performing the role of Robin Day/David Dimbleby. The panellists were David Ansbro, a solicitor who had filled chief executive roles with York, Kirklees and Leeds City Council and who at the time was managing partner of Eversheds, Professor Paul Fairest of Hull University, a recognised authority on consumer law and a member of the National Consumer Council, Edward McMillan-Scott MEP (Conservative) for

North Yorkshire[8] and Richard North, food safety consultant and co-author (with Christopher Booker) of *The Mad Officials*.

The event coincided with the publication by the Labour party of its draft proposals for reform of our legal system. Their stated aim was to make the law accessible to all – this was said to be "vital to strengthening public confidence in the justice system and strengthening respect for the rule of law, which must underpin any decent civic society and community regeneration". This of course was just two years before the general election of 1997 and the return to power of a Labour government under Tony Blair with its biggest parliamentary majority ever. The proposals were claimed to be a response to the perception that the system at the time was in crisis and characterised by exorbitant expense, waste, delay and, consequently, inaccessibility. At the time this perception was by no means confined to the Labour Party or to those whose political views were left of centre but readers will doubtless make up their own mind as to the extent to which these laudable ambitions have been achieved in the years that followed.

Questions from the audience focussed on four areas of concern: firstly, the surfeit of law and regulation and the difficulty and cost to the business and farming community of compliance – particularly in the face of apparent non-compliance in certain other EU states; secondly, problems associated with widespread rejection of much deeply unpopular law – ranging from practical non-compliance to full scale and wilful civil disobedience or even riot; thirdly, issues relating to the method of recruitment to the legal profession and its financing and fourthly to procedural problems associated with the criminal law and in particular to the right balance between prosecution and defence in relation to pre-trial disclosure.

The first issue – too much law and too much regulation – very quickly brought in the Brussels factor on which the main protagonists were Richard North and Edward McMillan-Scott. The latter claimed that many ills were popularly attributed to "Brussels" when it was entirely innocent and that no less than 119 Euro-myths had been identified in the previous eighteen months. Although Richard North was prepared to concede that "Europe" was not directly responsible for every example of *excès de zèle* in the regulatory field, he felt it was often the inspiration that lay behind it, as in the "Lanarkshire Blue" cheese case in which he had been recently involved in Scotland. There was a general tendency on the part of UK officials to use Euro-law as a power base. Both panellists accepted the phenomenon that Edward McMillan-Scott described as the "gold-plating" of Brussels directives by Whitehall – the creation of UK strains more virulent, or at any rate much more detailed than the originals. Examples cited included the directive that the walls of slaughterhouses be "washable" which in the UK became a requirement for stainless steel cladding; similarly a couple of pages of guidance to French farmers as to how to complete their IACS forms became eight in Ireland and 83 in the UK.

Whilst not disputing the gold-plating phenomenon, Paul Fairest raised a slightly different concern which he characterised as "pass-the-parcel". Sir Humphrey in *Yes Minister* used to have a quartet of infallible objections designed to stop ministers from doing things. These could be practical, administrative, political or legal. Legal objections were thought to be the best as they took ages to resolve and nobody but the lawyers understood them anyway. However the new way of stopping anything happening was to find some kind of Euro-reason why you could not do something that was sensible – like the fitting of seat-belts in coaches.[9] Equally, both Edward McMillan-Scott and Richard North seemed to think that the government could adopt a less supine attitude to problems of animal welfare involved in the live export of farm animals if they were so minded.

David Ansbro's concern with Euro-law was over different standards of enforcement. He cited the case in which he had been involved over the closure of the Case tractor factory in Meltham and its impact on the town. This was quite simply due to the French government breaking European rules and providing attractions in terms of investment to Case (based in the United States) and as a result some six or seven hundred people lost their jobs. The UK government was powerless to do anything about it and so was the Commission. The French were simply adapting the rules for their own benefit.

The next main topic for debate was the problem of civil disobedience as the natural reaction to unjust or over-burdensome laws.[10] Paul Fairest accepted that this was a possibility. Gilbert Gray put the question to him directly. "It seems to me that this discussion is moving in the direction of too much law, too little respect for the law and the prospect of wholesale breaking of the law. Do you think that is a direction in which we are moving?" Paul Fairest: "I think it might be." After further discussion Gilbert Gray asked the question again in a slightly different form: "Do you not just get a whiff of things moving in the wrong direction – dangerously?" Paul Fairest: "Yes, I do and I think it is getting worse." Quoting Dicey's principle that for the law to be accepted by the population it has to be accepted as good and that if people have no respect for the law they will flout it, Gilbert Gray observed "It seems to me – and I hope I am not magnifying it unduly – we have just heard a rather disturbing series of answers as to the direction in which we are moving." Nobody in the audience dissented.

Another issue prompted by a question from a retired major-general concerned recruitment to the legal profession and in particular to the Bar. Richard North (who claimed to be a major consumer of legal services) was the only non-lawyer on the panel and he took the view, very firmly, that anyone should be able to act as advocate or representative in court and that the only restriction should be that no-one should falsely lay claim to *qualifications* to which they were not entitled. This, however, seemed to be regarded by the other speakers, and particularly by the chairman, as an entirely heterodox, if not heretical, notion. All the lawyers acknowledged the very considerable difficulty for the young – in the case of the Bar of getting pupillages and in the case of solicitors, training contracts. Yet no particular solutions were proposed – there seemed to be an acceptance that the whole question of the volume of recruitment would ultimately be governed by market forces in any event. Both Paul Fairest and David Ansbro expressed strong views about the importance of the legal profession not becoming the preserve of the rich and the well-connected. Paul Fairest thought that most firms of solicitors had reasonably "serious" recruitment policies but added "The Bar's recruitment policy is not I think particularly transparent."

This last comment prompted the Chairman to invite Anton Lodge QC from the audience to make a public confession on behalf of the Bar. He accepted the invitation and conceded that until about ten years previously there might have been some grounds for the public perception that the Bar was a "toff's club" and for the old saw (quoted by Gilbert

Gray) that "barristers were gentlemen pretending to be lawyers and that solicitors were lawyers pretending to be gentlemen". The problem he thought was based on the Bar's three structural weaknesses: ignorance, disorganisation and meanness. Their ignorance was ignorance of *how* they selected people and the effect of such selection, their disorganisation was the result in part of the fragmented way in which they practised – as individuals and not in partnership – and their meanness stemmed in part also from their individuality. No individual barrister had a particular interest in recruitment as such. He went on to explain that in recent years these problems were being addressed – for example by the creation of the aspiring pupil's equivalent of the university UCCA form and by sponsorship during pupilage. The only misgiving he voiced on the latter was that "sponsorship" should not become a method of regulating entry to the profession.

David Ansbro referred to his own firm's (Eversheds) annual sponsorship of 16 trainee solicitors – pointing out that this represented a very heavy investment which was essentially disinterested. The demand for training contracts had by then reached the stage, however, where aspiring solicitors were writing in offering to spend the first year's training free of cost to the firm, although this was precluded at the time by Law Society rules. Similar policies were followed by other similar practices in Leeds and doubtless elsewhere. There was audible reaction to this from local solicitors in the audience from smaller practices and from some aspiring trainees – presumably on the grounds that this was all very well at the higher level but it still left a problem for smaller and rural practices which could no longer afford to take *any* trainees.

Next came a question on criminal procedure which sought the panel's views about the Home Secretary's proposals for more advance disclosure of the defence. This lead to a lively exchange between Richard North and the chairman which shed some light on how the law could work in different ways at different levels. Mr North had begun by recalling an early experience as a young man involved in his first prosecution when his senior officer remarked to him "Lad … there's now't wrong with a bad case that a bit o' perjury can't solve".

Gilbert Gray	"Do you suggest that this is limited to the prosecution?"
Richard North	"No indeed (*laughter*) – of course not! However, you must remember that we are not only talking about this very limited span of recognised criminal cases … murderers, rapists, thugs and what have you. The bulk of cases going through the law under the criminal code are not of this ilk".

After referring to prosecutions for administrative infractions which were still under the criminal code Richard North continued:

"Now fighting these cases, and I have fought dozens of them, one is working under the criminal code and the disclosure rules still apply, and as I say the disclosure we find wholly inadequate. We still find prosecutors, the authorities behind them, the ministers, the county councils and the local authorities are ready and willing to play the game of withholding information – so my view remains that we need more powers as defendants to get more information and until we do, justice is not always served."

Gilbert Gray	"Just so that people can follow it – if you are wanting something that is sensitive you may know about it and you can apply for it and then it is left to the discretion of the judge to decide whether you should have it, isn't it?"
Richard North	"Indeed".
Gilbert Gray	"Now I don't want to rehearse particular cases but I was concerned with the Matrix-Churchill case[11] and there the judge very wisely gave us a huge amount of material which eventually led to the Richard Scott inquiry. So I do not think you could expect every member of the Bar to say that PII [Public Interest Immunity] is not being fairly considered when it is left to the discretion of fairly experienced judges".
Richard North	"Well, this may be but you are working at a fairly rarified level …"

Gilbert Gray	"No, you have not seen me working ... " (*laughter*)
Richard North	"Certainly in that case you were but in the day-to-day nitty-gritty at magistrates level, down at the Crown Court – sometimes you find different rules apply and sometimes it can rest on what the clerk of the court will decide and it is very ... "
Gilbert Gray	"Again, I think it is fair to say that if the clerk gets it wrong you can seek to put it right either in the divisional court or on appeal?"
Richard North	"Easy for you to say as a lawyer but when you have to look at a case that might end up with a couple of thousand quid fine and then you have to put twenty thousand quid down on the table to take it to judicial review or to the court of appeal you often cut your losses".
Gilbert Gray	"I have your point".

In dealing with the same issue relating to the proposed requirement of greater disclosure by the defence both Paul Fairest and David Ansbro expressed themselves equally unhappy about the then Home Secretary, Michael Howard, although Paul Fairest thought that this specific proposal might be worth serious consideration: "I would not want to rule it out at this stage" he added. David Ansbro was not only unhappy about the approach of the Home Secretary, he was equally unhappy about the approach of the Lord Chancellor. [Lord Mackay of Clashfern] "My greatest fear, however, is that the Lord Chancellor and the present Home Secretary are not as interested in justice as they should be and if they put justice first and efficiency there to seek justice, I think that would be a much better way of going about it. But it seems to me that they put what they perceive to be efficiency first all the time and justice is taking a back seat."

The final question from the audience concerned attempts by animal rights demonstrators to prevent the export of live animals with the apparent tacit support of certain local authorities. None of the panellists appeared to be in favour of the export of live animals *as a policy* and it appeared to be accepted that most members of the public found the trade repugnant and would like to see it banned. There was a suggestion that the UK government could act independently within European law if it were so minded – but perhaps Sir Humphrey had been getting at the minister … As to civil disobedience it was left to Paul Fairest to state the classic moral, legal and philosophical position: "Break the law for conscience sake if you have to but be prepared to take the legal consequences".

This brought discussion back to its starting point. In introducing the symposium on behalf of the Society reference had been made to Robert Bolt's *A Man for all Seasons* where Thomas More's son-in-law, William Roper, was upbraiding him for being overly technical and standing on the letter of the law in defending himself against the machinations of Henry VIII and Thomas Cromwell:

More replies	The law, Roper, the law. I know what's legal not what's right. And I'll stick to what's legal … What would you do? Cut a great road through the law to get after the devil?
Roper	I'd cut down every law in England to do that!
More	Oh! And when the last law was down and the devil turned round, where would you hide, Roper, the laws all being flat? … do you really think you could stand upright in the winds that would blow then?

That, too, perhaps is a salutary reminder to all of us.

Earlier in this chapter I ventured to suggest that nothing had changed since Lord Roskill's lecture in 1986 on the occasion of the Society's bicentenary. If anything there has been a deterioration as regards the "mystery" and "avoidable complexity" of the law of which he complained and the reluctance of our politicians to pay any attention whatever to the informed opinions of those who actually have to apply it. His particular criticism at the time was directed at the Finance Acts which touch upon our wealth. Identical criticism could be directed at the veritable tsunami of legislation relating to criminal justice, the application and effective enforcement of which touches upon our liberties and our safety. Consider, for example, the following extract from a Court of Appeal judgment quoted by Carnwath J in the Law Section of *The Times* on 7 March 2000:

The Crime (Sentences) Act 1997, Schedule 4, paragraph 5(1)(b) as enacted would have amended the Criminal Justice Act 1967, s.56(2) so as to refer to section 17(3) of the Crime (Sentences) Act 1997. This section would have replaced the Criminal Justice Act 1991, s.40(3) if chapter 1 of part 2 of the Crime (Sentences) Act 1997 had been brought into force. The whole of the chapter (with the exception of section 9) was repealed by the Crime and Disorder Act 1998, Schedule 10 with effect from September 30, 1998.

The Crime (Sentences) Act 1997 (Commencement No.2 and Transitional Provisions Order) 1997 brought into force the amendment of the Criminal Justice Act 1997 s.56(2) made by Schedule 4, paragraph 5(1)(b) to the Act and then purported by paragraph 5(3)(b) to amend section 56(2) of the 1967 Act (as so amended) so that the reference to the Crime (Sentences) Act 1997, s.17(3) was replaced by a reference to the Criminal Justice Act 1991, s.40(3). The effect of this amendment would be that the Criminal Justice Act 1967, s.56(2) referred to the Criminal Justice Act 1991, s.40(3) instead of to the Criminal Justice Act 1967, s.62(6)

Lost somewhere in the above maze, the court had held that the Secretary of State had made an invalid commencement order, with the result that the sentence of the Crown Court had been imposed without jurisdiction. One lucky defendant at least was more appreciative of the mystery of the law as counsel was trying to explain to him in another case precisely why the Divisional Court had just thrown out the charges against him (for selling counterfeit Chanel No 5 off a barrow in the West End) on some equally arcane point: "Blimey guv" he observed with a grin, "ain't the law f---ing marvellous!"

Lord Roskill's comments were made thirty years ago. The mordant criticism of Carnwath J appeared sixteen years ago. Five years later in *R v Bradley* [2005] EWCA Crim 20 Rose LJ, Vice-President of the Court of Appeal observed:

> It is more than a decade since Lord Taylor of Gosforth CJ called for a reduction in the torrent of legislation affecting criminal justice. Regrettably, that call has gone unheeded by successive governments. Indeed the quantity of such legislation has increased and its quality, if anything, diminished.

More recently still the case of *R (Noone) v Governor of HMP Drake Hall and Another* [2010] UKSC 30 has provoked similar criticism from the President of the Supreme Court, Lord Phillips of Worth Matravers. Describing the road to hell as paved with good intentions – in the instant case the good intentions having been to introduce mandatory rehabilitation for very short term prisoners – hell was a fair description, according to his lordship, of the problem of statutory interpretation caused by transitional provisions introduced when "custody plus" as it had been baptised had to be put on hold because the resources necessary to implement the scheme did not exist.

The issue before the Supreme Court in 2010 had started its lamentable progression through the criminal justice system in a perfectly straightforward case in May 2007 before His Honour Judge Eades at Stafford Crown Court. Following her conviction, Rebecca Noone had been sentenced to a total of 27 months' imprisonment. Judge Eades might have imposed a sentence of 27 months for one offence of theft, with lesser concurrent sentences for the remaining offences. Unaware, however, of the Pandora's Box of legal complications which he was about to unleash – the result of endless statutory tinkering with the judicial process – he chose instead to impose a sentence of 22 months for theft, with consecutive sentences of four months and one month totalling a further five months. Notwithstanding the judge's conscientious effort to observe the "totality principle,"[12] the prison authorities were clearly overwhelmed by the morass of relevant legislation. They had given the prisoner a release date but later had to give her back word after further consideration of the Secretary of State's "policy" concerning the administration of the Home Detention Curfew Scheme – a policy which the one of the judges of the Supreme Court was eventually to castigate as "absurd". The result was an application for judicial review. MittingJ had allowed her application in 2008 but the Governor of the prison and the Secretary of State for Justice had appealed – an appeal which, absurdity notwithstanding, the Court of Appeal had upheld and so the case eventually landed in the Supreme Court. As Lord Phillips put it:

> The problem arose when sentences of less than 12 months and more than 12 months were imposed consecutively. The Criminal Justice Act 2003 (Commencement No 8 and Transitional and Saving Provisions) Order 2005 brought into force as from 4 April 2005 provisions of the Criminal

Justice Act 2003 that related to over 12-month sentences, as set out in Sch 1. At the same time ss 32 to 51 of the Criminal Justice Act 1991 were repealed. Sch 2 set out transitional and saving provisions. Para 14 provided "The coming into force of ss 244 to 268 of, and para 30 of Sch 32 to the 2003 Act, and the repeal of ss 33 to 51 of the 1991 Act, is of no effect in relation to any sentences of imprisonment of less than 12 months (whether or not such a sentence is imposed to run concurrently or consecutively with another such sentence)." Para 14 served one obvious purpose. Because s 181 and s 244(3)(b) of the 2003 Act had not been brought into force and ss 32 to 51 of the 1991 Act were repealed there was no provision for early release, or eligibility for home detention curfew release, for prisoners serving under 12-month sentences. Para 14 was clearly intended to make provision for such sentences, at least when not imposed concurrently or consecutively with over 12-month sentences, to continue to be dealt with exclusively under the 1991 Act. If imposed consecutively to other under-12 month sentences, these would be aggregated pursuant to the provisions of s 51(2) of the 1991 Act and the provisions of ss 33 and 34A, as inserted by section 99 of the Crime and Disorder Act 1998, applied to the aggregate. That would produce a similar result to that produced by ss 244 and 246 of the 2003 Act in relation to over 12-month sentences.

He proceeded to deal with the problem by a robust judicial redrafting of the wording of paragraph 14 to reflect what in his opinion the parliamentary draftsman had *meant* to say: "The effect of that [his own] interpretation … provided uniformity of approach, regardless of the order in which the individual sentences had been imposed, qualified the prisoner for the maximum grant of home detention curfew release, but at the same time subjected the prisoner to the latest sentence and licence expiry date."

Lord Judge, concurring, was equally trenchant in his criticism. After quoting from a Judicial Studies Board lecture by Professor John Spencer QC in which he had observed that the collection of statistics in preparation for his lecture was "not easy, because there had been so much criminal justice legislation over the last ten years that accurate figures are now hard to give. However, by my reckoning we have had since 1997 no less than 55 Acts of Parliament altering the rules of criminal justice for England and Wales." He went on to quote Mitting J in the original proceedings in the Administrative Court:

> These proceedings show that, in relation to perfectly ordinary consecutive sentences imposed since the coming into force of much of the Criminal Justice Act 2003, that task is impossible ... It is simply unacceptable in a society governed by the rule of law for it to be well nigh impossible to discern from statutory provisions what a sentence means in practice. That is the effect here ...

Lord Judge continued:

> I entirely agree with these observations. The explanation for the problem is simple. For too many years now the administration of criminal justice has been engulfed by a relentless tidal wave of legislation. The tide is always in flow; it has never ebbed ... I have studied the judgments of Lord Phillips and Lord Mance. Their judgments tell the lamentable story of how elementary principles of justice have come, in this case, to be buried in the legislative morass. They have achieved a construction of the relevant legislation which produces both justice and common sense. I should have been inclined to reject the Secretary of State's contention on the grounds of absurdity – absurd because it contravened elementary principles of justice in the sentencing process – but Lord Phillips and Lord Mance have provided more respectable solutions, either or both of which I gratefully adopt.
>
> Nevertheless the element of absurdity remains. It is outrageous that so much intellectual effort, as well as public time and resources, have had to be expended in order to discover a route through the legislative morass to what should be, both for the prisoner herself, and for those responsible for her custody, the prison authorities, the simplest and most certain of questions – the prisoner's release date.

He was perhaps wise not to have followed the example of Lord Atkin[13] in *Liversidge v Anderson* [1942] AC 206 in citing the authority of Humpty Dumpty "When I use a word," Humpty Dumpty said in rather a scornful tone, "it means just what I choose it to mean, neither more nor less.'" Lord Atkin was insisting that the relevant legislation meant what it said rather than what Humpty Dumpty chose it to mean. However, Lord Judge and his fellow members of the Supreme Court in the instant case were faced with a plethora of words which, once excavated and exposed to the light of day, didn't seem to mean anything at all. Nevertheless, he may have had Lord Atkin in mind when deciding that once again the executive had merited a good judicial chastisement.

We are fortunate indeed to live in a country in which such well-merited verbal chastisement of government can be administered by our judges without regard to consequences, whether it be directed at the nuts and bolts of legislation or more substantive issues. This is certainly not the case in many parts of the world, perhaps most, as the present Archbishop of York, the Most Reverend and Rt Hon Dr John Sentamu would doubtless be the first to confirm. Nor is it by any means merely the case in so-called third world countries. It is surely incumbent upon all citizens everywhere, and especially all lawyers (whether individually or as part of Edmund Burke's "small platoons') to do whatever is within their power to ensure the proper accountability of governments. Over two centuries ago the great Irish advocate, JP Curran[14] summed up our responsibilities in his speech on the right of election for the Lord Mayor of Dublin in 1790: " The condition upon which God hath given liberty to man is eternal vigilance; which condition if he break, servitude is at once the consequence of his crime and the punishment of his guilt." He was a fearless advocate who once observed: "Assassinate me you may; intimidate me you cannot." These were not mere words: in the course of his life he had fought no less than five duels rather than compromise his principles. A difficult act to follow perhaps in our own age but at least we can hold fast to his principle of eternal vigilance.

NOTES

1. Our law of evidence, on which entire books have been written, is often a source of bewilderment to foreign lawyers. In continental jurisdictions the law of evidence can often be summarised in one sentence: if it is relevant, it is admissible. English rules were developed for an age when all serious trials involved juries, even in civil cases.

2. See Chapter 3 p. 57.

3. *Proceedings and Papers of the Fifth Commonwealth Law Conference* Blackwood, Edinburgh 2000.

4. Henry de Bracton (or Bretton/Bratton) (c 1210-1268) was a Devon man and sometime Chancellor of the diocese of Exeter. At one time the Society

possessed a copy of this seminal treatise *De Legibus et Consuetudinibus Angliae* in Tottell's edition of 1569 – See Appendix C p. 393.

5. Alfred Thompson ('Tom') Denning (1899-1999) was a judge for thirty-eight years, twenty of them as Master of the Rolls. He was one of the best-known, popular and controversial judges of the 20th century and probably the only one to have become a household name over a prolonged period. One example of his use of Fuller's words was in *Gouriet v Union of Post Office Workers* [1977] 1 All ER 696 at 718. Denning was certainly not the first judge to have quoted Fuller in a judgment. Edmund Davies LJ had used it ten years earlier in *R v Metropolitan Police Commissioner ex parte Blackburn* [1968] 1 ALL ER 763 at 777 although on that occasion the target was a senior police officer rather than a trades union and the Attorney-General. Denning MR had himself had given the lead judgment in the latter case. Denning was guest of honour at the Society's annual dinner in 1982 to propose the toast of 'The Yorkshire Law Society'. In doing so he feigned surprise at the large turnout to greet him despite what he described as 'rival attractions'. He had clearly noticed that a newly released film was playing at the Regal cinema across the road from the Merchants Adventurers Hall, *The Best Little Whorehouse in Texas* featuring Dolly Parton. The dinner was a lively one. At the following committee meeting in January 1983 the Hon Treasurer was obliged to report 'a marked increase in the amount of alcohol consumed on the night' resulting in a slight deficit.

6. This lecture first appeared in print in *The King's Law Journal* (1996-7) Vol 7, 12-26; re-published in *The Business of Judging – Selected Essays and Speeches* Tom Bingham OUP 2000.

7. (1978) Cmnd 7054 – A similar scheme to that proposed was subsequently adopted in New Zealand.

8. Edward McMillan-Scott MEP fell out with the Conservative party and now sits as a Liberal Democrat MEP for the Yorkshire and Humber constituency. He has received a number of awards for his work in connection with human rights and since 2004 has been elected four times to the Vice-Presidency of the European Parliament.

9. By coincidence this long running euro-controversy was finally laid to rest on the very day of the symposium: the UK had notified the Commission of its plan to require the fitting of seat belts to buses and coaches used to carry *children* and the Commission had raised no objection. Commission press release 25 May WE/20/95.

10. The poll-tax riots of 1990 were still fresh in people's minds.

11. Matrix Churchill was a Coventry firm involved in the manufacture of machine tools. In 1991 three of its senior executives had been charged with exporting machine tools to Iraq which could be used for making military equipment; they had allegedly sought to deceive the government in their application for an export licences. The nub of their defence was that the government knew exactly what they had been doing – not least because one of the three, Paul Henderson, had been supplying information to British Intelligence on a regular basis. The prosecution had been something of a fiasco: the judge overturned Public Interest Immunity certificates signed by several government ministers, forcing them to hand over confidential documents to the defence. Subsequently Alan Clark MP, under cross-examination produced his much-quoted variation of the principle first enunciated by St Augustine and conceded that notes of one particular DTI meeting had been 'economical with the *actualité*'. The trial collapsed and it all resulted in due course in the Scott enquiry, the results of which were not published until the following year (1996).

12. A long established principle of sentencing which requires the court to have regard to the 'totality' of the defendant's conduct – a concept which has now received statutory recognition in S 120 (3) (b) of the Coroners and Justice Act 2009 – rather than basing its sentence on an individual analysis of every individual charge in the indictment and then adding them all together.

13. See Chapter 11 p. 219.

14. John Philpot Curran (1750-1817). Called to the Irish Bar in 1775, he subsequently became Master of the Rolls in Ireland in 1806, a post which he held until his retirement in 1814 when he moved to London and spent the last three years of his life there. He had the gift of repartee so characteristic of the Irish advocate. He was once dining with Toler CJ, a notorious Irish 'hanging' judge. Toler: "Curran, is that hung beef?" Curran: "do try it my lord, then it is sure to be".

EPILOGUE

"The more laws, the less justice."

Cicero – De Officiis 1.10.33

If Queen Victoria had been a man and not a woman when she succeeded to the throne in 1837 she would have been Elector of Hanover, but she was not. In Hanover the Salic law of succession applied, and this excluded women. Would any British government have allowed Bismark to have reunited Germany and subordinated His Majesty's realm in Germany to the King of Prussia? Equally, there is evidence, albeit not conclusive, to suggest that as a four year old child, Adolf Hitler may have been rescued from almost certain death when he fell through the ice into the River Inn at Passau in January 1894 by another boy who went on to become the parish priest of Passau, Father Johann Kuehberger.[1] Nobody can possibly say how the history of Europe might have unrolled if either or both of these events, the accession of a female rather than a male heir to the throne in 1837 or the rescue from certain drowning of Adolf Hitler in 1894 had not occurred.

We all know that both individually and collectively our lives are largely governed by such chance events. It is for this reason, that Niels Bohr, the Nobel Laureate was right to point out that prediction, especially of the future, is very difficult and this is why it would be a brave man who was prepared to predict the future of law and the legal profession.

As far as attorneys and solicitors were concerned, the skill and knowledge originally involved was relatively limited: the ability to read and write and a familiarity with the procedure of the relevant courts and their respective rule books. As Erasmus rather unkindly put it, "The study of English law is as far removed as can be from true learning", although he did add "but those who succeed in it are highly thought of." [2]

In 1516 Thomas More published his most famous work. It was originally written in Latin but the Greek name of his imaginary island, *Utopia* (*'eu'* or *'ou' topos* – lit *"good"* or *"no"* place) was his posthumous gift to the English language. The work first appeared in Louvain under the editorship of his friend Erasmus, but it was not until 1551 that the first English edition became available. More's professional trajectory, both as a lawyer and a politician, was nothing if not stellar. Himself the son of a judge, he was called to the Bar in 1502 at the age of 24 and became MP for Great Yarmouth two years later in 1504. By 1510 he was joint under sheriff for the City of London, Speaker of the House of Commons in 1523, Chancellor of the Duchy of Lancaster in 1525 and Lord Chancellor in 1529 – a fairly classic establishment career, replicated many times from that day to this. He was also a notable humanist with a European reputation. It was in this latter capacity rather than as a member of the Bar and MP that he made the following observations on law and lawyers in *Utopia*:

> They have but few laws and such is their constitution that they need not many. They very much condemn other nations whose laws, together with the commentaries on them, swell up to so many volumes; for they think it an unreasonable thing to oblige men to obey a body of laws that are both of such a bulk, and so dark as not to be read and understood by every one of the subjects.
>
> They have no lawyers among them for they consider them a sort of people whose profession it is to disguise matters, and to wrest the laws; and therefore they think it much better that every man should plead his own cause, and put it to the judge, as in other places the client trusts it to a counsellor.
>
> Every one of them is skilled in their law, for it is a very short study, so the plainest meaning of which words are capable is always the sense of their laws. And they argue thus: for all laws are promulgated for this end, that every man may know his duty; and therefore the plainest and most obvious sense of the words is that which ought to be put upon them.

As a practising lawyer and politician the author would have been all too aware that his tongue-in-cheek views on the need for simple law and an absence of lawyers were... well, utopian. But although he lived very much in the real world, even More could not have foreseen the extent to which our laws would "swell up to so many volumes", nor that they should become "of such a bulk, and so dark as not to be read and understood by every one of the subjects".

Gradually by fits and starts the absence of any "true learning" in English law, to which More's friend Erasmus had drawn attention, came to be remedied. A key figure in this process was Sir William Blackstone (1723-1780). Educated at Charterhouse and Pembroke College Oxford where he graduated as a Bachelor of Civil Law (the only law degree then available), he subsequently became a Fellow of All Souls. Although called to the Bar in 1746 as a Middle Templar, he never really practised at this stage of his career but remained an academic. In 1753 he began a series of lectures on English law at Oxford, the first time that the subject had ever been taught at university, and they quickly attracted favourable attention. Five years later he was formally appointed the first Vinerian Professor of English Law.[3] Attempts had already been made in the previous century to establish some basis of coherent principle from the mass of case law that had accumulated by then from mediæval times but Blackstone was the first to get to grips with the whole corpus of English law on any serious academic basis. The success of his four volume *Commentaries on the Laws of England*, the first volume of which was published in 1766, was astonishing. The complete work, republished during his lifetime in 1770, 1773, 1774, 1775 and 1778 was reckoned to have earned its author well over £1M in today's money. In 1841 Henry John Stephen[4] produced an updated edition with the title *New Commentaries on the Laws of England (partly founded on Blackstone)*, generally referred to simply as *Stephen's Commentaries*. This likewise was in four volumes and went through many editions. Both the original Blackstone and Stephen versions are available to this day and both are in a form and substance that the author of *Utopia* would have understood.

But the way in which English law has developed in the 20th and 21st centuries can best be gauged by the fact that the first real attempt to follow the pioneering efforts of Blackstone and Stephen did not occur until Stanley Bond, editor at Butterworths, the legal publishers, managed to track down Lord Halsbury, the former Lord Chancellor, on holiday in Nice and persuade him to become editor-in-chief of a project to provide a wholly new encyclopædic commentary under the simplified title *Laws of England*, known to generations of practitioners simply as *Halsbury's Laws*. The deal in Nice was concluded on the spot. Surprised to see him in the foyer of his hotel, Halsbury's first words were "Hello Bond, what are you doing here?" Bond explained his mission and Halsbury agreed. "Well Bond, I admire you for your cheek... and yes, I'll do it. Only Bond, the labourer is worthy of his hire, eh?" Asked to name his fee, the former Lord Chancellor did so, and it was a stiff one. Bond thereupon pulled out his cheque book and wrote out a cheque for the whole amount. A done deal.

Ever since then the editorship-in-chief has been held by a former Lord Chancellor, the present incumbent being Lord Mackay of Clashfern. But there was a major difference between the Butterworth/Halsbury enterprise which appeared in the early part of the 20th century and the Blackstone and Stephen versions of the 18th and 19th centuries. The first edition of *Halsbury's Laws* appeared not in four but in 31 volumes between 1907 and 1917. The second edition which appeared between 1932 and 1941 required 37 volumes; the third which appeared between 1952 and 1964 required 43 volumes; the fourth edition which appeared between 1973 and 1987 required 56 volumes. The fifth and current edition began to appear in 2008 and now contains 103 volumes.

Halsbury's Laws was joined in 1929 by Butterworth's companion series *Halsbury's Statutes*. The 20 volumes of this first edition had been completed by 1931 and was followed by the 28 volumes of the second edition which appeared between 1948 and 1951 and the 41 volumes of the third edition between 1968 and 1972. The completed fourth edition, comprising 50 volumes, appeared between 1985 and 1992, the publishers now being LexisNexis Butterworths. Finally, to complete the picture, there is *Halsbury's Statutory Instruments* – an enterprise the complexity of which almost defies human imagination since about 2,000 such instruments appear each year and about 21,000 are currently in force.[5] So much for Thomas More's utopian vision about a good society having "few laws".

As the publishing history of *Halsbury's Laws* outlined above illustrates, the sheer quantity of law has more than doubled from 43 volumes when I began my articles in 1963 to the current 103 volumes. Whole new subjects have appeared, including "Sports Law", "Information Technology

Law", "Financial Services and Institutions", "Judicial Review" and "Environmental Quality and Public Health". Equally, sections under traditional headings, such as "Criminal Procedure" and "Education" have increased in length and complexity to a degree which seems to defy all reason. As far as Education is concerned the trend can be observed by comparing the fourth and fifth editions. In 1990 the publishers reissued volume 15 of the fourth edition. It covered two topics: Education and Elections – and 300 paragraphs were devoted to Education. By 2001, however, the publishers found it necessary to have a reissue of the reissue and from half a volume in 1990 Education had expanded to two whole volumes on the subject, 15(1) and 15(2) containing altogether 1,160 paragraphs. Then came the fifth edition. Here the very title "Education" has slipped down the alphabetical list of subjects from volumes 15(1) and 15(2) to volumes 35 and 36. This alone shows how "the law" has expanded in the last 20 years or so and the paragraphs devoted to Education have increased from 1,160 to 1,630.

Another plangent example of the fallout from this legislative big bang is Employment Law which used to be a subheading in the Law of Contract but which has now become a subject in its own right – a rather sad example of how a well-meaning attempt to curb the abusive employer and provide a simple forum for determining workplace disputes has grown into a vast sea area of perilous and shifting sandbanks. This is just about navigable, with difficulty, by large employers with well-resourced HR departments but littered with the wrecks of small and medium-sized employers. They may have come to grief there as a consequence of manifest negligence or misconduct but all too often it is due to some minor procedural error or not having their paperwork in order.

Finally, of course, there is taxation. In an article by Daniel Sandler which appeared in the *Cambridge Law Journal* over twenty years ago the author began as follows: "Tax legislation is probably the lengthiest and most complex legislation enacted in the United Kingdom. But the sheer volume of the legislation has not brought certainty of meaning or predictability of application. The legislation is seriously wanting in clarity and simplicity."[6] Eight years earlier Lord Roskill, in a lecture at the University of York to mark the Society's bicentenary had been making a similar complaint: "Why should we all be afflicted by Finance Bills or Finance Acts which verge on the unintelligible?" Since the chorus of exasperated criticism from the likes of Lord Roskill, David Sandler and many others in the 1980s and 1990s the lack of clarity has markedly increased and any residual simplicity decreased. Tax law and practice affects most people one way or another, save of course for those global corporate behemoths who are in a position to use its very complexity to avoid the fiscal burdens which beset the rest of us, so it is a matter of concern to all. Furthermore, the way in which the Revenue actually manages the system which parliament has bestowed upon it has now reached such a state of chaos that even our politicians are beginning to be seriously alarmed.

HMRC as we now know it came into existence in 2005 at the instigation of Gordon Brown, then Chancellor of the Exchequer. It was formed by an amalgamation of the Inland Revenue and HM Customs & Excise, the latter, perhaps understandably in historical terms, having long had a more abrasive tradition in its dealings with "customers" than the former. The Chancellor's proposals were famously described by the *Financial Times* before they even came into effect as the equivalent of "mating the C&E terrier with the IR retriever". Unfortunately the genetic disposition of the terrier now seems to have been inherited by the new body. Certainly on the Revenue side a culture quickly took root which assumed that everyone with whom they have to deal is on the fiddle and should be treated accordingly. Such assumptions can easily become self-fulfilling.

For the last four years, until she announced her resignation January 2016, HMRC had been the responsibility of Lin Homer, its Chief Executive who qualified as a solicitor in 1980 at the age of 23 whilst working in local government and her last such appointment was in 2002 as Chief Executive of Birmingham City Council. It was here that she first had the misfortune of coming face to face with the nonsenses that governments can inflict on the unsuspecting. Her ultimate career choice, however, would seem to go beyond mere misfortune or carelessness and demonstrate either great recklessness or great courage. In her capacity as returning officer in Birmingham's local elections she became embroiled in a scandal which made headline news at the time and eventually found herself giving evidence before Election Commissioner Richard Mawrey QC. Of Ms Homer's contribution the Commissioner observed that "she threw the rule book out of the window" in order to deal with the overwhelming numbers of postal vote application forms that had been received, notwithstanding her claim that she had merely been "in strategic, not operational control" and had confined herself to "motivational management and fire fighting". There is little doubt, however, that the ultimate responsibility for that particular fiasco lay with the government who had greatly extended the availability of postal voting, ignoring advice that it would greatly increase the risk of fraud. Mr Mawrey was not impressed, describing the system as "wide open to fraud and any would-be political fraudster knows that". Of the government's insistence that "the current postal voting system was working", he went on to observe "Anybody who has sat through the case I have just tried and listened to evidence of electoral fraud that would disgrace a banana republic would find that statement surprising." In having to fight fires under such conditions, perhaps she had little option but to throw the rule and every other book out of the window.

Shortly afterwards Lin Homer resigned from Birmingham City Council. Having thus abandoned her career in local government, she joined the home civil service and quickly accepted an appointment as Director-General of the Immigration and Nationality Directorate of the Home Office, later to become the Border and Immigration Agency, later still renamed the UK Border Agency (UKBA). That perhaps was carelessness. This time her encounter was not with an Election Commissioner but with the House of Commons Home Affairs Select Committee which in 2013 criticised the UKBA for its "catastrophic leadership failure" during her incumbency. Keith Vaz MP, its chairman, described its performance as "more like the scene of a Whitehall farce than a government agency operating in the 21st century". By that stage in her career, however, Ms Homer was no longer in charge of borders and immigration but of HMRC. There her time at the helm overlapped with far-reaching changes, including a drastic reduction in the number of staff employed from 90,600 or so in 2005 to under 60,000 by 2014 – hardly circumstances conducive to "motivational management". This decline (mostly in staff dealing with personal tax) coincided with that inevitable concomitant of any government proposal to increase "efficiency", a new computer system. Such was its all-embracing newness and efficiency indeed that Ruth Owen, HMRC's Director of Personal Tax (formerly of Jobcentre Plus) found herself having to engage a large number of unpaid

18-24 year old NEETs (Not in Education, Employment or Training) from the government's Movement to Work programme to assist with the processing of PAYE records – which doubtless explains a lot.

Our politicians affect to believe in the principle of simplifying our law but what do we get? The Deregulation Act 2015 hardly makes a promising start with a title page which informs us that "Explanatory Notes" (More's "commentaries on them") have been produced to assist in the understanding of this Act and are available separately" before the Act itself continues to run for 116 sections and 23 schedules. Between the formal enactment provisions and the Section 1 heading appear the more promising words: "Measures affecting the workplace: general". Hopes, however, are hardly sustained by what follows. Section 1(1) proceeds to amend Section 3 of the Health and Safety at Work etc Act 1974 in accordance with subsections (2) and (3). So far, so promising but how is this to be achieved? Subsection (2) enlightens us: "In subsection (2) [ie of the 1974 Act] (which imposes a general duty with respect to health and safety on self-employed persons) – (a) after "self-employed person" insert "who conducts an undertaking of a prescribed description". After thus tweaking the nature of the self-employed undertaking intended to be deregulated, the subsection proceeds with a bold legislative contribution to the feminist cause in paragraph (b): for "his undertaking" we must now substitute "the undertaking".

After this less than promising start the Act moves swiftly on to extending the exemption for Sikhs with regard to the wearing of safety helmets from "on a construction site" to "at a workplace" (although not apparently if he "works, or is training to work, in an occupation that involves (to any extent) providing an urgent response to fire, riot or other hazardous situations..."). A further two pages or so of *primary legislation* are devoted to various "ifs" and "buts" relating to this particular topic for which I'm sure the Sikh community will be suitably grateful. The Act then turns its attention *inter alia* to the selling of knitting yarn, the subcontracting of private hire vehicles and the prohibition of unlicensed activities in outer space. As regards the latter, there is a nice touch which will certainly appeal to connoisseurs of the surreal. S12 (2) provides that any person referred to in S3 of the Outer Space Act 1986 is deregulated to the extent that any order under S10(1) of the 1986 Act *may* provide that it "does not apply" to the extent that that person "is carrying on activities that do not require a licence by virtue of the order." What a profound relief that must be.

To an impartial observer at least, it is far from clear that all this colossal legislative incontinence has necessarily led to a corresponding improvement in public welfare, whether here below or for that matter in the heavens above. What it has led to is a very great increase in the number of lawyers. In March 1963 when I began my articles there were 24,737 solicitors on the roll in England and Wales based on the Law Society's figures as at the previous 31 July,[7] of whom 19,790 held practising certificates. The corresponding figures for 2012 were 165,971 of whom 128,778 held practising certificates – more than a six-fold increase. I imagine that there has been a significant increase in the number of practising barristers likewise since 1963 although in both cases the trend has been reversed recently (largely as a result of the dramatic reduction in the availability of legal aid) but at least as far as solicitors are concerned it seems that numbers are now rising once again. It is against this background that Lord Thomas, the Lord Chief Justice, has suggested in a speech in New Zealand to the Legal Research Foundation on 25 September 2015 on *The Legacy of Magna Carta: Justice in the 21st Century* that "We have therefore to create a system which will remove certain judicial work from judges altogether and enable many cases to be dealt with by procedures which can function well, even if the parties do not have lawyers." I cannot help but wonder, given much recent legislative form, whether Lord Thomas has been devoting too much attention to Thomas More's *Utopia* or possibly to Richard Susskind. Faced with these learned opinions which seemingly conflict with what is actually happening, we can only adopt the replies of William Cowper's "churchbred youth":

> Fallible man
> Is still found fallible, however wise,
> And differing judgments serve but to declare,
> That truth lies somewhere, if we knew but where.[8]

Society has of course become much more complex since the early 1960s but, however complex the law may have to be to reflect the complexities of society, it still needs to be coherent and based upon discernable principles and substance rather than mere form if it is to retain the respect of the general public. Such principles as can in practice be discerned often owe more to judicial than political activism. So much new legislation seems to be driven by passing political expediency and reaction to events rather than any serious attempt at coherence. As a result it is certainly more difficult than it used to be for lawyers to form a judgment on any new problem presented to them by the application of basic legal principles.[9]

Practitioners of course are well aware that the great change that has come over legal publishing in recent years is the advent of information technology, the internet and the capabilities of online searching. These technical changes have led some commentators, notably Richard Susskind *The Future of Law* (1996), *The End of Lawyers? Rethinking the Nature of Legal Services* (2008) and (and now with his son, Daniel, a lecturer in Economics) *The future of the Professions* (2015) to predict seismic changes in how the legal profession is organised or even whether it will exist at all in the form we know today. Certainly in my professional lifetime there have been enormous changes – in the extent and nature of the law itself, in the way in which it is administered, in the way in which lawyers organise their affairs and finally in their relationship with clients. It is for the lawyers and politicians of the future to decide in which direction we wish all this to proceed but such decisions can only sensibly be made with an informed knowledge of where we are now and how we got there. But there is another problem: humility is not generally a defining characteristic of either lawyers or politicians. We tend to overestimate our ability to change the world – in effect to lead. In a democratic society politicians in particular have the additional burden of having to get themselves elected and for this reason alone the temptation to embrace populism and avoid the perils of genuine leadership can be almost overwhelming. This may account in part for the surfeit of law-making over the last century or so.

Lawyers may have escaped that particular temptation, but there have been plenty of others, not least of which perhaps has been its counterpart: inertia coupled with self-satisfaction. But then every profession has its weaknesses and temptations and over most of the Society's existence the story of lawyers' struggle for integrity within their own profession has been a reasonably honourable one. Writing in 1977 when he was editor of *The Times* in defence of his Catholic faith, the late William Rees Mogg[10] made the following comments about bankers and lawyers:

I have always felt a checking diffidence in writing about religion, and for good reason. I am not a theologian! I have made no adequate spiritual preparation for the task, I do not feel myself to have spiritual qualifications for it. I am in addition a member of that unilluminated group the comfortably off, middle aged, English professional class. It is natural that people should choose us as their worldly advisers, for we make some of the best lawyers or bankers that can be found; but for spiritual advisers we lack the necessary qualifications. We are unhumble, unmeek, and unpoor. Had we not produced our one great saint in Sir Thomas More, I might regard my background as a final disqualification. As it is I offer it as a warning. Anything that I write must be from a point of view that is in many ways spiritually inadequate.

By the time of his death in 2012 the author would no doubt have revised his opinion about English bankers at least, and he seems to have revised it about lawyers, at least as regards one aspect of their activities. In his memoirs[11] published the year before his death he observed that "many lawyers make indifferent politicians, too glib at making arguments..."

Bankers, however, are a different matter. The revelations about the activities of senior management at the Royal Bank of Scotland, Barclays, HBOS and the Co-operative Bank and failures of the Financial Services Authority make sombre reading. The Royal Bank of Scotland, coupled with the name of Fred Goodwin – "Fred the Shred" who has become a national folk villain – hardly needs comment, but the other three banks have fared no better. April 2013 saw the publication of the *Salz Review* – an independent review commissioned by Barclays following revelations about its involvement in the LIBOR scandal. Its principal author was Anthony Salz, Executive Vice-Chairman of NM Rothschild but formerly the senior partner of Freshfields and, following mergers in 2000, co-senior partner of Freshfields Bruckhaus Deringer. In a single sentence of Salz's review, there appeared the words "too clever by half", "arrogant" and "aggressive" – which of course were immediately picked up by a hostile media and converted into headlines. In truth this sentence, like the report itself, was rather more measured:

> We believe a culture developed within Barclays, quite possibly derived originally from the investment bank, which came across to some as being "clever" or what some people have termed "too clever by half", even arrogant and aggressive. (p.70)

Later, commenting more generally, he refers to "the gradual depersonalisation of the customer experience", a phenomenon with which every single bank customer must be all too familiar, and goes on to talk of "values", actually using the phrase "profession of banking":

> The culture of banks, it is said, drove the wrong behaviours. The sector lost sight of its sense of purpose and lost sight of the values that are needed to run a successful global financial system. Leaders built banks that pursued profit at the expense of all else, failing to see the systemic risks and forgetting the fundamental principles of the profession of banking. (p.177)

April 2013 also saw the publication of the Fourth Report of Session 2012–13 of the Parliamentary Commission on Banking Standards with the uncompromising sub-title *"An Accident Waiting to Happen": The Failure of HBOS*. On a subject which cries out for plain speaking, it is couched in plain English rather than in the colourless terms of so many official reports. It has the added virtue of being relatively short at 88 pages as against Salz's 244 pages. After referring (paragraph 5) to the FSA's announcement in March 2012 that it had completed its own investigation of HBOS and that "the firm" (sic) had been guilty of "very serious misconduct", the Commission's report then proceeded to express its own conclusions which were harshly critical of the bank's senior management and indeed the whole culture which it engendered. Also, and significantly, the report was equally critical of the Financial Services Authority. In Section 5 paragraph 83 under the subheading "A Failure of Regulation" the Commission turns its attention to the FSA:

- The picture that emerges is that the FSA's regulation of HBOS was thoroughly inadequate.

- The FSA took too much comfort from reports prepared by third parties whose interests were not aligned with those of the FSA.

- ... the appalling supervisory neglect of asset quality...

- The regulatory approach encouraged a focus on box ticking which detracted from consideration of the fundamental issues with the potential to bring the bank down. The FSA's approach also encouraged the Board of HBOS to believe that they could treat the regulator as a source of interference to be pushed back, rather than an independent source of guidance, and, latterly, a necessary constraint upon the company's mistaken courses of action.

Later on, refocussing on HBOS itself, the report continues its excoriation:

- The corporate governance of HBOS at board level serves as a model for the future, but not in the way in which Lord Stevenson and other former Board members appear to see it. It represents a model of self-delusion, of the triumph of process over purpose.

- Judging by the comments of some former Board members, membership of the Board of HBOS appears to have been a positive experience for many participants. We are shocked and surprised that, even after the ship has run aground, so many of those who were on the bridge still seem keen to congratulate themselves on their collective navigational skills.

When a solicitor, writing to another solicitor, expresses "surprise" or even "shock" we are inclined to treat it as somewhat formulaic; any solicitor who has been in practice for a few years dealing with the foibles of the human condition, knows well enough that we are rarely surprised or even shocked by anything, but when an all-party parliamentary commission expresses itself in such forthright terms, it is perhaps time to take notice. Unfortunately it is difficult to change underlying cultures and it would be rash to assume that we have heard the last of the great banking scandals, despite all protestations to the contrary. We have only just taken in the latest revelations about senior managers at Barclays and their infamous elephant "deal of the century". In the interests of protecting both ourselves and our financial system from exploitation by some of the world's most corrupt politicians, dictators, criminal gangs and terrorists, banks are supposed to exercise "enhanced due diligence" in dealing with the affairs of the "politically exposed" but is all too clear from the latest report of the Financial Conduct Authority (November 2015), that the only due diligence, enhanced or otherwise manifested by the Barclays' senior management, was directed at not being found out and covering their own traces. As the Final Notice imposing a fine of £72,069,400 dispassionately observed under the rubric *Failures in senior management oversight* "It was unclear who, if anyone, within the Barclays' front office senior management at the relevant time was responsible overall for overseeing Barclays' handling of the financial crime risks associated with the Business Relationship." (paragraph 4.19).

In dwelling in some detail upon the shortcomings of bankers, I would not wish to imply that lawyers are above reproach but on the whole our shortcomings don't have quite the same effect on the general population as those of bankers and politicians. Quite apart from the individual "rotten apples" that are always to be found in any human organisation, I recall with considerable shame, as I imagine do many of my professional colleagues, the misconduct of some solicitors in connection with miners' compensation claims which rightly made headline news some years ago. That too could properly be described as "a model of self-delusion" by lawyers who had lost sight of their "sense of purpose" and their "values" rather than simply succumbing to specific financial pressures. The real problem, however, is not so much blatant misconduct but rather an insidious shift in underlying culture. I referred in the Prologue to former Society President Peter Hannam's comment about "those who would prefer to regard lawyers simply as business people attempting to make as much money as they can at the expense of the consumer". To suppose that making as much money as possible at the expense of the consumer is the sole motivation of a business would be a travesty but it echoes the observation made a generation earlier by the economist ER Schumacher[12] referring to what had already become the western approach to industrial employment: "From the point of view of the employer it [ie the cost of employing people] is in any case simply an item of cost, to be reduced to a minimum if it cannot be eliminated altogether, say, by automation. From the point of view of the workman, it is a 'disutility'; to work is to make a sacrifice of one's leisure and comfort, and wages are a kind of compensation to the sacrifice." Schumacher's comment was made in his book *Small is Beautiful – a study of economics as if people mattered* which first appeared in 1973 and was subsequently described in *The Times Literary Supplement* for 6 October 1995 as "among the 100 most influential books published since World War II." In fact it had been inspired by a visit to Burma in 1955 at the pressing invitation of its Prime Minister, U Nu which he was able to accept as the NCB agreed to allow him three months' unpaid leave.

With unusual cultural sensitivity for a Western economist of the period, he quickly realised that such an approach to economic development in a country like Burma infused with Buddhist culture was not only inappropriate, it was dangerous. He could see nothing but trouble ahead if Burma were to adopt (or have imposed upon it) the Western "big business" model that has come to dominate world economic thinking even more in our own day than it had in the 1950s. His report was not well received by the Burmese government at the time because he wasn't telling them what they wanted to hear but the subsequent history of Burma (and indeed of much of the rest of the world) suggests that his fears were not altogether misplaced: whatever the cultural context may be, you disregard it at your peril. Schumacher was very aware of the temptations and problems which might be created by large scale and impersonal business enterprises, however essential they might be for a global economy. He was by no means the first: others had sensed this long before it came to its present size and importance. Sydney Smith (1771–1845) had once observed (quoting Lord Thurlow who died in 1806) "You remember Thurlow's answer to some one complaining of the injustice of a company. 'Why, you never expected justice from a company, did you? They have neither a soul to lose, nor a body to kick.'"[13] Later in the 19th century the Companies Act 1862 provoked no little controversy, its critics being particularly incensed by the notion that the owners/shareholders' liability should be *limited* – ie that they could escape liability for their company's debts. This view was still prevalent in the 1890s when Gilbert and Sullivan produced their penultimate Savoy opera *Utopia* (1893) which lampooned what Gilbert's libretto calls the "Joint Stock Company Act."

The problem for the legal profession in our own day is that we have inherited from the past a very specific and quite complex culture in which we owe allegiance both to our clients *and* to the law and to a certain concept of justice. If we come to regard ourselves *only* as a business whose purpose is to make money then any other purpose becomes an unwelcome incumbrance. The invitation to become more businesslike, whilst desirable (and often very necessary at one level) carries its own dangers. The concept of "business" as it has developed in the modern western world and been exported across the globe has brought with it some attributes with which we are familiar: a certain approach to the perceived economy of size, competition, advertising, capital expenditure, ways of organising how work is done and treatment of staff. If the "bottom line" becomes the sole preoccupation, there is inevitably a temptation to regard the latter as a necessary evil from whom the maximum effort is expected for the minimum reward, which is hardly conducive to overall human happiness and certainly not to loyalty. It is not an inevitable consequence of being more "businesslike" but the temptations are there and not always resisted – especially in the absence of any other vision than the fabled *el dorado* of the "bottom line". Certainly any business needs to bear in mind that you cannot have a *bottom* line unless you equally have a number of other lines above it and if it has any aspirations to longevity they are unlikely to be achieved without a firm sense that the interests of its customers and staff are just as important as the proprietors and theirs. Many commercial businesses nowadays make this claim as a necessary PR exercise but sadly there is often little substance to it.

The harsh reality, of course, is that it is not only bankers, lawyers and politicians who have fallen from grace in the modern world, it is far more generalised than that. There is much current talk, for example, of the National Health Service "having lost its soul" – an apt metaphor describing a collective amnesia about its purpose in life – a metaphor moreover which applies to so many professions and organisations which would benefit from a serious examination of conscience. Futhermore, despite their modish and populist claim to be in favour of *deregulation* our politicians seem in spite of themselves to be convinced that the solution to all these problems lies in *regulation*; and if the latest bout of regulation doesn't work, why, the answer must lie in a bigger and better bout. It is all sadly reminiscent of the generals of the First World War who convinced themselves that "one last push" would overcome all obstacles. But if regulators are drawn from the same underlying moral culture as those whom they are supposed to be regulating, they are unlikely to be effective. And where the government itself is acting as regulator, the results have hardly been reassuring, as witness the circumstances now coming to light about its prior knowledge relating to the affairs of Volkswagen, Kids Company and the seemingly unending banking scandals. So Juvenal's ancient conundrum remains: *Quis custodiet ipsos custodes?* – or, in its latterday form, *Who regulates the regulators?* You cannot after all infuse a soul or convey a higher purpose in life than making money, if necessary at other people's expense, simply by regulation. All that achieves is more law and more complication.

Ultimately professions and organisations are made up of individuals, so it is we as individuals who have to examine our consciences. This is not a very fashionable occupation nowadays but a desirable one nonetheless. Sir Matthew Hale in the 17th century was a great exponent of the practice both as regards his personal and his professional life, including those relating to his judicial responsibilities which he took very seriously.[14] Perhaps we can let Samuel Johnson have the last word in the form of an admirable prayer that he composed for attorneys.[15] It was devised of course for the benefit of the reasonably homogeneous Christian society of the 18th century, but to the extent that it encapsulates our professional purposes, its basic premise would serve well enough as a mission statement for our profession and bear being set out in every office manual and posted on the notice board of every law firm in the country:

> Almighty God, the Giver of Wisdom, without Whose help resolutions are vain, without Whose blessing study is ineffectual, enable me, if it be Thy will, to attain such knowledge as may qualify me to direct the doubtful and instruct the ignorant, to prevent wrongs and terminate contentions; and grant that I may use that knowledge which I shall attain to Thy glory and my own salvation; for Jesus Christ's sake. Amen.

Before ending on the subject of prayer, readers may care to contrast Dr Johnson's inspired composition on behalf of the legal profession with that said to have been composed by John Ward MP (1682–1755) who represented successively Reigate, Ludgershall and finally Weymouth and Melcombe Regis in the Tory interest. He quickly established a reputation for sharp practice even by the relaxed standards of the age before being expelled from the House of Commons in 1724 and subsequently convicted of forgery and condemned to the pillory. Even the semi-official *History of Parliament* describes his political career as "spectacularly controversial". His supplications to the Almighty which first appeared in *Fogg's Journal* in 1730 were markedly more self-interested than those of Dr Johnson:

> O Lord, Thou knowest that I have nine houses in the city of London, and that I have lately purchased an estate in fee simple in Essex. I beseech Thee to preserve the two counties of Middlesex and Essex from fire and earthquakes. And, as I have also a mortgage in Hertfordshire, I beg Thee also to have an eye of compassion on that county, and for the rest of the counties Thou mayest deal with them as Thou art pleased. O Lord, enable

the Banks to answer all their bills, and make all debtors good men. Give prosperous voyage and safe return to the *Mermaid* sloop because I have not insured it. And because Thou hast said: "The days of the wicked are but short", I trust Thee that Thou will not forget Thy promise, as I have an estate in reversion on the death of the profligate young man, Sir J.L....

Keep my friends from sinking, preserve me from thieves and housebreakers, and make all my servants so honest and faithful that they may always attend to my interests, and never cheat me out of my property night or day.

NOTES

1. Between 1892 and 1894 the young Adolf and his family were living in Kapuzinerstraße, Passau, Bavaria, just across the river from their native Austria. Mgr Max Tremmel (1902–1980), a well-known organist and composer, who succeeded Father Kuehberger as parish priest in Passau, recalled how shortly before his death, his predecessor had informed him how he had seen the young Hitler fall through the ice into the river and had managed to rescue him from almost certain death. The story was seemingly well-known in Passau at the time but lacked any corroboration until fairly recently when a local newspaper of the period, the *Donauzeitung*, surfaced in a German archive and was found to contain an account of the incident but unfortunately did not give the boy's name. Hitler did talk among his generals about how as a child he used to play on the river bank but is never recorded as mentioning a rescue story. Surprising perhaps if the story were true, except for the fact that by that stage in his life he had come to despise the Catholic Church and may not have wished to remind himself or others of an occasion when he was rescued by a future Catholic priest.

2. Quoted in *The Place of St Thomas More in English Literature and History* – RW Chambers – Longmans, Green and Co Ltd, London 1937.

3. For further details and for the foundation of the Vinerian professorship see Appendix C p. 404.

4. Henry John Stephen (1787–1864) was a shy and rather sensitive man whose diffidence seems to have prevented him from attaining the higher echelons of the profession although he did attain the distinction of Serjeant-at-Law in 1828. He never achieved high judicial office but became a commissioner in bankruptcy in Bristol in 1842, a position which he retained until his retirement in 1854. His *New Commentaries* were published volume by

volume over the period 1841-1845. Professor Dicey's verdict was that "Had the work been published as an original treatise, it would have stood on a level with Blackstone's work."

5. Much of the information about *Halsbury's Laws* and its companion publications is based on *History of a Publishing House* by H Kay and W Gordon 2nd ed. LexisNexis Butterworths 1997.

6. *The Revenue Giveth – the Revenue Taketh Away* Cambridge Law Journal 53(2) July 1994 pp. 273-281

7. The Law Society's records are based on a "snapshot" taken each year on this date.

8. William Cowper (1731-1800) *Hope* 1.423

9. For shattering examples of how even looking at the statute (or statutes) does not necessarily result in significant enlightenment, see Chapter 14 pp. 296-299 and it would be a bold judge nowadays who would claim to emulate Chief Justice Coke in the 17th century and answer any point of law, even common law, from his sick bed – see Appendix C p. 399.

10. William Rees Mogg (1928-2012). Later Lord Rees Mogg, he was editor of The Times from 1967 to 1981. The quotation is from his book *An Humbler Heaven – The Beginnings of Hope* Hamish Hamilton – London 1977.

11. *Good and Great* Diacha – London 2011.

12. For ER Schumacher see Chapter 11 p. 222.

13. Quoted in *Memoir of the Rev. Sydney Smith* by Lady Holland (his daughter) Longman, Brown, Green, and Longman – London 1855.

14. For Hale's judicial career and an extract from his *Things Necessary to be Continually had in Remembrance*, see Appendix C pp. 400-401.

15. From *The Life of Samuel Johnson* by James Boswell first published in 1791 – almost contemporary with the Society's foundation in 1786.

Appendix A

ENGLISH LAW AND THE ENGLISH LEGAL PROFESSION

Most readers, even non-lawyers, may well be familiar enough with the broad outline of our present court system and how the legal profession in England is organised – essentially between solicitors, paralegals, barristers and judges. Fewer, however, will be familiar with the detail of how we got to where we are or their recollection of what they once knew may have become hazy. It is a complex story which has developed over centuries and even today, as practitioners would doubtless agree, many aspects lack the logical coherence which one would expect from a system designed from scratch. Some modernisers, in a fit of zeal, have at times attempted wholesale reform but for the most part their efforts have had a distinct air of "make do and mend" about them. The prevailing attitude has usually been "if it works, don't fix it". Unfortunately, a reluctance to fix has often extended to aspects of the law and its administration which have clearly not been working. Perhaps this is the English way.

English or Common Law

The English or common law legal system is a historical curiosity and, but for a series of historical accidents, it might well not have survived into the modern world – certainly not to the world-wide extent that it now enjoys. One such accident, and a very important one, was the development of one of our first colonies in North America. The English and their law took root there in the 17th century and prospered. It might well have been otherwise. That the Pilgrim Fathers managed to establish their little colony in Massachusetts following their arrival in 1620 was nothing short of a miracle. They had the astonishing good fortune to have made early contact with a native American Patuxet called Squanto (or Tisquantum) who just happened to speak English and who was prepared to assist them in various ways, including brokering a deal with his fellow locals. A native American who spoke fluent English – quite possibly in Squanto's case with a Cockney accent – may have been more than a great rarity in those parts at that time, he may well have been unique. And of all the places on that long north-eastern seaboard of North America where the Pilgrims *might* have landed, fate decreed that they should arrive in Squanto's home territory. From an English or even a European perspective it is very easy to underestimate distances on the North American continent. The Gulf of St Lawrence alone, for example, from north to south is roughly the distance from London to the northern tip of mainland Scotland. As for the helpful Squanto, he had visited England not only once but twice. Returning after his first visit, he had been kidnaped by an English sea captain, Thomas Hunt, who took him to Spain with twenty other captives with a view to selling them all as slaves. On learning of Hunt's plans, some Spanish friars intervened with a view to taking them under their wing and converting them to Christianity. Squanto eventually found his way back to England where he stayed for some time with a family in London before eventually making his way back to his native Massachusetts via Newfoundland. Of such extraordinary chances is history made.

Not only that, but if the European colonial struggles of the 18th and 19th centuries had turned out differently, it might easily have been the French or Spanish languages and legal cultures based on Roman law which prevailed in most of North America. They very nearly did. Over half the current territory of the USA was acquired either in various deals or by conquest or annexation from France and Spain in the course of the 19th century. One such deal, of course, was the so-called "Louisiana purchase" in 1803 at a time when France was once again at war with the UK and Napoleon was desperately short of money. The American negotiators could hardly believe their luck at the terms offered – they were expecting to have to pay $2M or so simply for unlimited navigation rights along the Mississippi and were astonished to be offered the whole of "Louisiana"[1] for a mere $15M – a price which they quickly worked out was less than four cents an acre. It was apparently beyond their authority to agree such terms but they agreed them nevertheless and Congress duly ratified what must count as the greatest conveyancing transaction

Hoisting of American Colors over Louisiana by Thure de Thulstrup (1848-1930)

The painting, now in the Cabildo Museum in New Orleans, depicts the ceremony which took place there on 10 March 1804 in the main plaza (now Jackson Square). It was commissioned to mark the centenary of the completion of the Louisiana Purchase, perhaps "the greatest conveyancing transaction of all time" which resulted in the English common law being adopted throughout the United States with the paradoxical exception of the present state of Louisiana itself.

of all time. It was also a highly duplicitous one as far as Napoleon was concerned. From the Treaty of Paris of 1763 (which ended the Seven Years War) up to 1800 'Louisiana' has been a Spanish possession but by the highly secret Franco-Spanish Treaty of San Ildefonso of that year the territory had been re-ceded to France on the express understanding that it would not sell 'Louisiana' to another power.

The end result of all this wheeling, dealing and conquest was that the common law now governs virtually the whole of North America north of the Rio Grande. Today only the Canadian province of Quebec and to a lesser extent the present state of Louisiana stand apart. Quebec has its own civil code which derived from the Civil Code of Lower Canada adopted in 1866 which in turn was based on the Napoleonic Code of 1804, with contributions from the custom of Paris and the original Civil Codes of Louisiana and the French-speaking Swiss Canton of Vaud. Even the present state of Louisiana owes more to the civil law in many respects than it does to the common law. As in Scotland, for example, the doctrine of "protected heirs" still prevails and unlike the remaining 49 states of the union there is no reciprocity in the right to practise law. If you want to practise law in Louisiana you have to pass the Louisiana State Bar examinations. In Europe, on the other hand, it is the English or common law system which stands alone in that it does not owe its origin to the Romans, although certain aspects of it can be traced back to them.[2] Even Scots law has its basis in Roman law although, inevitably, its development has been influenced by English law concepts over the past three centuries since the Union in 1707. English law was different. Its basic structure, as we shall see, was forged in the twelfth and thirteenth centuries and has followed a different course ever since.

But it was not just to North America that English law followed in the footsteps of the empire builders. As a result countless other territories in every continent of the modern world are currently operating "our" legal system. Sometimes, as in South Africa where Roman Dutch law had already been established by the earlier Dutch settlers, the English newcomers yielded to the earlier arrivals, at least as regards substantive law. In the main, however, the fundamental system of English law flourished without competition. For many years its coherence was maintained by a system of ultimate appeals to the Judicial Committee of the Privy Council. Although in modern times the larger Commonwealth countries such as Australia and New Zealand have abolished such appeals, New Zealand as recently as 2003, there are still 27 colonies or former colonies and dependencies, where such appeals continue to be heard in London. Currently there are about 50 such appeals every year.

How the customary laws and legal tradition of the southern half of a relatively small off-shore island well away from the traditional heart of

Europe came to have such influence throughout the world is an intriguing story and worth the telling. In early mediæval England ultimate power was vested in the King but the feudal system, shared at the time with the rest of Europe, left much local jurisdiction in the hands of the barons and other grandees. It was Henry II (1133-1189) who first began, in modern terminology, to nationalise the legal system by seeking to break down feudalism by subordinating independent jurisdictions to himself.[3] From the 12th century onwards, if you had a grievance at the highest level it was to the King's Court that you had to go – wherever that happened to be. And if that meant, as at least one unfortunate litigant found to his cost, chasing the court around the highways and byways of France before he could get his case heard, then so be it. Henry also began the practice of sending his representatives as judges into the shires to "hear and determine" disputes ("oyer and terminer" in the Norman French of the time) although this was not formalised until 1285 by the Statute of Westminster II *De Donis Conditionalibus* (a statutory compendium of 50 chapters, of which two are still in force, Chapter 1 now bearing the short title of the Estates Tail Act 1285 and Chapter 46 as the Commons Act 1285). These judges were originally appointed to establish issues of fact in civil matters arising from writs issued in Westminster. The defendants were summoned to appear at Westminster *nisi prius* (unless before) the King's Justices came into their county. Such is the conservative nature of everything to do with law in England that nearly seven hundred years later, until the assizes themselves were abolished by the Courts Act 1971, it was still the practice of the Lord Chancellor's Department to issue High Court judges with personalised notebooks for use in court and those for civil cases were still being embossed in gold lettering on the front cover with the judge's name and the words *Nisi Prius*. Rather more widely known are the concepts of "due process", trial by a jury of one's peers and the principle that justice is not to be sold, established by Magna Carta under King John in 1215.

But who were these itinerant judges who travelled on circuit across the length and breadth of the kingdom? They were normally ecclesiastics (as they obviously needed to be able to read and write) and until the very recent changes in 2008 all judicial robes betrayed that origin; in the criminal courts they still do. The black "scarf" (to use the technical description) which judges in the criminal courts still wear around their neck and which falls almost to the bottom of their robes is nothing more than the stole familiar to any Anglican or Catholic priest. Also, even today, it is still the practice in the High Court to wear red robes on "red letter days" (ie the principal saints' days of the Church). One of these itinerant judges was Henry de Bracton[4] who was also largely responsible for the early development of the notion of "precedent".

The church also had a great influence in establishing notions of "equity". As an ordinary English word it simply means "fairness". Most people recognise instinctively that a rigid jobsworth approach to rules and regulations can lead to results that offend their moral sense, however logical the rules themselves may appear. We owe to the church and its ecclesiastical judges the development of "equity" in its more technical sense of a developed doctrine originally designed to run parallel to the law with a view to avoiding or at least mitigating any unintended unfairness. Its development was through the office of the Lord Chancellor or "the Keeper of the King's Conscience".

Until the appointment of Thomas More in 1528 following the fall of Cardinal Wolsey, the Lord Chancellor had always been a senior ecclesiastic. The Court of Chancery was gradually built up around the office of the Lord Chancellor who developed remedies unknown to the common law whose only remedy was damages. The mere payment of money was hopelessly inadequate where what the aggrieved party really needed to achieve (fairness) was an enforceable order requiring the offending party actually to do something or refrain from doing it. The most notable equitable remedies were the order for specific performance and the injunction. The Court of Chancery, however, was not merely concerned with remedies. It also concerned itself with the substantive law but usually with the notion of "individual conscience" lurking in the background. The common law, for example, was not overly subtle when dealing with property rights. If a man "owned" property, he was the owner with all the rights of an owner and could do what he liked with it but even if it could be shown that he had been given it for a specific purpose and was failing to keep his promise, the common law could not provide an effective remedy. But the Court of Chancery could: it would enforce the "trust" on the grounds that the "trustee" ought to be bound by his conscience if not by the law.

Over time a great number of equitable remedies were devised but they were only enforceable in the Court of Chancery. Not only that but the Lord Chancellor was only too ready to interfere if an aggrieved party could show that his opponent was threatening to enforce (in a common law court) a claim in a manner that he considered unfair or "inequitable". In complex litigation this meant that the parties could be shuttled backwards and forwards between the Court of Chancery and the Common Law Courts.

A further complication was the existence from the Middle Ages onwards of no less than three common law courts, the Court of King's Bench, the Court of Common Pleas and the Court of Exchequer. Originally established to ease the work load of the Court of King's Bench, the Court of Common Pleas became at times something of a legal backwater and other times an innovative court which attracted suitors. Depending on the nature of the claim, litigants were often able to choose between the two. As for the Court of Exchequer, this was originally intended, as its name suggests, to be the court which regulated the royal revenues and disputes relating to them – in modern terminology any dispute involving for example HMRC. One type of litigant which the court was prepared to entertain was the king's debtor or taxpayer who alleged that by reason of his being owed some money or having some other wrong done to him by some third party, he was unable or less able to satisfy his indebtedness to the king. If that were his problem he could apply to the court setting out the alleged debt owing or wrong done to him *quo minus sufficiens existit* – "whereby he was the less able" to pay his debt to the king. At first this court, always keen to involve itself in anything to do with tax liability, was not always over scrupulous in investigating the basis of its alleged jurisdiction and besides there were fees to be had. It was not long, therefore, before the suggestion that the plaintiff was indebted to the king became an irrebuttable presumption. From the point of view of the plaintiff, the court's attraction was the relative strength of its forearm and the size of its boots. It was as if in our own time claimants could apply to a court operated by HMRC, safe in the knowledge that if they obtained judgment, enforcement would be less of a problem.

These therefore were the main common law courts of record. There were others, with a general, albeit territorially limited jurisdiction, four of which continued to have an active life until abolished by S43 of the

Courts Act 1971. These were the Tolzey and Pie Poudre Courts of the City and County of Bristol, the Liverpool Court of Passage, the Norwich Guildhall Court and the Court of Record of the Hundred of Salford. It was, of course, this 1971 Act which abolished the old system of Assizes and Quarter Sessions and created the modern High Court and Crown Court.

In addition there were many local or customary courts of varied and limited jurisdiction. In particular there was no coherent and universal system for dealing with small claims. It was only by the County Courts Act 1846[5] that parliament began to address this particular problem. However, many of the pre-existing local courts which had fallen into total or partial disuse, including the York Courts of Husting, Guildhall and Conservancy, were not formally abolished until the Administration of Justice Act 1977. Even today some of them are still operative, including (in Yorkshire) the Courts Leet and Courts Baron with View of Frankpledge of the manors of Danby and Spaunton. Their jurisdiction is often largely administrative – managing the common grazing rights on the North Yorkshire Moors within their respective manors and related matters – but within their localities they can be of great practical importance.

Assizes

As we have seen, it was Henry II in the 12th century who had inaugurated the assize system by dispatching itinerant justices on circuit to every county in the realm. It was an arrangement which lasted from the late middle ages until 1971 – well within my own professional lifetime. In addition to their original legal function the assizes were to become notable social occasions invariably attended with much ceremony. The primary responsibility for the management of the entire proceedings was that of the High Sheriff of the county and it was not an appointment to be undertaken lightly. Sir Henry Slingsby, High Sheriff of the County of York in 1611-1612 was fined £200 for his non-attendance at the summer assize even though he had a reasonably serious excuse – he was involved at the time in litigation in London. More recently, at Winchester Winter Assizes in 1892, Sir Alfred Tichborne, the High Sheriff of Hampshire, was fined 500 guineas for being absent in South Africa in search of a warmer climate. The fact that the Under Sheriff was in personal attendance with the High

Sheriff's state carriage and the usual retinue – a mounted escort, javelin men – and the customary municipal hospitality – was not deemed to be a sufficient excuse. The unfortunate High Sheriff was still held to be in contempt and had to pay dearly for his winter sunshine. In the 1960s the High Sheriff of Hallamshire got off rather more lightly when the judges' official car broke down in Sheffield. Fortunately the High Sheriff's own car was in the judicial convoy, being driven by his personal chauffeur, and it was a relatively simple matter to transfer the judges swiftly to a respectable alternative mode of transport. Less fortunately, this had to be done in full view of a goodly crowd of citizens of the People's Republic of South Yorkshire and no doubt there was some audible mirth and perhaps ribaldry also. Neither of the judges had been long enough on the bench to see the funny side and the High Sheriff was duly given a telling off the following morning. He in turn passed the reprimand down the chain of command and Society member and Under Sheriff Charlie Dodsworth and Ron Scobey, the proprietor of the car hire company which had provided the offending vehicle, were duly summoned to appear before him that afternoon. Charlie Dodsworth, however, knew well-enough that "a soft answer turneth away wrath" and nobody was held to be in contempt.

The main official ceremony connected with the opening of the assize was the reading of the commission:

ALL PERSONS having anything to do before my Lords the Queen's Justices of Assize of Oyer Terminer and General Gaol Delivery for this County draw near and give your attendance.

My Lords the Queen's Justices do strictly charge and command all persons to keep silence while Her Majesty's Commission of Assize is produced and read upon pain of imprisonment.

ELIZABETH THE SECOND by the Grace of God of the United Kingdom of Great Britain and Northern Ireland and of Our other Realms and Territories Head of the Commonwealth Defender of the Faith to Our well beloved and faithful Counsellor the Lord High Chancellor of Great Britain

Our beloved and faithful Counsellor the Lord President of Our Council

Our most dear Cousin and Counsellor the Lord Keeper of Our Privy Seal

Our well beloved and faithful Counsellor the Lord Lieutenant of the County

Our well beloved and faithful Counsellor the Lord Chief Justice of England

Our Judges for the time being of Our Supreme Court of Judicature

Such of Our Counsel learned in the Law as are for the time being authorized by Our Royal Warrant or by the Warrant of Our Lord High Chancellor to be of the Commission and the Clerk of Assize and Circuit Officers of the Circuit

GREETING KNOW YE that We have assigned you and any two of you of whom one of Our Judges of Our Supreme Court of Judicature or one of Our said Counsel learned in the Law shall be one of OUR JUSTICES to enquire more fully the truth by the oath of good and lawful men of Our Counties of all offences and injuries whatsoever within Our said Counties and to hear and determine the premises and to deliver the Gaols of Our said Counties of the Prisoners therein being and to take all the Assize Juries and Certificates before whatsoever Justices arraigned within Our said Counties

AND THEREFORE WE COMMAND you that at certain days and places which you shall appoint for this purpose you and any two of you as aforesaid shall make diligent enquiries about the said injuries and offences and hear and determine the same within Our said Counties and deliver the Gaols of Our said Counties of the prisoners therein being and take all those Assize Juries and Certificates within Our said Counties doing therein what to justice does appertain according to the laws and customs of England saving to Us the amerciaments and other things from thence to Us accruing AND WE COMMAND AND EMPOWER you to do in the execution of this Commission all things which have heretofore been lawfully done in obedience to Our Commissions of Oyer and Terminer General Gaol Delivery Assize and Association and Our Writs of Association and *Si non Omnes*[6] AND WE WILL that this Commission shall be deemed to be a Commission of Oyer and Terminer a Commission of General Gaol Delivery and a Commission of Assize

IN WITNESS wherof We have caused these Our Letters to be made Patent WITNESS Ourself at Westminster

GOD SAVE THE QUEEN

Mr High Sheriff of this County be pleased to produce the several writs and precepts to you directed and delivered and returnable here this day so that my Lords the Queen's Justices may proceed thereon

Little attempt had been made over the years to update the wording. The reference to the Lord Privy Seal had been a sinecure and obsolete for centuries but still retains a ceremonial existence even today notwithstanding Ernest Bevin's quip in 1951 when he held the position for just over a month that he was "neither a Lord, nor a Privy, nor a Seal". Likewise 'Oyer' and 'Terminer' still remained in law French and the Commission still referred to gaol *delivery*. The latter was a hangover from earlier times when treason was punished by hanging, drawing and quartering or being

York Mansion House – February 1968

Lawton J receives a silver vinaigrette from the Lady Mayoress to help ward off gaol fever whilst presiding over York Assizes while Brabin J looks to camera with a suitably solemn expression not seemingly shared by the other participants including the recipient. (Photo © York Press)

burnt to death if you were a woman; felony was generally punished by hanging or transportation to the colonies and misdemeanours by branding, fining or being consigned to the stocks or the pillory. Imprisonment was what generally happened to you while you were *awaiting* trial. Hence the Commission was to *deliver* (ie clear) the gaols, rather than fill them which was what happened in more recent times. In York there was the complication that the city had its own Sheriff and therefore there were two Commissions to be read, the City one taking place in the Guildhall. It was time consuming and of course everybody was required to dress up appropriately. But at least France had disappeared from the territories over which jurisdiction was claimed,[7] as had the Empire of India and the title of Empress that accompanied it.

Other aspects were not so much legal as social but just as formal. In York the practice was to present the judges of assize with a silver vinaigrette. In earlier times they were doubtless filled with sweet-smelling herbs as some defence against gaolfever and the stench of unwashed 18th or 19th century humanity. In modern times the stench had more or less gone but the custom remained. A similar old custom survived at Newcastle Assizes. There the City Council presented the judges with an antique gold coin known as "dagger money" for the purpose of providing an armed escort to protect them from marauding Scots on the dangerous journey from Newcastle to Carlisle. The Marauding Scots had disappeared, save when a particular football match attracted unwelcome attention from across the border and gave the Geordies an opportunity to demonstrate that when provoked they likewise knew a thing or two about marauding. The practice, however, was discontinued with the abolition of the Assize system but has recently been re-instated, albeit in the more symbolic form of an illustrated certificate as befits these more austere times. In York too it was the custom until 1939 for the Lord Mayor to entertain the judges to breakfast on the first working day of the assize although in more recent times this particular act of hospitality was moved to a lunch at the Mansion House or later still to a dinner there.

The whole assize ceremonial was impressive but was modesty itself compared to that in the Society's earliest days:

> Taking the smallest view of the procedure, we must conclude that the procession on the judges' travelling day (commonly called "the riding day')

was formidable. There were the Sheriff's tenants, his approved tradesmen, at least 16 mounted halberdmen in uniform, the Sheriff's servants both in and out of livery, the gaoler, the sealkeeper and the Clerk of the County Court (if any) and the Under Sheriff also all mounted. Three trumpeters went on foot with the Sheriff's servants. Then came the Sheriff's coach and six horses, escorted by footmen, more servants and other coaches (if any) followed. Many of these people had to be hired and paid by the Under Sheriff and where appropriate, sent by him to be fitted for their uniform or livery: there were also horses to be hired.

The Sheriff appointed his tradesmen for the assizes and they were legion and probably old hands appointed by the previous Sheriffs: tailor and woollen draper, saddler, brewer, porter merchant, coal merchant, painter, shoemaker, hosier, hatter, glover, gaitermaker, hairdresser and engraver. There was also the inn to be selected, for there was much entertainment especially during the first week. The Under Sheriff had also to secure the services of sundry others and in some cases pay them, such as the Minster ringers (for bells always greeted the judges on arrival), singing boys, vergers, the city waits, Coney Street ringers, judges' crier and steward, butler, coachman and porter, the clerk of assize (for wine and assistance with the calendar), judges' attendants (who received glove money at a maiden assize), and prisoners in York Castle, the city gaol and Peter prison (if any) dinner bills on public days, footmen (when hired) and coal, turves and malt liquor for the judges' lodgings.

The judges arrived on a Saturday and, coming from the south, were met at Dringhouses. The City Sheriffs also went in their own coach to the ceremony and were presented. Wine and negus were provided for all and the judges were invited into the High Sheriff's coach for the journey to the Castle, each being presented with the calendar printed on "royal paper".[8]

The whole procession then moved off to the Castle for the opening of the County Commission and subsequently to the Guildhall for the opening of the City one. In an age when law enforcement was rudimentary it was clearly intended to impress – and it did. To gauge its impact on the city one has to imagine all this taking place in present day Malton – for York had roughly the same population at the time. It was impossible to be unaware that the majesty of the law was in town. Law students will doubtless recall, even if practitioners may have forgotten, the case of *Turberville v Savage* [1669] 1 Mod Rep 3; 86 ER 684, a seminal case on

YORK'S BLOODY ASSIZE

IN 1813 Baron Thompson, who had tried the two civil cases of *Burdon v Rhodes* and *Gilbert v Sykes* mentioned in Chapter One, was the judge of assize at York. On 8 January three Luddites were on trial for the murder of William Horsfall. One of them was George Mellor, 'King Ludd' himself. A week later, on 16 January, fourteen others were tried, convicted, sentenced to death and subsequently executed under the Frame Breaking Act 1812, the government's response to a wave of industrial sabotage by weavers thrown out of work by the rapid mechanisation of the weaving trade. Seventeen Luddites were sent to the gallows altogether. Both the law and the judge himself were uncompromising: "It is of infinite importance to society that no mercy should be shown . . . you have but a short time to remain in this world. I trust not only those who now hear me but all without these walls to whom the tidings of your fall may come, will be warned of your fate." Two troops of cavalry were drawn up around the gallows erected in the Castle precinct and approach roads were guarded by infantry. According to a report in the *Liverpool Mercury* of 22 January 1813, these executions left thirteen wives widowed and 50 children fatherless.

An attorney's silver *Medal of Admission* Court Security 1813 style

In my early days of practice as an attorney in York neither silver ID medals nor the presence of the military seemed to be required in connection with the functioning of the courts but unfortunately this happy state of affairs was not to last. One morning I was greeted by the amiable court keeper at the main entrance holding a clipboard and looking faintly sheepish: "Good morning Mr Lawton, I'm afraid I have to ask you your name." I almost heard the ghost of Captain Mainwaring muttering in my ear "Don't tell him Pike!" What innocent days they were.

The reverse of Mr Wm Fisher's *Medal of Admission* to the Assize Court

the law of assault and provocation. In the course of a furious argument Turberville had put his hand on his sword and yelled at Savage "If it were not assize-time I would not take such language from you!". The legal point was whether this constituted an assault. The King's Bench on appeal held that it was not – the appellant's declaration effectively was what he would *not* do to the respondent, the assize judges being in town. Nowadays even the most enthusiastic moderniser would concede that the fact that the lineal descendant of Judge Jeffreys himself is currently sitting in the Crown Court immediately adjacent to a supermarket car park in some northern industrial city is unlikely to have quite the same deterrent effect when the pubs close.

Perhaps it was the hope that the criminal classes of Yorkshire might be reminded of the majesty of the law that prompted the High Sheriff of Yorkshire, Captain Henry Whitworth MFH of Kilnwick Percy Hall, Pocklington (now a Buddhist retreat and meditation centre) to reintroduce what was described as "a state coach" for the purpose of conveying Acton J at the York Summer Assizes in 1924 from the Judges' Lodgings in Lendal to the Mansion House, a distance of about 80 yards or so, to attend the Lord Mayor's breakfast and thence to the Castle to proceed with the day's work. The account in the *Yorkshire Herald* for 26 June (complete with photograph) tells us that "The bright livery dresses of the coachman and attendants was an interesting feature of the proceedings, and the ancient mode of travel was more in keeping with customs and environment of an assize than the modern motor car." The breakfast, too, must have been an equally interesting feature of the proceedings, at least for those attending, which doubtless would have included at least one member of the Society, the under sheriff Edwin Gray.

> In accordance with custom, the judge was entertained at the breakfast by the Lord Mayor and Lady Mayoress, (Alderman and Mrs. W Dobbie) at the Mansion House. There were a large number of guests present. The entrance Hall had been tastefully decorated with choice flowers by the Corporation gardeners, and the tables in the State Room where breakfast was served, were neatly arranged. Mr Justice Acton was presented with a bouquet of pink carnations by the Lady Mayoress. The catering was done by the York Co-operative Society, and an orchestra composed of members of the N.U.R band played musical selections during breakfast.

What members of the National Union of Railwaymen in the band playing musical selections made of it all is not recorded.

One somewhat whimsical feature which intruded into the solemnities at York in the last days of the assizes was when their opening happened to coincide with a judge's birthday. On these occasions the sheriff's trumpeters abandoned the more customary sonorous fanfares and played instead "Happy birthday to you!" Again, what the prisoners awaiting trial made of this particular musical selection is not recorded either. It is possible that some of them at least, together with some of the NUR musicians, would have been slightly underwhelmed by these particular aspects of assize pomp and circumstance and shared the sentiments of a Staffordshire countryman of uncertain period: [9]

COUNTRYMAN: What mummery is this, 'tis fit only for guisers!

TOWNSMAN: No mummery Sir, 'tis the Stafford Assizes …

Another non-legal feature was the Assize Service which normally took place on the first Sunday of the Assize. In pre-reformation times, as we have seen, the link between church and the law was not only close, it was personal: the judges were themselves churchmen. Thomas More, Cardinal Wolsey's successor, was the first layman to be Lord Chancellor. Thereafter, albeit for somewhat different reasons, the state had good reason to preserve the link. At a time when law enforcement was rudimentary and the overwhelming majority of people were believers, that link was a useful one, even if at times it was regarded in a somewhat cynical light.

As with the assizes themselves, the York assize service in the 1780s at the time of the Society's foundation was attended with considerable formality. In summer the Archbishop would call at about 10.15 am at the judges' lodgings on his way to the Minster. The judges themselves would then proceed in full dress to the west door in the Sheriff's coach attended by a full retinue. It was normal practice for the sermon to be preached by the Sheriff's chaplain who, as often as not, would take the opportunity of reminding his listeners, particularly his judicial ones, that one day they too would have to give a solemn account of themselves at the day of judgment. On the whole the assize service was observed with due solemnity and decorum, but not always. At the height of the suffragettes' campaign the *Morning Post* for 20 October 1913 contained the following report of what happened on Sunday 19 October at the Assize Service at Norwich Cathedral:

> During the Collect for all sorts and conditions of men a group of Suffragists rose and chanted the words "Lord help and save Miriam Pratt and all those being tortured in prison for conscience sake". The Suffragists were seated immediately behind Mr Justice Bray who at Cambridge Assizes last week sentenced Pratt to eighteen months imprisonment for arson. Having finished their recital, the Suffragists resumed their seats. They were not asked to leave the building.

This was not, of course contempt in the face of the court and whatever Bray J's personal thoughts may have been, he was wise enough to keep them to himself, at least in public. Miriam Pratt was a 22 year old teacher and a suffragette activist who had attempted to set fire to an unoccupied house in Cambridge. She was only caught because on her return to Norwich her uncle (a police constable) noticed that her watch was missing and on hearing that a watch had been found near the scene of the crime, taxed her with having committed it.

The same issue of the *Morning Post* also reported a much more serious suffragette disturbance at St Paul's Cathedral that Sunday although no assize service was involved. Successive groups of six to eight "Suffragists" got up to chant and as each group was removed by the Cathedral authorities, it was immediately replaced by another group using the same tactics. Eventually serious fighting broke out and the Police had to be called; altogether it took over half an hour to restore some semblance of order.

Following the abolition of the assizes in 1971, the ecclesiastical tradition was preserved in York in the form of the annual legal service in the Minster, complete with judges, High Sheriffs, Chief Constables, the Lord Mayor of York (with full retinue) and other civic and legal dignitaries from all parts of the North Eastern Circuit. Many members of the Bar also attend (robed) where they process into the nave from the Chapter House which also serves as their robing room. Since 1971 this event has always been treated as an ecumenical one, at least as far as the sermon is concerned, preachers having being invited not only from the main Christian churches but also from the Jewish community. It was on this ecumenical basis that on one occasion the congregation had the benefit of hearing a sermon from the late Gilbert Gray QC (a Methodist lay preacher at the time who was later received into the Anglican Church). Many of us had heard him on other, more rumbustious, occasions. As he once explained to a meeting of members of the Society, he had originally thought of becoming a Methodist minister but then decided that "money wasn't everything" and became a barrister instead.

Quarter Sessions

Or to give them their full title, "the General Quarter Sessions of the Peace". Those of us whose professional memories go back to the days of Quarter Sessions tend to think of them primarily as an intermediate court, between the "Petty Sessions" or "Magistrates Courts" as they are known nowadays and the Assizes. It is easy to forget that until the creation of county councils as a result of the Local Government Act 1888, Quarter Sessions were also responsible for almost the entire governance of rural England. Putting it another way, outside the boundaries of boroughs, the county Quarter Sessions *were* the local authority and the exercising of their judicial function was almost incidental. Section 1 of the 1888 Act provided as follows:

> A council shall be established in every administrative county as defined by this Act and be entrusted with the management and financial business of that county, and shall consist of the chairman, aldermen and councillors.

It is Section 3, however, which brings home to us the full extent of the administrative responsibilities of Quarter Sessions:

> There shall be transferred to the council of each county on and after the appointed day, the administrative business of the justices of the county in quarter sessions assembled, that is to say, all business done by the quarter sessions or any committee appointed by the quarter sessions, in respect of the several matters following, namely …

There follow 16 sub-sections, some of them consisting of a quite lengthy list of seemingly disparate matters no longer to be the responsibility of Quarter Sessions. To give a flavour of what was entailed by this major transfer of functions, sub-section (xiii) provided for

The execution as local authority of the Acts relating to contagious diseases of animals, to destructive insects, to fish conservancy, to wild birds, to weights and measures and to the Local Stamp Act 1869;

One almost has the impression reading the above sub-section that the parliamentary draftsman had given up in despair at any attempt to group the wide-ranging responsibilities "of the justices of the county in quarter sessions assembled" in any form of logical order. Nevertheless it was an act of major constitutional and reforming importance in that it transferred the governance of rural England from the unelected magistracy to the new elected county councils. It was, moreover, as politicians of our own time should note, an act passed by a Conservative-led informal coalition with the support of the break-away Liberal Unionists.

To understand how these multifarious responsibilities of the county justices had came about it is necessary to go back to the 14th century. Section 1 of the Justices of the Peace Act 1361 provided as follows:

> First, that in every county of England shall be assigned for the keeping of the peace, one lord and with him three or four of the most worthy of the county with some learned in the law, and they shall have power to restrain the offenders, rioters and all other barrators and to pursue, arrest, take and chastise them according to their trespass or offence, and to cause them to be imprisoned and duly punished according to the law and customs of the realm...

The same section goes on to provide for the procedure of "binding over to keep the peace", a procedure which has been much used ever since. One interesting aspect is that it provides a good example of the purposive approach to statutory interpretation long before the days of Lord Hoffman. As enacted in Norman French the 1361 act could not be clearer: "& de prendre de touz ceux qi sont de bone fame ou ils sront trouvez, souffisant seurete & meinprise de lo bon port, devs le Roi & son people ... " However, for centuries the official English translation has read "and to take of all of them that be NOT of good fame, where they shall be found, sufficient Surety and Mainprise of their good Behaviour towards the King and his People ... " – the problem being, of course, that the vital word "not" is nowhere to be found in the words as enacted by parliament so only those of *good* fame or repute could be bound over. I have found no record of the point ever having been taken but presumably that was because being sent down or "chastised according to their trespass or offence" was a less appealing outcome in mediæval times than being merely bound over to keep the peace.

The requirement to meet quarterly (at Epiphany, Easter, Mid Summer and Michaelmas) came in later in the century under the Justices of the Peace (Quarter Sessions) Act 1388 and in that year and the following year the justices were made responsible the poor law and fixing the wages of labourers. Parliament had thus found a useful depository for administrative responsibilities.

By the 19th century county quarter sessions were thus broadly responsible *inter alia* for

- the repair of roads and bridges
- highway diversions
- the construction and maintenance of county buildings
- the administration of the county gaol
- the supervision of petty sessions
- the licensing of public houses
- the supervision of the poor law (until 1834)
- the county militia
- the police
- the setting of the county rate

In each administrative county (eg the Ridings of Yorkshire) there was a Clerk of the Peace appointed by the Justice of the Peace who happened to hold the office of *Custos Rotulorum* or Keeper of the County Records. In the nepotistic spirit of the age the Clerk of the Peace (who in the first half of the 19th century at least enjoyed a substantial fee income) was normally a friend or relative of the appointor. However, he often did not carry out the duties in person but appointed a solicitor to act as his deputy in return for a share of the fees.

For much of the 19th century Quarter Sessions had a poor reputation, certainly as regards their judicial role. Their Chairmen were not even obliged to be legally qualified, frequently owed their position more to their social standing in the county than any knowledge of the law and were often much criticised for their failure to take a proper note of evidence, their general antagonism towards the accused and the severity of their sentencing compared with judges of assize. Sometimes, too, sloppy administration resulted in bizarre outcomes. On one occasion a witness went into the box in an obvious state of intoxication. The Chairman was suitably outraged and told the warder to take him down to the cells until he had sobered up. There he remained until the end of the day, when all proceedings had been concluded and the case involving the intoxicated witness somehow disposed of without his assistance. The warder, however, having been told to take him to the cells, and not having received any further instructions, felt obliged to keep him there.

At the opening of the next sessions day, three months later, the faithful warder went to the Chairman's room to enquire about the prisoner. The Chairman was mystified: "What prisoner?" he enquired. The warder reminded him that it was the witness dispatched to the cells at the previous sessions for contempt. The Chairman, suddenly realising what had happened, was aghast. After consulting some of the other senior magistrates, they all agreed that there could be very serious *sequellae* indeed. A senior member of the Bar was then called in and he readily confirmed the seriousness of the situation. But a solution was found: on counsel's advice there was a quick whip-round which managed to produce a sum of about £25. The Chairman had the (now sober) witness brought up into the dock, to give him a thorough dressing-down on the lines that his behaviour in coming into a court of law in an inebriated condition to give evidence was quite outrageous and that he had been very properly punished. "However", he continued, "we cannot help feeling sorry for your wife and family, who were deprived of your help and earnings while you were in prison, and in order to compensate them we have made a subscription among ourselves which we propose to give you for the purpose of helping them. Understand this is not for yourself, nothing can be worse than the behaviour you showed, but it is to be given to your wife for her support." The witness clearly thought that he had been fairly, indeed generously treated and nothing further was heard of the matter.[10]

Many boroughs, however, held their own quarter sessions, independently of the county in which they were located. They were the realm of the recorder, a barrister appointed by the crown of a least five years' standing. This at least ensured that there was some measure of professionalism in the proceedings although in some cases at least antagonism towards the accused was not necessarily diminished thereby. Lord Justice Edmund Davies (1906-1992) once defined a recorder as "a rudimentary wind instrument", adding "and some are ruder than others". Following the Courts Act 1971 and the creation of the Crown Court in its modern form the title of "Recorder" was preserved and they are part-time judges who generally sit for between 15 and 30 days in the year. Their formal jurisdiction equates broadly to that of a circuit judge. Solicitors are eligible for appointment but barristers predominate.

One ancient feature of our criminal procedure whose demise predated by a few decades that of the Assizes and Quarter-Sessions was that of the grand jury which was not abolished in England and Wales until 1933.[11] Like so much in English law, it dated back to the time of Henry II. Its original purpose was investigatory – to investigate suspected crimes and determine whether a suspect should go for trial. As the late Lord Devlin pointed out, the grand jury effectively began to become redundant once a police force had been established following the Metropolitan Police Act 1829:

> It became their duty, as it is today, not only to arrest and charge the suspect but to take statements from the witnesses for the prosecution and to collect the evidence on which the justices are asked to commit.

> Thus the work of the grand jury became superfluous, for it merely duplicated the formal inquiry that was being conducted by the justices. Nevertheless, the grand jury lingered on in a life of ceremony. For the assizes this jury was usually made up of the justices of the county and other notables who assembled at the beginning of each assize chiefly to be entertained at luncheon by the High Sheriff after their morning's work. They were sworn by the judge's marshal … and they listened to a charge by the judge touching upon crime and morals in the county. They then retired to the grand jury room where, mindful of the sheriff's luncheon to come, they heard the witnesses for the prosecution, or some of them as nimbly as they could. Each bill, as they found it to be a true bill, was brought into court by two of their number and handed to the clerk of assize; it was not thought proper to dispatch it by a messenger, lest I suppose, some nefarious hand might write in an extra crime. The need for personal delivery was thought to be so imperative that in some courts in which access to the clerk was inconvenient, some contrivance was used to

ensure that the transit of the bill from the grand jury to the clerk should be kept out of alien hands. I have seen a sort of fishing net used; grand jurors appeared in the gallery above and with the aid of this instrument transmitted their bills directly into the hands of the clerk.[12]

In a footnote Lord Devlin observed that in the old grand-jury room at the Shire Hall in Warwick there is a long pole with what appears to be a pair of tongs on the end, which was used for the same purpose, adding "and no doubt there are many other similar weapons exhibited in other parts of the country".[13]

Ecclesiastical Courts

Until the major reforms of 1857 and 1859[14] the Ecclesiastical courts had exclusive jurisdiction over many matters which would not nowadays be considered as within their sphere of jurisdiction at all, notably marriage, wills and probate as well as admiralty matters. The work undertaken by barristers in the common law and chancery courts was generally conducted in the ecclesiastical courts by "advocates" and that undertaken by attorneys or solicitors by "proctors". These terms became obsolete when practising rights in the ecclesiastical courts (ie in their remaining jurisdiction) were given to barristers and solicitors. Ecclesiastical courts are still, of course, very much with us but since the 19th century reforms they are concerned exclusively with administering the particular law of the Church of England, principally with regard to clergy discipline and faculty jurisdiction – the Church of England's mechanism for regulating alterations to churches and churchyards. Each diocese has a consistory court, presided over by a Chancellor (normally a member of the Bar or someone who has held high judicial office) with a right of appeal to the Court of Arches (Canterbury Province) or to the Chancery Court at York (York Province). Such courts are solely concerned with the affairs of the Church of England and have no jurisdiction over other Christian denominations; however, they and the law they administer, are still very much part of the law of the land and, as such, ultimately under the control of parliament.

The Lawyers

In recent years the former strict demarcation between solicitors and barristers has become somewhat eroded, largely as a result of the Courts and Legal Services Act 1990 which made provision for solicitors to acquire rights of audience in the higher courts subject to rules relating to training and experience. This in turn has made it possible for some solicitors to be appointed as Queen's Counsel and to the ranks of the higher judiciary. It has also led to some solicitors practising exclusively as advocates in much the same way as barristers have traditionally practised, that is to say as individuals with common clerking and secretarial arrangements. Provided they are careful not to have any involvement with clients' money they can avoid some of the more onerous regulatory burdens governing the traditional solicitor's practice. The counterpart of these changes is that since 2004 provision has been made by the Bar Council, albeit subject to fairly stringent conditions, for barristers to accept instructions directly from the public rather than through a solicitor. Whether these changes will eventually lead to fusion of the two professions remains to be seen. Historically, fusion has occurred between attorneys, solicitors and proctors but that was largely driven by convergence and fusion of law and equity and their respective courts and the extension of their jurisdiction over much of what had previously been the exclusive domain of the ecclesiastical courts. Although there is a significant measure of common ground between barristers and solicitors, there is also a significant core difference of function, particularly in the general conduct of litigation and dealing with clients' affairs as to justify separate professional existence and separate modes of regulation.

Apart from barristers and solicitors the only other categories of practising lawyer are the notary public, the commissioner for oaths and members of the Chartered Institute of Legal Executives. The function of the notary public (in practice a solicitor with a specialist qualification) is explained in more detail in Chapter 6 p. 109. As for the commissioner for oaths, any solicitor holding a practising certificate is entitled to attest sworn statements and statutory declarations under the Statutory Declarations Act 1835 so the term is effectively obsolescent.

Trusts

If the basic structure of English law grew out of, and is peculiarly adapted to, English social and cultural conditions and not always readily exportable in its complexity to other cultures, it did produce one remarkable innovation, namely the trust. Although Roman law had a somewhat analogous concept of *fideicommissum*, largely concerned with inheritance issues, it never seems to have found its way into modern civil law systems. France, for example, has recently[15] purported to adopt new "trust" law based on the Roman law concept of *fideicommissum* or *contrat de fiducie* but in fact it bears no resemblance whatever to a trust in common law countries. The procedure is very formal in the French tradition and this is justified by appeals to the need for fiscal transparency and the prevention of money laundering.

The practical effect of the civil law jurisdictions' reluctance to embrace common law notions of trusteeship can be seen in everyday conveyancing transactions where everyone concerned has a "real" or legal interest in the property and must therefore be represented on completion. Since this involves actual presence before the attesting notary in person or under a power of attorney, the procedural complications to English eyes can be astonishing.[16] Furthermore, since children can have a legal interest in the property but at the same time lack the legal capacity to consent or execute a power of attorney, such procedural complications can have serious practical implications and delay practical dealings with property. Clients in England owe more to their lawyers' ingenuity over the centuries in developing the trust than they perhaps realise.

Land Law – General

English land law, even to day, is the perfect illustration of the old Irish response to those requiring complicated directions "Sure, if I wanted to go from here to Ballybunion I wouldn't be starting from here." It is quite impossible to disentangle it from its history and history is where one has to start. England is not unique in that respect. Within living memory it was necessary in the Channel Islands to obtain a degree in Norman law from the University of Caen (which was the only university which taught it) before one could practise there and even today conveyancing exams are conducted in French – a prospect which would doubtless instil even greater terror in students contemplating the Law Society's finals than that which they already suffer. Modern English simply has neither the vocabulary nor the concepts capable of doing it justice.

The modernisation of English land law has of course been going on for centuries but it has been a slow, piecemeal *ad hoc* process with occasional spurts as in 1925[17] rather than based on any attempt to start anew from scratch. In 1932 a new edition of Topham's *Real Property* was published. With an obeisance to the great reforms of 1925, it was re-christened *The New Law of Property*.

As Topham explains in his introduction:

Land cannot be owned by an individual other than the king.

> The early feudal law was the same in this respect. It assumed that all land was owned by the king, and in theory the same rule still applies. The rule underlies the whole of the English law of land prior to 1926, and accounts for many of its peculiarities, so that the law now in force cannot be thoroughly understood without some knowledge of the history of this theory.

This history Topham then proceeds to elaborate, explaining how those holding an inferior interest or "estate" from the king as "lord paramount" became his *tenentes* – ie "persons holding" or, in modern English "tenants". They did not normally pay any money rent as such but rather owed certain services in return for their rights of tenure. Some such tenures, such as "knight tenure" were what one might expect in a mediæval context; others, such as "pimp tenure"[18] less so. Such "tenants" did not hold for a fixed term of years, as in a modern lease, but in most cases had an interest in the land, which on their death would pass to their heirs. Furthermore these tenants in chief, or *in capite* as they were termed, would then make grants to inferior tenants in return for services rendered to them – and so on, down the line. As Topham explains, "It is impossible to discuss the English law of land without using many words which unknown to the ordinary English language", adding "The meanings of the following expressions must therefore be thoroughly mastered before the student can hope to understand the subject." On this the author in 1932 deemed it necessary to elaborate but more than 80 years on perhaps the necessity is less compelling as much of the old learning has now sunk below the legal horizon.[19] I merely record as a fact that in my early days in practice I really did have to concern myself from time to time with copyhold issues, estovers, courts leet and courts baron (naturally with view of frankpledge) to say nothing of rights of levancy and couchancy and quite a few other equally esoteric matters. On one occasion I even had to bar an entail and I sometimes wonder if I may possibly have been the last member of the Society ever to have done so.

Courts Leet together with levancy and couchancy, however, despite the terminology and grammar being entirely Norman French, are still very much with us, the former having survived the assault on local and peculiar jurisdictions by the Courts Act 1971 and the latter having occupied the attention of the House of Lords as recently as 2001 in the case of *Bettison and Others v Langton and Others*. [20]

One matter did surprise me when I came to York in 1966. In 1962 I had been preparing for my law finals at Messrs Gibson & Weldon's former tutorial establishment at Guildford. It had just amalgamated with the Law Society's School of Law to become the College of Law and later still the University of Law as we know it today.[21] In our real property lectures we had been taught about the Settled Land Act because it was part of the syllabus but we were more or less given to understand that strict settlements were "old hat" and we were unlikely to come across them in practice. In 1962 that may well have been the position in the wilds of Surrey but I quickly discovered that this was certainly not the case in Yorkshire where great landed estates were still very much part of the landscape.[22]

Nowadays dealings in land (ie real property) are subject to the Land Registration Acts – a system with its origins in the period of high Victorian law reform. It is a technical subject and dealt with separately in Appendix D.

NOTES

1. The term "Louisiana" in this context does not simply refer to the present US state of that name but the whole of the nominally French territory west of the Mississippi (ie excluding Spanish controlled territory). The French were understandably vague about its precise boundaries but even suggested that it extended as far as the present state of Washington on the Pacific coast.

2. The Canon Law of the Church of England (which forms part of our domestic law) is largely based on the mediæval Canon Law of the Roman Catholic Church, itself based on Roman law principles and until the mid-19th century probate and matrimonial law were governed not only by church law but equally by church courts. Thus many of the foundations of our modern law and practice on these topics are derived from Roman law, albeit by a rather circuitous route. See Chapter 6 p. 108-110.

3. The English temperament can at times be peculiarly resistant to all attempts at rationalisation. Henry II's efforts to institute a national court system did not ultimately reach fruition until the Courts Act 1971. Not only did that act finally lay to rest the very concept of *nisi prius*, and abolish a number of local or feudal jurisdictions, it even had to concern itself with some weird peculiarities connected with the Soke of Peterborough. The latter could trace their origin to the Saxon period when the lord of the hundred had the power or liberty of holding his own court. In course of time this privilege passed to the Abbot of Peterborough and (post-Reformation) to the Marquess of Exeter as Lord Paramount of Peterborough acting under a commission of oyer and terminer and gaol delivery. The magistrates of the liberty retained the power of hanging criminals in cases of murder, which they continued to exercise as late as 1812. Even in modern times their jurisdictional powers were greatly in excess of those enjoyed by other courts of Quarter Session. These peculiarities continued to cause some confusion for many years before passing into history in 1971.

4. Bracton is known to have sat as an itinerant justice in Nottinghamshire and Derbyshire in 1245, Northumberland, Westmoreland, Cumberland and Lancashire in 1246 and in the western counties between 1260 and 1267. He was appointed Chancellor of Exeter Cathedral in 1264. For further details of Bracton and other early judges, see Appendix C p. 393 *et seq*.

5. See Chapter 5 pp. 90-92.

6. *Si non omnes* – "if not all of you". The commission itself was addressed to a large number of the good and the great and its wording had hardly varied over the centuries. The Crown had long appreciated, however, the sheer impossibility of their all attending together in person to deal with the malefactors at any one assize and hence the writ *si non omnes* authorised the judges to proceed on their own and do whatever was necessary – no doubt to the relief of divers beloved and faithful counsellors, lord lieutenants and others who might otherwise have found themselves in contempt.

7. See Chapter 1 p. 16 and p. 30 n. 2.

8. *A History of Grays of York* WHC Cobb William Sessions Ltd (1989) p. 107.

9. Dudley Wilks *Fragments of Stafford's Past* Stafford 1932 quoted in *Albion's Fatal Tree – Crime and Society in Eighteenth-Century* England – Douglas Hay and Others – Allen Lane 1975.

10. His Honour Sir Ronald Bosanquet KC *The Oxford Circuit* The Thames Bank Publishing Co Ltd 1951.

11. It still, however, flourishes in the United States, notably at federal level. State practice varies – there is provision for grand juries in about half of them.

12. Patrick Devlin *The Criminal Prosecution in England* Yale University Press 1958. This account was, of course, written before the creation of the Crown Prosecution Service pursuant to the Prosecution of Offences Act 1985.

13. Lest it be thought that England has any monopoly in the undue preservation of such archaic legal practices, I myself once witnessed in the 1990s the curious spectacle of three candles being solemnly lit on the judge's dais in a court in Rouen in a complex procedure to regulate the judicial auction of debtors' properties under rules laid down by the *Code de Procedure Civile* in 1806. This much criticised, largely ineffective and potentially incendiary procedure, designed to prevent chicanery, was not abolished until 1 January 2007.

14. See Chapter 6 pp. 107-108.

15. Décret No 2010–219

16. I was once involved on behalf of English clients in the sale of property in Germany. Each "legal" owner – and I represented several – either had to travel to Germany to attend on completion or execute a power of attorney (Vollmacht) before an English notary; that document in turn had to be legalised by the Foreign and Commonwealth Office under the Hague Convention of 5 October 1961. As my clients only had (individually) a 120th interest in the property being sold, I can only assume that completion involved something akin to a mass meeting, much documentation or both.

17. For the benefit of non-lawyers, the relevant legislation consisted of the Law of Property Act 1925, the Settled Land Act 1925, the Land Registration Act 1925, the Land Charges Act 1925, the Administration of Estates Act 1925 and the Trustee Act 1925, sometimes referred to collectively as "the 1925 legislation".

18. Described in Wharton's *Law Lexicon* (1848) as "a very singular and odious kind of tenure mentioned by our old writers" – citing as an example: *Wilhelmus Hoppeshort tenet dimediam virgatum terrae per servitium custodiendi sex damisellas scil. meretrices ad usum domini regis*" – 12 Ed.1 – or in plain English "William Hoppeshort holds half a strip of land for keeping six young women, namely whores, for the use of our lord the king". Some later commentators have expressed doubts as to whether *meretrices* has been correctly translated and that it might have referred to laundry maids who followed the court. Certainly in classical Latin the word could mean simply "women who earned money" (i.e working women), although even at that period its primary meaning seems to have been 'whores'.

19. The problem of language remains. In the preface to his book *Understanding Land Law* (Cavendish Publishing Ltd 3rd edition 2000) the author Bryn Perrins observes "A closely associated problem is that of language ... It is struggle enough for the novice to try to cope with the curious concepts of property, without having them explained in a seemingly foreign language ... But property jargon is doubly deceitful, in that some expressions have ordinary, everyday meanings which differ significantly from their technical, property law meanings."

20. [2001] UKHL 24. The issue which their lordships had to determine was whether the Commons Registration Act 1965 had the effect (clearly unintended) of abolishing the ancient common law principles of levancy and couchancy according to which the right to graze stock on common land during the summer months was limited to the number of beasts "levant and couchant" (getting up and lying down) over winter on the land or farm to which such rights were appurtenant – ie which they were able to support. Except in rare cases such rights were not normally capable of being transferred independently of the land or farm to which they related. In case legal issues relating to grazing rights over common land might appear too much of a niche thing to lawyers concerned mainly with events connected with the City of London, Lord Nicholls of Birkenhead thought it prudent to record that "ancient common lands still cover 1.4 million acres over 4% of the total area of England and Wales ... What happens on the commons is of importance to the local farmers" and "a matter of general public concern." Indeed. In some parts of the country with "commons" but without an effective court leet or equivalent management structure, the number of cattle or sheep that a local farmer can graze on them is often the subject of endless friction.

21. Actually it bore no physical resemblance whatever to any campus of the University of Law which we know today. Lectures took place in a cramped Victorian villa where there was hardly room to swing a pen and there were no extra-curricular facilities whatsoever nor even, as I recall, a library to speak of. The standard of tuition, however, was as high as it is today. One of Gibson & Weldon's lecturers for a period after the war was RE (Ted) Megarry who developed refresher courses for returning servicemen. Megarry, a solicitor turned barrister, was later to go on the bench and become a most distinguished Vice Chancellor (head of the Chancery Division of the High Court). Not only that, but for generations of law students and practitioners he was a much respected academic authority on the law of real property. He was also, by all accounts, a brilliant teacher who was never dull and could always be relied upon to hold his audience. On one occasion in the course of demonstrating mooting technique to students at Lincoln's Inn, his opponent rashly cited one of Megarry's own works in support of his case. Megarry promptly objected under the long-established convention that a living author is not a citable authority in court. Whereupon his opponent promptly drew a toy gun and "shot" him – prompting a dramatic and doubtless well-rehearsed collapse and "death" which enabled his opponent to develop his argument based on that well-known authority, the *late* RE Megarry. This may help to explain why this distinguished and much respected lawyer only achieved a third class degree after reading law at Cambridge – he found the course indescribably dull and preferred to spend his time in sporting and musical activities. Later in his judicial and academic career – he was at one time President of the Society of Public Teachers of Law – Cambridge University saw the error of its ways and awarded him an LL.D.

22. "Settled" land or land subject to a strict settlement – ie land which by deed or will had been "settled" so as to be held typically by the eldest son only for his lifetime and thereafter for *his* eldest son's lifetime etc – was a common legal device designed to ensure that a family estate remained in the family to reinforce English notions of primogeniture. Since the sons in question were not absolute owners but merely "tenants for life" the practical effect was to make the make the land inalienable, often with undesirable social consequences. The Settled Land Acts 1882 and 1925 were designed to give tenants for life greater powers of disposal and management, the proceeds of sale being held by the trustees of the settlement to devolve in the same way as the land itself would have devolved had it not been settled.

William Gray (1751-1845) was admitted as an attorney in York in 1774 and later became a founder member of the Society. The original register of members bears his signature. The artist, John Russell, was a noted evangelical, as was William Gray, which was probably what brought them together. Russell's other sitters included William Wilberforce and George Whitefield.

William Gray (1751-1845) by John Russell RA, late 18th century. Portrait made available courtesy of David Gray. Photograph courtesy of Derek Balmer

John Brook (1766-1851) was admitted in 1791 and joined the Society the same year. Although he was only ten years youngers than William Gray, this portrait by William Etty was painted over forty years later. Men's fashions had changed significantly over that period and wigs in particular were no longer de rigeur. If worn at all they were confined to barristers, judges and liveried footmen.

John Brook (1766-1851) by William Etty 1838 Image courtesy of York Museums Trust

Appendix B

SOME FORMER MEMBERS

This appendix contains details of some former members of the Society which have been gathered from various sources selected partly at random and partly on available information. If any reader is able to supply additional information of general interest about former members which might be of interest, the Society would be glad to have it as an addition to its archives. A full list of members from 1786 to 2008 ia available on the Society's website – www.yorkshirelawsociety.org.uk/home/history

INDEX

Brook, John	1766-1851
Butterworth, (Sir) Alexander Kaye	1854-1946
Cobb, William Henry Crookenden	1917-1994
Dixon, Charles Robert	1920-2015
Dodsworth, Benjamin Charlesworth Ralph CBE, DL	1924-2014
Dodsworth, Ernest Ralph	1861-1939
Dryland, Michael Hubert	1927-2014
Dunnell, (Sir) Robert Francis Bt	1868-1960
Eddison, Edwin	1805-1867
Frost, Charles	1782-1862
Gibb, (Sir) George Stegmann Bt	1850-1925
Gilmour, Michael Hugh Barrie	1904-1982
Gray, Jonathan	1779-1835
Gray, William	1751-1845
Harrowell, Herbert Edward OBE	1880-1965
Hartley, John	c.1763-c.1840
Leeman, George	1809-1882
Lockward, William	1778-1836
Mortimer, Timothy	?-1788
Munby, Frederick James	1837-1914
Newton, Henry	c.1800-1881
Nicholson, Lucas	?-1819
Procter, Alfred	1861-1933

Raworth, Edwin	1863-1925	Spofforth, Robert	1740-1827
Robson, Thomas	1855-1924	Stovin, Aistroppe	1766-1828
Seymour, George Hicks	1793-1872	Townend, George	c.1749-1812
		Walker, William	1830-1897
Shannon, John	1918-2010	Ware, Innes Nöel	1896-1994

Brook, John (1766 -1851)

John Brook was admitted as a solicitor in 1791 and became a member of the Society in the same year. He seems to have been well-connected because the following year he was appointed as county clerk and seal keeper for Yorkshire. He also had a number of other interests. At the time of Napoleon's threatened invasion in 1803 he was a lieutenant in the Ouse and Derwent Volunteers. According to its chaplain, the Reverend Robert Elliott "The Corps was officered by the most respectable neighbouring Gentlemen, through whose zeal and disinterested attention to military duty and discipline, it deservedly obtained the highest degree of celebrity."[1] The corps had been raised and embodied at the sole expense of Richard Thompson of Escrick and was one of many such groups of volunteers prompted by a wave of patriotic fervour which had gripped the country as the threat of invasion increased. In 1812 he was joined in partnership in his office in Goodramgate by George Bulmer, the firm then becoming Brook & Bulmer, a practice which in due course became Ware & Co and now part of the present firm of Ware & Kay LLP. In 1828 Brook & Bulmer moved from Goodramgate to larger premises at 6 (now 9) New Street where they remained for many years. On Bulmer's retirement in 1833, Brook continued in practice on his own until his godson, Henry John Ware,[2] joined him in partnership in 1845. Brook died in 1851 and is buried in St Olave's churchyard York.

He was the solicitor for, as well as being a close friend of, the distinguished York artist and member of the Royal Academy, William Etty, whose portrait of him (reproduced on p. 356) will be familiar to many as until recently it occupied a prominent position in the York City Art Gallery although not currently on display.

Butterworth, Alexander Kaye (1854 -1946)

AK Butterworth was educated at Marlborough College and London University, taking his LLB there in 1877. The following year he was called to the Bar by the Inner Temple and subsequently worked in the office of the Solicitor of the Great Western Railway Company between 1883 and 1890, being formally admitted as a solicitor in 1884 after relinquishing the Bar. After a year as Clerk of the Peace for Bedfordshire from 1890 -1891, he was appointed as solicitor to the North Eastern Railway Company in 1891 and admitted to the Society the following year. He remained a member until 1906 when he was appointed General Manager of the company, a position which he retained until 1921. Knighted in 1914, Butterworth's responsibilities increased dramatically with the outbreak of war due to the NER's extensive dock ownership in Hull. In 1919 he was awarded the Order of Leopold (officer class) by the King of the Belgians for valuable services rendered to the allied war effort. He was one of six prominent 'railway' solicitors who were members of the Society in addition to George Hicks Seymour, George Leeman, Alexander Gibb, Francis Dunnell and Michael Gilmour (*q.v.*) all of whom except Dunnell and Gilmour went into railway management. In his younger days he was a keen rugby player, captain of the Marlborough Nomads which eventually amalgamated with Rosslyn Park in 1911. Butterworth was also responsible for drafting 'a revised code of laws for the Rugby Union Game' and served for a time on the Rugby Union's governing body. In the 1930s he was actively involved on behalf of the Pedestrian Association (now known as 'Living Streets') to urge 'no fault' compensation for the victims of road traffic accidents – albeit *excluding* drivers and their passengers. The Road Traffic Act 1930 had raised the previous speed limit for all motor cars at all times from 20 mph and fatalities on the roads, mostly pedestrians and cyclists, were averaging 7,000 a year – very considerably more than in our own day. At first the government was sympathetic and a bill was introduced and passed in the House of Lords but then the government took fright and further progress was blocked.

Cobb, William Henry Crookenden (1917-1994)

William Cobb very much represented the continuity of so many York professional families. His father and grandfather had been solicitors in the city (and members of the Society). Also, his great-grandfather, Henry Cobb (1790-1856) had been city sheriff (1825) and Alderman (1835) and his great-great-grandfather, John Cobb (1760-1830) had equally been city sheriff in 1822. Educated at Winchester College and New College Oxford (his father's college), where he read jurisprudence, William graduated in the summer of 1939. He was able to start his articles with his father in August but it was an inauspicious start. The outbreak of war at the beginning of the following month was soon followed by his enlistment in the Duke of Wellington's Regiment. Further disruption was to follow: just eleven days after he went off to join the colours his father died suddenly. In due course the articles were transferred but in the meantime William was serving with his regiment on the staff in India, Malaya and Java, eventually attaining the rank of major and being mentioned in dispatches. On his return from the war to resume his articles (which eventually were to spread over eight years) he was duly admitted both as a solicitor and as a member of the Society in 1948. By this time the family firm of Messrs WH Cobb & Son had been acquired by Messrs Gray & Dodsworth, in which William was offered and had accepted a partnership. This was the beginning of the firm of Gray Dodsworth & Cobb (subsequently Grays).

From 1948, the year of his admission, until 1959 William was Clerk to the Bulmer East magistrates, a position which his father had held until his sudden and unexpected death in 1939. At that point, at the beginning of the war and after hurried arrangements with the North Riding authorities responsible for county magistrates, Arthur Clayton, a member of the firm's staff had been appointed as clerk. At that time it was possible for an unadmitted person to be appointed provided that they had assisted a justices' clerk for a continuous period of ten years and Arthur was qualified on that basis. He himself, however, died in 1948 very shortly after William's admission and so William could and did apply for the clerkship. On appointment, therefore, William found himself following not only his father's rôle but his grandfather's rôle also, the appointment effectively having been held by the firm since 1872. William was also joint under sheriff of Yorkshire from 1962 to 1982 and President of the Society for the year 1975-6.

His non-legal appointments included a brief period as a member of York City Council, and from 1946-1952 he was Hon Secretary of the

Purey Cust Nursing Home and from 1962-1987 he was a Fellow of the Woodard Corporation (Northern Division). Perhaps his main extra-curricular interests involved York Minster. He was a devout Anglican and took a close and active interest in Minster affairs, being Hon Treasurer of the Friends from 1959-1972 and a trustee of the York Minster Fund from its foundation in 1967 until 1992. He also took a close interest in the Minster's music. Following his retirement as a solicitor in 1982 he devoted himself to writing *A History of Grays of York 1695-1988*.[3]

Dixon, Charles Robert (1920 -2015)

Like Michael Dryland, (*q.v.*) Charles Dixon "was a York man through and through". In this increasingly cosmopolitan world to describe anyone as being thus associated with a particular place can seem somehow to be a limiting factor but this is a modern and heretical notion. Roots are important and to be respected as part of everyone's personality. Born in York and a pupil at Nunthorpe Grammar School, Charles's early aspirations were to seek a vocation on the stage or in the ordained ministry of the Church. However, fate intervened in the form of a wholly unexpected offer of articles from John Hague, a York solicitor practising at the time from premises in Coney Street; he also generously offered to pay the stamp duty (£80) on Charles's articles and a modest stipend during them. Inevitably, however, as for so many of his generation, his articles were interrupted by the war. He was married and called up in the same month of August 1940 and served throughout the war with the King's Own Yorkshire Light Infantry, affectionately known as the KOYLIs. In 1944 his principal John Hague died but had providently arranged for a retired colleague to come out of retirement to ensure that the continuity of Charles's articles would be safeguarded. On completion of his interrupted articles Charles was duly admitted on 1 November 1946 and set up the practice known as Hague & Dixon, the name of Hague being retained out of respect for his first principal who had given him the chance to pursue a wholly unexpected career. Ten years or so later he was joined in partnership by Raymond Burn and the firm continued under the name of Hague, Dixon & Burn until 1 November 1980 when Raymond and his two sons left to set up the new firm of Burn & Co and Charles's firm reverted to its original name which it still retains.

In the early 1960s whilst still developing the practice Charles (supported by his wife Mary) became a founder (Charter) member of York Lions Club of which he served as President and subsequently as District Governor and ultimately Chairman of the Council of Governors for the British Isles and Ireland. In addition to other charitable and community interests, Charles and Mary were also founder members of the York Committee of the National Society for Cancer Relief (now known as Macmillan Cancer Support) and Charles also served as committee member of and solicitor for a youth club then known as York Boys Club, now known as Door 84, as President of Heworth Amateur Rugby League Club and Clerk to the Feofees of St Lawrence Church. He was also involved in the establishment of the Abbeyfields Society in York in addition to his lifelong interest in amateur dramatics.

Professionally Charles was well known to many members of the Society as Clerk to the Bulmer East and Ouse and Derwent Petty Sessional divisions until their respective benches were amalgamated with that of the City of York. In that capacity he was particularly noted for his calm and courteous way in dealing with everyone who had occasion to deal with those courts – in whatever capacity. President of the Society for the year 1976-1977, he also served on four occasions as Under Sheriff of the City of York and was responsible in his later years for opening a branch office of Hague & Dixon at Pickering. There he acted for many years as church warden with local parish churches and (as long as he was able to do so) continued to pursue his interest in local amateur dramatics.

Dodsworth, Benjamin Charlesworth (Charlie) Ralph CBE, DL (1924 -2014)

Charlie Dodsworth was the last bearer of that name to have practised as a solicitor in York. Not only were his grandfather, Ernest Ralph Dodsworth (*q.v.*), his father Benjamin Dodsworth (1882-1957) and his father's cousin Sir Leonard Lumley Savage Dodsworth (1890-1968) solicitors in the firm that included their names but his great-grandfather's brother, George Dodsworth (1805-1880) also practised in York at 4 High Ousegate York having been admitted as a member of the Society in 1827. The Dodsworths were a long established Yorkshire family, descended from Ralph Dodsworth of Beadlam of whom little is known except that he died some time after 1696 leaving two sons, William Dodsworth of Sinnington (from whom all the Dodsworths who practised as solicitors were descended) and John Dodsworth of Nawton (1696-1778) who also left two sons, Ralph (1732-1794) and John (1738-1813) both of whom served as Sheriffs in York, Ralph in 1777 and John in 1787. In addition Ralph served as Lord Mayor in 1792. On William Dodsworth's side of the family, his son George Dodsworth of Wheldrake (1754-1834), father of the solicitor George already mentioned, served as Sheriff of York in 1804, his grandson Benjamin Dodsworth (1810 -1880) in 1847, as did his grandson Ernest Ralph Dodsworth in 1896 and his great-grandson Benjamin Dodsworth (Charlie's father) in 1926. In other words no less than six Dodsworths served as Sheriffs of York at various times between 1754 and 1926.

Unlike his father, Charlie was never Sheriff of York but he was for many years Under Sheriff of Yorkshire (a position equally held by his father) from 1957 until his retirement in 1988, so perhaps it was only natural that it was in this latter capacity that he became best known, not only in Yorkshire but to every High Court Judge that ever came to Yorkshire on circuit. The responsibility of the Under Sheriff was to act as deputy for the High Sheriff of the county (an annual appointment) both in respect of his ceremonial duties, in particular attending upon High Court judges on circuit, and his law enforcement duties, that is to say executing all judgments of the High Court. Until the abolition of capital punishment, these included executing sentences of death – an extremely uncongenial task of which both Charlie and his father had experience. However, by far the greatest part of their law enforcement duties, at least until the Courts Act 2003, was the execution of High Court judgments relating to debt – writs of *fi. fa.* as they were known (Lat. *fieri facias* – 'cause to be done'). Enforcement involved seizing the goods of the judgment debtor or at least threatening to do so. This could give rise to interesting practical problems, eg if the goods in question involved live or perishable stock or there were issues as to whether they were in fact the property of the judgment debtor. Such work called for both speedy action and a detailed knowledge not only of a highly specialised branch of the law and equally (on the part of highly experienced sheriff's officers) a sufficient degree of low cunning to counter the dodges and subterfuges of the less scrupulous debtors, combined with a scrupulous adherence themselves to the letter of the law. Less frequent were writs of possession – cases where an unsuccessful defendant had been ordered to give up possession of land or premises of which he was in unlawful occupation but was refusing to do so. Occasionally these could lead to major confrontations as seen on television, involving not only the personal attendance of the under sheriff and the sheriff's officers in 'high-vis' jackets but equally the sheriff's *posse*, normally consisting in modern times of the local police.

A most gregarious man who was happy to assume a joint responsibility with the High Sheriffs for entertaining High Court judges on circuit, Charlie was a well-known and well-liked figure in Yorkshire but at the same time was scrupulous in performing his strictly professional as well as his ceremonial duties as Under Sheriff. Following the abolition of the Assizes in 1972 (and hence the Assize services) he was instrumental in securing the substitution of the Annual Legal Service in York Minster for the whole of the North Eastern Circuit, a practice which has been followed ever since. In recognition of his contribution to the Yorkshire shrievalty he was awarded a CBE in the 1987 New Year's Honours.

Dodsworth, Ernest Ralph (1861-1939)
Dodsworth was admitted as a solicitor in 1881 at the age of 20 and to the Yorkshire Law Society two years later in 1883. He did not join Edwin Gray in partnership at 75 Petergate until 1885, although the firm remained as W & E Gray until 1891. By the unusually early age of 30 he had joined the board of the York Union Banking Company which was eventually to become part of Barclays Bank in 1902. He continued to serve as a director of the bank for some years, both on the central board in London and as chairman of the local board in York. On one occasion as President of the Society in 1922-3, he marked his presidency by inviting all the unadmitted legal staff, including two clerks at the Probate Registry and the principal clerk at the High Court and County Court District Registry in York, to a dinner.

Dryland, Michael Hubert (1927-2014)
Michael was a York man through and through. He was born in York, worked in York for most of his professional life, married a York girl,

brought up his family in York, played sport for York served his articles in York and and finally died there peacefully in the house which had been his home for 50 years. For some such a life might possibly have proved somewhat restrictive but that was not Michael's style for he had many interests, most notably music, having won a top music scholarship at Worksop College in 1940 at the age of 13, following a choral scholarship at King's College Cambridge and before going on to gain a choral exhibition at Exeter College Oxford in 1944. Michael's studies, however, as with so many of his generation, were interrupted by the war and three years service in the Royal Navy much of it on minesweeping duties on *HMS Bamburgh* in the North Atlantic. In 1947 he was able to return to Exeter College to read Jurisprudence, graduating in 1949.

Back in York, Michael was articled to Innes Ware (*q.v.*) of Ware, Warner & Knowles. After qualification as a solicitor and brief sojourns in Bradford and Scarborough, he returned to York as a partner in the firm of Gillings, Walker & Dryland. Before very long, however, he was invited back to the firm where he was articled which in the meantime had become Ware & Peters and where he was eventually became senior partner. In addition to his music, his other interests outside the practice of the law were all followed with enthusiasm and dedication, including those of an all-round sportsman (rugby, hockey, tennis), Member and and some time Master of the Company of Merchant Taylors and a close involvement and trusteeship of the York Sea Cadets.

Dunnell, Robert Francis (1868-1960)

An alumnus of Rossall School, Francis (Frank) Dunnell was admitted in 1891 and joined the Society in 1892 as a young solicitor in the legal department of the North Eastern Railway Company. By 1900 he had been promoted to Assistant Solicitor to the company, Solicitor in 1905 and also Company Secretary in 1906 – the same year that George Gibb (*q.v.*) joined the Board. In 1917 the company lent his services to the Admiralty where he became Assistant Secretary and Secretary to the British Naval Mission to Washington. At the end of the war he was appointed Secretary to the Demobilisation Section of the War Cabinet and in the following year First Secretary and Solicitor to the newly created Ministry of Transport and at the same time appointed Knight

Commander of the Order of the Bath. It was 1921 before he was able to return to his old company. But the days of the North Eastern and the myriad independent railway companies in Britain were numbered. With very minor exceptions all were amalgamated with effect from 1 January 1923 into 'the big four' of which the London & North Eastern was one. Sir Francis Dunnell Bt (he had received his baronetcy in 1921 for services to the Ministry of Transport) was appointed Chief Legal Adviser to the newly amalgamated company, a position which he retained until his retirement in 1928 when he finally relinquished his membership of the Society. Throughout the time of his secondment to the Admiralty, the Demobilisation Section of the War Cabinet and the Ministry of Transport he had maintained his membership. Even on retirement from the LNER his career was not over. In 1930 he was appointed a Railway and Canal Commissioner. In 1947 he moved to Nairobi where he spent the remainder of his life.

Eddison, Edwin (1805 -1867)

Edwin Eddison had practised as a solicitor in Leeds ever since joining Richard Payne in partnership in 1826. Payne had been in practice there on his own account since 1816. This partnership was to mark the beginning of the firm which was eventually to become Ford & Warren. We do not know what prompted Eddison to join the Society in 1855 when he had already been in practice in Leeds for nearly thirty years. What we do know is that another Leeds solicitor, William North, who had been in the practice known as Payne, Eddison, North & Ford also joined the Society on the same day. North, however, had left the partnership with Payne, Eddison & Ford in the previous year, 1854, to set up in business with his son James. We equally know that North was proposed for membership of the Society by the prominent York-based railway solicitor, George Leeman *(q.v.)* – so possibly there was some railway connection. He became the Society's President in 1863.

But whatever his connection with York and the Yorkshire Law Society, his interest in Leeds was significant and definite. He served for some years as its Town Clerk from 1837, kept a farm at Adel where he practised animal husbandry and was closely involved in the founding of the Leeds Zoological and Botanical Gardens in Headingley which opened in the same year that he became town clerk. The idea behind it was suitably earnest and Victorian: "no one can fail to have observed how whilst the wealth, importance and population of this town has gradually increased, the opportunities for public recreation have in ratio diminished" was how the promoters put it. They were equally convinced that their project would "provide elevated pastimes for the operative classes and wean them from their grosser pursuits". All that remains to be seen today of this worthy attempt to elevate the pastimes of the operative classes of Leeds and wean them from their grosser pursuits are the bear pits in Cardigan Road Headingley, restored in 1966 by the Leeds Civic Trust. The venture was never a financial success, possibly owing to protracted disputes as to whether it should be open to the public on the Sabbath[4] and it eventually closed in 1858. Eddison was also a member of the Leeds Philosophical and Literary Society and in 1833 he read a paper to its members entitled *Observations on the Crime and Increase of Crime, with Suggestions for an Alteration in the Laws respecting Prison Discipline and Colonial Transportation.*

Frost, Charles FSA (1782-1862)

Charles Frost was the son of Thomas Frost (who joined the Society in July 1788). Again, as in the case of Edwin Eddison, there seems to be no record of when Charles Frost became a member of the Society but, like Eddison, he presumably did so as he was President in 1812. He followed his father as solicitor to the Hull Docks Company and was to hold this post for thirty-three years. He was also a noted antiquary and President of the Hull Literary and Philosophical Society for a total of ten years between 1830 and 1855. As a result of his research he was able to correct a universal misapprehension as to Hull's origins. Generations of historians, including William Camden had attributed its foundation to King Edward I but Frost had been able to establish that it was in fact much earlier. It was also largely through his efforts that Hull acquired one of its most outstanding 19th century buildings, the Royal Institution in Albion Street opened by Prince Albert on 24 October 1854. It was to be a great loss to Hull when it was bombed to destruction in the course of a Luftwaffe raid on 24 June 1943. For a number of years Frost was also President of the Hull Subscription Library which had its base in the building as did the Literary and Philosophical Society. The later still flourishes, albeit without a permanent home. He was clearly an energetic man of many parts, actively engaged in his legal practice until just ten days before he died at the age of eighty. Charles Frost was a member of the sub-committee appointed by the Society in 1814 to make representations to the authorities in London about costs and indeed it was the father and son's case of *Atkinson v Sadler* which was subsequently used as a test case on a review of taxation.[5] He subsequently published a book about payments to witnesses with the rather unwieldy title *Considerations on the Propriety of Making a Remuneration to Witnesses in Civil Actions for Loss of Time* (London 1815). It has been digitally re-published by Google Books in 2013 and 2015.

Gibb, George Stegmann (1850-1925)

In their Annual Report presented to members on 12 February 1926 the Committee had occasion to report the death of Sir George Stegmann Gibb. Although he had ceased to be a member of the Society and indeed to practise as a solicitor some years previously, they were surely right to do so. An alumnus of Aberdeen Grammar School and London University, Gibb had joined the office of the solicitor to the Great Western Railway in 1877. In 1882 he had been appointed solicitor to the North Eastern Railway Company, joining the Society that same year. By 1889 he was a member of its committee and served in that capacity for several years. His career, however, was to develop along railway management rather than legal lines. In 1891 he was appointed General Manager of the NER and quickly made his mark, joining the Board in 1906, having been knighted two years earlier.

It had been Gibb who had persuaded the NER directors six years earlier to authorise the construction of what has become a lasting memorial on York station and numerous others on the old North Eastern Railway's territory, from Berwick almost to Rotherham and from Carlisle to Withernsea: the impressive tiled map facing the tracks on the main concourse. How many of the Society's members, one wonders, must have passed through York station over the years – and indeed how often – without realising that one of its notable landmarks owes its existence to one of their own? Constructed of sixty-four 8" x 8" glazed tiles with further 8" x 4" tiles depicting the company's name at the top, it is a striking example of the exuberant commercial confidence of the age. It was not merely in railway décor and PR that Gibb's reputation was to rest. He was equally noted for his progressive views on equipment and operations. In 1902 he inaugurated a massive reorganisation of the company's traffic department based on the best American practice following a study tour in the US the previous year. Much railway management in late Victorian Britain is generally thought to have been weak and lethargic. As a recent study in 2007[6] observed "If railway companies generally have been seen as badly run, the North Eastern Railway has been seen as an outstanding exception, at least from the point when George Gibb became General Manager in 1891."

When Gibb eventually turned his attention to the London Underground even *The New York Times* reported his appointment by the board of the Underground Electric Railways Company[7] as their Deputy Chairman and Managing Director and Chairman and Managing Director of the Metropolitan District Railway Company. "He is accounted one of the most successful and up-to-date railroad officers . . . He is a man of wide attainment and has been noted in England for his progressive policies in railroad affairs. As manager of the North Eastern Railway he introduced the American system of ton and passenger mile statistics and during five years effected an increase of 52% in the freight train loads of his road." In one respect, at least, he seems to have been ahead of the Americans because the report continued "The autocar system for branch line passenger traffic now being taken up in this country was another of his innovations in England."

When members of the Society are travelling on the London Underground, especially on the Bakerloo and Piccadilly lines, they may care to reflect that a former member was closely involved in the pioneering work of 'the tube'.

Gilmour, Michael Hugh Barrie (1904-1982)

Michael Gilmour joined the Society in March 1953, having qualified as a solicitor in 1929. He remained a member for over ten years whilst based in York. As in the case of several other members mentioned here, he was to achieve high distinction either as a 'railway' solicitor or in senior railway management. Until nationalisation of the main railway companies by the post-war Labour government under the Transport Act 1947 which took effect in 1948, he had been solicitor to the Great Western Railway Company and a member of its board at a comparatively early age whereas the solicitors to the three other mainline railway companies were nearing retirement. He was therefore a strong candidate for the appointment, made in April 1949, as Chief Solicitor to the newly created British Transport Commission, the railway component of which (less London Transport) subsequently became the British Railways Board with effect from 1 January 1963. From 1943 until his death he was a member of the Garrick Club where he was a regular attender when in London.

After leaving York he was based at the British Railways Board's headquarters at 222, Marylebone Road in London where he was instrumental in establishing a distinct policy for dealing with claims against the Board. He strongly disapproved of the common practice, adopted by the less reputable insurance companies, of knowingly making inadequate offers to claimants in the hope that they would be accepted by the desperate or the ill-advised. His approach was to make fair and realistic offers once a proper assessment could be made – eg in a personal injury case. If the Board's offer was not accepted, there was a prompt payment into court which was rarely, if ever, increased unless new evidence came to light. Solicitors acting for the railway unions soon got the message and accordingly advised their clients that if they chose to refuse a payment into court, they should not assume that any further payment in would be made, nor that they could expect any better if the case went to trial. It was a sound policy which led to quicker fair settlements and a considerable reduction in costs overall.

Gray, Jonathan (1779-1835)

Jonathan Gray was the second of no less than five members of the Gray family to have been members of the Society, to have borne the 'Gray' name and practised in York. Further, although they did not bear the Gray name, three other members of the Society were descended from the first William Gray *(q.v.)*, namely Cecil Henry Cobb (1867-1939), William Henry Crookenden Cobb (1917-1994) *(q.v.)* and Benjamin Charlesworth (Charles) Ralph Dodsworth (1924-2014). The last two, William Cobb and Charles Dodsworth were both in due course to become partners in the firm which was to perpetuate the Gray name.

Jonathan, although outlived by his father William by ten years, was a man of many parts and managed to achieve much in his comparatively short professional career.[8] A foundation director of the York County Savings Bank (1816) subsequently part of Lloyds TSB and (since 2013) TSB Bank plc, the Yorkshire Fire and Life Insurance Company (now part of the Norwich Union/Aviva (1824), he established and made considerable contributions to the *Yorkshire Gazette* (1819). He was also the first Hon Treasurer of the Yorkshire Philosophical Society founded in 1822 by his partner, Anthony Thorpe, together with William Salmond, a retired colonel and amateur geologist, James Atkinson, a retired surgeon and William Vernon, son of the Archbishop of York. In his capacity as Hon Treasurer Jonathan was closely involved in the British Association[9] (subsequently the British Association for the Advancement of Science and now the British Science Association) having its inaugural meeting in York on 27 September 1831 and the Society now operates as a branch office of the Association. In 1829 the York Philosophical Society had been responsible of establishing the Yorkshire Museum and subsequently developing what are now known as the Museum Gardens. In 1961 both the Museum and the gardens were transferred on trust to York City Council.

Jonathan also took a close interest in the reform of 'lunatic asylums' as they were then known. Together with Samuel Tuke, and two other public spirited men he had led a campaign against the management of the York Asylum and the abusive régime practised there at the time. In May 1814 he was in attendance at parliamentary committee meetings connected with the passage of a bill which resulted in the County Asylums Amendment Act (55 Geo.3 c.46). The following year he published *A History of the York Lunatic Asylum*. If that were not enough, he also found time to be a Committee member of the York Musical Society, founded in 1765 and the oldest musical society in England which promoted three York Music Festivals (1823, 1825 and 1828).

Like his father William, Jonathan was an active member of the Society and served as President in 1817-1818. With two other members he was on the delegation dispatched to London in March 1815 to make representations about costs and which resulted in the *First Report of the Committee for obtaining an Augmention of the Allowance of Costs de Incremento*[10]. In 1817 the Society presented Jonathan with a handsome silver tankard,[11] suitably inscribed, in recognition of his services. About sixty years later it was returned to the Society by Jonathan's son William and nowadays it makes a regular appearance on the top table on the occasion of the Society's annual dinner.

Gray, William (1751-1845)

William, a founder member of the Society – see portrait on p. 356, was the father of Jonathan Gray (*q.v.*). Son of a weaver and a farmer's daughter in the East Riding, he had left school at twelve and found employment with a local attorney, William Iveson, as a 'writer'. William's father had paid a premium of 25 guineas for his articles but by modern standards they seem to have left much to be desired. He received little instruction or supervision from his principal who on one occasion when he was away in London for three months left William in sole charge of the office. William arrived in York from Hedon in 1772 before his articles had expired with a few personal possessions and just £3 in cash, all that was left of a loan of £10 or £15 from his former principal. He was lucky; he was acquainted with the Town Clerk of York, George Townend (*q.v.*) a Hull man who had moved to York and who was responsible for arranging the transfer of articles to John Graves a York attorney. Graves, whose practice was not very active, was generous and paid him an allowance of £60 pa. William quickly made his mark; admitted as an attorney in 1774, Graves immediately offered him an equal partnership. It was not clear, however, that this would equal his previous salary and again, very generously, Graves promised to make up the difference in the event of a shortfall. He need not have worried; thanks to William's diligence the partnership was to prosper. This was the beginning of a remarkable example of family continuity in the firm that bears its name to this day: Grays of York. Descendants of the first William Gray were partners in it continually from 1774 until the retirement of Charles Dodsworth (*q.v*) in 1987.

Harrowell, Herbert Edward OBE (1880-1965)

Son of a Methodist minister, Herbert Harrowell was admitted in 1906 and joined the Society in 1909, setting up his own practice, at first in Coppergate and later in Parliament Street. Like many enterprising and energetic solicitors of the period, he was active in the civic, charitable and business life of the city. He represented Clifton Ward on York City Council for twelve years, becoming City Sheriff in 1927 and Lord Mayor for two separate terms of office in the 1930s. He was awarded the OBE for civic services in the birthday honours in 1937, the year after joining the York bench as a JP and in due course becoming its Chairman. For over 30 years he was the Hon Secretary of the RSPCC and other active charitable interests included the chairmanship of the York Branch of the English Speaking Union, the presidency of the York Blue Coat School for Boys and York Grey Coat School for Girls. He was also clerk of the Feoffees of St Martin's and St Helen's and treasurer of the York Auxiliary Bible Society. Although towards the end of his life he relinquished many of his public appointments, he continued to be involved with the Merchant Taylors' Company until his death. It was during his time as Clerk between 1934 and 1961 that the Company's Hall underwent extensive restoration to become one of York's significant tourist attractions.

In his legal practice (which bears his name to this day) he was energetic and innovative. He pioneered the 'open practice' of being available to all comers on Saturday mornings to coincide with York's weekly market.

Hartley, John (c.1760 – c.1840)

John Hartley practised in Settle and became a member of the Society in March 1800, serving as President in 1816. On 25 April 1788, acting for a Mr Caley, one of the purchasers of part of the Wennington Estate in North Lancashire, he had spent the night at Hornby Castle in connection with the completion. There he had been joined by a number of solicitors acting for other purchasers, the intention being to complete the matter all together the following day. The lawyers concerned all had dinner together where they has been joined by their host, the estate owner and vendor John Marsden. The transaction was ultimately to involve Hartley as a witness in one of the great *causes célèbres* of late Georgian England – *Tatham v Wright* reported in part at 2 Russ & Mylne 1. It eventually transpired that Marsden had been of unsound mind for many years, being looked after by his aunt. The defendant in the proceedings was George Wright the steward employed on the estate. Wright, who had started in service as a shoe-boy, kitchen boy and butler before his appointment as steward, afterwards became the aunt's lover. At the start of the affair Wright was twenty-two and the aunt, Mrs Cookson, a widow of fifty-three. When Marsden died in 1826 he was found to have left a will leaving the entire estate to . . . George Wright. Predictably the will was contested by the deceased's cousin and heir-at-law, Admiral Sandford Tatham. The litigation,[12] which was to rumble on for twelve years, involved no less than four trials, one in York, before the plaintiff finally succeeded, having incurred legal costs of about £20,000 to secure an inheritance which was estimated to produce £8,000 a year.

In the proceedings at Lancaster in August 1834, before Baron Gurney and a special jury, over forty-six years after that pre-completion dinner at Hornby Castle in 1788, Hartley found himself giving evidence about it. It was notable for a reply that he gave under cross-examination to the defendant's counsel (Mr Pollock, Attorney-General for the County Palatine of Lancaster) when Hartley observed about a subsequent incident involving the defendant 'the only satisfaction I had was taking Wright by the nose and telling him that he was a forsworn villain; that was in coming down from the castle'. Counsel was clearly disconcerted by the witness's unflattering opinion of his client and responded, somewhat lamely, 'You took Mr Wright by the nose and told him he was a forsworn villain?' 'A forsworn villain.' 'I am obliged to you – that was not in my instructions. I wish to keep nothing back.' The admiral was ultimately successful in having the will set aside but it was a struggle, the 'forsworn villain' Wright using every subterfuge known to the creaking legal system of the day to obfuscate and delay proceedings. In 1837 they even reached the House of Lords and became an authority on the admissibility of hearsay. Throughout they were a lively and enduring topic of conversation in the drawing-rooms and clubs of the day.[13] Even the Prince of Wales became involved, lending his support to the embattled admiral.

Leeman, George (1809 -1882)

Son of a greengrocer, George Leeman joined the Society in July 1839, having been qualified as a solicitor in 1835 following articles to another York solicitor (not a member of the Society) Robert Henry Anderson. In due course he became senior partner in the firm of Leeman and Wilkinson with offices in York and Beverley. His name must be known to virtually the entire population of York and many of its visitors from all over the world as he is commemorated in the name of one of its principal streets in which is to be found the National Railway Museum. But even to those who are aware of the identity of the man from whom 'Leeman Road' takes its name, he is probably better known for his connection with politics and railways than as a solicitor. In York his name is always associated with that of his arch-rival George Hudson, the 'Railway King'. The animosity between these two men was to dominate York politics in the middle years of the 19th century. Even today the battles are still being waged by proxy.[14] In 1849 Leeman succeeded Hudson as Chairman of the York, Newcastle and Berwick Railway and promoted the mergers which created the North Eastern Railway Company in 1854 of which he then became a director which he remained until his death in 1882, being its chairman from 1874 to 1880. His other business interests included the development in the 1860s of iron ore mining in Rosedale to supply the steel works of Teeside and chairmanship of the Yorkshire Banking Company and a directorship of the *Yorkshire Herald* newspaper. In the course of his legal and business career he also managed to be a member of the city council (including 28 years as an alderman) and to represent York in parliament from 1865 to 1868 and again from 1871 to 1880. As far as I am aware he is the only member of the Society ever to have had a public statue erected in his honour in 1885 – the one familiar to many York residents on Station Road by York sculptor George Milburn paid for by public subscription following his death.

Lockwood, William (1778-1836)

A founder member of the Society from Easingwold, Lockwood was himself son of an attorney, also called William, with whom he served his articles, although it seems that at one time he had ambitions to go to university and the Bar. However, he seems to have earned a comfortable living as an Easingwold attorney. On his death in 1836 he left an estate valued at £14,000 – well over £1M in today's money or £10M by comparison with average earnings of the period. However, the Lockwood family was clearly prosperous – their family home still faces the market square at Easingwold. William seems to have been quite a practical man, his talents extending to the preparation of plans and valuations, tasks which nowadays would be undertaken by a surveyor or valuer. He even records in his diary for 25 February 1796 'Papered a Room in the other House' – the Lockwoods owned two properties in the Market Square. Admittedly he was an articled clerk at the time but even so, such DIY activity seems slightly unusual for an aspiring 18th century professional man. His practice survived to modern times under the name of Hileys (part of Harrowells since 2011) which also had an office in Thirsk.

Mortimer, Timothy (? -1788)

Mortimer, admitted to the Society on 13 March 1787, was the second President of the Society after George Townend that year. He clearly took an immediate and active interest in the Society's affairs: his is the first signature on the Society's first petition to parliament but died barely a year later. The *Gentleman's Magazine* for 1788 records his death at York after a short illness and described him as "an attorney of great eminence, extensive practice and universal good character". His practice was sufficiently extensive in 1786, the year of the Society's foundation, to send his son Charles to school at Rugby.

Munby, Frederick James (1837-1914)

At the time of his death in 1914 FJ Munby can justly be regarded as the father of the profession in York, having been admitted in 1860. He had become a member of the Committee and Hon Secretary in 1883, a position which he held until 1894, the year when he became the Society's President, an office which he again held in 1910, his Jubilee Year in the profession. It was during his first presidential year that he inaugurated the scheme later to be known as The Yorkshire Board of Legal Studies. In its early stages it was not met with the enthusiasm which he thought was its due and he suffered to some extent the proverbial fate of a prophet in his own country. But as the Committee was to report to the Society's members following his death "Mr Munby . . . when he once fully took up a cause which appealed to him, was a person of singular tenacity of purpose, and at the risk of being, and at the risk of being looked upon as a man with a hobby, he continued to push his scheme forward, and gradually gathered round him a body of men interested both in law and in education, and with their assistance and as their pioneer he succeeded in establishing Schools of Law at the Leeds and Sheffield Universities, and so induced the Law Society not only to support the Yorkshire Board but to establish similar Schools of Law in conection with the London and the Manchester Universities." Munby's interest in education also prompted him in 1903 to join with others, notably the Yorkshire Philosophical Society, in proposing the establishment of a Victoria University of Yorkshire, clearly with an eye to having a university based in York but this was one project too far and the city had to wait a further sixty years before that could come to fruition. Nevertheless he was to remain Chairman of the Yorkshire Board of Legal Studies until his death.

Munby also held the office of Clerk to the Justices for the City of York from the death of his father, Joseph Munby (his immediate predecessor) in 1875 until his resignation in 1910 which for some years he combined with the clerkship to the Justices of the Eastern Ainsty Petty Sessional Division. However, the office of which he was undoubtedly most proud was that of Clerk to the Yorkshire County Committee, an important but almost forgotten body which continued to exist until the final abolition of the Assize system as recommended by Lord Beeching and to which effect was given by the Courts Act 1971. Before the Local Government Act 1888 (which for the first time created county councils as a tier of local government) Munby had been Clerk to the Yorkshire Court of Gaol Sessions but S64(5) of the 1888 Act had provided that in the case of Yorkshire and Lincolnshire which were divided into ridings or parts there should be County Committees – corporations with perpetual succession and a common seal with power to acquire and hold land for the purposes of their constitution 'without licence in mortmain'. The Yorkshire County Committee thus became responsible for the ownership and management of the assize courts and the Judges' Lodgings. It was Munby's proud boast that he was the sole representative official of the County of York, the other county officials being only representatives of Ridings.

Like so many solicitors Munby did not confine his attention merely to the law; he equally had extensive charitable interests. These included a dedicated involvement with the Wilberforce School for the Blind or the Wilberforce Memorial as it was originally known. It had been set up in 1833 in memory of William Wilberforce immediately following his death in that year and held its first half-yearly meeting in August 1834. His father Joseph (also a member of the Society) had been Hon Secretary from the beginning and attended that first meeting in the Guildhall when William Gray (*q.v*) took the chair. At that point a total of £4,195 (roughly £200,000 in today's money) had already been raised by public subscription. On his father's death in 1875 FJ Munby followed him as Hon Secretary to the school and after 75 years of joint secretaryship he had been presented with a testimonial to mark the fact. In the event that was to continue for a further seven years, making it a continuous period of 82 years.

Another charitable involvement was the Boys' Industrial School which Munby served as Hon Secretary for a number of years. More controversially, he was a leading figure in the management of the York Refuge for Fallen Women. Many 'respectable' people in late Victorian society would doubtless have looked askance at a solicitor who interested himself in such a subject and it is perhaps significant that the Committee made no mention of it in their Annual Report in 1915[15] but as they themselves had noted 'Mr Munby was . . . a person of singular tenacity of purpose' and not easily discouraged by what others thought. In this matter he had been a close friend of another campaigner for 'fallen women', the Reverend Frederick Lawrence, the young Rector of St Mary's Castlegate from 1871 to 1881 of whom it has been written 'Much of his public work was extremely thankless, most of it against strong opposition and even hostility'.[16] Munby's former family home, Clifton Holme, was subsequently purchased by the Refuge Society in 1919 when it moved from its previous premises in Bishophill.

But perhaps the true nature of the man can best be judged by a dinner he gave on 19 December 1910, towards the end of his second presidential year when, supported by the Society's Hon Treasurer, Mr F Perkins and Hon Secretary, Mr HV Scott, he entertained at the Davy Hall York nearly fifty solicitors' clerks who had served for not less than twelve years. The senior clerk present, Mr J Logan, had served in Mr CR

Garwood's office for 56 years. He and Mr WB Pannett, who had served Mr Munby himself for over 30 years, sat on either side of him. After the loyal toasts the second-time President was congratulated and presented with an illuminated address which recalled a similar dinner he had given on the occasion of his first presidency sixteen years earlier. It also alluded to the Society's centenary celebrations in 1886 when he had been Hon Secretary and instrumental in arranging for solicitors' clerks in York to be entertained by their employers.

Newton, Henry (c.1800-1881)

Newton was admitted as an attorney and solicitor in 1824, becoming a member of the Society in August 1829 and its President in 1854. He had been articled to William Gray (*q.v.*) in 1821 who was his proposer for membership of the Society. For the rest of his life he seems to have maintained cordial relations with the Grays in their various manifestations Thorpe & Gray (1805-1828) J and W Gray (1829-1837) W Gray (1838-1872) and W and E Gray (1872-1891) and for some years was their near neighbours when the Grays' office was in Low Petergate York. In 1864 he became one of the four trustees of the York Savings Bank, William Gray Junior being another. He was under-sheriff for the City 1849 -1850. By 1853 Newton, together with his partner William Robinson had been appointed solicitors for the York and North Midland and York Newcastle and Berwick Railway Commission. Two years later these two undertakings had been incorporated and in due course became the North Eastern Railway Company, Newton & Robinson becoming the latter company's first solicitors. But probably best known among Newton's clients was Charlotte Brontë who was consulting him in November and December about her powers under her marriage settlement.[17]

Nicholson, Lucas (c.1750 -1819)

Nicholson was not only a prominent Leeds attorney but was also active as agent for the Royal Exchange, a chartered insurance company founded in 1720 and which continued to operate under that name until 1968 when it merged with Guardian Assurance Company to form Guardian Royal Assurance plc although the name finally disappeared in 1999 when the later was acquired bu the French multinational insurer AXA. In 1779

Nicholson joined another Leeds attorney, Nicholas Smith in partnership, subsequently becoming a member of the Society in 1787 and its President in 1795. He was also established a banking partnership in what in due course became known as the Leeds Bank of which he was Cashier. As far as I am aware he was the only member of the Society who has ever had the distinction of having his signature appearing on bank notes. Clearly a man of many parts, he also secured an appointment in 1792 as Town Clerk of Leeds. Unfortunately he and his banking partners all became bankrupt in 1812 in connection with their banking activities – a not uncommon fate in those days. However, it seems that his bankruptcy was not a total disaster. He had to resign as Town Clerk but was immediately replaced by his son Charles who was also able to continue with the insurance agency jointly with his father. Curiously, two major international law firms have a link with Nicholson: DLA Piper (through Dibb Lupton Alsop) and Addleshaw Goddard (through Booth & Co). Both of their Leeds components claimed original descent from Nicholas Smith and Lucas Nicholson.

Procter, Alfred (1861-1933)

Alfred Procter became a member of the Society in 1883, a year after his admission as a solicitor. By the time of his death in 1933 at the age of 71 he had become a very respected York figure. His funeral in York Minster on 15 February of that year attracted over a thousand mourners, including the Lord Mayor and other members of the city council with the ceremonial sword and mace draped in black. (As a young man he had been a member of the council until 1897). As a solicitor he had been senior partner of Messrs Holtby & Procter which shortly before his death had amalgamated with Messrs Francis, Ware & Lucas. At various times he had been HM Coroner for the City of York as well as parts of the North and East Ridings, and Clerk to the Justices of the Ouse and Derwent Division He had other interests, however, outside the law. Chairman of the York Gas Company since 1913, a member of the Board of Management of the York County Savings Bank, Chairman of Leak & Thorp, the York department store and Chairman of Bootham Park Hospital Board of Governors, a post that had previously been held by another Society member and President William Walker (*q.v.*). He had also been a prominent Mason, a member of both York and Amber Victor Lodges, as well as being an office bearer of the Grand Lodge of England, and Provincial Grand Master of Mark Masons for the North Riding. He was also an active member of the Society, serving as President between 1925 and 1927 and having also served earlier on the committee for several years from 1897 onwards.

Raworth, Edwin (1863-1925)

Edwin Raworth was the son of Richard H Raworth, a Harrogate builder. He qualified as a solicitor in 1885 and a year later was practising on his own in the town. He was soon joined by Jabez Butterworth to whom he gave articles who in turn qualified in 1905 and was admitted into partnership in 1911 to form what is now a leading Harrogate practice. Edwin joined the Society in 1898 and was an early member of the Harrogate Law Society (established in1918) and its President in from 1921. He became the first clerk to the Harrogate Justices whom he served in that capacity for 30 years and was also clerk to the School Board. In 1905 he had the misfortune to fall out of a third floor window in Edinburgh which resulted in concussion and the amputation of a leg. Elected as President of the Yorkshire Law Society in 1925, Edwin unfortunately died in October during his year of office, the presidency being assumed by Alfred Procter (*q.v.*). The Raworth family name is still very much in the public eye, before a much larger audience: Edwin's great-granddaughter is Sophie Raworth, the BBC presenter and newsreader.

Robson, Thomas (1855- 1924)

Thomas Robson was born at Full Sutton and articled to York solicitor Robert Holtby (member 1863) whose practice was at 15 Low Ousegate. Following his marriage to a farmer's daughter from Hatfield, near Doncaster, Robson moved to Pocklington. Admitted as a solicitor in 1880, he joined the Society in 1889 and served as President in 1906. At various times he was clerk to Pocklington Rural District Council, and to the Pocklington and Market Weighton justices as well as to the Governors of Pocklington School. On the occasion of Queen Victoria's diamond jubilee in 1897 he was Chairman of the Diamond Jubilee Committee responsible for the Victoria Memorial in Market Street. The latter part of his life was marked by tragedy: having lost his wife following a long illness in 1915, he was then to lose three of his five sons (all educated at Pocklington School) in the remaining course of the First World War. His eldest son Richard had qualified as a solicitor after articles in his father's firm and had become a partner in the London firm of Bell, Brodrick & Gray (now Wedlake Bell) but he had long suffered from ill-health and died in 1918 at the age of 34. His third son, Frederick William, had likewise qualified as a solicitor and been articled with his father's firm. In 1909 he had joined the TA but along with his battalion had become a regular soldier with the rank of captain. By 1918, having won the DSO, he was a Lieutenant Colonel but was posted as "missing, presumed killed" in March 1918. The fourth son, Edward, also a solicitor who had been articled in his father's firm, had joined up shortly after the outbreak of war. He survived the Battle of the Somme in 1916 where he had been awarded the Military Cross and promoted to captain, only to be killed in the last year of the war. All this was too much for their father; he retired from practice and left Pocklington in 1919 to go and live with his second son Thomas (junior), a farmer, at Hatfield, near Doncaster. However, he retained his membership of the Society following his retirement – the Annual Report for 1922 shows his residential address as Hatfield.

Seymour, George Hicks (1793-1872)

Admitted as a member on 9 August 1824, George Seymour established the firm of Seymour & Blyth with an office in Lendal (next to the Judges' Lodgings). Appointed Hon Secretary of the Society in 1830, he served in that capacity until 1836 (a total of seven years) and later served as Hon Treasurer from 1839 to 1871(a total of 32 years) or 39 years on the committee overall, thus becoming one of the longest serving officers of the Society ever. During his latter tenure as Treasurer he also served as President of the Society in 1845. But it was not just to the Society that he devoted his energies. In 1834 he was elected to the committee of the Yorkshire Philosophical Society and subsequently turned to railway management, becoming a director, first of the York and North Midland Railway and later of the North Eastern Railway. He was equally able to attend to civic affairs and served for many years on the city council, as Alderman from 1849 to 1862 and as Lord Mayor of York 1849-1850.

It was in the course of his year as Lord Mayor that he decided to repay hospitality he had received from the Lord Mayor of London on the occasion of a visit there to prepare for the Great Exhibition at the Crystal Palace the following year. Determined to show that anything London could do, York could do better, he organised a banquet the like of which York had probably never have seen since mediæval times – or indeed subsequently. It was held at the Guildhall on 25 November 1850. The guest of honour was Prince Albert and other guests included the Prime Minister, Lord Russell and 87 civic dignitaries from all over the British Isles. There was a choice of 72 dishes and a 'Royal Table' with a 'hundred guinea dish' including turtle heads and a great variety of birds from larks to turkeys. In overall charge of this remarkable repast was Alexis Soyer, the 19th century's best known celebrity chef, who had only just parted company with the Reform Club, albeit on fairly amicable terms, following a policy disagreement. It must have been mid-century Victorian bling at its most ostentatious and provoked a scurrilous (and anonymous) twelve verse poem "Dedicated (Without Permission) to the Rt Hon the Lady Mayoress [Seymour's wife Emma] by A Ragged Scholar". Two selected verses will serve to convey the general tone:

The Guildhall is deck'd	Some hundreds of dozens
In magnificent taste,	Of the choicest of wine,
And Soyer has cooked	Champagne, port and sherry
All his frogs and his paste ...	They swallow like swine.

It was perhaps a little unfortunate that Soyer should have been included as a target in this attack as he had a very strong social conscience and had made considerable personal sacrifices both previously (during the Irish famine) and subsequently (during the Crimean War) to put his culinary skills at the disposal of the suffering Irish and suffering soldiery but excess on this scale and at this particular time would undoubtedly have been a provocation to many.

Shannon, John CBE D.Univ. (York) (1918-2010)

John Shannon was quintessentially a York man. Admitted as a solicitor in 1944 and as a member in 1947, his name quickly became familiar to generations of solicitors in and around York as Hon Secretary of the Society – a position he held for just over 30 years from 1948 until 1978 – as joint Hon Secretary with the previous incumbent, Mr HC Scott, until 1958. But his reputation was to extend well beyond the law. His contribution to the city and more specifically to its conservation lead to his being awarded the OBE in 1970 and its advancement to CBE in 1996. In addition to these honours, York University conferred on him an honorary doctorate in 1977 and the city make him an honorary freeman in 2001. Although he played a leading rôle in many organisations, and was Sheriff of York in 1953, it is as the dynamic chairman of York Civic Trust for 38 years that his achievements will be familiar to York's inhabitants and equally its many visitors. You can hardly walk more than a few yards through York without seeing his influence on the fabric and feel of the city as Mr Darrell Buttery observed in the course of his heartfelt tribute in York Minster on the occasion of John Shannon's funeral on 14 June 2010 – adding that the fact that his funeral service could be conducted without disruption from traffic noise was largely thanks to his unremitting efforts to have Deangate closed as a major thoroughfare.

It was a typical John Shannon gesture to declare that when – and with John it was never a case of 'if' but 'when' – Deangate was closed, he and the Dean would have lunch together in the middle of the road. There is a famous press photograph of them both, heavily wrapped up against the freezing temperature, together having lunch together which was doubtless as cold as they both looked. John himself put the closing of Deangate as one of the Trust's two greatest achievements, the other one being of course the founding of York University. In reality all York's citizens are deeply in John's debt. His major battle honours gained in defending the city which he loved so much are extensive and include his pioneering work in establishing Stonegate as a foot street – a commonly accepted conservation measure nowadays but subject to considerable opposition at the time; the raising of the planning blight that had settled on Gillygate; the saving of Fairfax House and the Observatory in the Museum Gardens; the restoration of the Mansion House. And of course there are the myriad skirmishes which he led from the front, too numerous to mention here but well-known to the *cognoscenti*. At one AGM of the Civic Trust Archbishop Stuart Blanch put it very neatly. After listening to an account of the year's achievements he observed: "I really feel that if anyone deserves the title it should be JOHN EBOR and not STUART EBOR. To which many members of the Society over the years would have echoed 'Amen'.

Spofforth, Robert (1740-1827)

Admitted to the Society in March 1787, Spofforth was its President the following year. He was a member of a large and distinguished Yorkshire family, one branch of which had a longstanding connection with Howden of which he was Lord of the Manor. He was articled by his father to William Dunn of Howden for a premium of £30. In 1768 he married Hannah Markham of Howden Manor by whom he had ten children. Among other appointments, he was Clerk to Bishop Barrington of Durham. His death in 1827 at the age of 87 was noted by *The Gentleman's Magazine* in which he was described as 'an eminent solicitor'. His grandson, Edward Spofforth emigrated to Australia and fathered one of the 'greats' of Australian cricket, Frederick Robert (Fred) Spofforth (1853-1926) 'the demon bowler' who made his test début in Melbourne in 1877 in the second match of the first ever test series against England and is the subject of a detailed biography.

Stovin, Aistroppe (1766-1828)

Stovin was originally from the small village of Reedness near Goole in the East Riding and at first practised as an attorney at Gainsborough in Lincolnshire. Some time prior to 1793 however, he moved to Hull. By 1794 he had not only become a member of the Society but had begun an active involvement with the promotion of a private act of parliament which would eventually lead to the construction of a new street as the *Hull Advertiser* for 6 September 1794 described it "from the north side of a Street called Whytefryer-gate . . . opposite or nearly opposite to the site of a Building . . . of Trinity House . . . and also for building a row of Houses on each side of the said intended Street with suitable convenience". The proposal required an act of parliament because it involved what we would now call 'compulsory purchase'. The Hull Dock Company which had been responsible in 1778 for constructing the city's first dock, was strongly in favour as it considered that "it would be in every point of view, one of the most eligible improvements which this town has undergone for several years . . . it would be the means of removing from one of the most beautiful Streets in the town, a place which is, at present, a receptacle for every wretchedness. The houses of a new Street, on account of their contiguity to the dock would be a very desirable situation for people in business, and no doubt would be taken with the greatest avidity". One of the early subscribers was William Wilberforce, one of Hull's most famous sons and Stovin himself, as well as being the clerk to the subscribers, took a share himself in the tontine arrangement which was the financial basis of the scheme. The 'new' street is now known as Parliament Street and has been described as a 'Georgian Gem'. Certainly the Hull Dock Company's prediction in 1794 that it would be 'a very desirable situation for people in business' has proved to be correct: the whole area, including Parliament Street itself, is home to a number of well-known law firms. Stovin was also an active member of the Hull Philosophical Society and made a number of contributions to the Gainsborough weekly known as the *Country Spectator* as well as being the author of *The Law Respecting Horses* (1794) – digitalised version available from Amazon – and *The Analysis of the Law on the Abandonment of Ships and Freight* (1801).

Townend, George (c.1749-1812)

George Townend, originally from Hull, had the privilege of being elected as the Society's first President when he was Town Clerk of York having succeeded his father-in-law to the post in 1781 although he also continued in private practice. In the latter capacity he had been appointed a Master Extraordinary of the Court of Chancery and a Commissioner for taking Affidavits in the Court of Exchequer on 14 December 1773. His younger brother Richard also practised as an attorney in York and became Town Clerk on his brother's retirement in 1806, a position which he held until his death in 1827. It was George Townend who had been responsible for recommending John Graves to accept William Gray as an articled clerk when the latter was seeking a transfer of his articles.

Walker, William (1830-1897)

William Walker was a York solicitor of some prominence in the latter part of the 19th century. Articled to the firm of Leeman & Clark, he was admitted as an attorney and solicitor in 1848 and began practising on his own account in 1852 or 1853, becaming a member of the Society on 15 March 1853 and its President in 1880 and again in 1886, its centenary year – a rare distinction. A significant part of his practice was acting on behalf of the Roman Catholic Church, firstly on behalf of the Diocese of Beverley (comprising the whole of Yorkshire) and then after 1878 when the two separate dioceses of Leeds and Middlesbrough were created, for both. Indeed, he had been heavily involved in the division which had not been without controversy. The actual division proposed by Bishop Cornthwaite and Rome had been strongly opposed by some of the Yorkshire Catholic gentry who had their own ideas as to what would constitute two new viable dioceses. The leader of this opposition was the Hon Charles Langdale (son of Charles Stourton, the 17th Baron – he had taken his mother's maiden name to comply with the terms of a will) – a formidable opponent, well-connected, Jesuit educated at Stonyhurst and described by Archbishop Manning, as having been for 50 years the foremost man among the Catholic laity in England. It seems that Walker's advice was sought by both sides in the argument although he remained loyal to Bishop Cornthwaite, having sought to dissuade Langdale from proceeding with his objections and declining to add his own name to the latter's petition. Considerable diplomacy must have been required.

But Walker's career was not all church politics. Justice of the Peace, a Liberal city councillor for the Guildhall ward and alderman (Lord Mayor in 1871), Vice-President of the Yorkshire Philosophical Society, Fellow of the Geological Society of London, a Manager of the York Savings Bank, a Director of the York Gas Company, Vice-Chairman of York Charity Trustees, he was for thirty years a Governor of the York Asylum and for eleven its Chairman. A portrait of William Walker by Richard Jack currently hangs in Bootham Park Hospital as it is now known. A York Asylum committee minute for May 1896 records a resolution that in recognition of the services given by the Chairman, Mr William Walker, his portrait in oils be painted and hung within the asylum as "a lasting record of the great improvements which have been effected under his direction and supervision ." It is perhaps noteworthy that four former Presidents of the Society in the 19th and 20th centuries, William Walker, Jonathan Gray (*q.v.*) and Alfred Procter (*q.v.*) and Henry John Ware (President 1868) all took such a close and personal interest in mental health, Ware having been the Asylum's Treasurer for some years.

In 1866 Walker married Emma Weatherley, daughter of master builder Joseph Weatherley (who himself served as Sheriff and Lord Mayor of the City) responsible for both St George's and St Wilfrid's churches in York. After his marriage he lived at 14 Bootham Terrace, within easy reach of both his office at 11 Lendal and York Asylum.

Ware, Innes Noel OBE, TD (1896- 1994)

Colonel Innes Ware was the last member of the Society to have fought in the First World War – a dire memory that stayed with him all his life. A full colonel in the Territorial Army (Royal Artillery) he was awarded the military OBE for his distinguished services. Living as he did to the good age of 97, he was also the last member of the Society to have qualified as a solicitor before the Law of Property Act, the Settled Land Act and the Administration of Estates Act 1925. He thus had to have an intimate working knowledge of the 'old' land law, complete with such legal delicacies as the law of dower, co-parceners, copyhold, and tenancies by the entireties, to say nothing of the barring of entails and the rule in Shelley's case.[18] True, later practitioners who were involved in any way with property had to have a reasonable knowledge of the previous law if only for the purpose of investigating titles but it cannot have had quite the same immediacy as it did for Colonel Ware's generation.

Innes Ware was the son of Francis Ware and the grandson of Henry John Ware and had joined his father's firm (originally founded by John Brook (*q.v.*) then known as Francis Ware & Lucas, as an articled clerk in January 1914. One of his first tasks was to prepare the abstract of title of the White House in Clifton York only to find that the earlier title had been dealt with by his grandfather Henry John Ware in 1845. He also learnt during his articles how to do up parcels of deeds and seal them with hot sealing wax without setting them alight or spilling the wax. His mentor, the head clerk also taught him the rudiments of professional etiquette: for example the importance of removing his hat when entering a bank – a habit he maintained to the end of his days. As a result of his articles being interrupted by war service, he was not able to qualify until 1921 and join the Society until 1922 but in the course of a long career in the law he was able to achieve much. Two years after the death of his partner Clarence Lucas in 1931 his firm amalgamated with the next door firm of Holtby & Procter of whom Alfred Procter (*q.v.*) was by then the sole surviving partner. Unfortunately, Procter died just ten weeks after the amalgamation, facing Ware with the problem of buying his next door premises as well as his goodwill, just at the time when his wife had presented him with twins and the consequent necessity of buying a house for his own family.

Nothing daunted, in the course of his career and in addition to his close involvement with the TA, he was at various times President of the Society, Clerk to the Ouse and Derwent Justices, HM Coroner for the City of York, the Escrick Division of the East Riding and the Southern Division of the North Riding, as well as being the Archbishop of York's legal secretary and Registrar of the Diocese and Province of York and treasurer, prior to the establishment of the NHS, of Bootham Park Hospital (Asylum). Like Alfred Procter his former neighbour and short-term partner, Ware was a prominent mason. He was also a devout member of the Church of England and appointed a lay canon by Archbishop Coggan – a rare honour. His leisure activities included cooking (a fairly rare skill for a professional man of his generation) and fishing.

NOTES

1. *The Battle of Stamford Bridge* by Robert Elliott – W Blanchard & Son 1810. Another local volunteer corps at this period was the Stockton Forest Riflemen. It is known that the two units, the Ouse & Derwent Volunteers and the Stockton Forest Riflemen held a church parade together at Scarborough on 9 June 1805. Doubtless the precise rôle of these and other estimable volunteer units in deterring Napoleon's *Grande Armée* of over half a million men from an attempted an invasion of Britain will continue to be the subject of debate among military historians for years to come. Certainly one such regiment of volunteers raised in Hertfordshire seems to have had a certain flavour of *Dad's Army* about it: its surviving casualty lists indicate that its members were apt to forget whether they were exercising with blank or ball ammunition – see *Confessions of an Un-Common Attorney* by Reginald L Hine – JM Dent and Sons Ltd 1945.

2. One of Henry John Ware's brothers, the Reverend William Ware, was responsible for raising a company of the Stockton regiment, known as The Reverend John Ware's Stockton-on-Forest Rifle Volunteers in 1850.

3. Much of this entry is based on William Cobb's book.

4. Since Saturdays were generally working days for most members of the operative classes at the time, it is hardly surprising that the establishment's *clientèle* was for the most part made up of members of the more middle and upper class of Leeds inhabitant.

5. See Chapter Three *Costs Conveyancers & Low Practitioners*.

6. *Were British Railway Companies Well Managed in the Early Twentieth Century?* Working Paper 10/07 by Nicholas Crafts, Timothy Leunig and Abay Mulatu – Department of Economic History, London School of Economics.

7. Originally the system we now know as 'the London Underground' was not a 'system' at all. The first providers of underground railway services perceived themselves as operating a 'shuttle' between two fixed points of high density traffic. Little or no thought was given to the provision of 'junctions'. Sir George Gibb arrived on the London scene when notions of a "system" were beginning to take root. He was a man of many parts; he was later to turn his attention to roads.

8. *Papers and Diaries of a York Family* by Mrs Edwin Gray – London, The Sheldon Press 1927 and *A History of Grays of York 1695-1988* by William Cobb – William Sessions Ltd 1989 *passim*.

9. The Association's objects at the time of its foundation were "To give a stronger impulse and a more systematic direction to scientific inquiry; to promote the intercourse of those who cultivate Science in different parts of the British Empire with one another and with foreign philosophers; to obtain more general attention for the objects of Science and the removal of any disadvantages of a public kind that may impede its progress." It is reasonable to assume that, as a solicitor and founder member (along with his partner Anthony Thorpe) Gray would have had a hand in drafting these objects. Among the Association's contributions to the modern world were the first establishment of the words "scientist" and "dinosaur" and, in 1894, the first demonstration of wireless transmission.

10. As Note 5 above.

11. This and other items of silver can be viewed on the Society's web-site www.yorkshirelawsociety.org.uk/home/history

12. A detailed account of the whole saga can be found in *John Marsden's Will – The Hornby Castle Dispute 1780-1840* by Emmeline Garnett – Hambledon Continuum 1998.

13. Emily Brontë was to incorporate aspects of the story (without the sex) in *Wuthering Heights*.

14. In defence of George Leeman is Dr Alf Peacock (*George Leeman and York Politics: 1833-1880*); *George Hudson* Vols 1 & 2 AJ Peacock 1988-9; *George Hudson and the Historians* York History 1974; *George Hudson of York* Dalesman Books 1971. In defence of George Hudson is Robert Beaumont *The Railway King*. Review 2002 – a somewhat revisionist view but nevertheless supported by former Hon Secretary and President of the Society, the late Dr John Shannon.

15. Still less was any connection made with FJ Munby's great uncle, Arthur J Munby (1828-1910), a member of the Bar now well-known to social historians for his voluminous diaries and his obsessive interest in 'working women' – not prostitutes particularly, but working-class women in menial or labouring employment, one of whom, Hannah Cullwick he married in secret. He was the subject of a Channel 4 television programme in 2008, the last in a series *Upstairs Downstairs Love*. Clearly there was a psycho-sexual element in his obsession of which, in a pre-Freudian age, he was probably unaware but there is no evidence of moral impropriety.

16. *Poverty and Prostitution – A Study of Victorian Prostitutes in York* by Frances Finnegan – Cambridge University Press 1979.

17. The Letters of Charlotte Brontë Vol 1 1820-1847 Margaret Smith ed. OUP 1995.

18. Even today there are a handful of US states and some Canadian provinces where lawyers have to concern themselves with such recondite matters. Rather closer to home, the Republic of Ireland only managed to rid itself of this particular incubus with its Land and Conveyancing Law Reform Act 2009 where poor Shelley is finally given a decent burial by S.67(3) together with much else besides extending as far back as the 13 Edw. 1 c.1 (De Donis Conditionalibus 1285) and 18 Edw. 1 c.1 (Quia Emptores 1290). The pace of law reform can be vey slow at times.

Appendix C

THE SOCIETY'S LIBRARY

A note on some of the historic legal works formerly in the Society's library largely based on a report prepared in 1933 by George Laycock Brown. As to the library generally and its early history, see Chapter 5.

1. *De Legibus et Consuetudinibus Angliæ* by **Henry de Bracton**

Henry de Bracton (or Bretton/Bratton) (c.1210-1268) was a judge and ecclesiastic, almost an exact contemporary and friend of Henry III (1207-1272). A Devon man, he received the degree of Doctor of Laws at Oxford University. In 1245 he was appointed to the bench – it was usual in those days for judges to be ecclesiastics as literacy was not the norm. His famous treatise bears evident traces of the influence of the civil (and indeed canon) law with which clerical judges would of necessity been familiar, using them to supplement the inadequacies of the common law. In 1264 he became Archdeacon of Barnstable but resigned the same year on taking up the post of Chancellor of the Diocese of Exeter.

Part of Bracton's genius was to articulate the great constitutional principle that the sovereign himself was not above the law in his famous dictum *ipse autem rex non debet esse sub homine sed sub deo et sub lege, quia lex facit regem* – The king himself should not be subject to any man but to God and the law because it is the law which maketh the king. This principle was to endure more or less intact until the advent of Tudor despotism under Henry VIII in the 16th century and re-established, albeit in somewhat different form, with the Glorious Revolution of 1688. Bracton's great work, written between 1250 and 1260 was never completed, probably due to the Barons' Wars, but Maitland[1] nevertheless described it as the "crown and flower of mediæval jurisprudence". It was during the reign of

Henry III that despite continuing civil strife, the common law was taking shape and being transmitted throughout the kingdom by the itinerant justices established in the time of Henry II. These judges regarded their function as applying the king's law, or common law (ie as administered in the king's court or *curia regis* in London) throughout the realm but were quite prepared to apply the principles of Roman law with which they were familiar to fill any perceived gaps. Indeed, they went further: as ecclesiastics they were prepared to introduce notions of conscionableness, based on Christian principles, with which they were equally familiar, where circumstances seemed to require it – a foreshadowing of the concepts of equity familiar to later generations of English lawyers. It is often not fully appreciated in these secular days the extent to which our law is imbued with fundamental Christian ethics and traditions. For example, one of the laws promulgated by King Alfred in 901:[2] "Thæt ge willen, thæt othre men eow ne don, ne doth ge thæt othrum monnum" or, as we would say nowadays, "That which you do not wish other men to do to you, do not do it to them". (St Luke expressed exactly the same sentiment in its positive form "And as ye would that men should do to you, do ye also to them likewise").[3] Even the very buildings where law was dispensed often contain clues of their Christian basis. Westminster Hall itself, where the king's courts sat from mediæval times until the 19th century, has a remarkable hammer-beam roof whose thirteen massive oak trusses were probably intended to represent Christ and the twelve apostles. It has seen many famous trials, including those of Thomas More and Charles I and although it no longer operates as a courthouse, the Lord Chancellor's "Judges' Breakfast" is now usually held there after the service in Westminster Abbey to mark the opening of the legal year in October. That HM judges require a breakfast on this occasion is an echo of the original Catholic practice of fasting from midnight before taking communion.

Inevitably, these "newfangled" interventions by Bracton and his judicial contemporaries in the latter half of the 13th century came under exactly the same criticisms as those faced by Lord Denning and his judicial supporters in the 20th century: inventing new legal remedies, said the critics, was no business of the judges who, while professing to declare existing law, were in fact creating new law. One does indeed come to recognise the truth of the dictum attributed to Mark Twain that history does not often repeat itself but it usually rhymes.

Another aspect of *De Legibus* which was to have profound consequences for the future was Bracton's reference to previous cases, especially where they had been heard by judges whom he held in high regard. He cited about five hundred, as opposed to one by Glanvil,[4] eleven by Littleton[5] and none by Britton.[6] This was to become the foundation of what we now call "case law"; it was not so much a concept of *stare decisis* or binding authority, but simply the notion that if anything similar had happened before it should be judged in a similar manner. Certainly it encouraged the lawyers of the 13th and 14th centuries to discuss the cases to which reference was made in this treatise and this would lead in turn to the *Year Books*[7] and the development of a doctrine of precedent as we know it today.

The treatise was first printed in 1569 by Richard Tottell in folio but the Society's copy dating from the same year was in large quarto, the text in mediæval Latin, the type in black letter or "Old English" script which made reading difficult, although a variant known as "Gothic" or "Schwabacher" continued in regular use in Germany until well into the 20th century.

2. *The Year Books*

The term is applied to a series of reports of cases tried between 1292 and 1534 and have been described by Sir Frederick Pollock as "our glory, for no other country has anything like them." They were written in Norman French and once again the type was black letter. They were first printed by Richard Pynson, stated by Brown to have been an assistant of Caxton but this is now thought to have been unlikely. Pynson (1448-1529) was one of the earliest printers of books in England but was in fact a Norman and did not become naturalised until 1513. His is believed to have learned his trade from Guillaume le Talleur in Rouen. This, however, did not prevent him from having a seminal influence on the modern English language by standardising much of its spelling and it was he too who introduced Roman type into English printing. As "King's Printer" to both Henry VII and Henry VIII he had been responsible for over 500 books all told, although his most famous one of all, the *Morton Missal* of 1500, was a religious one rather than legal or official. The publisher of the Society's set, from 1553, was Richard Tottell – see *supra* – but nevertheless interesting according to Brown.

Volume 1 which commenced the series was the splendid folio edition (1678) of Sir John Maynard,[8] being the unique edition of the reports of Richard de Winchedon covering substantially the whole reign of Edward II to Trinity term 1326, together with excerpts from the Exchequer records of Edward I.

The other ten volumes covered the reigns of Edward III, Henry IV, Henry V, Henry VI, Edward IV, Edward V, Richard III, Henry VII and part of the reign of Henry VIII. These volumes were published by various printers in the reigns of Elizabeth, James I and Charles I, four of them by Richard Tottell.

All the above, with the exception of the first volume appear to have belonged to Eustatius Strickland of York whose name and the date "1822" were written in each volume. Strickland was appointed City Counsel in 1832 at a salary of £5 p.a and held office until the coming into force of the Municipal Corporations Act 1835.

3. *Seldon's Fleta*

A quarto volume printed in 1647. The text was in Latin and the type Roman. Fleta is the name of a Latin textbook of English law based on Bracton.[9] It is said to have been written in the Fleet Prison in 1290 or thereabouts – hence its name. It was printed with a long dissertation in Latin by John Selden[10] in 1647 and again in 1685. The Society's copy was that of 1647.

4. *Britton*

This book was normally known as "Britton" and was supposed to have been written by Johannes Bretoun (or John le Breton or Britton) who was appointed Bishop of Hereford in 1268 and was also a justice of the King's Bench. The Society's copy was the second edition of this work by Edmund Wingate published in 1640. The text is Norman French and the type black letter. The title page was described by Brown as being "worthy of attention" showing an altar with texts in Hebrew and Latin.

5. *Fortescue de Laudibus Legum Angliæ*

This book was written for the instruction of Edward, Prince of Wales, son of Henry VI, when in exile. It was first printed in 1537 and many times thereafter. The author Sir John Fortescue (1394-1476) was Chief Justice of the King's Bench. The Society's copy was a small volume printed in 1616 with references and notes by Selden but without his name. The text was in Latin with an English translation, the type black letter. For a 15th century judge Fortescue is remarkable for having articulated in an English legal context the fundamental concept of modern constitutional monarchy and democratic government. In a treatise known under its later (printed) title *On the Governance of England* he wrote:

> There bith two kyndes off kyndoms, of wich that on is a lordship called in laten *dominium regale*, and that other is callid *dominium politicum et regale*. And thai diversen in that the first kynge may rule his peple bi such lawes as he maketh hym self. And therefore he may sett uppon thaim tayles and other imposicions such as he wol hym self, withowt thair assent. The secounde kynge may not rule his peple by other lawes than such as thai assenten unto. And therefore he may sett upon thaim non imposicions withowte thair owne assent. This diversitie is wel taught bi Seynt Thomas [Aquinas] in his boke wich he wrote *ad regem Cipri de Regimine Principum*.

6. *Hengham*

Appended to this book were the Magna and Parva of Hengham "written in barbarous Latin" according to Brown. They are stated to be practical manuals. Ralph de Hengham (or Hingham) (?-1311) was Archdeacon of Worcester who was appointed a justice of the King's Bench and transferred by Edward I to the Common Pleas, later becoming Chief Justice of the King's Bench, but he fell into disgrace and was fined and imprisoned. He was the reputed author of the original *Registrum Omnium Brevium*, a register of writs which was first printed in 1531 and was said by Coke[11] to be the most ancient book of the law. These two manuals of Hengham were edited by Selden in 1616.

7. *Fitzherbert's Abridgment*

La Grande Abridgment, first printed in 1514, is a digest of the Year Books. The original work was reprinted by Tottell in 1565. It was reprinted again in 1573, 1577 and 1786. The Society's copy was Tottell's first folio edition of 1565. Sir Anthony Fitzherbert (1470-1538) was a member of Gray's Inn and a justice of the Common Pleas. He had a profound knowledge of English law combined with a strong logical faculty and a remarkable power of lucid exposition.

8. *Brooke's Abridgment*

This *Grande Abridgment* is merely a revision of *Fitzherbert's Abridgment* but is considered superior in lucidity to that of Fitzherbert and contains valuable original matter. Brooke was first printed in 1568. The Society's copy was Richard Tottell's quarto edition of 1568. The text is in Norman French and the type black letter. Sir Robert Brooke (or Broke) (?-1558) was of the Middle Temple and at various times Common Serjeant, Recorder of London (representing the City in various parliaments) and Chief Justice of the Common Pleas.

9. *A Briefe Treatise of Testaments and Willes by Henry Swinburne*

The Society's edition of Swinburne was the fourth edition of 1677. The first edition appeared in 1590. Henry Swinburne (c.1560-1623) was an ecclesiastical lawyer (wills and probate were under the jurisdiction of the ecclesiastical courts until the Court of Probate Act 1857). He was the author of two books, the other being *A Treatise of Spousals or Matrimonial Contracts* – both being the first written in England on their respective subjects. Brown's comment on this book has a slightly odd ring to the modern legal ear. He says of it (writing in 1933) "Owing to changes in the Law the Treatise on Wills is to a great extent out of date". However, he does go on to add "but it still contains some useful statements of law and shrewd observations. It is a marvel of condensation and is the work of a profound lawyer."

Swinburne was a York man, born and educated there before going up to Oxford where he matriculated in December 1576 and subsequently took his BCL. In due course he returned to York where he practised as a proctor. He eventually became Commissary of the Exchequer and judge of the Consistory Court at York. He died in 1623 and was buried in York Minster, where his monument in the North Choir Aisle can still be seen, as can his house in High Petergate, subsequently occupied by Sir Thomas Herbert, the faithful attendant of Charles I. This property is now the Rectory of St Wilfrid's Catholic Church in Duncombe Place.

10. *Coke's Institutes* (4 vols)

The Society's first volume was printed by the Society of Stationers in 1670. Sir Edward Coke (pronounced "Cook")[12] (1552-1634) was a member of the Inner Temple, Attorney-General and subsequently Speaker of the House of Commons, Chief Justice of the Common Pleas and later of the King's Bench under James I. His relationship with James and later with Charles I was at times stormy. Life on the Bench under Stuart monarchs could be trying: he was suspended twice from his judicial functions and even spent time in the Tower. Yet at times he was clearly on reasonably intimate terms with King James I. It is said that on one occasion the king called on him at home when he was ill, asking to be advised on a point of law. "Is it a point of common law or statute law?" asked Coke. "Why, what difference does it make?" replied the king. "Well Your Majesty" said Coke, "if it's a point of common law, I can answer it from my bed, but if it's a point of statute law I shall have to get out of bed and look at the statute" – a precautionary approach which all lawyers should perhaps bear in mind.

Coke is probably best known for authorship of *The First Part of the Institutes of the Laws of England* which is generally referred to simply as *Coke upon Littleton*. It appeared in 1628 and was intended as a first book for law students. The second part appeared in 1642 and the third and unfinished fourth part in 1644. The first part is a reprint of *Littleton's Treatise on Tenures* with a translation and a commentary. The text is Norman French with the English translation in Roman character with voluminous notes by Coke in English in black letter type.

Volume 2, printed by Flesher & Young in 1642 contained the text of various statutes from Magna Carta to the time of James I with a full exposition.

Volume 3, dated 1644, was a treatise on the criminal law and deals with High Treason and other Pleas of the Crown.

Volume 4, dated 1644, is a treatise on the jurisdiction of the courts of law.

11. Coke upon Littleton Thomas Coventry

This edition was in English, based on Coke's first Institute published in three volumes in 1818 by Thomas Coventry, being a systematic arrangement on the plan of Sir Matthew Hale's analysis with the annotations of Mr Hargrave, Hale LCJ and Nottingham LC. The Society also had a later edition of 1830.

12. *De juri Belli ac Pacis Grotius*

"On the Law of War and Peace" the famous treatise by the Dutch author Hugh Grotius (Huig de Groot) (1583-1645) who is generally regarded as the father of international law. His interest in the subject was first aroused when in 1604 he became involved (as a young lawyer) in litigation concerning the seizure by Dutch merchants of a Portuguese vessel and her cargo in the Straits of Singapore.

13. *Rolle's Abridgment 1668*

This work was in two fine folios. It was an abridgment of cases of the common law by Henry Rolle (1589-1656) of the Inner Temple, Serjeant-at-Law and subsequently a King's Bench judge. The text is in Norman French and the type black letter. There is an introductory preface addressed to students of the common law and a memoir of Rolle by Sir Matthew Hale – see item 14 *post*.

14. *Hale's Pleas of the Crown (Historia Placitorum Coronæ)*

This *Editio Princeps* of 1736 was produced by Sollum Emlyn. Sir Matthew Hale (1609-1678) of Magdalen College Oxford and Lincoln's Inn was a profound lawyer. A Justice of the Common Pleas under Cromwell, he then became a Baron of the Exchequer at the Restoration and eventually Chief Justice of the King's Bench. *Bishop Burnet's Lives*[13] contains a sympathetic account, including Hale's *Things Necessary to be Continually had in Remembrance* – a fascinating aide-memoire for conduct on the bench which might usefully be issued by the Ministry of Justice to newly appointed judges even today. Among the things listed are the following:

> VI That I suffer not myself to be prepossessed with any judgment at all, till the whole business, and both parties be heard.
>
> XI That popular, or court applause, or distaste, have no influence into anything I do, in point of distribution of justice.
>
> XVII To charge my servants:
> 1. Not to interpose in any business whatsoever;
> 2. Not to take more than their known fees;
> 3. Not to give any undue precedence to causes;
> 4. Not to recommend counsel.

15. *William Sheppard*

The Society's library had three works by William Sheppard (?-1675):

1. *A Graunde Abridgment* of the common and statute law in four parts printed in London in 1675 by Flesher and others. The text was partly in English and the type partly Roman and partly black letter.
2. *A Practical Counsellor in the Law* – "touching Fines, Common recoveries, judgments and the execution thereof, Statutes, recognizances and Bargain and Sale, collected out of the many great volumes of the Law" (1671). The text is in English and the type black letter.
3. *The Touchstone of Common Assurances* being a treatise on conveyancing with notes in two volumes (1826 edition). Sheppard was a Serjeant-at-Law and a puisne judge of the County Palatine. He was a prolific author and has been called "Cromwell's Law Reformer".

Among his other works was *The Faithful Councellor: or the Marrow of the Law in English* first published in 1651, with a second edition in 1653. The earthy flavour of the law of this period can be judged from the section on defamation:

> It [ie an action] lieth for saying of a brewer, He sells naughty beer, M.15. Car.B.R. or my mare doth piss as good Beer as he doth Brew, ... To say

of a woman Inn-keeper, She is a pocky unwholsom woman, doth wear a skarfe to hide blanches in her neck, it is a pocky household may happily bear an action. M.9.Jac. Ludman's Case

But the author goes on "Out of which it is to be observed, that where ever this Action lieth for a slander to a man in his Trade, there must be a special Averment of some loss by the words spoken ... But others upon better reason and authority hold the contrary. But all agree it to be best to alledge some special damage if the case will bear it". We can see here a renewed attempt to establish principle out of a mass of case law that had accumulated over the centuries from the days of the Year Books and subsequently. The modern law on this particular point is now settled: slander, or oral as opposed to written defamation, is not actionable unless the claimant can prove actual pecuniary loss unless the slander relates to the claimant's trade or profession – brewer, inn-keeper, hedge fund manager or whatever.

16. *Comyns Digest*

This was Hammond's edition of 1822. Sir John Comyns (c. 1667-1740) was educated at Queen's College Cambridge and member of Lincoln's Inn. A Serjeant-at-Law, he became successively Baron of the Exchequer, a judge of the Common Pleas and lastly Lord Chief Baron of the Exchequer. In addition to his Digest, he also produced reports of cases in the King's Bench, Common Pleas and Exchequer. Both were originally written in Law French, but subsequently translated by his nephew J Comyns of the Inner Temple.

Lesser Works

Brown's report also contains what he described as "a few brief notes concerning some old works of less importance than the preceding volumes". As the Scots lawyers still say in their pleadings, *causa brevitatis*, I shall simply give the barest details for the record.

Liber Regis – Thesaurus Rerum Ecclesiasticum by John Bacon (1786) Printed version of original MS transcribed by a monk of Westminster on the eve of the Reformation.

Collectanea Juridica (2 vols) by Francis Hargrave, a member of Lincoln's Inn who made his reputation acting for the black slave James Somerset in *Somerset v Stewart* – see Chapter 1 p. 18.

A Digest of the Laws of England respecting Real Property (7 vols – one missing) by William Cruise (?-1824)

Reportorium Canonicum or Abridgment of the Ecclesiastical Laws of England by John Godolphin (1617-1678) 3rd ed. 1687

A Treatise on Equity (2 vols) by John de Grenier Fonblanque (1760-1837)

Pleas of the Crown (2 vols) by William Hawkins (1673-1746)

Crown Law by Sir Michael Foster (1689-1763) Clarendon Press Oxford 1762. A revision of the proceedings of Oyer and Terminer and gaol delivery of the rebels in the year 1746 in the County of Surrey and other crown cases.

Forest Law by John Manwood (?-1616) printed by the Society of Stationers 1615.

An Analytical Digested Index to the Courts of King's Bench, Common Pleas and Exchequer (2 vols) by Anthony Hammond (1758-1838)

Essay on the Law of Bailments by Sir William Jones FRS (1746-1794) 4th ed with notes by William Theobald – the first edition appeared in 1781 and was often reprinted both here and in the United States. As well as being an eminent lawyer (Middle Temple, a Commissioner of Bankrupts in England, a judge of the High Court of Calcutta) Sir William Jones was one of our greatest oriental scholars, being the founder in 1784 of the Asiatick Society (subsequently the Asiatic Society of Bengal and now known simply as the Asiatic Society), one of the first English scholars to master Sanskrit and the author of the first grammar in English on the Persian language. It was said of him that no subject was too abstruse for him to investigate.

Principles of Equity by Lord Kames (1696-1782) Edinburgh 1760.

Johnson's Collection of Ecclesiastical Laws (2 vols) by the Reverend John Johnson MA Vicar of Cranbrook (1720).

Two Books both by John Lilly (1) A general abridgment of the law with the rules of the courts down to 1719 (1735) and (2) A collection of Modern Entries or Select Pleadings in the Courts of King's Bench, Common Pleas and Exchequer (1771). The last volume bears the signature "Robert Sinclair" who was Recorder of York and a friend of Lord Eldon.

Preston on Abstracts (3 vols) by Richard Preston.

Termes de la Ley attributed to William Rastall (?-1565) a nephew of St Thomas More whose works he edited. He was a judge of the Queen's Bench under Mary but (as a Catholic) was obliged to exile himself on the accession of Edward VI in Flanders where he eventually died at Louvain. This edition was published in 1721 and is an explanation of difficult and obscure terms in the common and statute law of the realm. The *Termes* are in Law French and the explanations in English. Note: Brown has his name as "Rastal" and describes him as having been a judge of the Common Pleas but the *Dictionary of National Biography* has it as Rastell and a judge of the King's Bench (as does Fuller's *Worthies of England*).

Viner's Abridgment by Charles Viner (1678-1756) "which today is valueless as an authority" according to Brown. He reminds us, however, that the residue of Viner's estate (about £12,000) went to found the Vinerian Law Professorship at Oxford, the oldest professorship in the law of any common law jurisdiction. The first professor being Sir William Blackstone. The current holder of the chair is Professor Hugh Collins who succeeded Andrew Ashworth QC.

Doctor and Student or Dialogues between a Doctor of Divinity and a Student of the Laws of England by Christopher St Germain or German (c.1460-1540) This book was first published in Latin. This is the 6th edition 1671.

Selected Precedents of Deeds and Instruments concerning the most considerable estates in England by Sir Orlando Bridgeman (c.1606-1674) Lord Chief Justice of the Common Pleas from 1660 to 1668 who presided over the trial of the regicides. This 5th edition published in 1735 was the finest and was presented to the Society by FJ Munby who was for many years its highly esteemed Hon Secretary and twice President.

Deposited Works

In addition to the above there are a number of works deposited at various times with (a) the Borthwick Institute of Historical Research (part of the University of York) (b) with the main library of the University and (c) with the Minster Library. The details are as follows:

Borthwick Institute

The Clergyman's Law by W Watson (London 1747)

Ordo Judiciorum (2 vols) by Thomas Oughton (London 1728)

Ecclesiastical Canons (2 vols) by J Johnson (London 1720)

Law Dictionary by Dr Cowel (London 1708)

Law Dictionary (2 vols) by TE Tomlins (London 1708)

The Civil Law (2 vols) by Jean Domat (tr by William Strahan) (London 1722)

Lex Maneriorum by William Nelson (London 1726)

De Officio Hominis et Civis by Samuel von Puffendorf (London 1748)

A Treaty on the Law of Wills and Codicils (2 vols) by William Roberts (London 1837)

An Essay towards a General History of Feudal Property in Great Britain by John Dalrymple (London 1748)

Collections relating to the Dioceses of York and Ripon by George Lawton (1840). George Lawton was never a member of the Society but he seems to have been a member of the York Law Library, established in 1828 as a separate organisation albeit with a large common membership until it effectively amalgamated with the Society in 1883 – see Chapter 5, p. 87.

A Collection of Decrees by the Court of Exchequer in Tithe-Causes by Hutton Wood (London 1798) [NB only 2 out of 4 vols]

Treatise on the Law of Tithes by William Eagle (London 1830) [NB only 1 of 2 vols]

Royal Commission Reports

Ecclesiastical Courts (England and Wales) (1832)

Admiralty Courts 1833

Further Report of the Commissioners for Inquiring concerning Charities (1828)

Ditto 1829

Return of Registered Charities and Charitable Trusts (1829)

Index to the London Gazette 1830-1883 (1885)

Law Lists

1780, 1785, 1789, 1790, 1800 (2 copies), 1803, 1805, 1806, 1808, 1809, 1811, 1814-1823, 1825-1834, 1837-1842, 1844-1855, 1857-1864, 1868-1882

University Library

Special Collections Room

Les Reports des Cases & Matters en Ley by Sir John Davies (Flesher 1674) and Index 1677

Les Commentaries ou Reports by Edmund Plowden[14] (London Rawlins 1684)

Mirfield Room

On the Statute of Sewers 23 Hen. VIII c.5 A lecture originally given by "the Famous and Learned Robert Callis Esq upon the Statute of Sewers 23 Hen.c.5 as it was delivered by him at Gray's Inn in August 1622" by William John Broderip (London 1824)

The Law Magazine or Quarterly Review of Jurisprudence Vols 1-28, 30, 34, 36-42, 44-55 (1828-1856)

The Law Quarterly Review Vols 1-10 (1885-1894)

The Law Times Vols 1-2, 5-6, 9-31, 37-38, 41-46, 68-74, 78-93, 95, 105,

107-110, 112-118, 121-125, 127, 130-131, 134-214 (1843-1952)

Rare Books Store

77 volumes of Private and Local Acts of Parliament (uncatalogued – originally deposited with the Borthwick Institute in 1958)

The Monthly Law Magazine and Political Review Vols 4-5 (1839)

York Minster Library

A General Abridgment of Law and Equity by Charles Viner Vols 1-4, 6, 8-10. 12-15, 19-23 (London 1746-1756)

An Abridgment of the Modern Determinations in the Courts of Law and Equity being a supplement to Viner's Abridgment 6 vols (London 1799-1806)

THE SOCIETY'S ARCHIVES

The Society does still have in its possession as part of its archives one item donated to the library by a York member, JE Jones in 1895. It consists of two rather frail sheets, together forming instructions to counsel and counsel's opinion dated 13 May 1762. The instructions, measuring approximately 7½ in by 3½ in contain but seven lines of text in in small neat handwriting, the reverse being endorsed "ord original 10th May copy Bond sent *Johnston v Exors of Thompson*." Counsel's opinion is likewise on a single sheet measuring approximately 15 ins by 10 ins the opinion itself headed "Furnivals Inn 13th May 1762" and covers just half of one side of the sheet, the other half containing the address "To Mr Draper of York". Both the instructing solicitor and counsel seem to have been somewhat less prolix than they have become of late, the opinion consisting of just 24 lines. The signature of counsel is difficult to read but is probably that of Stafford Squire who is known to have been a member of Furnival's Inn, one of the Inns of Chancery in Holborn attached to Lincoln's Inn. Founded in the 14th century, it counted Thomas More as one of its Readers and Charles Dickens as one of its tenants. It survived until 1817 but was wound up when Lincoln's Inn declined to renew its lease.

And finally …

Some of the deposits had been made in 1977 at a time when the future of the Society's library (which had been in premises on the ground floor at 17, Stonegate since 1944 when it had become a tenant of York Medical Society) was under active discussion. It was decided, reasonably enough, that no decision on the future of the library could be taken without canvassing the views of members. The result was a decision to improve the facilities rather than to close the library but this involved *inter alia* making more space available. There was an understandable reluctance to dispose of the more important historical works – hence the deposits with the Borthwick Institute, the University and the Minster Library. The problem, however, would not go away.

In 1986, the Society's bicentenary year as it happened, the problem of the library was to come once again to the fore. This time it was perceived as essentially financial: the books included a comprehensive collection of law reports. The older volumes were leather-bound and were beginning to need urgent attention if they were to be preserved for future use – as it was assumed they would have to be. The age of Bill Gates, Richard Susskind and information technology had not quite dawned. At the same time the output of new law was expanding exponentially which in turn required more shelf-space. The committee and members decided reluctantly that the only solution was for the Society to cease to act as a custodian of antiquities by selling the remaining historic works on the basis that their proceeds of sale would then be available for the necessary re-binding. The library sub-committee was asked to arrange the disposal which realised a total of £7,648.

It was assumed at the time that this would assist in preserving a working library which would be of practical use to members but it was not to be. The IT revolution coincided more of less with the arrival in York of a branch of the College of Law at Bishopthorpe. The problem of maintaining a modern law library with the resources available to a local law society in York was becoming impossible. The committee accordingly decided in 1989 to open negotiations with the College to take over the contents of the Society's Library in return for user rights by the Society's members. These negotiations were speedily and happily concluded. Sadly this arrangement was not to be so beneficial to the Society following the College of Law's decision to relocate in Leeds.

Brown, whose original report was clearly a labour of love, ended it by thanking the Society's librarian, Robert Booker, and, addressing the committee, saying "I have done what I could in bringing before your notice some of theses old treatises. If I am instrumental in saving the more important of them from destruction, [many of them according to his report were in poor repair] my labours will not have been fruitless."

A Note on the Language of the Law

Those unfamiliar with English legal history may be puzzled by references in the above account to Latin and even more so to Norman or Law French. As with so many English peculiarities, the explanation is historical. Following the Norman conquest in 1066 the use of Norman French was imposed in all legal proceedings until the time of Edward III. Then in 1362 came the Statute of Pleading, 36 Edw. 3 c.15, which required all cases to be pleaded, shown, defended, answered, debated and judged in English but to be entered and enrolled in Latin by substituting "la lange du paiis" for "la lange francais qest trop desconue" [sic]. The government of the day had no doubt made a correct assessment about French being "trop desconue". Perhaps it was all the fault of the schools. The Cornishman John Travisa (translator, scholar and Fellow of Exeter and subsequently Queen's College Oxford) writing in the late 14th century observed:

> John Cornwaile, a maister of grammar, chaunged the lore in gramer scole and construccion of Frensche into Englische ... so that now, the yere of our Lorde a thowsand thre hundred and foure score and fyve, in alle the gramere scoles of Englond children leveth Frensche and construe and lerneth in Englische, and haveth thereby advauntage in oon side and disadvauntage in another side; here advauntage is that they lerneth the gramere in lesse tyme than children were i-woned to doo; disadvauntage in that now children of gramere scole conneth no more Frensche than can their left heele, and that is harm for hem and [if] they shulde passe the see and travaille in straunge lands and in many other places ...

Changes in the national curriculum notwithstanding, for lawyers, the Norman or Law French, being the more familiar language as applied to the law, they continued to use it in making notes of cases which were then recorded and in due course published in the Year Books. This practice continued uninterrupted until Cromwell's time, gradually degenerating into a barbarous and arbitrary mixture of Latin, French and English. A good example can be seen from the 16th century case of *Hawes v Davye* in 1565.[15]

> En dett sur obligation le defendant ad oyer del obligation enter verbatim, et del condition in hec verba scilicet

> If the obligour doe pay or cause to be payd unto the obligee the whole somme of lx li. of lawful money of England in one whole payment to be made the xxiiij day of September next ensuing the date hereof, without any further delay, in the house of the obligee in Plymouth in Devon, or at any time on this side the xxiiij day of September, if the abovenamed barke fortune to take any purchace or price worth in value 500 li. that then etc [the bond should be void]

> Defendens dicit quod actio non, quia dicit quod post confectionem scripti praedicti et ante diem impetrationis brevis originalis dicti querentis le barke vocat "le dragon" non cepit aliquam perquisitionem sive captionem Anglica vocata a prize ad valenciam 500li, et hoc etc., sur que le plaintife demurre en ley. Et lopinion del court fuit pur le plaintife, eo que il appert bien que la somme de 60li.fuit due devant lobligation fait, et lextremitie del payment deferre tanque le 24 jour de Septembre contingent ou happe il est payable pluistot.

It requires a certain imagination as well as some familiarity with Latin, English and French to work out that the case involved disputed liability under a bond of £60 due on or before 24 September but if the barque *Dragon* succeeded in making any "purchace" or prize worth over £500, then the bond would be void. The plaintiff sued on the bond but the defendant averred that he had no claim since after the bond had been granted and before the writ was issued the *Dragon* did not make any purchace or prize to the value of £500, to which the plaintiff demurred in law. The court found for the plaintiff on the grounds that the sum of £60 was due before the bond was issued and the liability of the payment was deferred until 24 September and upon the contingency or chance event it was payable sooner. And no, I am not altogether sure that I understand the legal point of it all either. A few years earlier, in the course of the West Country Prayer Book Rebellion of 1549, Archbishop Cranmer, contending with the disaffected Devonians anxious *inter alia* to preserve the Latin mass, had observed "I have heard suitors murmur at the bar because their attornies pleaded their causes in the French tongue which they understood not". On the basis of the report of *Hawes v Davye* the murmuring suitors may have had a point. Almost incredibly a very attenuated form of this barbarous language was still being taught to law students in my day, supposedly for the purpose of note taking. An imaginary example was provided. I cannot remember its source but it has stuck in my mind ever since and went something like this:

> *Semble* [it would seem] the phrase "carcase or portion of a carcase" for the purposes of this statute does not include a sausage – see Tripe LJ *obiter* in *Sage v Onions* (CA) *sed contra* [but on the contrary] in *Ham v Eggs* (Div Ct); *aliter* [otherwise] if the sausage meat is not yet minced.

Such is the force of habit of things learnt at an impressionable age that I still find myself actually using the old "shorthand" subsequently when making rough notes for my own use. And even today there are counsel who will endorse their brief with the result bearing the heading "Coram Scroggs J" (Before Scroggs J) to identify the judge before whom their case was tried.

At the end of the 17th century John Northleigh (1657-1705) physician and barrister writing about France, had commented:

> The French tongue spreads it self mightily, and becomes almost universal ... 'Tis not above an hundred years ago, their public Acts ran all in Latin, but since for the promoting their own language, they have abolish'd that, tho' always used among Civil Lawyers, and have ordered all Process to run in French, whereas we retain yet, tho' their old Enemies, our old French Law their Norman introduc'd.

Although Northleigh does not give the date, the requirement in France for "all Process to run in French" was earlier than he suggests and dates back to the Ordinance of Villers-Cotterêts 1539 in the reign of François I. As part of a major act of law reform, Articles 110 and 111 prescribed the use of French in all judicial acts, notarised contracts and official legislation. Part of the actual text is perhaps worth quoting:

Nous voulons et ordonnons qu'ilz soient faitcz et escrits si clerement qu'il n'y ait ne puisse avoir aucune ambiguité ou incertitude, ni lieu à en demander interpretation. Et pour ce que telles choses sont souventesfoys advenues sur l'intelligence des motz latins contenuz esdictz aretz, Nous voulons que doresenavant tous arretz ensembles toutes autres procedeures, soyent de nous cours souveraines ou autres subalternes et inferieures soyent de registres, enquestes contractz, commissions, sentences, testamens et autres quelzconques actes et exploictz de justice ou qui en dependent, soient proncez, enrigistrez et delivrez aux parties en langage maternels francoys et non autrement.

[We desire and order that they [ie edicts laws etc] be written so clearly that there can be no ambiguity or uncertainty, nor occasion for any request for interpretation. And forasmuch as the meaning of edicts and laws often depend on Latin words, We desire that henceforth all laws and legal documentation, whether issuing from our royal courts or other subordinate and inferior jurisdictions, or from registers, inquiries, contracts, commissions, sentences, wills or other formal or legal documents, or documents which depend on them, be expressed, registered and delivered to the respective parties in their French mother tongue and not otherwise.]

As far as England and "Law French" was concerned, Cromwell did make a similar but less all-embracing attempt to put a stop to our own egregious linguistic nonsense, albeit over a century later. In 1650 he persuaded the Rump Parliament to pass an act forbidding its use in printed books – the same parliament incidentally that made fornication and adultery capital offences – but parliament at the Restoration took a dim view of the previous régime[16] and former practices were promptly resumed, but at least as regards matters linguistic, not for very long. By 1704 all law reports were in English and by 1711 John Woodward, a doctor and antiquarian was observing "our Booksellers care not to meddle with any Thing that is in Latin". Eventually parliament made a second attempt to deal with the problem. By the Proceedings in Courts of Justice Act 1730 4 Geo. 2 c.26 English was at least established as the basic language of our courts. The preamble recited

> Whereas many and great mischiefs do frequently happen to subjects of this kingdom from the proceedings in courts of justice being in an

unknown language, those who are summoned and impleaded having no knowledge or understanding of what is alleged for or against them in the pleadings of their lawyers and attorneys … be it enacted by the king's most excellent Majesty … that from and after the twenty-fifth day of March one thousand seven hundred and thirty-three all writs process and returns etc etc … shall be in the English tongue and language only and not in Latin or French …

The penalty for non-compliance was a fine of £50. The act also proscribed the use of "court hand" – a form of hand-writing peculiar to lawyers and virtually unintelligible to anyone else – but as far as law in French was concerned did not extend for some reason to the giving of royal assent to acts of parliament. Even today this is done by the Clerk of Parliaments on behalf of the Queen with the words "La Reine le veult" (The Queen wishes it) except in the case of money bills where a more polite formula is employed: "La Reine remercie ses bons sujets, accepte leur benevolence, et ainsi le veult" (The Queen thanks her good subjects, accepts their benevolence and so wishes it). Non-assent is equally polite: "La Reine s'avisera" (The Queen will consider the matter) but that has not had to be used since Queen Anne refused her assent to the Militia Bill in 1707.

The 1730 Act, however, was too sweeping; it was quickly realised that exceptions would have to be made for "ordinary" legal terminology and a further act was hurriedly passed two years later (6 Geo. 2 c.14) to avoid bankrupting the legal profession with £50 fines – which is how words such as *affidavit* and *ex parte* survived until finally suppressed by Lord Woolf in the form of the Civil Procedure Rules 1998 where the main target was Latin.[17] At least any breach of the latter will not incur the penalty imposed by Stanton J in the 15th century. Committing an unfortunate attorney for some procedural irregularity, the irate judge called him a *malvois ribaud* (wicked rascal) and added that he would remain in gaol *tanqe vous seez bien chastiez* (until you are well chastised).[18]

But if Latin has disappeared for the purposes of post-lupine litigation, leaving us with just the bleached prose of the Civil Procedure Rules, we still have a rich legacy of Law French. Even its grammar has left its trace: the senior law officer for example is the "Attorney-General", not the "General-Attorney" and we still talk about a "court martial", 'fee simple" and "treasure trove". Consider the following "Law French" terms, some of which are recognisably French but many others carry an effective English disguise: appeal, arrest, arson, attainder, attorney, autrefois acquit/convict, bail, bailiff, cestui que trust, counsel, covenant, culprit[19] cy-près, debtor, demand, defendant, disclaimer, escheat, escrow, estoppel, felony, feme couvert[20], feme sole, force majeure, heir, indictment, joinder, laches, larceny, lessee, merger, mortgage[21], mortmain, negligence, nuisance, ouster, perjury, profit à prendre, proof, recovery, remainder, suit, tender, tort, trespass and trove (as in treasure trove). The English disguise can be very effective: ever since the 15th century English lawyers had given up any pretence of pronouncing Law French in a way which would be intelligible to a Frenchman. For example, the pronunciation of *autrefois aquit* was (and is) "oaterfoyz ak-wit" and "laches" becomes "laycheese" with no nonsense about "ohtrerfwa a-key" or "lashay".

It was in this glorious tradition that the Attorney-General (Sir Reginald Manningham-Buller) in 1960 appearing on behalf of HM Secretary of State for Home Affairs in an extradition case, when confronted with some genuine French, had no hesitation whatever in pronouncing such terms as *arrêt de contumace* and *jugement par défaut* exactly as if they they were standard English terminology: "arr-ett de con-tew-mace and judgment par de-foat.[22] I rather think that nowadays in the age of eurolaw, some attempt at least might be made to pronounce them in the French manner.

NOTES

1. Frederick William Maitland (1850-1906). He is still regarded as a pre-eminent authority on the history of English law. A member of Lincoln's Inn, he became Reader in English Law and later Downing Professor of the Laws of England at Cambridge. His *Bracton's Note-Book*, originally published in 1887, was re-issued by Cambridge University Press in 2010.

2. Quoted in *Gesetze Anglesachsen* by F Liebermann 1.44 (1903).

3. Luke 6 v.31 (AV)

4. Ranulf de Glanvil (Glanvill or Glanville) (?-1190) Chief Justiciar of England.

5. Sir Thomas Littleton (1422-1481) judge and legal author. His treaty on Tenures with Coke's comments on it, generally known as *Coke upon Littleton* long remained the principal authority on the English law of real property.

6. See item 4.

7. See item 2.

8. Sir John Maynard (1602-1690) of Exeter College, Oxford and the Middle Temple. He became a judge and a Lord Commissioner of the Great Seal. As doyen of the Bar he was presented to the Prince of Orange on his arrival in London. William congratulated him on having outlived so many rivals. Maynard replied "And I had like to have outlived the Law itself had not your Highness come over."

9. See item 1.

10. John Selden (1584-1654) was a member of the Inner Temple and a notable scholar, jurist, politician, antiquary and orientalist. His friends included Henry Rolle, afterwards Lord Chief Justice, Sir Edward Littleton, afterwards Lord Keeper, Edward Herbert, afterwards Attorney-General, and Ben Johnson. The Selden Society, established by FW Maitland in 1887 and the only learned society and publisher devoted entirely to English legal history, is named in his honour.

11. See item 10 on p. 399.

12. According to John Aubrey's *Brief Lives* the pronunciation of his name gave his second wife a chance to pun at his expense on their wedding night: "He married his second wife, Elizabeth, the relict of Sir William Hatton, who was with child when he married her: laying his hand on her belly (when he came to bed) and finding a child stir, 'What,' said he, 'flesh in the pot?' 'Yes,' quoth she, 'or else I would not have married a cook.'"

13. *Lives, Characters and an Address to Posterity* by Gilbert Burnet DD. Bishop Burnet's account of Sir Matthew Hale was largely based on his funeral sermon.

14. Edmund Plowden (1518-1585). His career was notable in that he also qualified as a surgeon and physician as well as a lawyer. At one time he was Member of Parliament for Wallingford, and subsequently Reading and Wooton Bassett before eventually resigning as he disapproved of its proceedings. Most astonishing of all, perhaps, was the fact that he was a devout Catholic at a time when this was not the most obvious way to advance one's career in the public service. At one point Queen Elizabeth wanted to appoint him Lord Chancellor – but only on condition of renouncing his faith. This he refused to do, making a spirited (and very brave) defence of it, coupled with a denunciation of religious persecution. Nevertheless, the

Queen continued to employ him as a lawyer. Not content with risking his career and possibly his life by such defiance, he was also vigorous in defending his co-religionists prosecuted under the draconian penal laws against Catholics. In one such case he managed to elicit in court the fact that the prosecution was the result of a fraudulent attempt at entrapment. His client was accused of attending "mass" but it had been conducted by a collusive layman masquerading as a "priest'. When this emerged Plowden is reported to have exclaimed "The case is altered – no priest, no mass!" thereby securing an acquittal. Thereafter and for many years the phrase "'The case is altered'" quoth Plowden" became a staple comment at the Bar whenever new evidence emerged at trial. Even more surprisingly *The Case is Altered* has also survived as the name of a pub in various parts of the country, at Eastcote (Pinner, Greater London), Five Ways (Warwickshire) and Bentley (Suffolk) and there may be others. Less surprisingly he is also commemorated in the Plowden Buildings in the Middle Temple overlooking Middle Temple Gardens.

15. A case from the Court of Common Pleas from *Reports of the Lost Notebooks of Sir James Dyer* (1510-1582) (Selden Society Vols 109-110– JH Baker ed. 1994). Dyer was the principal judge in the case of *Hales v Pettit* (1565) Plowden 253 heard a year before – a case on the law of inheritance on which the plot of Shakespeares's *Hamlet* is largely based.

16. The Legal Proceedings During Commonwealth Act 1660 (12 Chas. 2 c.12) (only repealed by the Statute Law Revision Act 1948) ended by lamenting that it was "necessary to mention Diverse Acts and Ordinances" of the previous rulers and declare their titles "most Rebellious, Wicked, Trayterous and Abominable Usurpations Detested by this present Parliament as opposite as possible in the Highest Degree to His Sacred Majestyes most Just and Undoubted Right to whom and to his Heires and Lawful Successors the Imperiall Crownes belonged."

17. Attempts to control the use of language are rarely attended with total success. It is said that on the day when the 1998 Civil Procedure Rules came into force a certain judge decided to remind the lawyers in his court of the importance of complying with the new rules, including the avoidance of Latin. Having delivered his lecture to a somewhat restless audience, the judge continued "I shall now hear the *ex parte* applications ... "

18. Quoted by RE Megarry in *Miscellany-at-Law* – Stevens & Sons Ltd London 1955.

19. In modern usage "culprit" denotes established guilt but this was not its original meaning. It is in fact an extreme contraction of Latin and Law French and simply means "the accused': culpabilis (Latin) and "prist" (Law French) – the full phrase being "prist del averer" "(I am) ready to prove'.

20. By about 1500 English lawyers had given up trying to cope with the French rules dealing with the gender of nouns so we find such egregious errors as "une home" and "un feme'. As a result of changing social patterns even the French themselves are now having trouble: for example a French woman lawyer is addressed as Maître Chantal Dupont and not as "Maîtresse", which is perhaps just as well, and a woman colonel is Madame le colonel (Madame la colonel being reserved for the (male) colonel's wife. Confusing.

21. A good example of how Law French is often unintelligible to a modern French speaker. The modern French word for "mortgage" is *hypothèque*.

22. *R v Governor of Brixton Prison ex parte Caborn-Waterfield* [1960] 2 QB 498. It would seem that French was altogether rather outside the Attorney-General's comfort zone. Sitting in the House of Lords as Viscount Dilhorne in *James Buchanan & Co Ltd v Babcock Forwarding and Shipping (UK) Ltd* [1978] AC 141 he was obliged to consider (but not decide) firstly whether it was permissible for an English judge to refer to the French text of an international contention as an aid to construing the English version scheduled to an Act of Parliament; and secondly, if it was, whether the judge was entitled to use his own knowledge of French in reaching any conclusion: "I confess to some doubt as to the propriety of doing so when Parliament has only scheduled the English text to the Act and declared that is to have the force of law. If it is proper to do so, I do not regard my knowledge of the nuances of the French language to be a reliable guide to the meaning to be given to these English words."

Appendix D

LAND REGISTRATION

In recent years house prices have become a modish (not to say irritating) topic of conversation amongst those who own or aspire to own their own homes or who have adult children still living with them because they lack the means to do so. However, land law as such is generally acknowledged to be a conversational turn-off for all non-lawyers and indeed many who practise more immediately appealing aspects of the law. Although its efficient working is of great practical importance to many of us, its reform has long proved to be astonishingly intractable. One reason for this is inherent – the very large number of vested interests. And of all aspects of land law, one of the most contentious over a very long period was any proposal for compulsory registration. For the benefit of those with a direct interest in our land law it is right that the background to this contention should be accessible.

The idea of land registration in the form with which we are now familiar began its long gestation with the appointment in 1854 of the Royal Commission on Registration of Title. It marked a significant departure from earlier notions, which focused on the registration of deeds rather than of title as such. There may well be quite a few conveyancers outside London and the home counties under the impression that land registration first made its appearance with the coming into force of the Land Registration Act 1925. Rather more perhaps will attribute its origin to the Land Transfer Act 1897. In fact our present system of land registration (as opposed to the registration of deeds) goes back much earlier – to the Land Registry Act 1862, introduced under the guiding hand of the Lord Chancellor, Lord Westbury.[1] Its genesis, however, went back even further than that to the Royal Commission on Registration of Title which had been set up in 1854[2] which reported in 1857. The 1862

Act (which was voluntary) was not a success and only a few hundred titles were ever registered under its provisions. The very first (Title No 1) was issued to Sir Fitzroy Kelly MP in that year and was in respect of his properties Crane Hall and The Chantry near Ipswich. By 2012 the number of registered titles exceeded 23 million.

In 1868 a yet further Royal Commission was appointed to investigate and report on the reasons for its failure. It duly reported in 1870 and one impediment to which it drew attention was the expense entailed by the strictness of the rules relating to the investigation of title before any registration could be completed. The standard applied was the proof which the Court of Chancery would require before obliging a reluctant purchaser to accept a proffered title. The reality of course was that any *voluntary* system of first registration imposes an 'up-front' expense on a purchaser which will not be off-set by any obvious advantage until he comes to sell.

The report of the proceedings[3] of the Leeds Law Society for 1893 clearly shows their members' concerns over the introduction by the Lord Chancellor of the Land Transfer Bill "to simplify titles and to facilitate the transfer of land in England". The report states that though the Bill was less ambitious and extensive in scope than Lord Halsbury's Bill which was withdrawn in 1889:

> ... it retains however in principle, although in a somewhat modified shape, the most objectionable feature of its predecessor – compulsory registration... the views of your Committee on the subject of land transfer have been frequently expressed. They approve and will assist any efforts which may be made to improve the law of real property and to facilitate conveyancing practice but they consider that these objects will be best attained by allowing those concerned to be free agents in the matter. It is impossible moreover not to see in the Bill a first and not inconsiderable step of establishing a government office for transacting the conveyancing business of the country. Officials of the Land Registry have made it plain in more ways than one that they intend to enter into active competition with solicitors for conveyancing business. It is certainly anomalous that professional men who are rightly taxed for the privilege of exercising their calling and subjected by the State to so many restrictions in exchange for the privileges assumed to be conferred on them should be subject to competition on the part of the body from whom their rights and privileges are derived.

This distrust of the compulsory registration of land was widespread amongst the profession almost until modern times. Looking back it is not always easy to understand the intense hostility which the subject engendered in so many. It was visceral rather than being based on any detailed analysis, owing much to general political instinct. Members of a proudly independent profession had no natural affinity with *any* involvement of the state in what they regarded as private property-based transactions between citizens. Members of the Yorkshire Law Society evidently felt much the same as their brethren in Leeds as their reports at this period amply demonstrate.

Annual Report 1895

LAND TRANSFER BILL

This measure has peculiar interest for Lawyers in Yorkshire, inasmuch as it is evidently intended, when passed, that some portion of the country shall be chosen as a corpus vile upon which to experiment, and it is more than probable that Yorkshire, being already a Register County, and containing within its limits every class of real property, will prove to be the victim for the Vivisectionist's knife. Your Committee have, therefore, been particularly active in its opposition to this Bill, and in pursuance of the resolution passed at the July meeting of the Society, and believing that the apparent favour in which this measure is held by both parties in Parliament is due in no small degree to ignorance, your Committee, in September of last year, convened a Conference of the Law Societies of Yorkshire and the M.P.'s of Yorkshire to discuss this matter. All the 14 Law Societies in the County were represented and Mr. B.G. Lake and Mr. E.W. Williamson, of London, and Mr. Wing, of Nottingham, kindly attended, and the former gave an admirable address on the subject. Your then President, also in a statesmanlike speech, pointed out the impossibility of accomplishing by statutory provision an alteration in the nature of the property dealt with by the Conveyancing Law. Unfortunately, none of our Legislators were able to be present except the York City Members, Mr J.G. Butcher and Mr. (now Sir) Frank Lockwood, Q.C., together with Col. Gunter. Many of those who wrote expressing their regret at being unable to be present, manifested in their replies the urgent necessity for education on the subject, one honourable Legislator going so far as to say he should support the Bill as the only cure for the present Agricultural distress, a statement the humour of which the Members of this Society will no doubt appreciate. The following Resolution was passed, and copies were sent to the Lord Chancellor and to the then heads of both political parties: –

That this Conference of Representatives of Law Societies in the County of York, assembled on the invitation of the Yorkshire Law Society, while ready to further the simplifications of dealing in land, to minimise the consequent expense, and to perfect, so far as possible, the existing system of registration of Titles, strongly deprecates any attempt to make the system established by the Act of 1875 compulsory, and urges the necessity of a thorough enquiry, by Royal Commission or otherwise as to the desirability, of any compulsion in the matter.

The Bill has already been re-introduced, and your Committee, in conjunction with the Law Societies having the best interests of clients at heart, will offer its most determined opposition, and do its utmost to secure its rejection.

Annual Report 1896

LAND TRANSFER BILL

By the pressure brought to bear upon the late Government through the Society, the Government were induced to appoint a Committee to inquire into the matter, and the evidence taken by that Committee will, it is hoped, have removed many of the misapprehensions which appear to surround the subject in the minds of the uninitiated.

The advent to power of a strong Government, which is pledged equally with their predecessors to deal with the question, has now rendered it absolutely imperative for the profession to abandon the policy of simple opposition to the measure. No opposition which Solicitors could bring to bear will avail aught against the overwhelming majority of the Government backed up by a great part of the present opposition. It has, therefore, become a choice of two evils: either to have the Land Transfer scheme, already proposed, passed in its naked ugliness; or to formulate some scheme, which, while it would remove some of the anomalies now existing in regard to the law of Land Transfer, would avoid some of the worse evils which Solicitors believe would be entailed upon their clients by registration of title pure and simple, and which would mitigate the disastrous effects which they fear such a scheme would bring upon the future members of the legal profession. The Incorporated Law Society,

U.K.. with the concurrence of the Associated Provincial Law Societies, have chosen the latter alternative as being the lesser evil, and a Bill is being promoted in the present Session of Parliament with a view to carrying out this decision.

Annual Report 1898

LAND TRANSFER

This troublesome measure, like the poor, seems to be always with us, and during the past year it has given more than the usual amount of worry, trouble and expense. It will be remembered by all who have closely followed the course of this measure that in former years the Incorporated Law Society (U.K.) has, with the assistance of the Associated Provincial Law Societies, presented a determined and successful opposition to the passing of it, and provided a valuable body of evidence which was given before the Select Committee in 1895. The Land Transfer Bill of 1897, however, was framed on slightly different lines, and the Incorporated Law Society (U.K.) thought it better to endeavour to secure certain amendments rather than to oppose the measure with an absolute negative. It is admitted that the amendments proposed and secured were of much importance, but it is believed by your Committee that the ultimate action of the Incorporated Law Society (U.K.) was somewhat affected by the belief that the first experiment of the Act would be in Yorkshire. The amendments in question were as follows:–

1. – The original area to be limited to one County.

2. – Such area not to be extended for three years.

3. – No compulsory registration, either original or subsequent, to be introduced in a County if the County Council decide at a Meeting specially called for the purpose, and at which two-thirds of the whole number of members shall be present, against such introduction.

4. – The right of conducting business for reward, either directly or indirectly, to be limited to Solicitors.

The Yorkshire Solicitors, however, felt that their opposition must be continued and intensified, and the various Societies in Yorkshire determined to continue to oppose, and your Committee promised to provide a proportion of the necessary funds for the purpose. A small Executive Committee, consisting of Mr. Arthur Middleton, President of the Leeds Law Society, Mr H. Bramley, President of the Sheffield Law Society, Mr. Ianson, President of the Wakefield Law Society, and Mr. J.T. Atkinson, your President, was formed for the purpose of taking active steps to make this opposition effective. They were indefatigable in their efforts, as may be seen from the following quotation from Mr. A.J. Balfour's speech:

> "everybody would be glad to recognise the action taken by the great County of York in dealing with this question of Land Transfer. He thought they owed the County a debt of gratitude for the energy and public spirit it had shown and for the steps it had taken to advance to a rational solution to this question,"

The result of the opposition was that before the Bill was passed it was secured that the first district to be named by the Order in Council was the County of London. Thus the danger, so far as Yorkshire was immediately concerned, seemed to be averted.

The danger, however, is not over yet, as the County Council of London have the opportunity within three months of the receipt of the draft Order of resolving in the specified manner that, in their opinion, compulsory Registration of Title would not be desirable in their County. It now appears that the Incorporated Law Society (U.K.), and the other bodies who have been approached for advice on the subject by the County Council, are naturally doing their best to prevent the application of the Act being made in their County, and it is quite within the bounds of probability that they will be successful in their efforts. Should this be the case, it is almost certain that one of the Ridings of Yorkshire will be gazetted, and the fight will begin anew, but upon a new battle field. The County Council of the Riding chosen must then be "educated" upon the question, and must be shown that their fetish is an idle, mischievous delusion, and not a panacea for all the ills from which real property suffers as some of them at present ignorantly imagine. Should the London County Council be convinced of this fact however, that, in itself, will be the strongest argument which can be brought to bear upon any other County Council similarly threatened.

The small Executive Committee now consisting of A. Middleton, E. Bramley, H. Plews and J.T. Atkinson, your President, has been re-appointed.

Your Committee will continue to watch the progress of events, and to use every legitimate means in their power for protecting not only the interests of the profession, but more particularly the interests of the clients, which, in the long run, represents in the fullest sense the interests of the profession at large and individually.

The Act does considerably more than affect the question of registration. It establishes a real representative upon whom all real estate now devolves as if it were a chattel real. The importance of this alteration of the law will be apparent to all conveyancers. The Act came into operation on the 1st instant and provisional rules have already been issued.

Annual Report 1899

LAND TRANSFER

Your Committee think it well to impress upon the Members the fact that the present position of Land Transfer, or otherwise the registration of title to land, by no means constitutes a settlement of the subject, because the putting into operation of the recent Act within certain prescribed limits is no more than a trial. It will probable be necessary that a vigilant watch should be kept and examination made of the progress of the work in the first trial, and for this purpose that complete and accurate records should be kept both as to its working and results. And with this object the Incorporated Law Society (U.K.) has issued to all its Members forms on which it requests that particulars may be furnished to the Society of all transactions involving registration, showing the expense, time involved, and other necessary data, to enable it to tabulate results and present a body of evidence, when any further extension of the Act is proposed.

The *Times* of 19th December, 1898, contained a leading article upon the Act and the working of it, which is deserving of study. The following is the concluding paragraph:–

> The first effect of this Act will probably be that Solicitors much engaged in conveyancing will drive a brisk business, and unless the Measure is materially modified there will always remain outside its purview many dealings of a kind not the least profitable to the

Solicitor. Where transactions are large, purchasers will continue to pay handsomely for integrity and professional skill. But there is no hiding from oneself the possibility that as years go on and as qualified titles are perfected the Registry will cut down seriously the profits of many Solicitors. Not merely will titles become in course of time simplified, but there will be a tendency, especially as to small properties, for the officials to do inside the office, gratis or for fees, not a little that is now, and for some time will be, done outside it. Ten or fifteen years hence the Conveyancer's province cannot be the land flowing with milk and honey, which it is supposed to have been in the past. As to one aspect of the change it is impossible to withhold sympathy from the class affected. Solicitors see the Legislature always anxious to supersede them, jealous of their privileges, and vigilant in curtailing or regulating their remuneration. Yet it is not only Solicitors who are concerned with dealings in land; Surveyors, Auctioneers, Land Agents, and Members of other professions all derive their income, more or less, from such transactions. And while the professional charges of these classes steadily grow, while the Auctioneer or Land Agent is practically permitted to exact as much as he can induce those who employ him to pay for his services, the Solicitor is treated as if he were an extortioner. As the full effect of the Land Transfer Act is experienced the resentment which Solicitors feel at this treatment will grow stronger, and will not be altogether unreasonable.

The latter part of this article is particularly worthy of attention, for while a Land Agent would have no hesitation in charging and no difficulty in obtaining 2½ per cent. upon the sale of an estate for £100,000, say £2,500, a Solicitor who had carried out the same transaction would be limited by Statute to a charge of £290.

The Land Transfer Act 1897 having finally passed into law, parliament became too preoccupied in the immediate aftermath with even more pressing (and overtly 'political') concerns inspired by radical liberalism, constitutional issues relating to the House of Lords and Ireland, the South African war and the increasing external threat from Germany to devote much attention to property law reform. This was not to become an issue again until the 1920s when parliament once more embarked on a programme which was to lead to the radical real property legislation headed by the Law of Property Act 1925. In July 1920, however, it was the specific question of land registration was once again before the House of Lords. In a debate on 20th July Lord Buckmaster, a former Lord Chancellor in the wartime coalition government pointed out that "Nearly every Chancellor for the last century has been trying to reform the law" [of real property]. He went on to observe:

> The land laws of this country are an interesting subject for investigation by the antiquarian or the historian, but to plain-dealing men who are accustomed to plain language, they are nothing but an affront, for they have so complicated the whole history of real estate with phrases that have no meaning to the mind of anybody excepting those who have been trained in learning what they mean, that the layman is completely baffled and bewildered by the technicality of the phraseology in which, without a system of registration and without this Bill, it becomes essential that you should clothe your transactions relating to the transfer of real estate.

In the event this concerted opposition to the whole concept of land registration resulted in a parliamentary hiatus. There was no further attempt to extend the 1897 experiment until 1925 and thereafter progress was very slow and continued to be beset by professional opposition. It was only during the last quarter of the 20th century that any real momentum was achieved. Looking back, it seems remarkable that there was ever an assumption at the time when the Land Registration Act 1925 passed into law that universal registration would be achieved by 1955! The Land Registry had set itself a target of having all land in England and Wales 'on the register' by 2012 – exactly 150 years since the passing of the Land Registry Act 1862. Predictably this target has still not been met. The length of time taken to complete this exercise has certainly been due in part to professional opposition, particularly during the earlier period but solicitors were by no means alone in their suspicions. Even today many owners are not entirely happy at the loss of privacy. If their title is registered, anyone with a computer and the nominal land registry fee to spare can ascertain the names of the proprietors, precise details of the property, whether it is subject to any mortgage or charge and in many cases the price last paid. There are other problems: in practice, as opposed to Land Registry theory, there *are* cases where it is necessary to consult the original deeds which are often not available, either because they have been discarded as redundant or because their possession was not passed on. The wariness of our Victorian predecessors was not entirely groundless.

Today, of course, we have entered into the uncharted waters of electronic conveyancing. Despite some initial fears, particularly with regard to the discharge of mortgages, no new problems seem to have emerged but perhaps it is still early days. And of course the possibility of human error and technical disaster will never disappear.

NOTES

1. Richard Bethell, first Baron Westbury (1800-1873). Called to the Bar in the Middle Temple in 1823, he became a Liberal MP in 1851 and subsequently served in government as Vice-Chancellor of the Duchy of Lancaster, Solicitor-General, Attorney-General and eventually becoming Lord Chancellor in 1861.

2. An earlier Royal Commission had been appointed in 1850 but it had only considered registration of deeds akin to the older system of registration first enacted for the West Riding of Yorkshire (1704), the East Riding (1707), Middlesex (1708) and the North Riding (1735). It was recognised that this was not the way forward. In Yorkshire at least these older systems survived until their final abolition in 1970. A few older members of the Society, doubtless no longer in practice, will have been familiar with their operation although curiously the system never applied to the City of York which was not in any Riding.

3. Reported in the President's Column of *Leeds & Yorkshire Lawyer* Issue 77 (December 2008).

SOURCES & SELECT BIBLIOGRAPHY

A. *Primary Sources (Yorkshire Law Society)*

Minute Book 1786-1839

Minutes of the Proceedings of the Yorkshire Law Society 1839-1871

Minute Book 1872-1982

Minutes of the Proceedings of the Committee for General Purposes 1815-1849

Committee Minute Book December 1908 to March 1924

Committee Minute Book May 1924 to April 1949

Committee Minute Book June 1950 to May 1963

Committee Minute Book July 1963 to September 1973

AGM Minute Book January 1974 to April 1999

First Report of the Committee for obtaining an augmentation of the allowance of costs *de Incremento*. 13 March 1815

Second Report of the Committee for obtaining an augmentation of the allowance of costs *de Incremento* And for General Purposes 8 July 1815

Deed of Assignment – The Yorkshire Law Society Library to The Yorkshire Law Society 20 August 1885

Library Catalogue 1886

Scrap-Book Centenary Celebrations 1886

Printed Annual or Biannual Reports 1871-2010*

President's file Bicentenary Celebrations 1986

* From 1895 onwards printed Committee Reports have been produced in booklet form and refer to Annual General Meetings. Four are missing *viz* 1904, 1906, 1939 and 1990. Publication was suspended between 1942 and 1946 inclusive due to the war.

B.   Published Sources

Abel, Richard L and Lewis, Philip SC *The Making of the English Legal Profession 1800-1988* Beard Books 1988

Allen, CK *Law and Orders* Stevens& Sons Ltd London 1945

Ballantine, Serjeant William *Some Experiences of a Barrister's Life* Richard Bentley & Son London 1882

Beaumont, Robert The Railway King – *A Biography of George Hudson* Headline Book Publishing 2002

Bingham, Tom *The Business of Judging– Selected Essays and Speeches* Oxford University Press 2000

Blanqui, Adolphe *Voyage d'un Jeune Français en Angleterre et en Écosse* Dondey-Dupré Père et Fils Paris 1824

Burke, Edmund *Reflections on the Revolution in France* 1791

Cannadine, David *Class in Britain* Yale University Press New Haven and London 1998

Cobb, William *A History of Grays of York 1695-1988* William Sessions Ltd 1989

Devlin, Patrick *The Criminal Prosecution in England* Yale University Press 1958

Gillett, Edward and MacMahon *A History of Hull* Oxford University Press for University of Hull Oxford 1980

Gray, Mrs Edwin (Almyra) *Papers and Diaries of a York Family* Sheldon 1927

Gunn, Simon and Bell, Rachel *Middle Classes – Their Rise and Sprawl* Cassell & Co 2002

Hague, William *William Pitt the Younger – A Biography* Harper Collins 2004

Hague, William *William Wilberforce The Life of the Great Anti-Slave Trade Campaigner* Harper Collins 2007

Hattersley, Roy *The Great Outsider David Lloyd George* Little Brown 2010

Kingsdown, Lord *Recollections of his Life at the Bar and in Parliament* (1868) Republished 2009 by Bibliobazaar

Kirk, Harry *Portrait of a Profession – A History of the Solicitors Profession 1100 to the Present Day* Oyez 1976

Kirk, Helen (ed) *"Ye dear Object of my Affections" – The Diary of William Lockwood of Easingwold 1778-1836. From 1st January 1796 to 30th September 1797* Forest of Galtres Society 1996

Levine, Joshua *The Secret History of the Blitz* Simon & Schuster UK Ltd. London 2015

Megarry, RE *Miscellany-at-Law* Stevens & Sons Ltd 1955

Megarry, RE *A Second Miscellany-at-Law* Stevens & Sons Ltd 1973

Murray, Venetia *Castle Howard – The Life and Times of a Stately Home* Viking 1994

Murray, Venetia *High Society – A Social History of the Regency Period 1788-1830* Viking 1998

Napley, David *Not Without Prejudice* George G. Harrap & Co 1982

Nield, Basil *Farewell to the Assizes* Garnstone Press London 1972

'O' [Theo Mathew] *Forensic Fables* Butterworths London 1961 (reprint)

Perrins, Bryn *Understanding Land Law* 3rd ed. Cavendish Publishing Ltd London & Sydney.

Polden, Patrick *A History of the County Court 1846-1971* Cambridge University Press 1999

Poser, Norman S *Lord Mansfield – Justice in the Age of Reason* McGill-Queen's University Press Montreal & Kingston, London, Ithaca 2013

Robson, Robert *The Attorney in Eighteenth Century England* Cambridge University Press 1959

Schumacher, EF *Small is Beautiful – A study of Economics as if People Mattered* Blond & Briggs London 1973

Slinn, Judy *A History of Freshfields* Vanessa Charles 1984

Solicitors' War Memorial Fund *Record of Service of Solicitors and Articled Clerks with His Majesty's Forces 1914-1919* Spottiswood, Ballantyne & Co Ltd London 1920

Stacpoole, Alberic & Others *The Noble City of York* Cerialis Press York 1972

Sykes, Christopher Simon *The Big House – The Story of a Country House and its Family* Harper Collins 2004

Topham, Alfred Frank *The New Law of Property* 1932.

Trevelyan, GM *English Social History* Longmans, Green and Co 1944

Turner, ES *May it Please Your Lordship* Michael Joseph 1971

Walvin, James *Black Ivory – Slavery in the British Empire* Blackwell 2nd ed. 2001

Wilson, AN *The Victorians* Hutchinson London 2002

Wilson, AN *After the Victorians – 1901-1953* Hutchinson London 2005

Yorkshire Weekly Herald *Reprint of The Yorkshire Law Society on the occasion of its 125th anniversary 1911*

TABLE OF STATUTES

Acts of Parliament Numbering and Citation Act 1962
    10 & 11 Eliz. 2 c.34   440
Administration of Estates Act 1925 15 & 16 Geo.5 c.23   259, 353
Administration of Justice Act 1970 c.31   109-110
Administration of Justice Act 1977 c.38   332
Administration of Justice (Miscellaneous Provisions) Act 1933
    23 & 24 Geo. 5 c.36   97, 121n.
An Acte for Poysonyng 1530 22 Hen. 8 c.9   122n.
Attorneys and Solicitors Act 1729 2 Geo. 2 c.23   40

Capital Punishment (Amendment) Act 1868 31 & 32 Vict. c.24   113, 119
Chancery Regulation Act 1862 25 & 26 Vict. c.42   105
Combinations of Workmen Act 1825 6 Geo 4 c.129   193
Common Law Procedure Act 1854 17 & 18 Vict. c.125   93
Commons Registration Act 1965 c.64   354n.
Companies Act 1862 25 & 26 Vict. c.89   319
Contagious Diseases Act 1864 27 & 28 Vict. c.85   121n.
Continuance of Acts etc Act 1749 23 Geo. 2 c. 26   439
Coroners and Justice Act 2009 c.25   303n.
Costs Act 1531 23 Hen.8 c.15   237
County Asylums Amendment Act 1815 55 Geo. 3 c.46   371
County Courts Act 1846 9 & 10 Vict. c.95   89, 92, 94, 332
County Courts Act 1866 29 & 30 Vict. c.14   93
Court of Probate Act 1857 20 & 21 Vict. c.77   107, 398
Courts Act 1971 c.23   33n. 270
Courts Act 2003 c.39   363
Courts and Legal Services Act 1990 c.41   348
Crime and Disorder Act 1998 c.37   20, 119, 297, 299
Crime (Sentences) Act 1997 c.42   297

Criminal Evidence Act 1898 61 & 62 Vict c.36   241
Criminal Justice Act 1967 c.80   297
Criminal Justice Act 1991 c.53   297, 299
Criminal Justice Act 2003 c.44   98, 298
Criminal Law Act 1723 (The Waltham Black Act) 9 Geo. 1 c.22   240
Criminal Law Act 1967 c.58   258

Deceased Brother's Widow's Marriage Act 1921
    11 & 12 Geo. 5 c.24   259
Deceased Wife's Sister's Marriage Act 1907 7 Edw. 7 c.47   259
Defence of the Realm Consolidation Act 1914 5 Geo 5 c.8   221
Deregulation Act 2015 c.20   312
Disarming the Highlands etc Act 1745 19 Geo 2 c.39   31n.
Divorce Reform Act 1969 c.55   260

Ecclesiastical Licenses Act 1533 21 Hen.8 c. 21   109
Education Act 1902 2 Edw. 7 c.42   147
Education Act 1944 7 & 8 Geo.6 c.31   263
Elementary Education Act 1870 33 & 34 Vict. c.75   157
Emergency Powers (Defence) Act 1939
    2 & 3 Geo. 6 c.62   219
Employers' Liability Act 1880 43 & 44 Vict. c.42   286
Evidence Act 1851 14 & 15 Vict. c.99   97

Firearms Act 1920 10 & 11 Geo. 5 c.43   154
Frame Breaking Act 1812 52 Geo. 3 c.130   338

Gambling Act 2005 c.19   33n.
Gaming Act 1710 9 Anne c.19   33n.
Gaming Act 1845 8 & 9 Vict c.109   33n.
Government of Ireland Act 1914 4 & 5 Geo. 5 c.90   145
Gun Licence Act 1870 33 & 34 Vict. c.57   154

Health and Safety at Work etc. Act 1974 c.37   312
High Court of Admiralty Act 1859 22 & 23 Vict. c.6   107
Highways Act 1662 14 Car.2 c.6   66
Housing of the Working Classes Act 1903 3 Edw. 7 c.39

434

Increase of Rent and Mortgage Interest
    (War Restrictions) Act 5 & 6 Geo. 5 c.97   191
Inheritance (Family Provision) Act 1938 1 & 2 Geo. 6 c.45   259
Interpretation Act 1889 52 & 53 Vict. c.63   440

Juries Act 1949 12 & 13 Geo. 6 c.27   33n.
Justices of the Peace Act 1361 34 Edw. 3 c.1   343
Justices of the Peace Act 1906 6 Edw. 7 c.16   155
Justices of the Peace (Quarter Sessions) Act 1388 12 Ric. 2 c.10   344

Labourers, Artificers etc Act 1349 25 Edw. 3 cc. 1-7   193
Land and Conveyancing Law Reform Act 2009 No 27 of 2009
    (Republic of Ireland)   391
Land Registration Act 1925 15 & 16 Geo. 5 c.21   419, 427, 353n.
Land Registry Act 1862 25 & 26 Vict. c.53   419, 427
Land Transfer Act 1897 60 & 61 Vict. c.65   419
Law of Property Act 1925 15 & 16 Geo. 5 c.20   353n., 427
Law Reform (Husband and Wife) Act 1962 10 & 11 Eliz. 2 c.48   259
Law Reform (Married Women and Tortfeasors) Act 1935 25 & 26
    Geo.5 c.30   259
Legal Aid and Advice Act 1949 12, 13 & 14 Geo. 6 c.51 99n., 238, 240
Legal Proceedings During Commonwealth Act 1660 12
    Chas. 2 c.12   416n.
Life Peerage Act 1958 6 & 7 Eliz 2 c.21   235
Local Stamp Act 1869 32&33 Vict. c.49   343
Locomotives on Highways Act 1896 59 & 60 Vict. c.36   160n.
London to Harwich Roads Act 1695 7 & 8 Will. 3 c. 9   67

Magna Carta 1215   313, 329, 399
Marriage Act 1753 (Lord Hardwicke's Act) 26 Geo 2 c. 33   46
Married Women (Maintenance in Case of Desertion) Act 1886 49 &
    50 Vict. c. 52   112
Married Women's Property Act 1870 33 & 34 Vict. c.93   111
Married Women's Property Act (1870)
    Amendment Act 1874 37 & 38 Vict. c.50   111
Married Women's Property Act 1882 45 & 46 Vict. c.75   111
Married Women's Property Act 1893 56 & 57 Vict. c.63   113

Married Women (Restraint upon Anticipation)
    Act 1949 12, 13 & 14 Geo. 6 c.78   113, 259
Matrimonial Causes Act 1857 20 & 21 Vict. c.85   258
Matrimonial Causes Act 1937 1 Edw. 8 & 1 Geo. 6 c.57   239, 259
Matrimonial Causes (Property and Maintenance) Act 1958 6 & 7 Eliz.
    2 c.35   259
Matrimonial Proceedings and Property Act 1970 c.45   259
Metropolitan Police Act 1829 10 Geo 4 c.44   346
Motor-Car Act 1903 3 Edw. 7 c.36   152
Municipal Corporations Act 1835 5 & 6 Will. 4 c. 76   396
Murder (Abolition of Death Penalty) Act 1965 c.71   119

National Service (No 2) Act1941 5 & 6 Geo. 6 c.4   213
Northern Ireland (Emergency Provisions) Act 1973 c.53   119
Norwich and Swaffham Road Act 1835 5 & 6 Will. 4 c. 40   67

Obscene Publications Act 1959 7 & 8 Eliz. 2 c.66   252
Outer Space Act 1986 c.38   312

Parliament Act 1911 1 & 2 Geo. 5 c. 13   145, 147
Peerage Act 1963 c.48   236
Piracy Act 1837 7 Will. 4 & 1 Vict. c.88   119
Pistols Act 1903 3 Edw. 7 c.18   153, 154
Poor Prisoners Defence Act 1903 3 Edw. 7 c.38   99n., 152, 160n. 241
Poor Prisoners' Defence Act 1930 20 & 21 Geo. 5 c.32   241
Prevention of Corruption Act 1906 6 Edw. 7 c.34   155
Prisoners' Counsel Act 1836 6 & 7 Will. 4 c.114   240
Proceedings in Courts of Justice Act 1730 4 Geo. 2 c.26   412
Prosecution of Offences Act 1985 c.23   353n.

Race Relations Act 1965 c.73   253
Race Relations Act 1976 c.74   253
Railways Clauses Consolidation Act 1845
    8 & 9 Vict. c.20 66
Redundancy Payments Act 1965 253
Repeal of Statutes as to Treasons, Felonies etc Act 1547 1
    Edw. 1 c.12   122n.

Representation of the People Act 1832 2 & 3 Will. 4 c.45   94, 137
Representation of the People Act 1867 30 & 31 Vict. c.103   137
Representation of the People Act 1884 48 & 49 Vict. c.3   137
Road Traffic Act 1930 20 & 21 Geo. 5 c.43   160n. 359
Roman Catholic Relief Act 1829 10 Geo. 4 c.7   140

Settled Land Act 1882 45 & 46 Vict. c.38   355
Settled Land Act 1925 15 & 16 Geo. 5 c.18   353, 355
Short Titles Act 1892 55 & 56 Vict. c.10   440
Short Titles Act 1896 59 & 60 Vict. c.14   440
Slave Trade Act 1807 47 Geo.3 c.36   20
Solicitors Act 1843 6 & 7 Vict. c.75   234
Solicitors Act 1906 6 Edw. 7 c.24   156
Solicitors Act 1932 22 & 23 Geo.5 c.37   197
Solicitors Act 1941 4 & 5 Geo. 6 c.46   197
Solicitors Remuneration Act 1881 44 & 45 Vict. c.44   192, 193
Stamp Act 1804 44 Geo. 3 c.98   59
Statute Law (Repeals) Act 2008 c.12   67
Statute Law Revision Act 1863 26 & 27 Vict. c.125   122n.
Statute Law Revision Act 1948 c.62   416
Statute of Additions (Details on original writs etc) 1413 1 Hen.
    5 c.1   42
Statute of Pleading 1362 36 Edw. 3 c. 15   409
Statute of Sewers 1531 23 Hen. 8 c.5   406
Statute of Westminster II 1285 13 Edw. 1 c.30   329, 391
        A statutory compendium of 50 chapters of which
        two are still in force *viz*
        Estate Tail Act 1285 c.1 (still inforce)
        Commons Act 1285 c.46 (repealed 2006)
Statutory Declarations Act 1835 5 & 6 Will. 4 c. 62   348
Suing in Forma Pauperis Act 1495 11 Hen. 7 c.12   237
Suitors in Chancery Relief Act 1852 15 & 16 Vict. c.87   105
Supreme Court of Judicature Act 1873 36 & 37 Vict. c.66   120
Supreme Court of Judicature Act 1875 38 & 39 Vict. c.77   120
Suspensory Act 1914 4 & 5 Geo. 5 c.88   145
Trade Union Act 1871 34 & 35 Vict. c.31   194
Trades Disputes Act 1906 6 Edw.7 c.47   194

Transport Act 1947 10 & 11 Geo. 6 c.49 370
Treachery Act 1940 3 & 4 Geo. 6 c.2 225
Treason Act 1790 30 Geo.3 c.48 439
Treason Act (Ireland) 1537 28 Hen.8 c.7 119
Turnpike Roads Act 1773 13 Geo. 3 c.84 66

Union with Ireland Act 1800 39 & 40 Geo. 3 c.67 12
Union with Scotland Act 1706 6 Anne c.11 11
Use of Highland Dress Act 1782 22 Geo 3 c. 63 31

Welsh Church Act 1914 4 & 5 Geo.5 c.91 145
Workmen's Compensation Act 1897 60 & 61 Vict. c.37 156, 286
Workmen's Compensation Act 1906 6 Edw. 7 c.58 155

NOTE

The titles and citation of statutes can be confusing as practice has changed in several respects over the years.

Titles

It was only in the 1840s that Acts of Parliament began to be accorded short titles. At first this only applied to new legislation. Hence, for example, the Treason Act 1790 (30 Geo.3 c.48) which abolished the sentence of burning at the stake imposed on women convicted of high or petty treason continued at first to have only a long title: "An Act for discontinuing the Judgement which has been required by Law to be given against Women convicted of certain Crimes, and substituting another Judgement thereof." This was highly inconvenient, particularly in respect of Acts passed in the earlier part of the 18th century where the practice of dealing with one subject at a time had yet to be established. A particularly shattering example of this legislative multi-tasking was the Continuance of Acts etc Act 1749 23 Geo.2 c. 26 the long title of which would put the contents of any modern "Miscellaneous Provisions" Act to shame:

> An Act to continue several Laws for the better regulation of Pilots, for the conducting of Ships and Vessels from Dover, Deal and the Isle of Thanet, up the Rivers of Thames and Medway; and for permitting Rum or Spirits of the British Sugar Plantations to be landed before the Duties of Excise are paid thereon; and to continue and amend an Act for preventing Frauds in the Admeasrement of Coals within the City and Liberty of Wesminster, and several Parishes near thereunto; and to continue several Laws for preventing Exactions of Occupiers of Locks and Wears upon the River Thames Westward; and for ascertaining the Rates of Water Carriage upon the said River; and for the better Regulation and Government of Seamen in the Merchants Service; and also to amend so much of an Act made in the first Year of the Reign of King George the First, as relates to the better Preservation of Salmon in the River Ribble; and to regulate Fees in Trials of Assizes and Nisi Prius, upon Records issuing out of the Office of Pleas of the Court of Exchequer; and for the apprehending of Persons in any County or Place, upon Warrants granted by Justices of the Peace in any other County or Place; and to repeal so much of an Act made in the twelfth Year of the Reign of King Charles the Second, as relates to the Time during which the Office of Excise is to be kept open each Day, and to appoint for how long Time the same shall be kept open each Day for the future; and to prevent the stealing or desroying of Turnips; and to amend an Act made in the second Year of his present Majesty, for better Regulation of Attornies and Solicitors.

By the end of the 19th century, however, parliament decided that the time had come to deal with older acts still without 'short titles'. The result was the Short Titles Act 1892 55 & 56 Vict. c.10 but four years later this was repealed and replaced by the Short Titles Act 1896 which conferred short titles on about 2,000 earlier acts.

Citation

Another piece of legal flummery which long outlived its sell-by date was the giving of acts of parliament chapter numbers relating to the sessions of parliament identified by the regnal year in which any particular act received the royal assent. This might have mattered somewhat less if the parliamentary clerks had been able to settle on an agreed method of computation but in that they failed. As a result the year and chapter printed in different editions of the statutes has been known to vary. And anyway, this anarchic practice continued long after it ceased to be customary to reckon all time from the date of the sovereign's accession to the throne – the beginning of the regnal year. Just how long can be judged from the fact that its sheer inconvenience was first drawn to public attention by astrologer and mathematician Arthur Hopton (c.1588-1614), a member of Clement's Inn and friend of John Selden. In his book *A Concordancy of Yeares*, published posthumously in 1615 and dedicated to Chief Justice Coke, a fellow member of his Inn, Hopton spoke of "the inconveniences that happen to vulgar wits and mean capacities" of such a practice. No matter: parliamentarians chose to ignore "the inconveniences" – doubtless under the impression that they were imbued with more refined wits and greater capacities than the ordinary run of humankind – at least until the Bill which was to become the Interpretation Act 1889 first came before them. The Bill had proposed future citation by calendar year. This eminently sensible suggestion survived scrutiny in committee but somehow the parliamentarians of the day took fright at the prospect of meddling with ancient tradition and it never made it into law.

There the matter rested until it came before parliament once again in 1962 and resulted in the Acts of Parliament Numbering and Citation Act of that year. However, in deference to the parliamentary prejudice against retrospective legislation, this requires to be formally cited as 'the Act 10 & 11 Eliz.2 c.34'. Nevertheless, as acts of parliament go, it should have earned itself a prize for succinctness, clarity and absence of controversy. The first and only operative section (the second section merely gives the short title) provides that:

> "The chapter numbers assigned to Acts of Parliament in the year nineteen hundred and sixty-three and every subsequent year shall be assigned by reference to the calendar year, and not the Session, in which they are passed; and any such Act may, in any Act, instrument or document, be cited accordingly."

Would that everything enacted in parliament were that simple. Even so, the irritating lawyers' practice of writing out dates in words rather than in figures still managed to prevail even in the year one thousand nine hundred and sixty-two.

TABLE OF CASES

Atkinson v Sadler (1814) (unrep.)   57, 60, 368

Bebb v The Law Society [1914] 1 Ch 286   233
Bettison & Ors v Langton & Ors [2001] UKHL 24   351
Burdon v Rhodes (1791) (unrep.)   xiv, 9, 21, 26, 34

Cattanach v Melchior [2003] HCA 38; 215 CLR 1   35

Egerton v Brownlow (1853) 4 HLC 124   35

Gilbert v Sykes (1812) (unrep.)   9, 26, 34n.
Gouriet v Union of Post Office Workers [1977] 1 All ER 697   302n.
Gregson v Gilbert (1783) 3 Doug 233; (1783) 99 ER 629   17, 21

Hales v Pettit (1565) Plowden 253   416n.
Hawes v Davye (1565) Dyer 119   410, 411

IRC v Rossminster Ltd [1980] AC 952   221

Kennedy v Broun (1863) 13 CBNS 677; 143 ER 268   275n. 277

Liversidge v Anderson [1942] AC 206   219, 221, 300
Loving et Uxor v Virginia (1967) 388 US 1   253, 274n.
Priestly v Fowler (1837) 3 M&W 1   284

Radcliffe v Ribble Motor Services Ltd [1939] AC 215   285

re L (A Child) [2015] EWFC 15   265

R v Governor of Brixton Prison ex parte Caborn-Waterfield [1960] 2QB 498   417n.

R (at the prosecution of Arthur Zadig) v Halliday [1917] AC 260   221

R v Metropolitan Police Commissioner ex parte Blackburn [1968] 1 All ER 763   302

R v Murphy (1789) (unrep.)   20, 21

Rylands v Fletcher (1866) LR 1 Ex 265; (1868) 3 HL 330   97n.

Santos v Illidge (1860) CB (NS) 861; 29 LJCP 346   32n.

Shackell v Rosier (1836) 2 Bing NC 634   34n.

Simpson v Ebbw Vale Steel, Iron & Coal Co [1905] 1 KB 453   156

Somerset v Stewart Loft 1 sub nom Sommersett's Case (1772) 20 State Trials 1; (1772) 98 ER 499   18

Swinfen v Lord Chelmsford (1860) 5 H&N 890; 29 ER   382

Swinfen v Swinfen (1856) 2 D & J 381   276

Taff Vale Railway Company v Amalgamated Society of Railway Servants [1901] AC 426   194

Tatham v Wright 2 Russ & Mylne 1   373

Tuton v Sanoner (1858) 3 H & N 280; 27 LJ Ex.293   48n.

INDEX

Note - Where it is known that a named individual in this index is a solicitor (whether or not a member of the Society) his or her name is followed by the description 'solicitor' or 'attorney' in brackets. The names of solicitors' firms are dealt with similarly.

A

Abinger, Lord 29, 62n.5, 284, 285
 - *see also* Scarlett, James
Acton, Mr Justice 198, 339
Addleshaw Goddard (solicitors) 380
Adie, Kate 217
Admiralty
 - courts and litigation 97, 107, 108-110
 - Lord Sempill employed at 224-225
 - Society member employed at 365, 366
adultery
 - capital offence under Cromwell 412
 - ecclesiastical courts cognizant 108
 - Scotland 277 n.10
 - sharing double bed as evidence of 260
 - wife's adultery bar to maintenance 113
 - women's increased opportunities for 262
advertising by solicitors 255, 257
Advisory Committee, Society's
 - *see* war
advocates
 - Doctors' Commons 108, 347
 - Scotland 121 n.8
 - *see also* barristers
Albert, HRH Prince 124, 147, 367, 383
Alderson, Baron 88
Alfred, King - laws of 394, 414 n.2
All Souls 108, 307
Allen, CK 220, 222
America, United States of
 - *Chargé d'Affaires* in London 27
 - civil war in 140
 - Declaration of Independence 34 n.14
 - law in 274 n.3, 325-328

 - Pilgrim Fathers 325
 - repayment of war loan 231
 - supply of glass by US army 228 n.2
 - Supreme Court 253, 274 n.3
 - war with Mexico 182 n.5
 - war with UK 28
Amiens, Treaty of 26, 30 n.2
Anderson, Elizabeth Garrett 248 n.1
Anderson, Sir John 219-221
Anderson, Robert Henry (solicitor) 375
Anderton, James (solicitor)
 - petition to parliament 60-61
Anglo-Irish war - *see* war
animals, export of live 295
Ansbro, David (solicitor) 289, 291, 292, 293, 295
Anschluss 201, 203
anti-semitism xii, 185-188, 197-198, 205 n. 3, 224
Antoine d'Orléans-Bragance, Prince 158 n.3
appeasement policy 200-201
Appleby, Sir Humphrey 291, 296
Arab-Israeli conflict 165
archdeacons, pack of 24, 38
Armistice Day - *see* war
Armley Gaol, executions at 113-115
Armstrong, Sir Robert 17
Articles of clerkship
 - payment during 236, 267
 - premiums 267, 249 n.4
 - stamp duty 59, 236, 361
Ashton, Mr Commissioner KC 168, 179.180
Askern, Thomas 115
Aspinall, James 16

445

Asquith, Herbert 142, 143, 154
assizes
   - abolition 268-270
   - ceremonial 332-342 *passim*
   - gaol delivery, meaning 335
   - oyer and terminer, meaning 329
Associated Provincial Law Societies 423
Atkin, Lord 219-221, 229 n.7
attorney hugging - *see* touting
Auschwitz 206
Australia
   - cricket 385
   - gastronomy 248
   - law reports 29
   - protonotaries 62
Austria 186, 201, 203, 322 n.1
Austro Hungarian Empire 145, 165

B
Badger, HW (solicitor) 133
Baedeker raid - *see* York
Bailey, CG (solicitor) 226
Bailey, Mr Justice 58
Baldwin, Stanley 200
Balfour, Arthur J Rt Hon 157, 424
Balfour Declaration 188
Ballantine, Serjeant William 94, 98 n.11, 99 n.12
banana republic
   - electoral system that would disgrace 311
bankers' failings
   - Barclays 315
   - Co-operative 315
   - general 315-318
   - HBOS 315
   - Royal Bank of Scotland 315
Bankruptcy Court
   - bankrupt more favourably placed than judgment debtor in county court 93
banks and banking 9, 12 n.9, 314-318
Bar Convent, bombing 213
Bar Council 348
Barclays Bank
   - LIBOR and 315
   - London as international financial centre 195
   - York Union Banking Company 364
   - *see also* bankers' failings
Bardell v Pickwick - *see* Dickens
Barnett, Lady (Isobel), prosecution 273
barristers 33 n.11, 43, 45, 88, 98 n.12, 108, 121 n.8, 180, 245, 249 n.2, 293, 313, 325, 342, 345, 346, 347,348, 411
Bartram, Mrs J (solicitor) 258
Bayley, Mr Justice 28, 57, 88
Beeching, Dr Richard 34 n.15, 135, 268, 377
Behan, Brendan
   - 'Anglo-Irish horse Protestants' 140
Belgium 70, 107, 164
Bell, Brodrick & Gray (solicitors) 382
Belle, Dido Elizabeth 19, 31 n.5
Bench, interruptions by 30, 103
benefit of clergy 122 n.11, 240
Berent, Margarete 248 n.1
Bethell, Richard - Westbury
Bevan, Aneurin 200
Beveridge Report 227
Beverley, RC Diocese of 387
Bevin, Ernest
   - cautious about Beveridge Report 230 n.15
   - 'not a lord, nor a privy, nor a seal' 335
Bevis Marks Synagogue 249 n.4
big government 149, 150, 159 n.9
Bingham, Lord 229 n.8, 239, 250 n.10, 287
Birkett, Lord 249, 275 n.7
Birmingham City Council, voting scandal 310-311
Bismark, Otto Edward Leopold von, Prince 305
Black and Tans - Ireland
Black Death, labour problems occasioned by 193
black letter type 399-401 *passim*
Black River, slave ship *Zong* arrives at 17, 18
Blackburn, Sir Colin 88, 97 n.7
Blackpool, compared with Scarborough 70
Blackstone, Sir William
   - attempts to start hearing at 7am 32 n.8
   - chastisement of wives by lower rank of people 111
   - first Vinerian professor and author 307, 308, 323 n.4, 404
   - unsuccessful plaintiffs suing *in forma pauperis* 238
Black Swan Inn - *see* York
Blakeston,WH (solicitor) 252
Blanqui, Jérôme-Adolphe
   - visit to York 81-83, 96 n.1
Bleak House - *see* Dickens
Bloor, Kenneth (solicitor) 215, 216, 275 n.4
Bodmin, public executions at 114

Boer War - *see* war - South Africa
Bohr, Niels, prediction of future difficult 305
Bolt, Robert 13 n.11, 296
Bonaparte, Napoleon
 - ambitions 'feeble' compared to Hitler 202
 - applies as teenager to join Royal Navy 134 n.1
 - *Code Napoleon* 106-107
 - defeat at Waterloo 35 n.18, 70, 81, 101, 124
 - escape from Elba 70
 - failure to invade Britain 389 n.1
 - French commanders in Crimea served under 78
 - Louisiana purchase 326-328
 - rise of 81
 - sea power 124
 - Sir Humphry Davy invited to visit Paris 77 n.10
 - subject of litigation in York 26-30
 - white charger belonging to 35 n.18
Bond, Stanley - *see* Halsbury's Laws etc
Booker, Christopher 290
Booker, Robert, Society's librarian 409
Booth & Co (solicitors) - *see* Addleshaw Goddard
Bootham Park Hospital - *see* York - Asylum
Borthwick Institute
 - Society's books deposited 405, 407, 408
Boswell, James 16, 31 n.3, 41, 48 n.10
Boulogne and Calais
 - visit of Jonathan Gray to 70-74, 77 n.9
Boxer Rebellion 143
Boycott, Captain Charles 140-141
Boyle, James Patrick - *see* Glasgow, Earl
Brabin, Mr Justice 335
Bracton, Henry de 287, 301 n.4, 330, 352 n.4, 393-396, 414 n.1
Bradford 1, 157, 210, 365
Bramley, H (solicitor) 424
branding as punishment 336
Braunschweig-Querum Law Society 215-216
Bray, Mr Justice 168, 180, 341
Brazil, slavery in 31 n.6
Brès, Madeleine
 - first woman to practice medicine in France 248
Bridlington 253
Bristol
 - Assizes 32 n.8

 - Edmund Burke MP 3
 - Law Society 2
 - slave trade 20
 - solicitors attending Society's Centenary 2
 - Tolzey and Pie Poudre Court 332
British Association - *see* British Science Association
British Railways Board 264, 267, 370
British Red Cross Society 216
British Science Association 371
British South Africa Company 138
Britton, John 396
Brixton Prison 219
Brontë, Charlotte 379, 391 n.17
Brontë, Emily 391 n.13
Brook & Bulmer (solicitors) 358
Brook, John (solicitor) 356, 358
Brougham, Lord 29, 127
Brown, Gordon MP 310
Buller, Mr Justice 18
Bulmer, George (solicitor) 358
Burdon, Thomas 21
Bureau International d'Education 216
Burke, Edmund 3, 301
Burke, TH, assassination in Dublin 142
Burma *see* Schumacher, Ernst
Burnet, Bishop Gilbert 400, 415 n.13
burning of women at stake - *see* capital punishment
Butcher, JG, MP 421
Butterworth, Alexander Kaye (solicitor) 357, 359
Butterworth, Jabez (solicitor) 381
Butterworths, as legal publishers 307, 308

C

cabinet meetings, conducted in French 16
Caen University, Norman law taught at 349
Cairns, Lord 149
Cambridge University 45, 47 n.4, 48 n.8, 240, 268, 355 n.21, 365
Camden, William 367
Cameron, David 12 n.6
Campbell-Bannerman, Henry 154
Canada
 - law 328
 - war loan repaid 231
candles, judicial use in France 353 n.13
Canning, George 29
Canterbury 70, 73, 229 n.10

447

Canterbury, Archbishop 109
Cape Colony 138
capital punishment 16, 20, 21, 32 n.7, 99, 113-119, 122 nn.14 & 16, 241, 439
Caraman, Rev Philip SJ 10, 13 n.11
Cardiff - *see* anti-semitism
Cardwell reforms (army) 102
Carnwath, Mr Justice 296, 297
Caroline, Queen 29
case law - *see* stare decisis
Cassels, Mr Justice 247

Catholic Church
 - canon law 108, 352 n.2, 393
 - Catholic Emancipation 3, 140
 - Hitler and 305, 322 n.1
 - influence on English law 330, 394
 - Yorkshire diocese of Beverley divided 387
Caudine Forks, Battle 205 n.2
cavalry charge, last mounted 158 n.3
cavalrymen, supposed influence on British army in First World War 184-185
Cavendish, Frederick (Lord), assassination in Dublin 141-142
Cavendish, Henry
 - not a gentleman according to cousin 37, 39
 - distinguished scientific career 47 n.4
Caxton, William 395
Centaur, winner of disputed sweepstake 21, 38
champerty - *see* maintenance and champerty
Chancery Court 54, 102-108, 347
Chancery Division 46, 110, 355 n.21
channel crossings 70-74, 77 n.9, 82, 135 n.7
Channel Islands
 - conveyancing exams still in French 349
 - France seeks to recover 31 n.2
Charles I, Court of King's Bench under 220
Charlie, Bonnie Prince 16
Chartered Institute of Legal Executives 348
Chartism 101
Chatsworth, French prisoner on parole at 78
Chauvin, Jeanne
 - first woman at French Bar 248 n.1
Chelmsford, Lord 276 n.8
child employment, restrictions 152
Childers, Erskine, execution of 146, 159 n.7
Christianity, influence on English law 260, 394

Churchill, Winston,
 - fifth column danger exaggerated 225
 - French different from English 5
circuit
 - judges on 329
 - Northern and North Eastern 62 n.6, 341
civil law
 - distinguished from common law 107, 108, 109, 307, 328, 349, 411
Civil Procedure Rules 413, 416
Clark, Alan MP 303 n.11
Clausewitz, Carl von 184
Clemenceau, Georges 183-184
Clerk of the Peace 268, 344, 359
coaching services 63-65, 69
Cobb, Cecil Henry (solicitor) 207 n.8, 370
Cobb, WHC (solicitor) 77 n.8, 353 n.8, 359-360, 370, 390 nn.3 & 8,
Cobb, WH (solicitor) 132,
Cockburn, Sir Alexander 276 n.8
Coke, Sir Edward 42, 323, 397, 399, 400, 414 n.5, 440
Code Napoléon 106, 107, 328, 353 n.13
coining offences as High Treason 20
Colditz Castle, light relief at 216, 228 n.5
collective bargaining - *see* Trade Unions
College of Law 228, 351, 355 n.21, 408
Collingwood, Luke 16
Collins, Professor Hugh 404
Collins, Lord Master of the Rolls 157
Colquhoun, Patrick 9, 12 n.8, 124, 134 n.2
commissions in army, purchase 102
Committee of Public Safety, government's powers compared to 221
common employment, doctrine 282, 284-286
Common Pleas, Court of 29, 32 n.6, 35 n.23, 51, 55, 97 n.6, 331, 416 n.15,
common sense
 - aid to statutory construction 300
 - basis for matrimonial law reform 261
 - examination in, desirable 274
commons, still over 4% of land area 354 n.20
Commonwealth, legislation during 412, 416 n.16
companies, not to expect justice from 319
computers, introduction 266
Comyn, James QC (later Comyn J) 146, 151, 160 n.10
Comyn, James (Senior) 146
Comyn, Michael KC 146
Comyns, Sir John Chief Baron 402

concentration camps
- Germany 223
- not established in Moravia 186
- South Africa 139
conditional fee agreements 258, 276
Congress, US 326
conscription - *see* war
constitutional crisis (1909-1911) 147
Cook, Thomas 75
Co-operative Bank - *see* bankers' failings
Cornthwaite, Rt Rev Robert 387
Corpus Christi College, Cambridge 268
Cosgrave, Liam - demands British military intervention in Northern Ireland 159 n.4
couchancy - *see* levancy and couchancy
County Courts 43, 89-94, 112, 125, 152, 332, 364
Court of Arches 347
court hand, use forbidden 413
court hours 32 n.8
Courts Leet 332, 351, 354 n.20
coverture, doctrine of 111
Craigmyle, Lord - *see* Shaw of Dunfermline, Lord
Crane, Dr CB 257, 258
Cranmer, Archbishop Thomas 410
Crathorne, Maria 78 n.10
Cresswell, Sir Cresswell 88, 97 n.6
cricket
- Society's contribution to Australian 385
- teaching French to play 5
- Wisden approach 12 n.5
Crimean War - *see* war
Crombie, CNP (solicitor) 234
Crombie, NT (solicitor) 197
Cromwell, Oliver 400, 401, 410, 412
Cromwell, Thomas 296
Crossman, Richard 200
Crown Court 269, 295, 297, 298, 332, 339, 346
Culloden, Battle 16
Curragh Mutiny 144, 158 n.3
Curran, JP 301, 303 n.14
Cusack, Mr Justice 269
customers, solicitors' clients to be regarded as 8
Custos Rotulorum - *see* Clerk of the Peace
Czechoslovakia 201, 202, 203

D
Dahrendorf, Lord,
- Jephcott Lecture on English professions 7-8
Daily Herald 183-184
Daladier, Édouard, reaction to Munich agreement 201, 202
Dale, R Percy (solicitor) 128, 129, 133, 152
Dallas, Mr Justice 60
Dampier, Mr Justice 57, 60
Davy, Sir Humphry, visit to Paris 77
deceased wife's sister, bar on marrying 259, 277 n.11
Denning, Lord 264, 287, 302 n.5, 394
deregulation 312-313, 320
Detroit, British forces capture 28
Devlin, Lord 346-347, 353 n.12
Devonshire, fifth Duke 37, 39
Devonshire, seventh Duke 142
Devonshire, ninth Duke 198
Dicey, AV
- constitutional principles 292
- on *Stephen's Commentaries* 323 n.4
Dickens, Charles
- *Bardell v Pickwick* 97 n.8
- *Bleak House* 102-103
- capital punishment and 117, 122 n.14
- chancery reform 102-103, 121n.7
- *Jarndyce v Jarndyce* 102
Diplock, Lord 221, 287
discrimination
- Lord Mansfield and 18, 19, 31 n.5
- race and gender 253
Disraeli, Benjamin 124
Disraeli, Isaac 249 n.4
District Manpower Board - *see* war
divorce 258-262, 278 n.15
DLA Piper (solicitors) 380
Dobbie, Alderman and Mrs W 339
dock brief 99 n.13, 240
Doctors Commons 107
Dodsworth, Ben (solicitor) 192, 210, 212, 357, 362, 363
Dodsworth, Charles "Charlie", (solicitor) 212, 275 n.4, 333, 362, 371, 372
Dodsworth, Ernest Ralph (solicitor) 179, 196, 197, 357, 362, 363, 364
Dodsworth family 362-363
Dodsworth, Sir Lumley (solicitor) 233, 246, 362
Domvile, Admiral Sir Barry, KBE, CB, CMG

- interned under Regulation 18b 223, 224
Dorset, Duke - cricketing ambassador in Paris 5
doughboys 167, 182 n.5
Dover 5, 70, 71, 77 n.9, 439
Dreyfus, Capt. Alfred 185, 186, 205 n.3
Dryland, Michael (solicitor) 236, 357, 361, 364-365
Duck, Dr Arthur 108
due diligence
 - banks' liability to observe 317
Duncombe, Augustus, Dean of York 30
Duncombe Place - *see* York
Dunkirk 210, 219, 225
Dunn, William (solicitor) 385
Dyson, Arthur, execution of 113
Dyson, Will, cartoonist 183, 184

E
Eades, His Honour Judge 298
Easingwold 1, 375-376
East Coast Main Line 135
Easter Rising - *see* Ireland
ecclesiastical courts 108-110, 258, 347, 348, 398
Eddison, Edwin (solicitor) 366-367
Edinbro' Mail 63-65, 69
Edmund Davies, Lord Justice 302, 346
Edward VII, King 151
Election Commissioner
 - *see* Mawrey, Richard QC
Elisabeth (of Austria), Empress 181 n.3, 186
Elizabeth, Queen Mother 231, 251
Elizabeth II, Queen 333
Ellenborough, Lord 28, 55, 56, 57
 (*see also* Law, Edward)
employment law 244, 309
English law, development 325-332
Erasmus, Desiderius 305, 306, 307
Erskine, Thomas 33 n.8, 46
estovers 351
Etty, William 96 n.2, 356, 358
European Convention on Human Rights 119
European Court of Human Rights 12 n.4
Evans, John (solicitor) Town Clerk of York 269
Eversheds (solicitors) 289, 293
Exchequer Chamber, Court 32 n.6, 97 n.7
Exchequer, Court 29, 35 n.23, 62 n.5, 331, 386, 400, 402, 403, 404, 405, 439
Exodus, Book of 237, 250 n.8

F
Fabian Society
 - Oswald Mosley a member 199
Fairest, Professor Paul 289, 291, 292, 295, 296
Faraday, Michael
 - *see* Davy, Sir Humphrey
fascism 198, 200
fax, solicitors use of 266
felony 240, 366, 414
Financial Conduct Authority 317
Financial Services Authority 315
Financial Services and Institutions 309
Financial Times 310
firearms, control of 154
Fisk, Robert 159 n.4
Fitt, Gerry 159 n.4
Fogg's Journal 321
Foljambe, Sir Geoffrey 39
Foljambe, John (attorney) 38-39
Ford & Warren (solicitors) 114
fornication, capital offence under Cromwell 412
Fortescue. Sir John 397
Foster, William MP and compulsory education 157
Foulis, John Robert 27, 34 n.17
Foulis, Sir William 23
France
 - authority of state 6
 - Britain at war with 124
 - George III's claim to throne 16
 - Latin in legal procedure banned 411
 - women lawyers in 248 n.1
Francis Ware & Lucas (solicitors) 380
Franco-Prussian War - *see* war
Franz Ferdinand, Archduke 145, 164, 165
Franz Jozef, Kaiser
 - family misfortunes 181 n.3
 - friendship with British royals 165,
 - dismayed by anti-semitism 186, 187
Frederick III, Kaiser
 - married to Princess Royal 124
freemasonry - *see* Petre, Baron Robert Edward
French Revolution
 - lasting effect 3-6
 - foundation of Society predates 16
 - 'Rights of Man' and 34 n.14
Freshfields (solicitors) 213, 228 n.3, 315
Frost, Charles (solicitor) 54, 56, 100 n.14, 367-368

Frost, Thomas (solicitor) 367
Fuller, Thomas 287,302 n.5
Furnival's Inn 407

G
Galicia, Jewish refugees in Vienna 186
Galloping Jack - *see* Seely, Colonel John
gaol delivery, meaning - *see* assizes
Gardiner, Lord 268
Garland, Emma, translates Ovid 96
Garland, Richard (solicitor)
- memorial to judges 54, 99 n.13
- travel in Teesdale 74
Garrow, Sir William 29
Gates, Bill 408
Gatty, George, compensation for loss of office 105
gentlemen
- barristers not quite 25
- litigation over definition 21-26
- attorneys and solicitors as 125-126,
George I, King
- Hanoverian 147
- unable to speak English 16, 45
George III, King 16, 31 n.2
George V, King 147, 164, 165, 224
George VI King, Society seeks guidance for mourning 231, 246
Germany
- army, state of 203
- empire 147
- inflation in Weimar Republic 185
- use of Gothic or Schwarbacher type 395
- women lawyers in 248 n.1
Gibb, George Stegmann (solicitor) 357, 368-369
Gibson & Weldon 351. 355 n.21
- *see also* Law Society - School of Law
Gilbert, Rev Robert, Vicar of Settrington
- *Gilbert v Sykes* 26-30
Gilbert & Sullivan
- *Iolanthe* 157
- *Utopia* 319
Gilmour, MHB (solicitor) 357, 359, 369-370
Gladstone, William, 112, 137, 142, 158 n.1
Glasgow, Earl 235
Glorious Revolution 240, 393
Goderich, Viscount 134
Godfrey, Elizabeth, execution 21
Goebbels, Joseph 202
gold plating, European law 291

Goodwin, Fred 315
Gough, Brigadier-General 144
grand jury - *see* jury
Gray, Dodsworth & Cobb (solicitors) - *see* Grays
Gray, Edwin (solicitor) 339, 364
Gray, Gilbert QC 289-295 *passim*, 342
Gray, Jonathan (solicitor) 54, 63, 68, 70, 71, 73, 76, n.6, 83, 100 n.14, 229 n.10, 370-372, 387,
Gray, William (solicitor) 15, 16, 20, 67, 68, 115, 356, 370, 372, 378, 379, 386
Gray, William (solicitor)
- (grandson of above) 86, 89, 114-115
Gray, W & E (solicitors) - Grays
Grays (solicitors) xii, xiii, 75, 77 n.8, 212, 353 n.8, 360, 361, 372, 379, 390 n.8
Great Exhibition (1851) 101, 383
Great Famine - *see* Ireland
Great Western Railway Company 359, 370
Gregorian University 10
Gregson, John, William and James 16
Grey, Viscount 147, 148, 159 n.8
Griffith, Arthur
- President of Dáil Éireann 159 n.7
Grotius, Hugh 400
Guildhall - *see* York
Gunning 'Fog Index' 278 n.17
Gunter, Colonel MP 421
Gurney, Baron 374
Gurr, TR 124

H
Habeas Corpus 18, 221
Hague Convention (5 October 1961) 353 n.16
Hale, Sir Matthew 321, 400, 415 n.13
Hallamshire - *see* High Sheriffs
Halsbury's Laws, Statutes and Statutory Instruments, publishing history 307-309
Hamilton, Lord 98 n.10
Hammett, Sir Benjamin 21
Hankey, Maurice 183, 184, 205 n.2
Hannam, Peter (solicitor) 8, 318
Hanover, Elector 45, 305
Hardy, Thomas 147
Hartley, John (solicitor) 373-374
Hartlepool, Scarborough & Whitby, German bombardment of 165
Hastie (solicitor) AH 125
Hawkins, Henry 94, 98 n.12

451

HBOS - *see* bankers' failings
Healey, Maurice 11 n.3
Henry II, King 329, 332, 346, 352 n.3, 394
Henry III, King 393, 394
Henry IV, King 396,
Henry V, King 396
Henry VI, King 47, 396, 397
Henry VII, King 395, 396
Henry VIII, King 109, 277, 278 n.11, 296, 393, 395, 396
Herbert, Sir Thomas 399
Herring, Elizabeth, execution 20
Heslington Hall - *see* Yarburgh, Henry
High Sheriffs
  - fined for non-attendance 332-333
  - Hallamshire 333
  - trumpeters 16, 337, 340
high treason - *see* treason
highland dress, legal control over 31 n.3
Hileys (solicitors) 376
Hinchcliffe, Mr Justice 258
Hinrichsen, Dr Klaus E 226
Hispaniola, mistaken for Jamaica by captain of *Zong* 17
Hitler, Adolf 148, 185, 186, 199, 200-203, 305, 322 n.1
HMRC 310, 311, 331
Hobson, John A 206 n.4
Hoffman, Lord 12 n.4, 46, 343
Holden, Lt-Colonel RB (solicitor) 234, 253
Holtby & Procter (solicitors) 380, 389
Holtby, Robert (solicitor) 381
Holtby, Sam 207 n.8
Home Affairs Select Committee 311
Home Detention Curfew Scheme 298
Home, Earl - *see* peers, their privilege to embrace women
Home Office Immigration and Nationality Department
  - *see* UK Border Agency
Homer, Lin, CB 310, 311
Hopton, Arthur 440
Hornby Castle 373-374
Horsfall, William - *see* Luddites
horses, slaves compared to 18
Hudson, George 375, 391 n.14
human rights - *see* 'rights of man'
Hull
  - attornies and solicitors entitled to join Society 51
  - bomb damage to 213, 231, 367
  - Docks Company 367
  - George Muff MP 222
  - Literary and Philosophical Society 367
  - Parliament Street 386
  - standard of attornies 40
  - Subscription Library 367
  - William Wilberforce and 20, 386
Hullock, Sir John 29
Humpty Dumpty
  - authority for judicial interpretation 219-221,
  - Lord Judge wise not to cite 300
Hunt, Thomas 326
Hutchinson, Rev HN 163
Hutchinson, Thomas - *see* Massachusetts

I
Incorporated Law Society - *see* Law Society
Immigration and Nationality Directorate
  - *see* UK Border Agency
Independent Labour Party
  - Elizabeth Wolstenholme member 121 n.9
  - Oswald Mosley member 199
India 81, 164, 199, 336, 360
Institute of Electrical Engineers (US) 7
internet 314
internment
  - First World War 221
  - Napoleonic wars 73, 74, 77 n.10
  - Second World War 219-226
Ireland
  - Act of Union (1800) 12 n.3
  - Black and Tans 199
  - Easter Rising 145
  - Great Famine 140
  - gun-running 144-145
  - Home Rule 142, 144, 145, 158 n.2,
  - Irish Free State 146, 159 n.7
  - Parliamentary Party 138
  - Republican Brotherhood 142
  - Ulster 11, 140, 142, 143, 158 n.2
Irwin Mitchell (solicitors) 237, 249 n.7
Isle of Man 70, 226
Italy
  - kingdom 164
  - Papal States incorporated 122 n.15, 181 n.2
Iveson, William (attorney) 372

J
Jacob, Sir Jack 97
Jacobite Rebellion 16, 31 n.3, 46
Jacobs, Mrs Barbara (solicitor) 263
Jamaica, voyage of *Zong* to 16, 17
James II, King 287
Jameson, Sir Leander Starr 138,
Japan
- *Code Napoléon* in 107
- naval secrets passed to 224-225
- Society's dinner to await end of war 228
Jarman, Thomas, death intestate 96
Jarndyce v Jarndyce - *see* Dickens
Jenkins, Roy 146, 200
Jephcott Lecture - *see* Dahrendorf, Lord
Jewish Question - *see* anti-semitism
Jobcentre Plus 311
Johannesburg 138, 139
Johnson, Dr Samuel
- opinion on attornies 41, 48 n.10
- prayer for attornies 321
- visit with Boswell to Hebrides 16, 31 n.3
Johnston, WR (solicitor) 232
Jones, Sir William FRS
- founder of Asiatick Society 403
Joyce, Mr Justice 233
Judge, Lord 299
judges
- breakfast 394
- donations to Society's library 88-89
- lodgings xi, 25, 34 n.15, 221, 269, 270, 337, 339, 340, 377, 382
Judicature Acts 106, 109, 120,
Judicial Review 282, 287, 295, 298, 309
Judicial Studies Board 12 n.4, 299
jury
- City of London special 33 n.10
- grand 274 n.3, 346-347
- Scotland in 98 n.10
- special 22, 24, 26, 33 n.9 & n.10, 374
- trials (civil) 97 n.10
justices of the peace 155, 343, 344, 439

K
Kay, NB (solicitor) 234
Kaye, Joseph (solicitor) Bank of England 59
Keen, Mrs Sandra (solicitor) 263
Kelly, Sir Fitzroy MP
- holder of first registered title 420
Kemp, HT 168
Kennedy, Charles Raun - *see* Swinfen family

Kennedy, Mr Justice 280
Kent, Tyler 225
Kenwood House 19, 32, 49 n.19
Kenya executions in 119
Keynes, Maynard 222, 223
Kids' Company 320
kilt - *see* highland dress
Kinder Scout, mass trespass on 198
King, General Sir Frank 159 n.4
Kipling, Rudyard 143, 158 n.2
Knavesmire
- executions 20, 77 n.6, 117, 119
- racing 21-22, 38
Knowles, Peter (solicitor) 215, 216
Knox, John 235, 249 n.3, 277 n.10,
Kuehberger, Fr Johan
- rescues Hitler as a child 305, 322 n.1

L
Labour Party 194, 199, 200, 290
Lady Chatterley's Lover, prosecution 252
Lake, BG 421
lancer regiments, lances re-adopted 148
Land Registration 119, 134, 226, 230 n.14, 351, 353 n.17, 419-428
Langdale, Hon Charles 387
Langleys (solicitors) 211
language of law
- Norman French 329, 343, 351, 395-400 *passim*, 409-410, 413, 414, 417 n.19
- Latin 44, 62 n.2, 161 n.15, 354 n.18, 395, 396, 397, 404, 409-410, 413, 416 n.17
- in France 411-412
Latin - *see* language of law
Law, Edward 24, 34 n.13
(*see also* Ellenborough, Lord)
law clerks - *see* legal executives
Law Society
- accounting requirements 197, 233
- advice sought on mourning death of King George VI 231, 246
- altered playing field, operating in 9
- annual conference at York 75, 125-132
- Beveridge Report, consultation on 227
- compulsory membership of, Yorkshire Law Society in favour 197
- David Napley President 48 n.16
- final examinations, subjects in 274, 350
- land registration 422, 423, 424, 425
- legal aid societies 226

- national emergency 210
- national service in wartime 210, 213, 214,
- Poor Man's Lawyer Scheme 237, 239, 242, 243
- practice rules 160 n.14
- prisoners of war 215
- School of Law 351
- solicitor numbers 313, 323 n.7
- statutory disciplinary committee 156
- sympathy with York following air raid 213
- Thomas Lund Secretary 228 n.4, 251
- trainee salaries 293
- women not permitted to take examinations 233-234

Law Society Gazette 48, 61, 160
Law Times 110
Lawton, Mr Justice 335
Lawton, William John 242
lawyers' testamentary disasters 96 n.4
Le Blanc, Master 56, 57
Le Blanc, Mr Justice 28, 57
Lee, John, Recorder of Doncaster, 'slaves chattels or goods' 18
Leeds
   - Civic Trust 367
   - Jewish settlement 187
   - Law Society 1, 2, 420, 424
   - Philosophical and Literary Society 367
   - population in 1801census 21
   - Zoological and Botanical Gardens 366
Leeman, George (solicitor) 359, 366, 375, 391 n.14
Leeman & Clark (solicitors) 386
Legal Aid
   - origins of 99 n.13, 237-242
   - Poor Man's Lawyer Scheme 237, 243-244
   - reduction in availability 313
legal executives 192-195, 348
legal practice as a trade 46-47, 256
Legal Research Foundation 313
Léger, Alexis
   - French Prime Minister's aide 202
legislative multi-tasking, example 439
Leslie, CA (solicitor) President of Law Society 280
levancy and couchancy 351, 354 n.20

Levine, Joshua 223, 229 n.11
Levy, Madeleine 206 n.3
LexisNexis Butterworths - *see* Butterworths
Liberal Party 137, 154, 158 n.1, 194
LIBOR - *see* Barclays Bank
Lietzmann, Heinrich 204-205
Lightfoot, William and James, conviction 116
limited liability, objections to principle 319
Lincoln's Inn
   - mooting technique demonstrated 355 n.21
   - Furnival's Inn attached to 407
   - German lawyer called as member 204
Lindsay, Sir John RN 19
Linklaters & Paines (solicitors) 213
Littledale, Sir Joseph 29
Liverpool
   - coaches from York to 63
   - Court of Passage 332
   - slave trade 16, 20
Liversidge, Robert 219, 221, 300
Living Streets - *see* Pedestrian Association
Lloyd George, David 42, 148, 154, 183, 185, 201
Lloyds TSB Bank 371
Lobban, Professor Michael 121 n.7
Local Government Board 153
Lock, Fossett, His Honour Judge 168
Lockward, William (solicitor) 357, 375-376
Lockwood, Sir Frank, QC, MP 421
Lodge, Anton QC 292-293
London Irish, TA regiment 203
London Bridge, Fenian attempt to blow up 142
London Evening Standard 187-188
Long, Breckinridge
   - US Assistant Secretary of State 225
Lord Chancellor
   - Department 214, 329
   - office held by ecclesiastics 340
Lord Privy Seal 335
Loughborough, Lord 32 n.7
Louis XVI, King 5, 16, 31 n.2
Louis XVIII King 31 n.2
Louis Philippe, King 158 n.3
Louisiana - law in 107, 328
Louisiana Purchase 326, 327, 351 n.1
Lucas, Clarence (solicitor) 197, 388
Ludendorff, General Erich von 158, 167
Luddites, trial at York 338
Lueger, Karl 186
Lund, TG "Tommy" 48 n.12, 213, 214, 215, 228 n.4, 251

454

Lute, Herr Meyer 129
Luxembourg, Grand Duchy 107, 164

M
McAdam, John 65
MacDonald, Ramsay 199
McDonalds, built on former bomb site 211
Mackay of Clashfern, Lord 295, 308
McCardie, Mr Justice 168
Macdonald, Flora 16
Macmillan, Harold 200
McMillan-Scott, Edward MEP 290, 291, 302 n.8
maintenance and champerty 258, 275-277 n.8
Maitland, FW 11 n.1, 393, 414 n.1, 415 n.10
Malton 1, 3, 5, 29, 62 n.5, 128, 135 n.7, 227, 232, 337
Mann, JW (solicitor) 132
Manning, Most Rev Dr Henry Edward 387
Manning, FG and M, execution of 117
Manningham-Buller, Sir Reginald 414
Mansfield, Lord 18, 19, 20, 31 n.5, 32 n.8, 33 n.8, 46, 49 n.19, 103
Marwood, John 114-115
Mara, Gertrud Elisabeth 83
Marie Antoinette, supposed gift of cricket bat to 5
Markiewicz, Countess 145
married women, status 111-112
Marsden, John 373-374
Marsh, William 88
Marwood, William 114, 115
Massachusetts,
 - colony established 325-326
 - Thomas Hutchinson Governor-General 20
Master of the Rolls 160 n.14, 197, 302 n.5, 303 n.14
Mathew, Theo 'O' 256, 275 n.7
Matrix Chambers 34 n.14
Matrix Churchill case 294, 303 n.11
Maugham, Viscount
 - public criticism of fellow Law Lord 221
Mau-Mau rebellion – *see* Kenya
Mawrey, Richard QC 310-311
Maxse, Lt-General Ivor 189
Maynard, Sir John 396, 415 n.8
Mee, Arthur 168
Meek, WA 168
Megarry, RE (Ted) 46, 96 n.4, 355 n.21, 416 n.18

Merchant Adventurers Hall 234
messenger boys, more use in Britain than telephones 252
middle class
 - attitude to trade 263
 - daughters as solicitors 236
 - expansion of 262
Middlesex Deeds Registry 428 n.2
Middleton, Arthur (solicitor) 424
Milburn, George sculptor 375
Minster - *see* York
misdemeanours, punishment 336
Mitting, Mr Justice 298, 299
More, St Thomas 122 n.11, 296, 306, 308, 313, 315, 322 n.2, 330, 340, 394, 404, 407
Moore, Mrs GL (solicitor) first woman member of Society 233, 234, 235, 257
motor-vehicles
 - reckless driving 152
 - speed limits 153, 160 n.13
Motor Vehicle (Construction and Use) Regulations 271
Mottistone, Lord - *see* Seely, Colonel John
Mozart, WA, as child prodigy 16
Muff, George MP 222
Munby, Frederick James (solicitor) 86, 133, 357, 376-379, 391 n.15, 404
Munby, Joseph (solicitor) 377
Munby. Mr Justice 265
Munby & Scott (solicitors) 211-212
Munich Agreement 201-203
Munnings, Sir Alfred 158
Murphy, Catherine
 - execution by burning 21
Murray, Lady Elizabeth 19
Murray, Gilbert 147
music festivals - *see* York
Mussolini, Benito 200

N
nanny state - big government
Napier, Michael (solicitor) 237, 249 n.7, 250 n.8
Napoleon - *see* Bonaparte
Natal, colony 139
National Health Service 200, 230 n.15, 320
National Railway Museum 375
National Union of Railwaymen 339-340
Neave, Airey MP, light relief at Colditz POW camp 228 n.5

NEETs (Not in Education, Employment or Training) used by HMRC 312
Newgate prison 21
Newton, Henry (solicitor) 357, 379
Newton & Robinson (solicitors) 379
Neyle, Gilbert Neville 59
Nicholls of Birkenhead, Lord 354
Nicholson, Lucas (solicitor) 2, 357, 380
North Eastern Circuit 62 n.6, 289, 341, 364
North Eastern Railway Company 135 n.6, 359, 365, 368, 369, 375, 379, 382
Northern Star 101
Northleigh, John 411
Norway
- German invasion 202
- monarchy 164
- secession from Sweden 181 n.1
Norwich
- disturbance at assize service 341
- Guildhall Court of Record 332
- public executions at 116
Norwich Union/Aviva 371
notary public 109, 348, 353 n.16
Nu, U, Prime Minister of Burma 318
Nussbaum, David 198
Nuttgens, Professor Patrick 81, 83

O
'O' - *see* Mathew, Theo
O'Connell, Daniel 140
Oflag 79
- *see* Braunschweig-Querum Law Society
Old Bailey 94, 99 n.13, 241, 252
ordinary (eating house) equivalent to modern day pub 24
Orlando, Vittorio Emmanuele 183
'other ranks', solicitors described as
- *see* Taylor, AJP
Ottoman Empire 163
Ouse and Derwent Volunteers
- *see* volunteer corps
outer space, deregulation of 312
Owen, Ruth 311
oyer and terminer - *see* assizes

P
Paget, General Sir Arthur 143, 144
Paine, Thomas 34 n.14,
Pankhurst, Emmeline 121 n.9
Park, Sir James Alan 29
Paris
- cricket international of 1789 with France cancelled 5
- custom of 328
- Napoleon reviewing troops 27
- reaction to Munich agreement 202

Parliamentary Commission on Banking Standards 316
parliamentary draftsman
- as cause of litigation 279
- struggles with disparate responsibilities of Quarter Sessions 343
Parton, Dolly, as rival attraction to Lord Denning 302 n.5
Passchendaele, Battle 166, 176
Payne Eddison North & Ford (solicitors) 366
Payne, Richard (solicitor) 366
Peace, Charles, execution of 113-115
Peacock, Dr Alf 391 n.14
Pearson Report, cool reception by legal profession 288
Pedestrian Association 359
Peel, Sir Robert 240
peers, privilege to embrace women 235
Peking - Boxer Rebellion
Penguin Books - *see* Lady Chatterley's Lover
Perkins, F (solicitor) 152, 378
Perlzweig, Jack - *see* Liversidge, Robert
Peterborough, Soke, jurisdictional peculiarities 352 n.3
Peters, JC (solicitor) 234
Petre, Baron Robert Edward 69, 77 n.7
petty treason - *see* treason
Phillips of Matravers, Lord 62 n.5, 298, 300
Phillips, William (solicitor) 88-89
Pilgrim Fathers, arrival in Massachusetts 325
pimp tenure 350, 354 n.18
Pinkney, William (solicitor) 253, 254
pistols - *see* firearms
Pitt, William 3, 65, 69, 76 n.2
Platt, Baron 88
Plews, H (solicitor) 425
Plowden, Edmund 415 n.14
Pocklington 1, 211, 232, 339, 381
politicians
- reluctance to heed informed opinion 296
Poll Tax riots 143, 303 n.10
Pollock, (Jonathan) Frederick
- A-G for County Palatine of Lancaster 374
- Chief Baron 48 n.17

Pollock, Sir Frederick 395
Pontius, Gaius 205 n.2
Pope
   - appointment of notaries by 109
   - foresees major war 164
   - head of the Catholic Church 108
   - infrastructure inherited from
      Roman Empire 108
   - jurisdiction 109
Poor Man's Lawyer Scheme,
   - *see* Legal Aid
postal arrangements
   - abuse by parliamentarians 69
   - high cost of 68, 69
   - Intel fax service 266
   - introduction of postage stamps 69
   - postage payable by addressee 69
Powell, HS (solicitor) 211
Powell & Young (solicitors) 211
practising certificates - *see* solicitors
Prague
   - internment of MP for 222
   - possible Anglo-French
      intervention in 202
Pratt, Miriam 341
prayer for attorneys - *see* Johnson, Samuel
Prayer Book Rebellion 410
precedent - *see* stare decisis
premiums on articles
   - *see* articles of clerkship
Prescott, Rt Hon John MP 229 n.9
Privy Council appeals 328
Procter, Alfred (solicitor) 133, 192, 357,
   380-381, 387, 389
proctors 88, 108, 347, 348, 399
professions, nature of xi, 3, 6, 25, 40, 41, 42,
   43, 45, 46, 48 n.8, 51-53, 56, 59, 83, 91,
   102
prostitutes, women suspected
   of being 121 n.9
protonotaries 51, 55, 62 n.2
Prussia 124, 147, 164, 305
public executions - *see* capital punishment
Public Trustee
   - Society's objection to 149-150
Putlitz, Wolfgang 202
Pynson (or Pinson), Richard
   - French printer responsible
      for modern English spelling 395

Q
Quarter Sessions, 42, 253, 268, 269, 270, 278
   n.16, 332, 342-346
Quebec, *Code Napoléon* in 107, 328
Queen's Own Yorkshire Dragoon Guards 148

R
Radzinowicz, Professor Sir Leon 240, 250 n.11
Railway King - *see* Hudson, George
railway solicitors
   - Butterworth, AK 359; Dunnell, RF 365-
      366;
      Gibb,GS 368-369; Gilmour, MHB 369-
370;
      Leeman, G 375; Newton, H 379;
Seymour,
      GH 382-383
railways
   - coming of 12 n.9, 66, 69, 78 n.11, 123
   - Duke of Wellington objects to 75
Ramsay, Captain Archibald MP 223-224
Rathbone, Eleanor MP 223
Raworth, Edwin (solicitor) 358, 381
Raworth, Sophie 381
Recorders 18, 31 n.3, 45, 168-169, 268, 345-
346
Red Cross 214, 215, 216, 254
Rees Mogg, William 314, 323 n.10
registration of land - *see* Land Registration
Rent Acts - *see* war, housing problems
rhinoceros, witness compares
   himself to 24
Rhodes, Cecil 138
Rhodes, Robert, Clerk of the Course at York
   21
Richardson, Lt-General Sir George 143
Richmond Golf Club Rules 209, 217-218
Right Club 224-225
Rights of Man 3, 25, 34 n.14
Ringrose's House 2, 15, 30 n.1, 65, 96 n.3, 279
Ripon
   - centenary visit to 75, 128, 129
   - Dean 133
   - Marquess 123, 126-127, 132
Ritz Hotel, justice compared to 237, 249 n.6
road traffic fatalities 359
roads, improvement to 64-69
Rob Roy - first cross Channel steamer (1821)
   77 n.9 Roberts, Field Marshal Lord 143
Robertshaw, Abraham, sentenced to
   death for forgery 26

Robinson, GFS - *see* Ripon, Marquess
Robson, Thomas (solicitor) 381
Rochester
- Bishop's cook executed by boiling 122 n.11
Roman Dutch law - *see* South Africa, law in
Roman Empire 108-109
Roman law 108, 121 n.8
Romilly, Sir Samuel 34 n.16, 127
Roosevelt, President 225
Roper, William 296
Rose, Lord Justice 297
Roskill, Lord 98 n.10, 278 n.17, 279, 280-289 *passim*, 296, 297, 309, 310
Rotherham, attorney's practice at,
- *see* Foljambe, John (attorney)
Rothman, Benny 198, 199
Rothschild, NM 315
rotten boroughs 83-84
Rouen 353 n.13, 395
Rowe, Harry, fought at Culloden 16
Rowntree, "Kitty" 21-25, 34 n.17
Rowntree, Seebohm 191
Royal Bank of Scotland - *see* bankers' failings
Royal Commission
- on Assizes and Quarter Sessions (1970) 268, 269
- on Marriage and Divorce (1955) 260
- on Registration of Title (1857) 419-420
Royal Exchange Insurance Company 2
Royal Flying Corps 199
Royal Naval/Royal Air Force Volunteer Reserve 210
Royal Society of Medicine
- *see* Dahrendorf, Lord
Rugby Union Rules 359
Rule of Law
- as basis of civilisation 287, 290, 300
Russell, Bertrand 147
Russell, William Howard 102
Russia, pogroms 185
Russian officer, charters channel packet 71-72

S
Sacks, Jonathan 124
Salford Hundred Court 332
Salic law 305
Salz, Anthony 315-316
St John of Jerusalem, Order of 216
St Olave's Churchyard 358

St Paul's Cathedral,
- binge drinking near 134 n.2
- suffragettes disrupt service 341
San Marino, Republic 164
Sandler, Daniel 309, 310
Sarajevo 145, 165
Sargisson, James, botched execution 115
Saul, Professor Berwick 280
Saxe-Coburg, HRH Prince Albert 124, 147, 367, 383
scale fees (conveyancing) 160, 193, 227, 254, 255
Scarborough, bombardment
- *see* Hartlepool, Scarborough & Whitby
- Society's centenary visit 128-129
Scarborough & Whitby Railway Company 135 n.6
Scarlett, James
- counsel for Sir Mark Sykes 29
- counsel for Society 57, 58
- MP for Malton 29, 62 n.5
- urbanity 30
- views on court attire 62 n.5
- *see also* Abinger, Lord
Scarlett, Major-General James Yorke 62
Schönbrunn Palace
- Kaiser prepared to accommodate Jewish refugees 186
Schwitters, Kurt
- interned in York, Bury and IOM 226
Schumacher, Ernst
- advises British government 222
- advises Burmese Government 318, 319
- interned as enemy alien 222, 223
Scobey, Ron, not in contempt for car breakdown 333
Scone Palace,
- portrait of Elizabeth Belle 19
Scotland
- basis of law 121 n.8
- benefit of free trade in 11 n.3
- marriage 277
- legal status of wagers 33 n.12
- use of civil juries 98 n.10
Scott, Henry C (solicitor) 233
Scott, Henry Venn (solicitor) 378
Seely, Colonel John 143, 144, 158 n.3
Selden, John 396, 397, 415 n.10
Sempill, Lord 224, 225
Sentamu, Dr John 301
settled land 351, 353, 355 n.22

Seymour, Admiral Sir Edward 143
Seymour, George Hicks (solicitor) 358, 359, 382-283
Shakespeare, William 39, 198, 278 n.11, 416 n.15
Shannon, John OBE (solicitor) 48 n.8, 212, 234, 257, 269-270, 280, 358, 383-385, 391 n.14
Shaw of Dunfermline, Lord 221
Sheffield
- Chaucer, mentions 11 n.2
- breakdown of judges' car 333
- Law Society 2, 424
Shelley's Case, rule in 388, 391 n.18
Sheppard, William 401-402
Sheriffs
- *see* High Sheriffs and Under Sheriffs
Sherman, General, 'war is hell' 213
shorthand, curious legal 411
Sikhs, wearing of safety helmets 312
Simon, Lord 219
Sinclair, Robert, Recorder of York 404
Slaughter & May (solicitors) 213
slave trade 16, 20, 31 nn.5 & 6,
Sledmere
- dinner party results in litigation 26-30,
Slingsby, Sir Henry
- *see* High Sheriffs
Smethwick
- Oswald Mosley contests seat for Labour 199
Smith, Ernest (solicitor) 271, 272
Smith, FE 143, 274
Smith, Nicholas (attorney) 379, 380
Smith, Rev Sydney 68, 70, 76 n.4, 77 n.8, 319
soldiers' wills 109
solicitors
- accounts, regulation of 233
- acting *pro bono* 237-242 *passim*
- collective bargaining by staff 192-193
- conveyancing costs 75,
- cost of qualifying as 41, 59,
- defaulting 195-196
- etiquette 255, 388
- gentlemen 41, 42, 125, 293
- justices of the peace, acting as 155
- practising certificates 156 -
proceedings against dishonest 156
- Saturday closing of offices 266
- service in First World War 166, 168-181
- wartime staffing difficulties 166, 213-214

- women qualifying and practising as 233-236
- work 'boring' 42
- 'drudgery' 98 n.12
- 'laborious' frontispiece
Somerset, James 18, 31 n.5
Somme, Battle of 166, 170-176 *passim*, 185, 382
South Africa
- law in 328
- war in 138, 139
Spain 164, 326
Spanish Civil War 210
special branch officer (armed)
- attendance at annual dinner 272-273
special jury - *see* jury
Spencer, Professor John QC 299
Spofforth, Robert (solicitor) 358,385
Squanto, English speaking Patuxet assists Pilgrim Fathers 326
Stable, Mr Justice
- letter to Lord Atkin 221
Stalingrad, battle 214
stamp duty - *see* articles of clerkship
Stanley, RM (solicitor) 280
Stanton, Mr Justice 413
stare decisis 395
statutory interpretation 278, 282-288 *passim*, 296-300 *passim*
Stephen, Sir James
- history of the criminal aw 239
Stephenson, George 128
sterling, pre-eminence of 195
Stockton Forest Riflemen -
see volunteer corps
Stoecker, Adolf 187
Stonyhurst 387
Stourton, Charles, 17th Baron 387
Stovin, Aistroppe (attorney) 358, 385-386
Strickland, Eustacius 396
Strickland, Sir William 40
Stewart, Robin QC 280
successful rebellion against government
- *see* Fisk, Robert
suffragettes 147, 159 n.6, 340-341
Sudetenland, Hitler's annexation of 201,202
sugar
- British acquire taste for 31 n.6
- excise duty on rum and spirits 439
- wartime rationing ends 232
Sugden, Sir Edward B 89

Sullivan, Serjeant AM, 161 n.15
Sunningdale Agreement 158, 159
Susskind, Richard 313, 314, 408
Sweden 164, 181 n.1
Swift, HL (solicitor) 196,197
Swinburne, Henry 398
Swinfen family 275 n.8
Switzerland 70, 164
Sybil - *see* Disraeli, Benjamin 124
Sykes, Sir Mark Masterman 26-29 passim, 34 n.17
Sykes, Lee & Brydson solicitors 34 n.15

T
TA - *see* Territorial Army
Tadcaster, turnpike from York 67
Taff Vale Railway Company 194
Tankerville, Earl 5, 12 n.5
tartan - *see* highland dress
Tasburgh-Anne, Michael 78 n.10
Tate Britain 31 n.6
Taylor, AJP
 - adopts popular error about cavalry generals 185
 - considers solicitors as 'other ranks' 42, 43
Taylor of Gosforth, Lord Chief Justice 297
Teasdale, R (solicitor) 210
telegraphs
 - development of railways and use in war 78 n.11
telephones
 - Britain has no need to have 252
 - in Society's library 152
 - solicitors, use by 252
Templar, His Honour Judge 168
Territorial Army 203, 388
Thesiger, Sir Frederick
 - *see* Chelmsford, Lord
Thompson, Richard 358
Thomson, Sir Alexander (Baron) 33 n.9, 338
Thomson, Sir George, FRS 268
Thorpe & Gray (solicitors) 379
Thurlow, Lord 45, 319
Thwaites, Doctor 234, 257
Tichbourne, Sir Alfred
 - *see* High Sheriffs
Tichbourne case 98 n.12
Tisquantum - *see* Squanto
Toler, C 303 n.14
Topping, James

 - counsel in *Gilbert v Sykes* 28, 30
touting 43, 160, 226, 227, 254-256, 267
Townend, George (solicitor) and
 Town Clerk 37, 51, 358, 372, 376, 386
trade unions
 - attitude to Beveridge Report 227
 - parliament's views on 6, 193-194
 - Society and collective bargaining 192-195
training contracts
 - *see* Articles of Clerkship
treason, high and petty distinguished 20
Tremmel, Mgr Max 322 n.1
trousers on fire - *see* Dodsworth, Ben
TUC 157
Tuke, AW, pre-eminence of London as financial centre 195
Tuke, Daniel 70, 71
Tuke Samuel 371
Turkey - *see* Ottoman Empire
Turpin, Dick 65, 76 n.6
turnpikes 65-68

U
UK Border Agency 311
Ulster Workers' Council, general strike organised by 158
Under Sheriffs 16, 114, 115, 306, 332, 333, 337, 339, 360, 362, 363, 364, 379
United States - *see* America
university degrees, not norm for solicitors 236
University of York 309, 377, 279, 384, 405
Ustinov, Klop
 - working for British Intelligence 202
Ustinov, Peter 202
Utopia
 - More, Sir Thomas
 - Savoy opera 319

V
Vansittart, Rt Hon Nicholas 59, 62 n.7
Vatican
 - capital punishment abolished 122 n.15
 - Charles Dickens attends execution 122 n.14
 - political pressure on Kaiser Franz Jozef 186
 - protonotaries in 62 n.2
 - status in international law 181 n.2
Vaz, Keith, MP 311
Versailles

460

- last public execution in France 122 n.16
- Peace Conference 165
- Treaty ending First World War 185, 200, 203
- Treaty ends US war of independence 16

vicarious liability 285-286

Victoria, HM Queen
- death 135 n.7, 151
- diamond jubilee 381
- Princess Royal marries Kaiser Frederick III 124, 164
- requests Lord Chief Justice to attend second court martial of Captain Dreyfus 205 n.3
- Salic law prevents succession to Electorate of Hanover 305

Villers-Cotterêts (1539 Ordinance) bans Latin in French legal proceedings 411

vinaigrette
- warding off gaol fever 335-336

Vinerian Law Professorship -
see Blackstone, Sir William

Virginia
- attempt to return slave from England 18, 31 n.4
- mixed race marriage law unconstitutional 253, 274 n.3

volenti non fit injuria, only topic of conversation
- see Sullivan, Serjeant

Volkswagen, scandal 320

volunteer corps 358, 389 n.1

W

wagers, enforcement at law 33 n.12

Walker, Emma (Lady Mayoress) 128, 130-131

Walker, William (solicitor) 128, 132, 133, 380, 386-387

Wall Street crash 195

Walster, AE (solicitor) 189

war
- Anglo-Irish 145
- Armistice Day 176
- Battle of Britain 210
- conscription 166, 210, 233, 252
- casualties 165-176, 179-181, 210, 211
- Crimean 79, 101, 124, 383
- District Manpower Board 214
- Franco-Prussian 124, 138, 144, 147
- housing problems caused by 189, 190
- prisoners of war 71, 77 n.10, 214-216, 228 n.5
- members of Society as 215-216
- rationing in and after 210, 231-232
- reporting of 78-79
- Society's Advisory Committee 167, 188-189
- Society's war memorial 167-181 passim
- South Africa 138-139, 143, 148, 426
- see also internment

Ward, FSH (solicitor) 232

Ward MP, John 321-322

Ware, Francis (solicitor) 380, 388

Ware, Henry John (solicitor) 358, 387, 388, 389 n.2

Ware, Innes OBE, TD (solicitor) 365, 388-389

Ware, Rev John 389

Ware & Kay LLP (solicitors) 34 n.15, 358

Ware, Miss AMI (solicitor) 233

Warren, William (solicitor) 113-114

Washington
- British forces occupy 28
- mixed race marriages permitted but not in neighbouring Virginia 274 n.3
- Society member at British Naval Mission 365

Waterloo
- final defeat of Napoleon 81, 124
- Jonathan Gray visits battlefield 70

Wayper, Miss V (solicitor) 233

Weatherley, Emma 388
(*see also* Walker, Emma Lady Mayoress)

Weatherley, Joseph 388

Weiskirchner, Richard 186

Wellington, 1st Duke 29, 75, 78, 101

Wellington, 5th Duke 224

Wenlock, Lord and Lady 133

Wennington Estate, litigation 373

West Indies 19, 32 n.6, 81

Westbury, Baron xiv, 93, 96 n.4, 419, 428 n.1

Westminster Hall 59, 61, 394

Whigs 3, 32 n.7, 137,

whipping, or pilloring unsuccessful plaintiffs *in forma pauperis* liable to 238

Whitby, Society's centenary visit 75, 128

White Bear, Stillington
- turnpike trustees meet at 68, 69

White House, British troops burn 28

Whitfield, Peter (solicitor) 267

461

Whitworth, Captain Henry, MFH 339
Wickenden, WE 7
Wightman, Mr Justice 88
Wilberforce, William 20, 21, 30 n.1, 65, 356, 378, 386
Wilhelm I, King and Kaiser 124
Wilhelm II, Kaiser 124, 163, 187
Wilkinson, KET (solicitor) 197, 210
Williamson, EW (solicitor) 421
Willes, Mr Justice 18
wills, defective 96 n.4
Wilson, Christopher 23
Wilson, Harold 158 n.4
Wilson, John (solicitor) - frontispiece
Wilson, President Woodrow 183
Wisden - *see* cricket
Witwatersrand - *see* Johannesburg
Wolkoff, Anna 225
Woolf, Lord 413
Wolsey, Cardinal 330, 340
Wolstenholme, Elizabeth 112, 121 n.9
women
- admission as solicitors 234
- as medical practitioners 248 n.1
- as peers 235-236
- ceasing to work on marriage 236, 249 n.5
- conscription 213-214
- members of the Society 233, 234
- monstrous regiment 249 n.3
- not persons, judicial decision 233-234
- percentage as solicitors 234
Women's Franchise League 121 n.9
Woodall, Alderman JP 129
Wooton, Baroness 236
workmen *inopes consilii* 157, 161 n.15
workmen's compensation 155, 156, 286,
Wright, George 374
writs of association and *si non omnes* 334, 352 n.6
Wuthering Heights - *see* Brontë, Emily

Y

Yarburgh, Henry 76 n.4
Year Books 395, 396, 398, 402, 409
Yes Minister - *see* Appleby, Sir Humphrey
YMCA 216
York
- Assembly Rooms 30 n.1, 133, 279
- assizes at 1, 26, 37, 56, 57, 85, 336-340
- Asylum 371, 387, 388
- Baedeker raid 211-213, 231
- Black Swan Inn 63
- Blake Street, bomb damage 211
- bloody assize - *see* Luddites
- Castle Museum
    - Dick Turpin's cell 77 n.6
    - Society's War Memorial 181
- Chancery Court 347
- Charity Trustees 387
- Clark's Hotel, Society's meeting at 57
- Clifford's Tower, massacre of Jews 188
- Courts of Husting, Guildhall and Conservancy 332
- Duncombe Place 30, 212, 267, 268, 280, 399
- Goodramgate 133, 358
- Guildhall
    - Assize Commission in roofless 218
    - bombing 213, 251
    - George Seymour's banquet 383
- Hebrew Congregation 188
- High Petergate 399
- Judges Lodgings xi, 25, 34 n.15, 269, 270, 339, 377
- Law Courts, Clifford Street 245
- Leeman Road - *see* Leeman, George
- Lord Mayor 128, 189, 247, 336, 339, 341, 363, 373, 380, 382, 383, 387, 388,
- Mansion House 128, 142, 335, 336, 339, 384,
- Micklegate 251, 252,
- Minster 30 n.1, 82, 89, 211, 221, 280, 337, 340, 341, 361, 364, 380, 384, 399,
- Museum Street 30, 96 n.3, 280
- music festivals 83, 89, 371
- St Wilfrid's Church 388, 399
- Sheriff of 336, 363, 384
- Station Hotel 151
- Tavern 30 n.1
- Town Clerk 37, 51, 218, 245, 372, 386
York Co-operative Society 339
York County Savings Bank 371, 379, 380, 387
York & District Law Clerks Association 192-194
York, Dean 30 n.1, 133, 189
York Lunatic Asylum/Bootham Park Hospital 371, 380, 387, 389
York Medical Society 227-228, 247, 257, 258, 408,
York Minster Library 407, 408
York Newcastle & Berwick Railway 375, 379

York & North Midland Railway 76 n.3, 379, 382
York Savings Bank - *see* York County Savings Bank
York Union Banking Company - *see* Barclays Bank
York University - *see* University of York
Yorkshire Union of Law Societies 226
Yorkshire
- Catholic gentry 387
- Deeds Registries 75, 428 n.2
- East Riding 40, 167, 253, 270, 372, 380, 385, 389
- North Riding 75, 155, 360, 381, 389
- West Riding 1, 134 n.4, 142, 253
Yorkshire Banking Company 375
Yorkshire Evening Press 190
Yorkshire Fire and Life Insurance Company 371
Yorkshire Gazette 12 n.9, 130-131, 371
Yorkshire Herald 179, 190, 339, 375
Yorkshire Law Society
- annual dinner 151, 189, 191, 228, 235, 247, 254, 257, 264, 269-272, 302, 372
- badge of office, gift of JT Atkinson 150
- bicentenary 61 n.1, 279-296 *passim*, 309, 408
- centenary 123-135 *passim*
- foundation 5, 15, 16, 37
- incorporation 150
- land registration 419-428
- library, acquisition 86-87
- silver 390 n.11
- War Memorial 168-181
Yorkshire Philosophical Society 133, 387
Yorktown, surrender at 16
Young, Arthur Edwin (solicitor) 211
Yugoslavia 165

Z
Zong, voyage of 16-18, 20